Essays on the
Power of Images
by Maurice Berger

# RACE STORIES

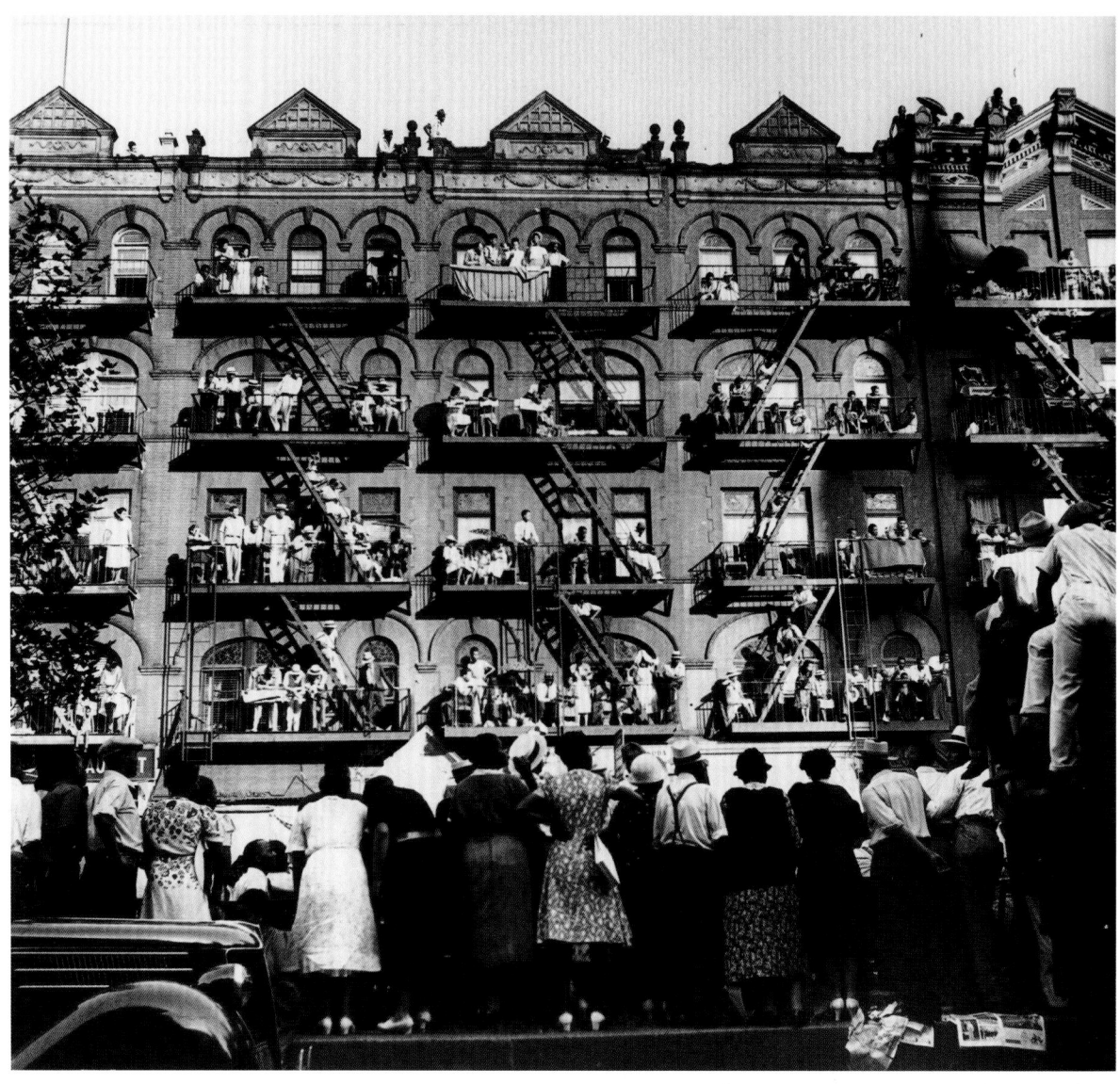

Jack Manning, *Elks Parade, Harlem*; from the series *Harlem Document*, 1939

# Essays on the Power of Images by Maurice Berger

A Vision & Justice Book

Edited by
Marvin Heiferman

Series Editors' Note by
Sarah Lewis
Leigh Raiford
Deborah Willis

Foreword by
Henry Louis Gates, Jr.

Afterword by
Dawoud Bey
Nona Faustine
Peter W. Kunhardt, Jr.

# RACE STORIES

The New York Times

*aperture*

## About the Vision & Justice Book Series

The Vision & Justice Book Series, created and coedited by Drs. Sarah Lewis, Leigh Raiford, and Deborah Willis, is designed to reexamine and redress historical narratives of photography, race, and justice. The series aims to address past omissions and contribute to the ongoing work of telling a richer, more racially inclusive story of photography.

The series presents vital new books that center lens-based Black artists whose work has had significant impact on the history of the medium and on modern and contemporary culture at large. The books extend a critical canon-building movement, redefining the historical record—both central concepts and artistic practices—and disseminating the often unheralded work by Black artists, while inspiring and modeling ongoing excellence and innovation.

## Advisory Board

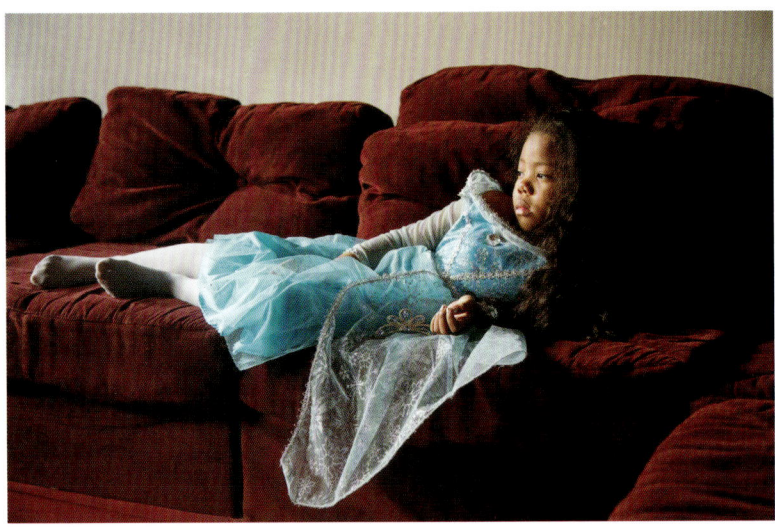

Nona Faustine, *Blue Queen*, 2015

# Series Editors' Note

Few understand the power of images, race, and justice more than Maurice Berger. Few ever may. As a cultural historian, curator, and writer, Berger's mission was a clear presentation of complex ideas about racial equity for the public.

For a decade, he shared extraordinary, award-winning short essays with the public in his monthly online column in the *New York Times*, "Race Stories." The book, edited by curator and scholar Marvin Heiferman, Berger's husband, brings together this collection of incisive essays, written between 2012 and 2019, for the first time. This anthology is also the first volume of the Vision & Justice Book Series that presents a new history of images, race, and justice in America.

Berger was a leader in his exploration of the transformational role of visual culture in shaping ideas and attitudes about race, justice, and belonging in the United States. He challenged readers and viewers to reconsider both cultural and personal assumptions and prejudices. He made space to examine how photographs, from works by Gordon Parks to LaToya Ruby Frazier, Nona Faustine to Dawoud Bey, allow us to see the world anew.

Yet he identified a critical part of the unfinished work in the history of race and representation: audience. He wanted to ensure that people within and, most importantly, beyond the art world saw how we understand race through pictures today, and have over time. He understood that "racial literacy could come from visual literacy." This book is a primer; each essay models how this is done.

Berger's writing and scholarship was courageous. He was committed to do that rarest of things in American life: to deploy and, at times, sacrifice his position to say, with fire, what many would not dare, come what may. As a professor, writer, and curator, he marshaled his command of the history of photography to state the absolute truth that needed to be heard, not just for that moment, but for all time. Maya Angelou once said that "courage is the most important of all the virtues, because without courage, you can't practice any other virtue consistently." Maurice had courage in spades. He led with his heart and backed it up with his brilliance. It gave his work fire. It made him a force.

In all of his work, Berger had a common refrain: he urged us all to take down everything that prevents us from honoring life. He had an ethical clarity, the rigorous study required to back it, and the rhetorical style required to make people pay attention. We salute our colleague and dear friend Maurice Berger and hope that this volume inspires further scholarship of the kind that he pioneered for the sake of the arts, and for justice.

Sarah Lewis
Leigh Raiford
Deborah Willis

# Contents

5    Series Editors' Note by Sarah Lewis,
     Leigh Raiford, and Deborah Willis
8    Foreword by Henry Louis Gates, Jr.
10   Introduction by Maurice Berger

## Chapter 1
## Revisiting Images:
## The Past Seen Anew

20   A Radically Prosaic Approach to Civil
     Rights Images
24   The Woman in a Jim Crow Photo
28   Reconsidering the Black Panthers
     through Photos
32   Chronicling the Virtuosity and Struggles
     of 1970s Soul and Funk Musicians
38   Holding a Mirror to Race
42   Photographing Civil Rights, Up North
     and Beyond Dixie
46   Whiteness and Race, between
     the Storms
50   The Heartbeat of Our Being, in Black
     and White
54   Black Performers, Fading from Frame,
     and Memory
58   The Cinematic Images of Gordon Parks
62   A Momentous Day Driven by
     Ordinary People
66   Robert Frank, Telling It Like It Was

## Chapter 2
## Visibility: Strategies
## of Representation

72   Malcolm X as Visual Strategist
76   Zanele Muholi: Paying Homage to the
     History of Black Women
80   When Glamour Speaks Your Name
84   The Quiet Heroism of Arthur Ashe
90   Making a Confederate Flag Invisible
94   Making Chicano Life Visible
98   Three Generations of Black Women in
     Family Photos
102  One Drop, but Many Views on Race
106  Black Fathers, Present and Accountable
110  Black Dandies, Style Rebels with
     a Cause
114  Framing—and Reflecting—Beauty
118  These 1970s Pageants Celebrated Black
     Women's Beauty
122  Pictures of Men, Friends or Lovers
126  Gordon Parks's Harlem Argument
130  Dr. King's Complex Relationship with
     the Camera

## Chapter 3
## History and Memory:
## Engaging the Past to
## Understand the Present

136  Reimagining a Tragedy, Fifty Years Later
140  Rarely Seen Photos of Japanese
     Internment
144  An Elegy to India's Vanishing Cinemas
148  The Modern Spirits of *Ebony* and *Jet*
152  The Lasting Power of Emmett Till's
     Image
156  This Photo of a Seven-Year-Old Girl
     Transformed the Abolition Movement
160  Anonymous Men, Made Real
164  Images of Emancipation
168  A Civil Rights Photographer, and a
     Struggle, Are Remembered
172  Finding Inspiration in the Struggle at
     Resurrection City
176  A Cultural History of Civil Rights

180 Black Soldiers: Fighting America's Enemies Abroad and Racism at Home

184 Lynchings in the West, Erased from History and Photos

188 Fifty Years after Their Mug Shots, Portraits of Mississippi's Freedom Riders

192 Lee Friedlander's Overlooked Civil Rights Photos

196 Escaping to Freedom, in the Shadows of the Night

# Chapter 4
# Witnessing: Images as Catalysts for Change

202 Meditation on President Obama's Portrait

206 A Meditation on Race, in Shades of White

210 Bearing Witness to Jim Crow in Mississippi with Uncompromising Candor

214 Documenting Selma, from the Inside

218 Photos That Challenge Stereotypes about African American Youths

222 Intimate Photos of Community and Resilience in New York's Chinatown in the 1980s

226 In Ferguson, Photographs as Powerful Agents

230 Capturing the Struggle for Racial Equality, Past and Present

234 A Photographer Who Made "Ghosts" Visible

238 The Holocaust's Paradox of Good and Evil, in Photographs

242 The Faces of Bigotry: When the Hoods Come Off

246 Civil Rights, One Person and One Photo at a Time

# Chapter 5
# Community: Visualizing the Connections between Us

254 Jamel Shabazz's Forty Years of Sights and Styles in New York

258 Complicating the Picture of Urban Life

262 Born by a River, Watching the Change

266 Past and Present Collide in Pittsburgh

270 A Photographer's Search for the Magic in Everyday Life

274 Artists of Color as Avatars of Originality

278 American Culture, Riding a Mushroom Cloud

282 A Russian American Photographing Native Alaska

286 Documenting the Dynamic Black Community of 1940s Seattle

290 What the Camera Sees, and Doesn't See

294 LaToya Ruby Frazier's Notion of Family

298 Kamoinge's Half-Century of African American Photography

304 Afterword: Reflections on Maurice Berger and His Work by Dawoud Bey, Nona Faustine, and Peter W. Kunhardt, Jr.

308 Contributor Bios

310 Acknowledgments

311 Image Credits

# Foreword

Reading this marvelous collection of Maurice Berger's essays straight through underscores his role as a veritable philosopher, and something of a prophet, of what is now commonly called the "social construction of race." But rather than merely claim this truism as if the phrase's meaning is self-evident, as so very many commentators do, Berger demonstrates, in essay after essay, how and what it can mean in the widest array of guises—many counterintuitive, which is a hallmark of his originality. In other words, rather than making specious claims and repeating clichés, Berger *renders* the way "race" is so broadly defined through close readings of an astonishing range of visual images. His language is as clear, focused, and crisp as the photographs that he is so gifted at reading. As he says in his essay on Yaba Blay's book (p. 102), the visual "attest[s] to the many faces, colors, and stories of Blackness," specifically, and of race, more generally. And that is Berger's message, propounded throughout this book in engaging, thoughtful prose without being repetitive or reverting to tiresome jargon. His readers can count on him for new insights about America's favorite topic: the *whys* and *wherefores* of the facial features that compose, collectively, our country's beautifully variegated citizenry. And he never disappoints.

Maurice, whom I was fortunate enough to call a friend, left us way too soon, as this collection attests. We needed his insights about the ways race has been read historically— from the clash of cultures that defined the contacts between Europeans and Native Americans to the construction of this country's economic prosperity on a foundation of enslavement of red and black and brown humans. We still so urgently need those insights today, as we witness the rise of xenophobia drawn upon as a tool by unscrupulous politicians. This collection establishes not only Maurice Berger's place in the history of the criticism of photography but also his role as a social philosopher determined to underscore, essay by essay, all that unites us as human beings. While those of us who adored him continue to miss him, this volume is both a testament to his brilliance and a living reminder of the resonant sublimity of his vision and his voice.

Henry Louis Gates, Jr.

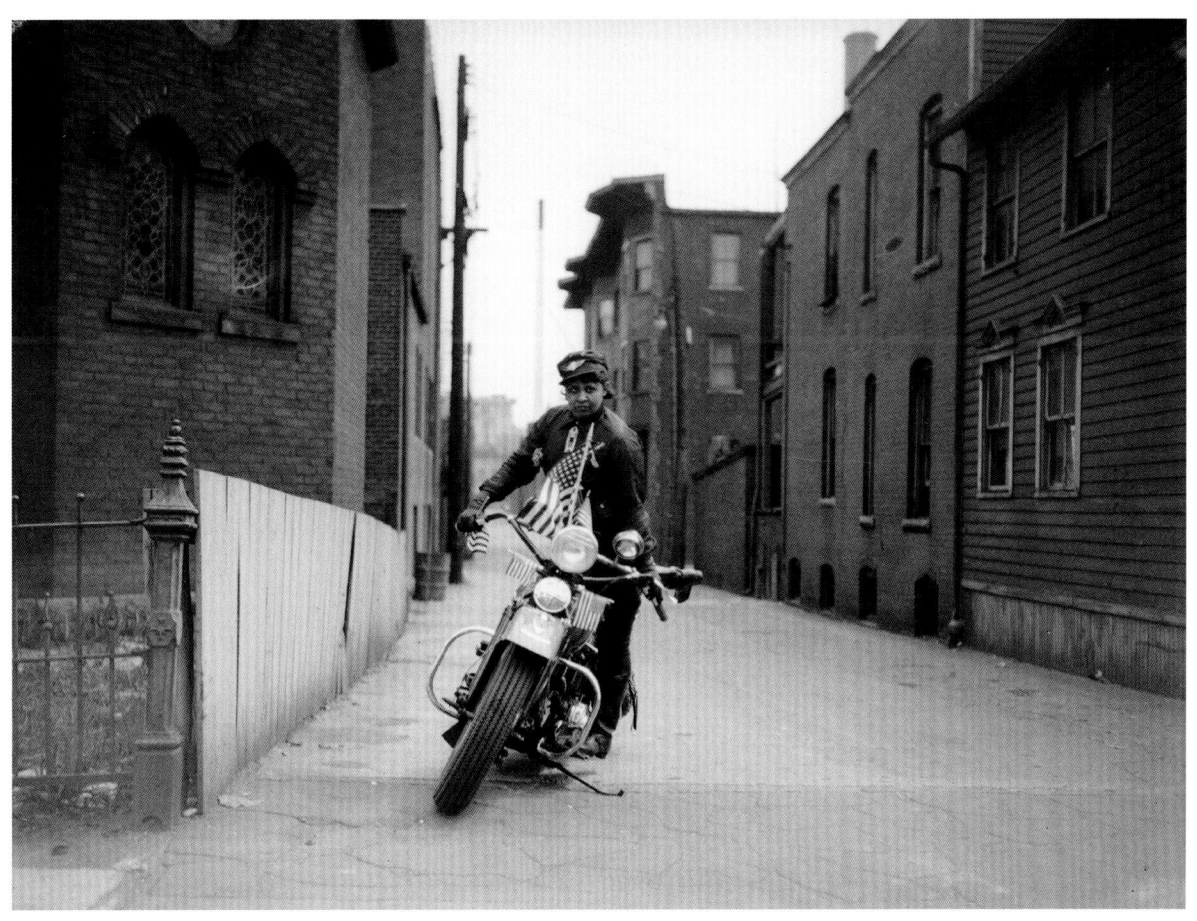

Charles "Teenie" Harris, *Woman Mounting Motorcycle*. Woman wearing dark cap with eagle, mounting motorcycle decorated with flags in an alley, Pittsburgh, Pennsylvania, ca. 1940–46

# The Story of
# Race Stories
# by Maurice Berger

Adapted from audio recorded in 2018, during the filming of an interview honoring Berger's Infinity Award for Critical Writing from the International Center of Photography

My childhood shaped and informed the way I see and understand race in America. I didn't grow up like most of my white friends. I grew up in a predominantly Black and Puerto Rican low-income housing project on the Lower East Side of Manhattan, an experience that shaped the way I see the reality of race: a complex reality, a troubling reality, a reality that has stayed with me for my entire life. As a gay man and as a Jew, I've experienced homophobia and anti-Semitism in my life, but the racism the kids I grew up with experienced, in front of my eyes, left me realizing that nothing quite compared to that in terms of prejudice. From the time I was a boy, I've tried to understand the violence, the pain, the aggressions and microaggressions, the gross acts of hatred, the subtle dismissals and slights. I was lucky in the sense that my white skin protected me from that, but it also made me realize how, in the society we live in,

the color of your skin can make a whole lot of difference. I realized, at a very young age, that race was a very visual thing. And that, years later, would inform my view of photography.

My greatest passion as a child was writing. I dreamt of writing a column in a national newspaper, and in an extraordinary confluence of events, decades later, that dream turned into a reality. In 2012, I curated a public art project about Gordon Parks for the International Center of Photography. I presented his images on three screens in windows that faced Sixth Avenue in Midtown Manhattan and, over the course of one year, millions of people walked by and saw them. Shortly after the window project was installed, I got a call from James Estrin, an editor of the *New York Times* Lens blog, for an interview. When we spoke—about public art, Gordon Parks, and race—I guess he liked

Introduction

Gordon Parks, *Untitled*, Harlem, New York, 1948

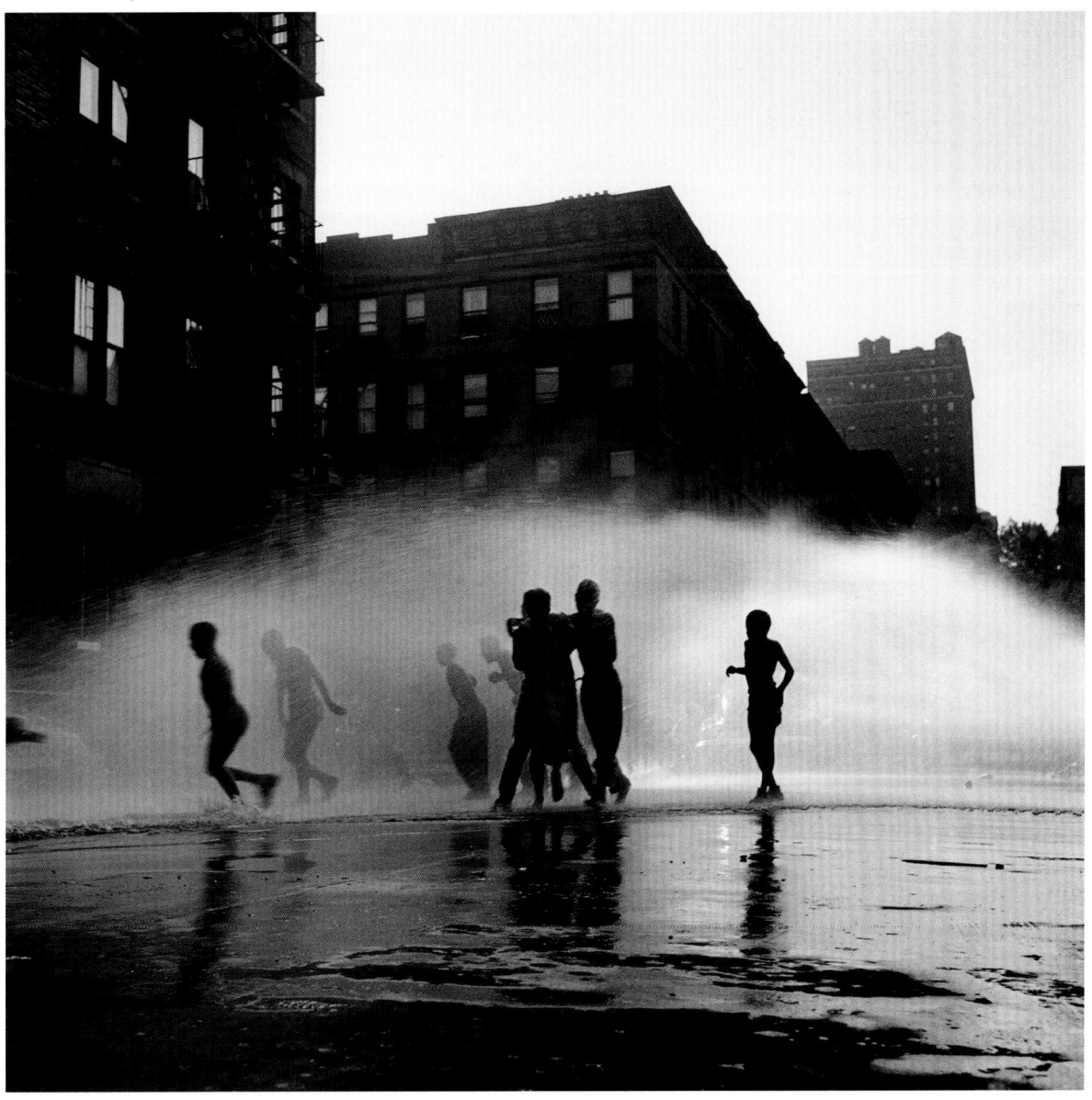

what I said, because he suggested I consider writing something for Lens.

A few weeks later, as we talked in the light-filled cafeteria in the Times Building, I described how I'd always wanted to write a column about race and visual images. I proposed writing about a recently found series of Parks's color photographs of a family's life in Alabama during Jim Crow segregation in the mid-'50s. I remember the day that piece came out because something unexpected and extraordinary happened: It not only wound up on the home page of the *Times* website, but right under the masthead, where it stayed up for hours on the day of its publication. After a few more pieces, I asked if what I was doing could become a monthly column and also for my own rubric, *Race Stories*—a

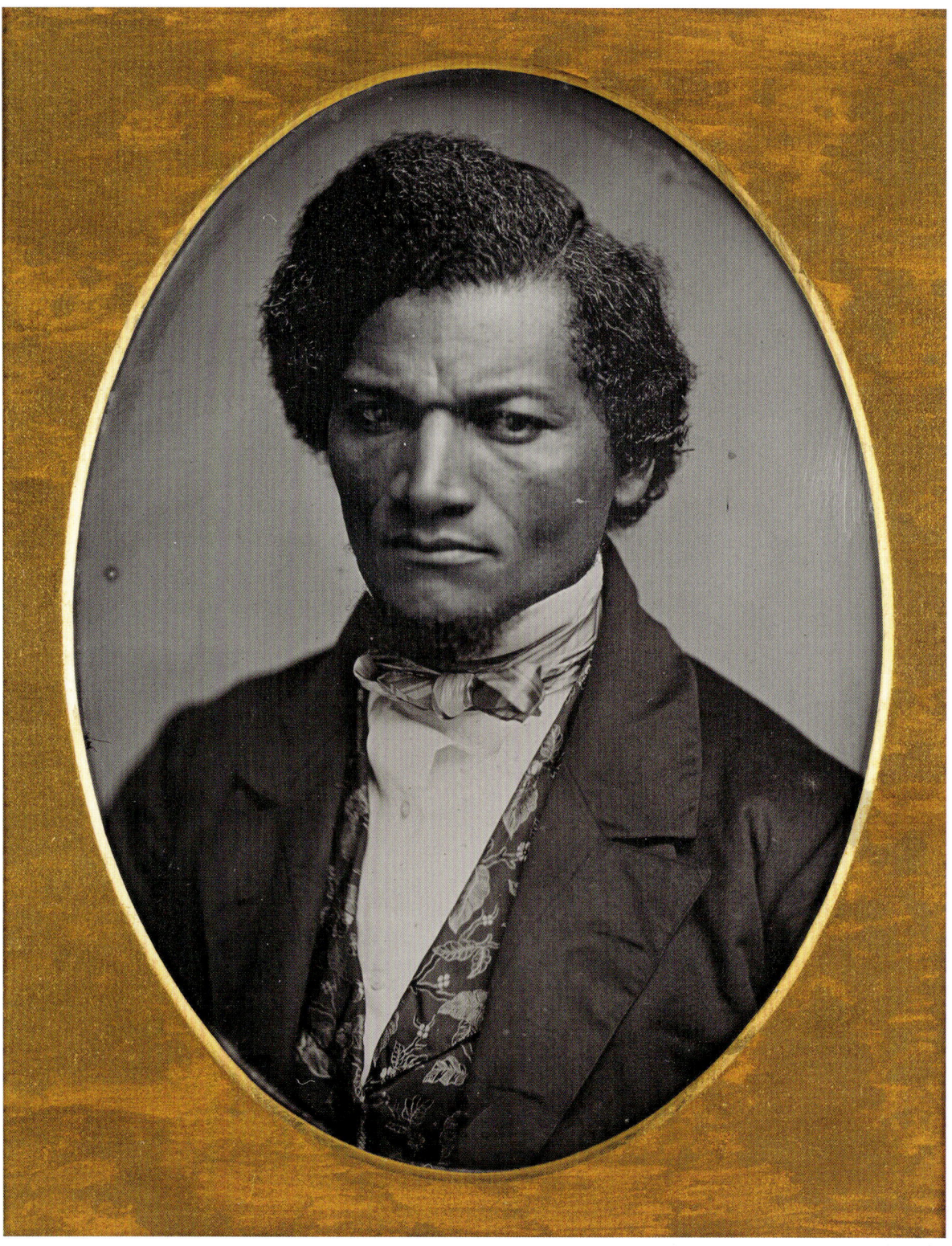

Introduction

title I'd had in mind for a while. Every month, I handed in an essay and both my editors, Jim Estrin with David Gonzales, became champions of what I do. They're extraordinarily sensitive and understood my aspirations for *Race Stories*. I owe them a great debt.

I could easily argue that, starting in the mid-twentieth century, it was graphic and dramatic televised footage of, let's say, the Birmingham conflagration in 1963, seen night after night, that changed hearts and minds around the country. But photographs do things that television and video cannot do. Photographs are all about focusing. They have the remarkable ability to cut through to realities by slowing things down, by being so still that details you never would have noticed are suddenly right before your eyes. And sometimes, if the right moment is captured, the story an image tells is more valuable than words could summon.

Photography has long worked that way in the African American community, telling the story of race in America. It's why Frederick Douglass was the most photographed American of the nineteenth century. It's why the great leader and intellectual W. E. B. Du Bois chose to curate an exhibition of portraits at the Paris Exposition in 1900 and later used photographs strategically in his work as the editor of the *Crisis*, the magazine of the National Association for the Advancement of Colored People (NAACP). It's why photographers like Gordon Parks and Roy DeCarava understood they had, as Parks called it, a "weapon of choice" in their hands. The camera could be used not just to sway white people's opinion, but to allow African Americans, under the gaze of a mainstream culture that ignored or denigrated or subjected them to all manner of stereotypes, to represent themselves as they wanted to be seen.

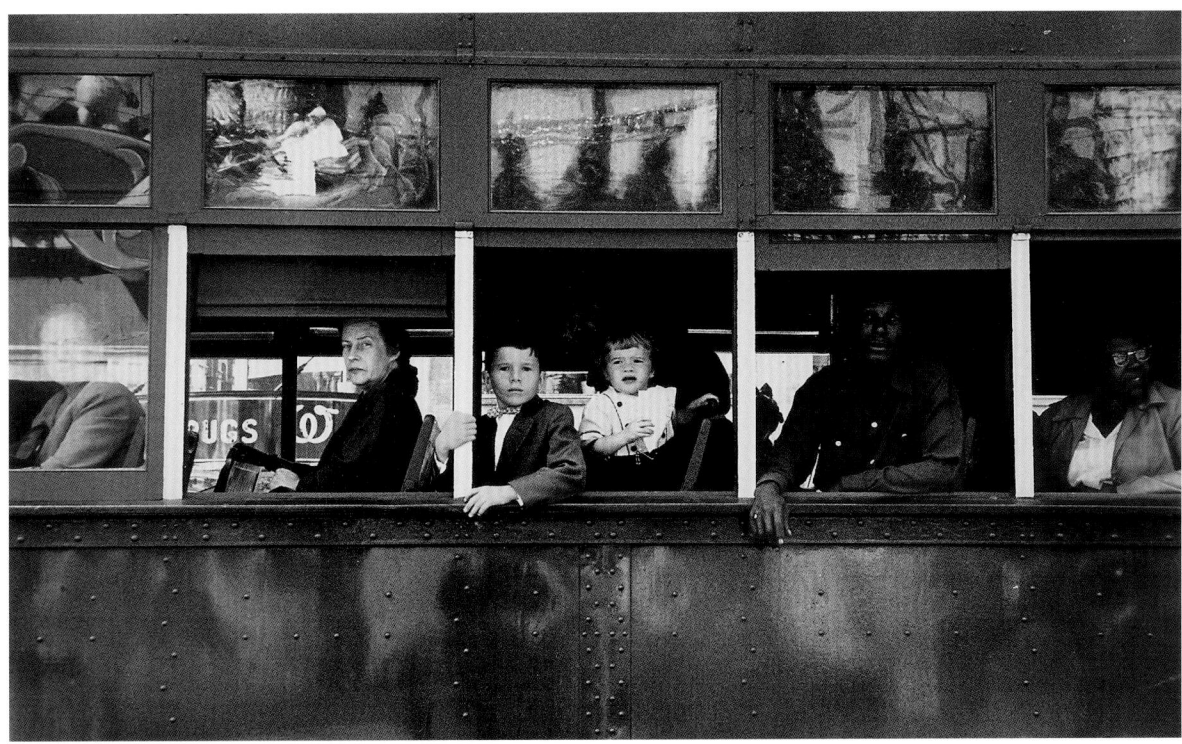

Robert Frank, *Trolley—New Orleans*, 1955

African American photo studios cropped up across the United States, solely for the purpose of allowing African Americans to represent themselves in the world. Snapshot, Polaroid, and home movie cameras all became powerful means of transcending the strictures of segregation in the South and the racism and de facto segregation in the North. The camera was, in many ways, so sacred that African American homes would have altars set up consisting of photographs of families: mothers and fathers, children and grandchildren, grandparents, aunts and uncles. Those altars were, in a way, moments of grace in a world, which wasn't always very graceful, accepting, or forgiving.

Images like those allowed people to take representation into their own hands. And equally extraordinary is what happens when gifted men and women, like Parks, DeCarava, and Ming Smith, took cameras into their own hands as artists, a tradition that continues to the present day and is a beautiful thing to watch and write about. Nothing gives me greater joy than writing about younger photographers like LaToya Ruby Frazier and Nona Faustine as they take photography to a new level, using the camera as their weapon of choice in a transference of the power of the camera from generation to generation.

The camera is a remarkable tool of political persuasion and activism. And when used in a savvy or compassionate way, the camera can do extraordinary things. The great photographers of race and civil rights understood it wasn't only about photographing somebody getting hit over the head with billy clubs, bitten by dogs in Birmingham, or being thrown to the ground. The story of race, of civil rights, of identity is a big story, so I like to write about photographers who tell big stories—not just about the conflagrations, violence, and protests, but about what happens every single day in the lives of people.

There's brilliance and beauty and profundity; it's all out there. I'm interested in writing about what is not normally written about in the mainstream press, about photographers who aren't famous enough, about issues of race that people are uncomfortable with. My greatest passion is to be an educator. I see my *New York Times* pieces as a form of teaching. How do you teach visual literacy, then racial literacy through visual literacy? Many photographers have little interest in the subject of race. But the photographers who *do* have a very profound sense of what photography can do as a medium, not just to further our awareness of the reality of racism, but to respect those different from ourselves and, in the case of people of color, to further self-esteem in a world that bombards them with stereotypes that are destructive and cruel.

What would it mean to people of color to see people like themselves, doing what they're doing, living in the world? Thriving. Succeeding. Transcending even the worst racism. Conversely, what would it do if white people saw the same thing? Gordon Parks felt strongly that images like that could inspire something not all that common in American life in the middle of the twentieth century: empathy. Photography could, by saying "look at these folks who are just like you," undermine the very concept of difference that drives the motor of racism and segregation and bigotry by disarming the idea of difference itself.

Whenever I've written about whiteness as a racial concept in *Race Stories*, those essays have asked my white readers to take a look at themselves and consider that whiteness is not invisible, not meaningless, and not the default. What I choose to do is put out ideas that I hope will help readers to

Introduction

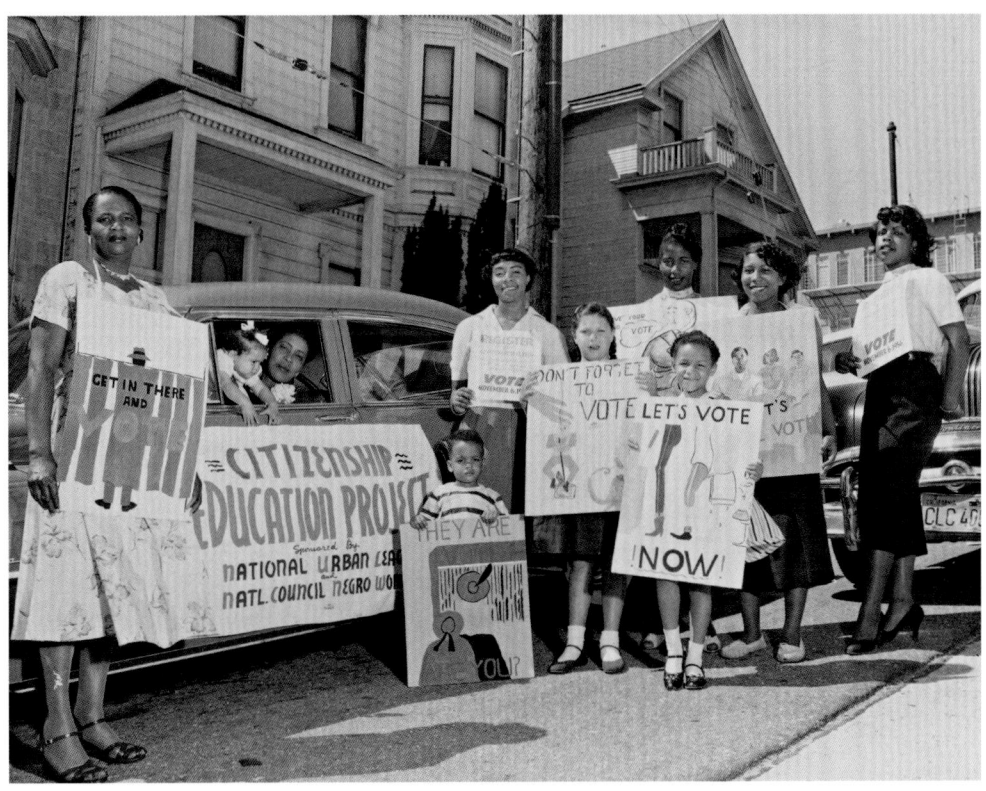

Photographer unknown, Women and children at voter registration motorcade, September 8, 1956

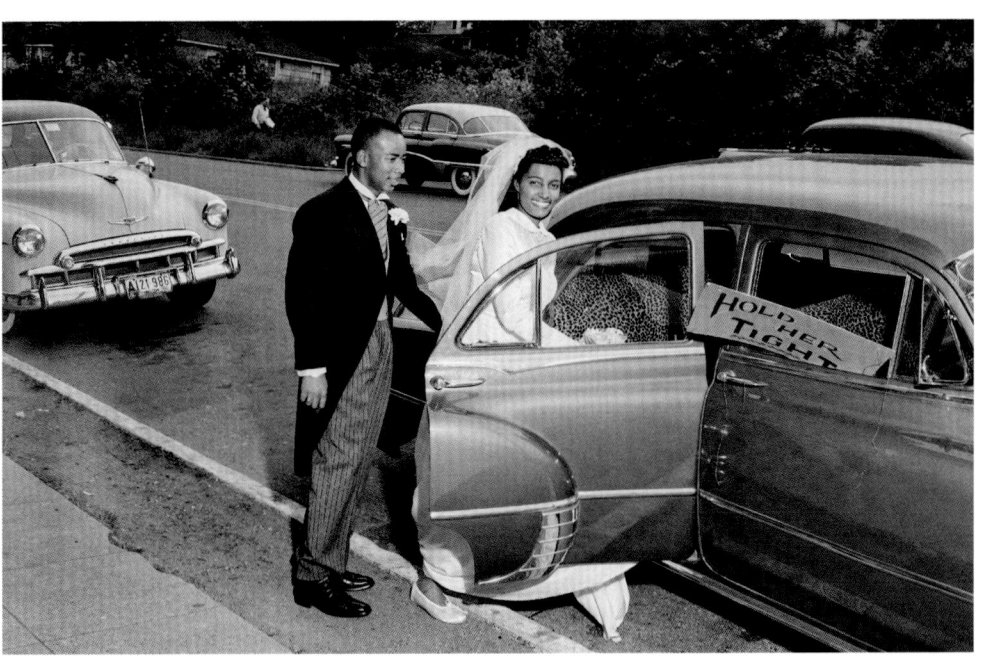

Al Smith, *Delois and Rhone Berry entering car on their wedding day, Seattle,* June 15, 1952

understand their own motivations and blind spots, to look at photographs and be thinking about themselves, thinking about their own racial attitudes in that moment. The problem of racism is not over. In some ways, it's worse now because people think it's over. And if you believe something is over, then you do not acknowledge the problem. It's my hope that in addition to empowering people of color—by showing a history of images that don't matter as much as they should or have not necessarily been part of the mainstream media—I'm also empowering white people: to be brave enough to walk themselves out of their racism by examining not only themselves, but the world of images and incredible stories about race that are all around them.

That is why I see young people as my ultimate readers. It's going to be up to them to try to understand the realities of race, often through images. And if I can do something, just one tiny little thing that might inspire a high school student in Iowa, or in the Bronx or Texas, to think about race differently or become a photographer or start writing or see their Black and white classmates differently, I think I will have done something. Maybe in reading what I have to say, a person might think, What am I doing that's hurting someone else? What can I do that might change things?

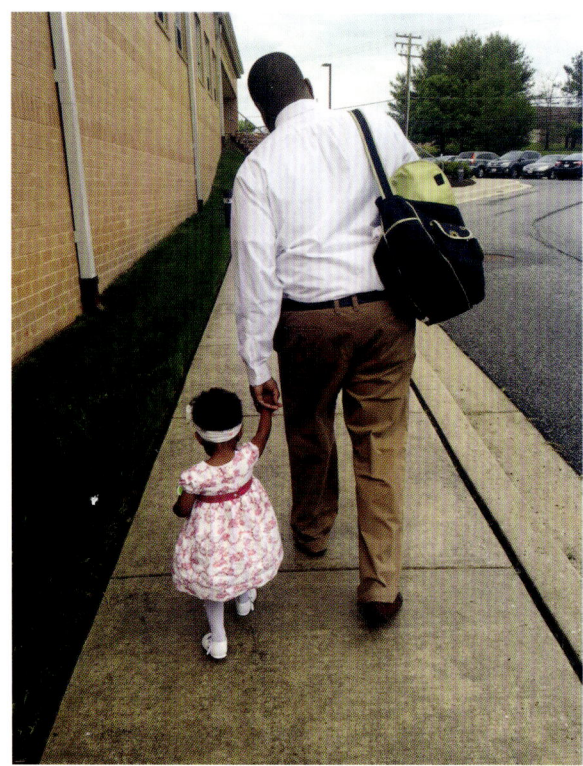

Twenty Eight Ink, *Jermaine and Janaya*, 2018

Matt Herron, March on Washington marcher with hand-lettered sign: Like, Man, I'm Tired (of Waiting),
Washington, DC, August 28, 1963

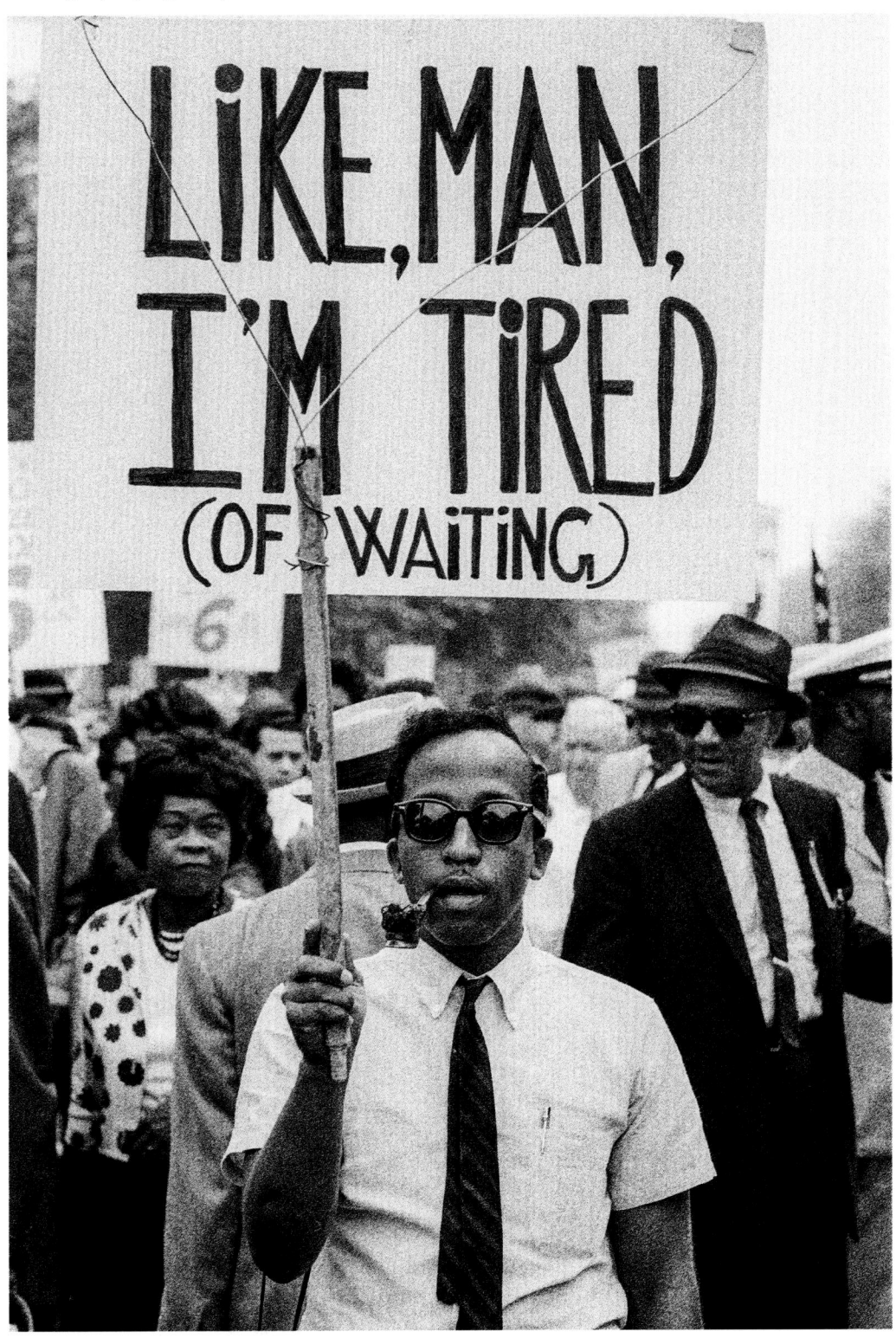

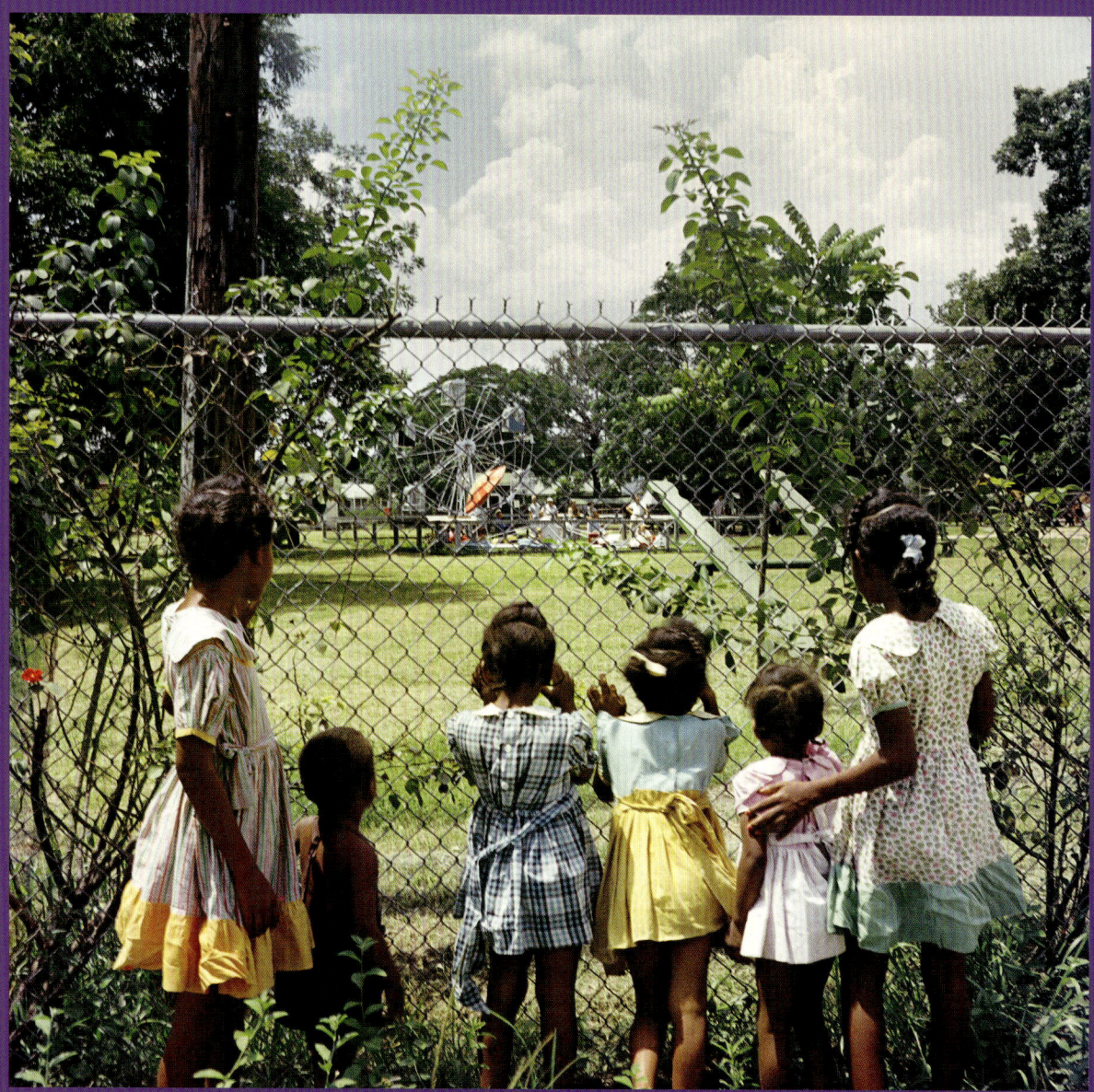

Gordon Parks, *Outside Looking In*, Mobile, Alabama, 1956

Revisiting Images:
The Past Seen Anew

# CHAPTER ONE

# A Radically Prosaic Approach to Civil Rights Images

Published July 16, 2012

Gordon Parks's portrait of Mr. and Mrs. Albert Thornton Sr., an older Black couple in their Mobile, Alabama, home in 1956, appears to have little in common with the images we have come to associate with civil rights photography.

It is in color, unlike most photographs of the movement. Its subject matter was neither newsworthy nor historic, unlike more widely published journalistic images of the racial murders, police brutality, demonstrations, and boycotts that characterized the epic battle for racial justice and equality.

Yet, as effectively as any civil rights photograph, the portrait was a forceful "weapon of choice," as Mr. Parks would say, in the struggle against racism and segregation. He took the picture on assignment for a September 1956 *Life* magazine photo-essay, "The Restraints: Open and Hidden," which documented the everyday activities and rituals of one extended Black family living in the rural South under Jim Crow segregation.

While twenty photographs were eventually published in *Life*, the bulk of Mr. Parks's work from that shoot was thought to have been lost. That is, until this spring, when the Gordon Parks Foundation discovered more than seventy color transparencies at the bottom of an old storage box, wrapped in paper and masking tape and marked *Segregation Series*.

Not all of the *Segregation* photographs are as prosaic as the Thornton portrait. Some are ominous and intense, providing stark evidence of the unjustness of segregation and the ways it endangered democracy: the "Colored Only" signs that marginalized one community as assuredly as they enrich another; the backbreaking labor; the squalor and overcrowding; and the unequal, ramshackle accommodations.

Chapter 1

But most of the images are optimistic and affirmative, like the portrait of Mr. and Mrs. Thornton. They focus on the family's everyday activities, and their resolve to get on with their lives as normally as possible, in spite of an environment that restricts and intimidates: Mrs. Thornton cradling her newborn great-grandchild; her son, now a father himself, on a stroll with his children; a couple filling out tax returns; a Sunday church service; boys fishing in a creek; a woman and her granddaughter window shopping; teenagers hanging out in front of a country store; and mourners at a funeral.

These quiet, compelling photographs elicit a reaction that Mr. Parks believed was critical to the undoing of racial prejudice: empathy. Throughout his career, he

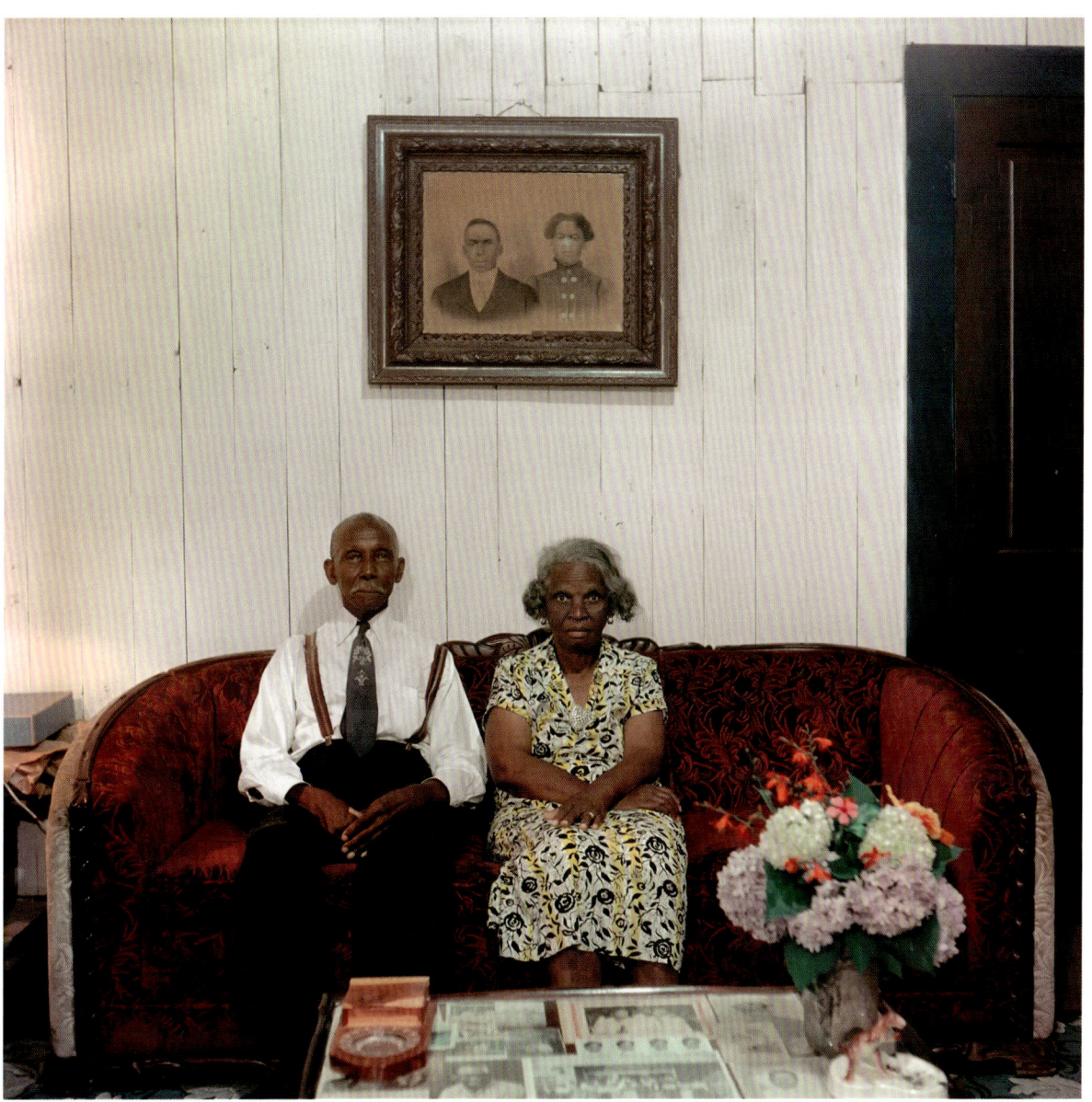

Gordon Parks, *Mr. and Mrs. Albert Thornton*, Mobile, Alabama, 1956

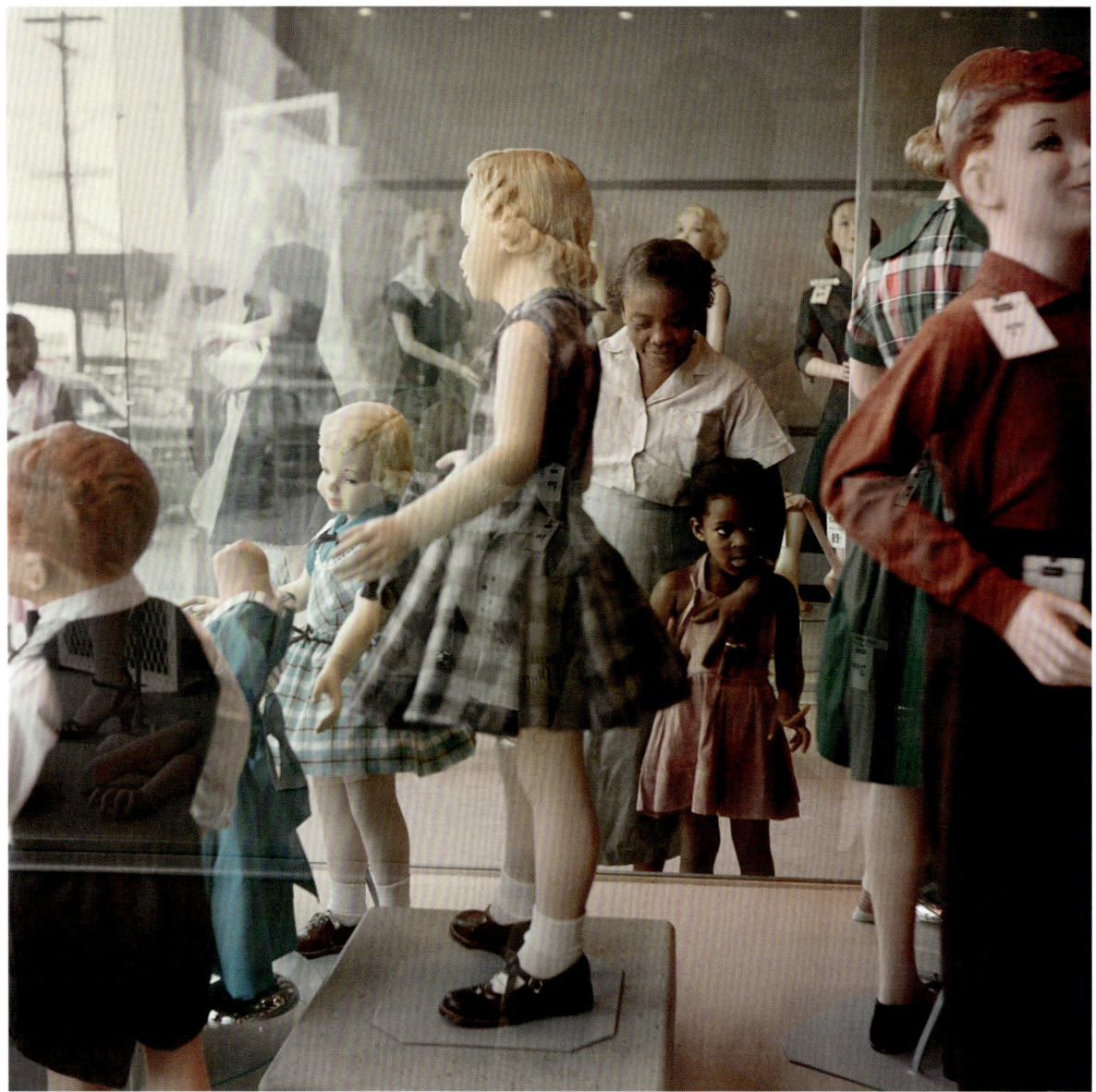

endeavored to help viewers, white and Black, to understand and share the feelings of others. It was with this goal in mind that he set out to document the lives of the Thornton family, creating images meant to alter the way Americans viewed one another and, ultimately, themselves.

More than anything, the *Segregation Series* challenged the abiding myth of racism:

that we are innately unequal, a delusion that allows one group to declare its superiority over another by capriciously ascribing to it negative traits, abnormalities, or pathologies. It is the very fullness, even ordinariness, of the lives of the Thornton family that most effectively contests these notions of difference, which had flourished in a popular culture that offered no more than an

Chapter 1

incomplete or distorted view of African American life.

As the writer Thulani Davis observes, white Americans, in the civil rights era, had little awareness that Black people "lived in a complete universe." In our private lives "we were whole. We enjoyed a richness that the mainstream almost never showed, but that we took for granted just as white people did."

As the holistic depiction of Black life in the rural South in the *Segregation Series* demonstrates, the aspirations, responsibilities, vocations, and rituals of the Thornton family were no different from those of white Americans. Yet, these religious and law-abiding people, and others like them, were persecuted. It is this incongruity, made visible by Mr. Parks's photographs, that may have appealed to the empathy and fairness of some of *Life*'s white readers. It challenged them to reconsider both their attitudes about segregation and the stereotypes they assigned to people who were little different from them.

The complete and positive images also helped to bolster the morale of Black people in the face of withering prejudice. This is one reason Mr. Parks's quiet portrait of the Thorntons is an important civil rights image, demonstrating as it does the historic role of photography in Black culture.

Throughout a century of oppression, photography served as a ray of light for Black Americans, illuminating the humanity, beauty, and achievements long hidden in the culture at large. By allowing a people to record and celebrate the affirmative aspects of their lives, the camera helped to countermand the toxic effects of stereotypes on their self-esteem.

One detail in Mr. Parks's photograph of the Thorntons underscores the medium's restorative power: the ornately framed picture of the couple that hangs on the wall above them. The image dates to the year of their wedding, 1903, when he was twenty-nine and she was seventeen. A close examination reveals that it was spliced together from two separate images. And so, what first appears to be a wedding picture is, in fact, the restitution of a lost history. The image serves as both a commemoration of the couple's union and a poignant metaphor of the resilience and urgency of their bond against a tide spanning decades of intolerance and adversity.

Another object, the coffee table in the foreground with family snapshots proudly displayed under its glass top, underscores photography's esteemed place in Black life. These details remind us of the extent to which Blacks were able to represent themselves in a positive light, requiring neither the cooperation of the media nor the work of photographers like Mr. Parks, who died at age ninety-three in 2006.

As the popularity of inexpensive and easily accessible cameras swept across the nation in the 1900s, Black Americans, like their white counterparts, relied on snapshots to document and memorialize their lives. Millions of Black people used their own cameras (and before that patronized a nationwide syndicate of Black-owned photo studios) to accomplish for themselves what a century and a half of mainstream representation usually could not: the creation of positive, multifaceted images that could embolden a people against the forces of intolerance.

# The Woman in a Jim Crow Photo

Published June 6, 2013

When Joanne Wilson stepped out to enjoy a balmy summer afternoon with her niece in 1956, she stepped into history. The two stood in front of a movie theater in downtown Mobile, Alabama, dressed in their Sunday best. But the neon sign that loomed overhead—"Colored Entrance"—cast a despairing shadow. "I wasn't going in," Mrs. Wilson recalled. "I didn't want to take my niece through the back entrance. She smelled popcorn and wanted some. All I could think was where I could go to get her popcorn."

That moment was captured by Gordon Parks, who was working on a *Life* photo-essay that documented everyday life among an extended African American family in the rural South. Although it was not among the final selections published in September 1956 as "The Restraints: Open and Hidden," the photograph of Mrs. Wilson and her niece,

Shirley Diane Kirksey, is among the most compelling of the project.

We usually associate civil rights photography with dramatic scenes of historic events. But this image helps us to understand that the battle for racial equality and justice was waged not just through epic demonstrations, speeches, and conflagrations, but also through the quiet actions of individuals.

More than half a century later, the Gordon Parks Foundation honored Mrs. Wilson with a gift of that color print during its celebrity-filled annual awards dinner at the Plaza Hotel in New York City. Speaking in a lilting but strong voice, Mrs. Wilson recounted on Tuesday night what it was like to encounter and work with Mr. Parks—how comfortable he made her feel and her need to teach him, the Northerner, "the things we could do and the things we could not do" under the watchful eyes of segregationists.

Chapter 1

Gordon Parks, *Department Store*, Mobile, Alabama, 1956

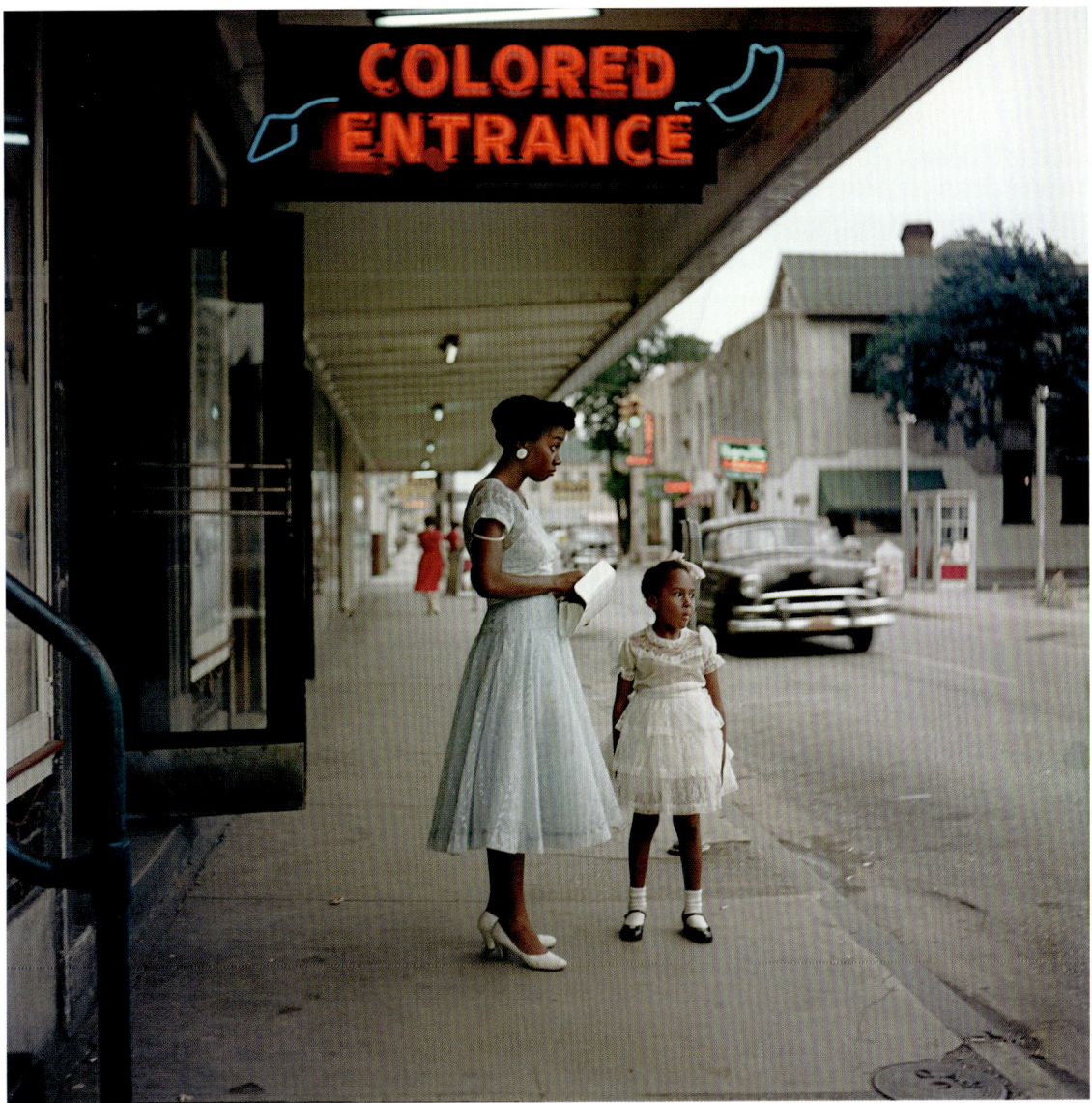

White supremacists understood the power of the camera to expose their violent prejudices and turn the nation against them. As Mr. Parks recalled later, the risk of retaliation for participating in the *Life* story was great, both for the photographer and for his subjects. But neither he nor Mrs. Wilson would be intimidated. "My family saw the photo-essay as an opportunity to advance the cause of civil rights," said Michael Wilson,

Mrs. Wilson's son and the family historian. "These pictures were going to be published in a national magazine. People across the country would clearly see the problem. They could see our plight. Maybe then we could get help."

Despite the poverty and racial enmity all around her, Mrs. Wilson endeavored to make life for her family as normal as possible. In 1956, she married Troy Wilson, a longshoreman. They had two children. After receiving her college degree, she taught American government and economics for thirty-six years at Mattie T. Blount High School, which served a predominantly Black and low-income community in Prichard, Alabama.

Like her father, Albert Thornton Sr., she believed in the power of education to uplift African Americans and prepare them to overcome racism and segregation. Each year, she organized a bake sale to finance a trip to Atlanta for her female students and introduce them to the city's historically Black colleges.

Mrs. Wilson, who was not featured in the final photo-essay, survived its publication relatively unscathed. Her sister and brother-in-law, Allie Lee Causey and Willie Causey, were less fortunate. Mrs. Causey, a teacher in a ramshackle one-room schoolhouse in Shady Grove, Alabama, was quoted in the piece as advocating integration as "the only way through which Negroes will receive justice." One of the most outspoken members of the Thornton family, she helped to organize voter drives and teach community members the Bill of Rights, the recital of which from memory was a prerequisite for African Americans to vote in many Southern states.

As *Life* later reported, Mrs. Causey's candor and activism infuriated white supremacists, who taunted the couple about their participation in the photo-essay. Service stations refused to sell gas to Mr. Causey, a woodcutter and farmer. He was soon accused of owing money on his truck, which was seized by alleged creditors. Without it, he was unable to work. Two weeks after the photo-essay was published, Mrs. Causey was fired from her teaching job. Unable to make a living and fearing for their safety, the couple moved out of Alabama. Mrs. Causey, who died in 2006, never taught again.

Despite these setbacks, the family had no misgivings about appearing in the piece.

"Everyone was very impressed with the article," Mr. Wilson said. "They felt that they had made a friend. Gordon had become part of the family." After the essay was published, Mr. Parks would periodically check in with Mrs. Wilson's parents.

Mrs. Wilson's only quibble with the photograph of her and her niece was that Mr. Parks did not tell her the strap of her slip had fallen. "I always wanted to look neat and nice," she said. "I did not want to be mistaken for a servant. Dressing well made me feel first class. I wanted to set an example."

But Mr. Parks may have had a reason for the oversight: a desire to stress the human side of an image that, in its refinement and flair, could at first be mistaken for one of his fashion photographs. In this context, Mrs. Wilson was not just challenging racism and stereotypes through meticulous self-presentation. She was also going about her daily life, like millions of women, Black and white—tending to the needs of an energetic young child, but in a hostile environment. The price she paid for meeting this responsibility, as anyone who has cared for a child knows, was the distraction that made her overlook the fallen strap. Yet, it is this poignant detail that helps us to identify with her. And it is this appeal to empathy, a central goal of Mr. Parks's civil rights work, that helped him to challenge racism's abiding myth: that we are fundamentally different.

The decision of the Gordon Parks Foundation to honor Mrs. Wilson challenges another misconception: that history is principally the domain of the famous and powerful. As the *Life* photo-essay shows, history is also made through the daily, unheralded acts of ordinary people. What we see in Mr. Parks's image is a determined and self-possessed woman, challenging stereotypes and fortifying herself against the poisonous tide of

Chapter 1

oppression that threatened to engulf her and her family.

Mrs. Wilson's humanity was under assault, and she chose, in her own way, to fight back. Fifty-seven years later, that moment is potent proof that even the smallest gesture, seen through the right eyes, can change the world.

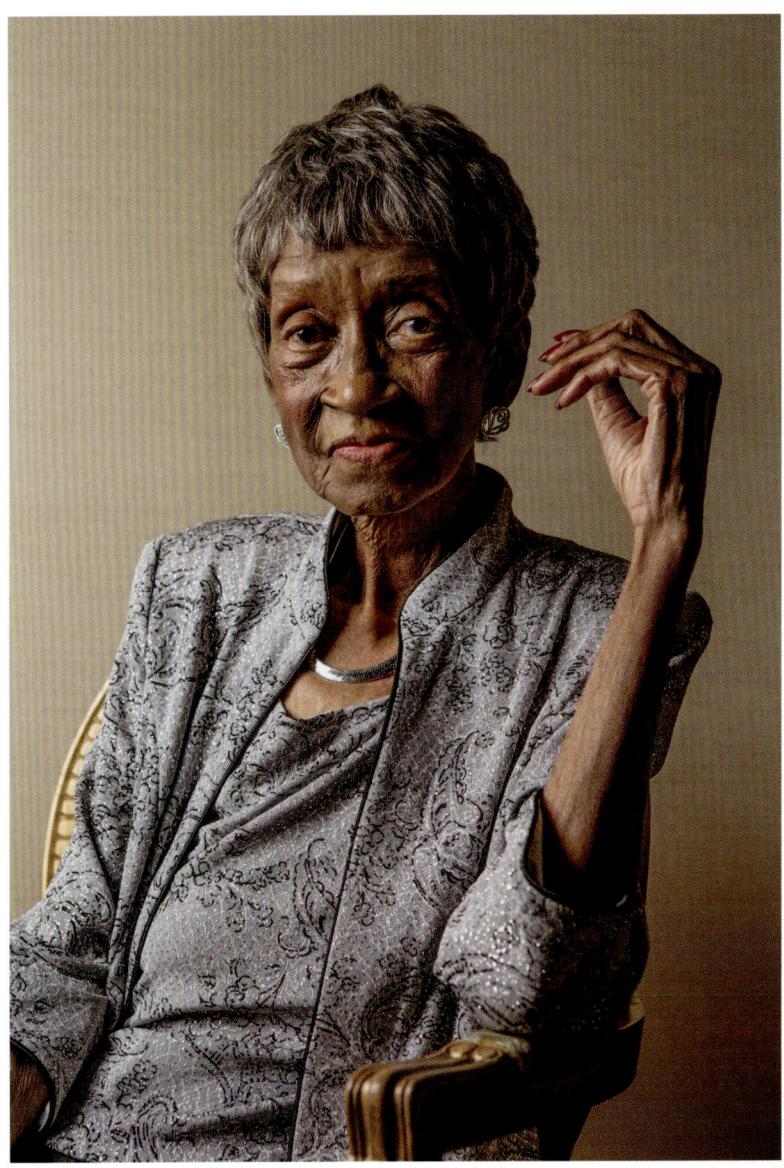

Fred R. Conrad, Mrs. Wilson at the Plaza Hotel in New York City for the Gordon Parks Foundation Awards Dinner, 2013

# Reconsidering the Black Panthers through Photos

Published September 8, 2016

A Black man helps an older African American woman as she shops in an Oakland, California, supermarket. The image from 1973, by Stephen Shames, documents an initiative to protect the elderly in a crime-ridden neighborhood. It doesn't just show community activism, it also challenges lurid media stereotypes about the organization responsible for the initiative: the Black Panther Party.

This is one of many photographs in an important new book by Mr. Shames and Bobby Seale, *Power to the People: The World of the Black Panthers*, that help us to better understand one of the most innovative, if controversial, American movements for racial equality and justice. An accompanying exhibition of Mr. Shames's Panther photographs opens this month at the Steven Kasher Gallery in New York.

Published on the fiftieth anniversary of the party's founding, *Power to the People* constitutes an impressionistic visual and oral history of the Panthers. It combines in-depth commentary by Mr. Seale, a major figure within the Panthers; the photographs and observations of Mr. Shames, the group's principal visual chronicler; excerpts of interviews Mr. Shames conducted with party leaders— including Kathleen Cleaver, Emory Douglas, Elbert "Big Man" Howard, Ericka Huggins, Billy X Jennings, and Jamal Joseph—as well as the words of Huey P. Newton and Eldridge Cleaver.

Mr. Shames was a student at the University of California, Berkeley, when he became active in politics. He met Mr. Seale and Mr. Newton in San Francisco during the Spring Mobilization Committee to End the War in Vietnam six months after they founded the Black Panther Party for Self Defense in October 1966. "I started hanging out with the Panthers, attending their

Chapter 1

rallies," Mr. Shames recalled in the text. "Bobby Seale became my mentor and friend . . . I was granted incredible access. Over the next seven years, culminating in Bobby Seale's 1973 campaign for mayor of Oakland, I documented this group of young men and women, who were at the forefront of the Black Power movement and who became the vanguard of the revolution that was sweeping America."

The aims of the Black Panther Party were diverse and complex. On one level, the group advocated armed resistance against police misconduct and abuse, as well as a revolution to achieve the racial equality and justice that it felt the nonviolent civil rights movement had failed to achieve. As the party gained momentum, J. Edgar Hoover, director of the FBI, deemed it "the greatest threat to the internal security of the country." Vowing that 1969 would be the last year of the Panthers' existence, Hoover made it a principal target of the bureau's COINTELPRO initiative, established in the 1950s to monitor, infiltrate, and discredit radical political organizations.

But the movement endured, in part because its objectives went far beyond armed self-defense and insurrection. To some extent stymied by the 1967 Mulford Act—the bill, which repealed the right to publicly bear firearms in California, was created largely in response to Panther members who were conducting armed patrols of Oakland neighborhoods—the party increasingly emphasized community-based activism, voter registration drives, and more than sixty "survival programs." Those programs included free medical, eye, and dental care; legal aid; food cooperatives; employment referral; plumbing; pest control; home maintenance programs; screening for sickle cell anemia; a child development center; and a well-regarded school.

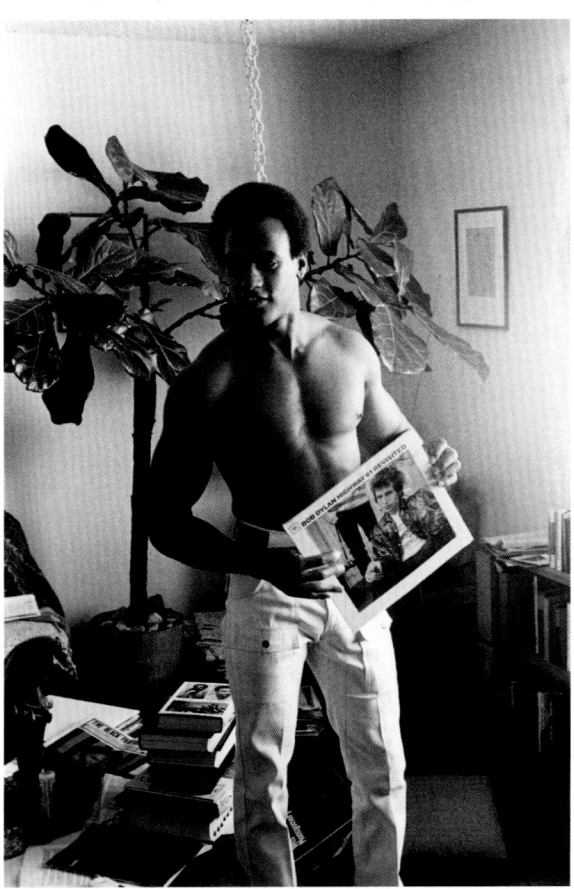

Stephen Shames, Huey P. Newton, cofounder and minister of defense of the Black Panther Party, listening to Bob Dylan's record *Highway 61 Revisited* in his house in Berkeley, California, shortly after his release from prison, August 1970

Granted, among such a group of strong-willed leaders with a particular vision, "the Panthers suffered from the factionalism, disorganization, and personality cults that so often afflict oppositional movements," wrote the *New York Times* critic A. O. Scott in his review of the 2015 documentary *The Black Panthers: Vanguard of the Revolution*.

But Mr. Shames's pictures affirmed the movement's complexity, countering an unrelenting stream of mainstream images of menacing, gun-toting men, women, and children. If some in the news media viewed the party as an influential force for Black autonomy, others saw it as a criminal organization. *Power to*

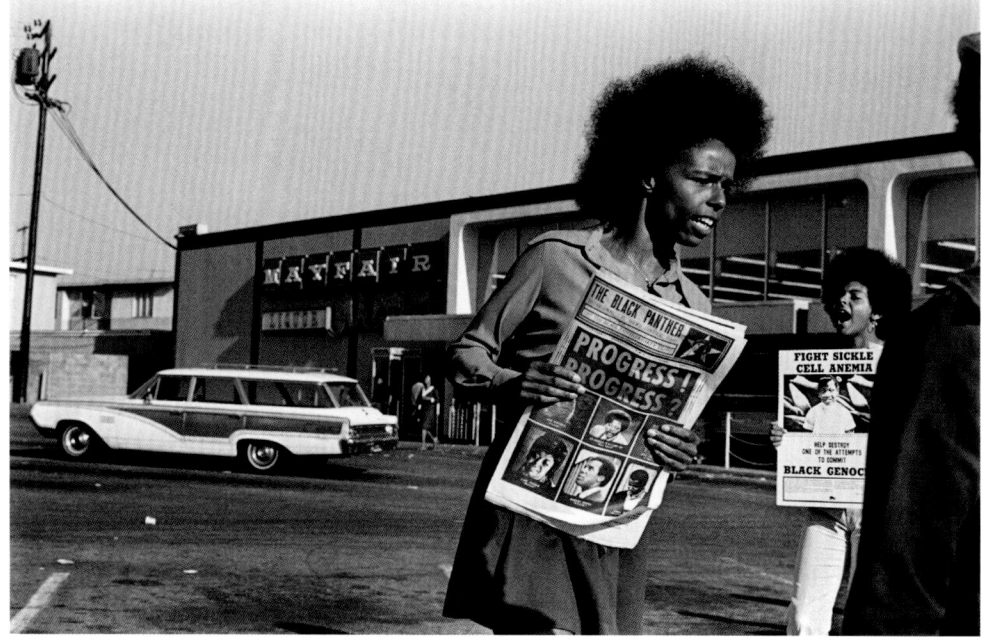

Stephen Shames, The Black Panther Gloria Abernathy selling papers at the Mayfair supermarket boycott in Oakland. Tamara Lacey was in the background holding a poster, 1971

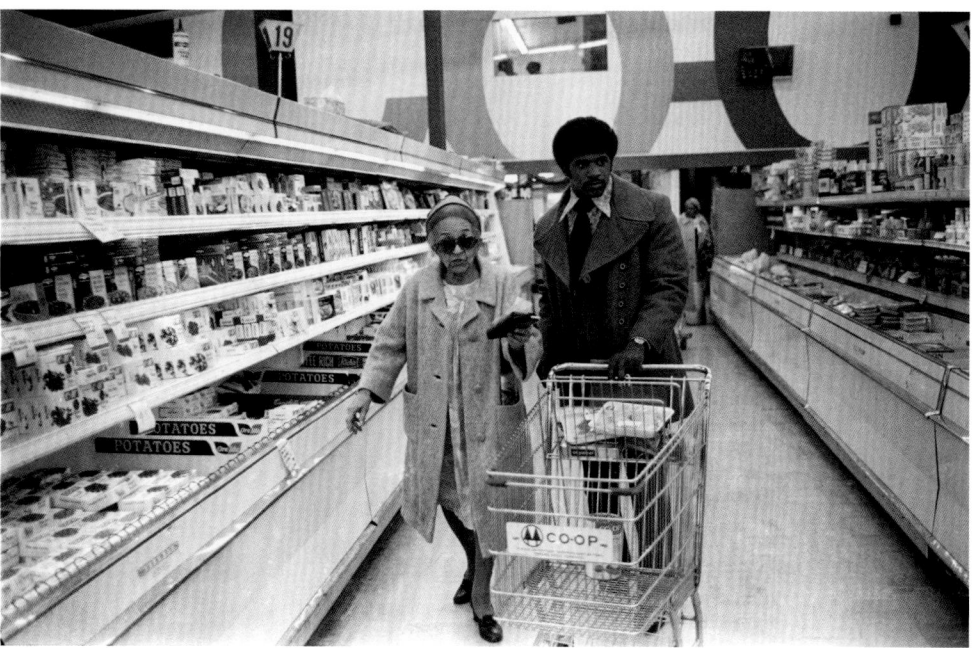

Stephen Shames, Leonard Colar helping a woman with her shopping as part of the Black Panther Senior Escort program in Oakland, 1973

*the People* offers a relatively nuanced view of a militant national organization that advocated insurrection and armed resistance but also fought for empowered, self-reliant, and culturally expressive Black communities.

The photographs in *Power to the People* attest to the movement's accomplishments and ingenuity: children engaged in programs designed to educate, bolster self-esteem, and teach the Black history and culture that were virtually absent from public schools; people carrying grocery bags emblazoned with the Panther logo and filled with free food; suave, self-possessed, and media-savvy leaders who challenged prevailing stereotypes; and protest rallies and boycotts.

In the end, Mr. Shames's exacting photographs were in keeping with a movement that often disseminated its ideas through imagery. As the artist and writer Colette Gaiter has documented, every detail of the party's visual campaign was rigorously considered, from the impeccable uniforms of its leaders to the vivid graphic design of its national weekly newspaper, *The Black Panther*, for which Emory Douglas, the "master craftsman" of the party's visual identity and its minister of culture, was the art director.

"Before a correct visual interpretation of the struggle can be given, we must recognize that Revolutionary Art is an art that flows from the people," Mr. Douglas observed in 1968. "It must be a whole and living part of the people's lives, their daily struggle to survive." To emphasize this point, the Kasher Gallery has mounted a companion exhibition, in tandem with Mr. Shames's photographs, of Mr. Douglas's illustrations for the newspaper.

Through its retrospective view of the party, which disbanded in the 1980s, *Power to the People* has much to say about our present-day racial crisis. Over the past half-century, much has changed, yet little has changed, as the campaign to end systemic racism and violence against people of color, exemplified by the Black Lives Matter movement, remains as vital as ever.

And fifty years after he helped found the party, Mr. Seale sees it as relevant as ever. "Now we must reach for the future," he wrote in the book's afterword. "Progressive people around the world understand that we must continue our liberation struggle. We must organize people's programs and evolve greater participatory community control democracies, void of racist, bigoted, and chauvinistic practices. This is the true legacy of my Black Panther Party."

# Chronicling the Virtuosity and Struggles of 1970s Soul and Funk Musicians

Published September 6, 2018

The photograph is as unusual as it is illuminating: a close-up of the bassist Louis Johnson's cut and blistered thumb after playing a concert. Taken in 1977 at Funk Fest in Los Angeles by Bruce W. Talamon, the image reminds us that there is more to the music business than glamour. It was a world driven by hard work, sacrifice, and relentless ambition—one that Mr. Talamon came to know well as one of the preeminent chroniclers of R&B, soul, and funk musicians in the 1970s.

Mr. Talamon's pictures are distinguished by their intimacy, as the image of Mr. Johnson's injured finger suggests, offering a view into the hidden moments of a music scene that had been largely understood through promotional photos and visual clichés. The trust he earned from his famous subjects afforded him extensive access, allowing him to document moments often unavailable to other photographers and reporters. "Man, I got more private concerts than the law allowed," Mr. Talamon said in a profile in the *Guardian* this summer. "People like Marvin Gaye would say, 'Listen to this,' and they'd play something hip. I'd be in the room when they were trying something out, working on some idea."

His photographs from that heady period are the subject of a new book, *Soul, R&B, Funk*, edited by Reuel Golden with a foreword by the photographer, a chronology of his life, and an interview with Mr. Talamon by the playwright Pearl Cleage. The images depict musicians onstage and off, in performance, greeting fans, in quiet reflective moments, and living their lives: an exhausted Al Green, slumped against the door of his dressing room after a grueling performance; Aretha Franklin, her hand thrust gracefully into the air, white feathers cradling her radiant face, singing on a television special; Bootsy Collins,

Chapter 1

in typically outrageous costume, performing at the Forum in Inglewood, California; Stevie Wonder having a late night at Roscoe's House of Chicken & Waffles in Hollywood; and Patti LaBelle, relaxing in a sleek conference room at CBS Records after a long day of interviews.

Mr. Talamon, who majored in political science at Whittier College and intended to become a lawyer, began photographing musicians in 1971 on a whim and with no formal training. A chance encounter with Howard L. Bingham, the respected photographer and biographer of Muhammad Ali, led to a life-changing mentorship and an introduction to the publication that launched his career: *Soul*, a pioneering Black-owned newspaper published in Los Angeles from 1966 to 1982.

Founded by Regina and Ken Jones, *Soul* published interviews, articles, and photographs about Black entertainers. By 1972, Ms. Jones had become editor in chief, overseeing all aspects of the biweekly paper's production, which included the hiring of young writers and photographers like Mr. Talamon. His intimate and humanistic images typified *Soul*'s sensibility, an important outlet for Black artistic expression during a period when the mainstream media was not always paying attention.

In a 2012 interview conducted by UCLA's Center for Oral History Research, Ms. Jones recounted how at the time of *Soul*'s founding, there were no Black publicists working for record companies. "When we first started, most of the time they didn't even have a

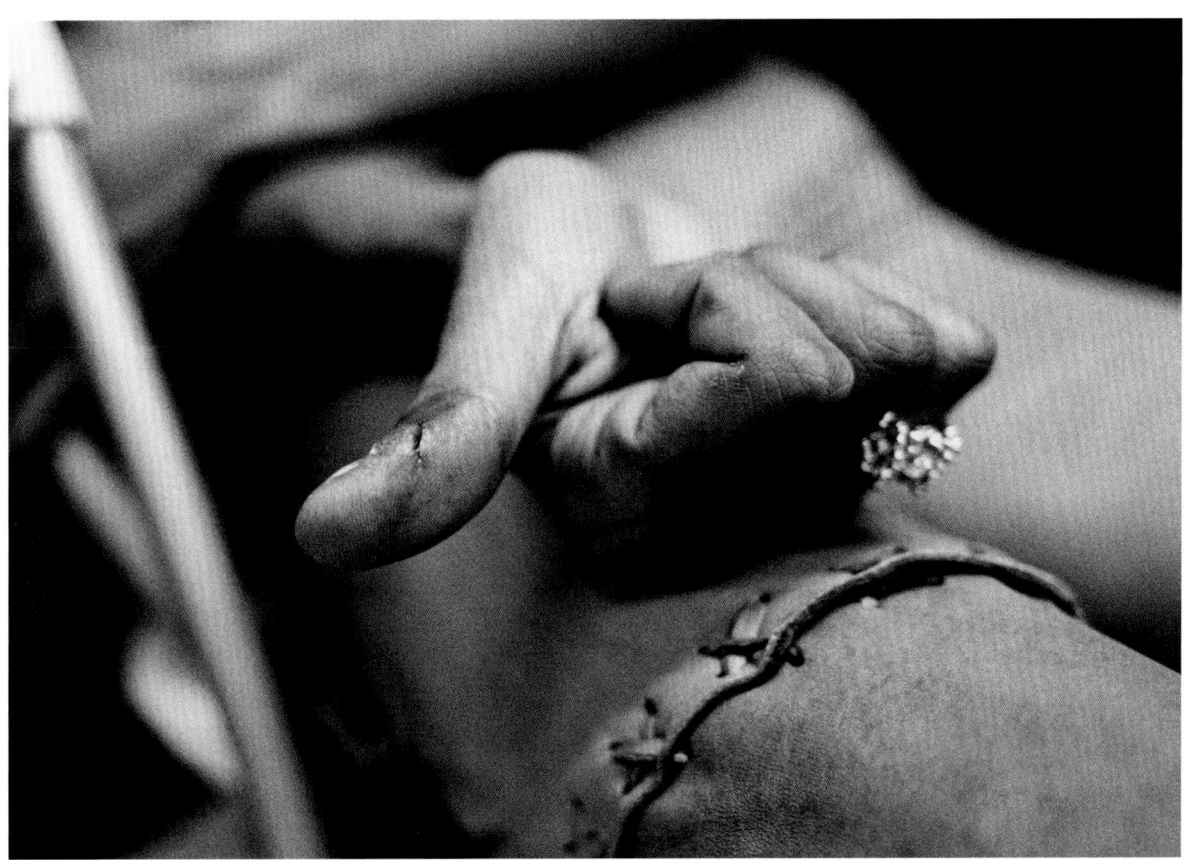

Bruce W. Talamon, Louis Johnson's blistered thumb after performing at the P-Funk Earth Tour, Los Angeles Coliseum, 1977

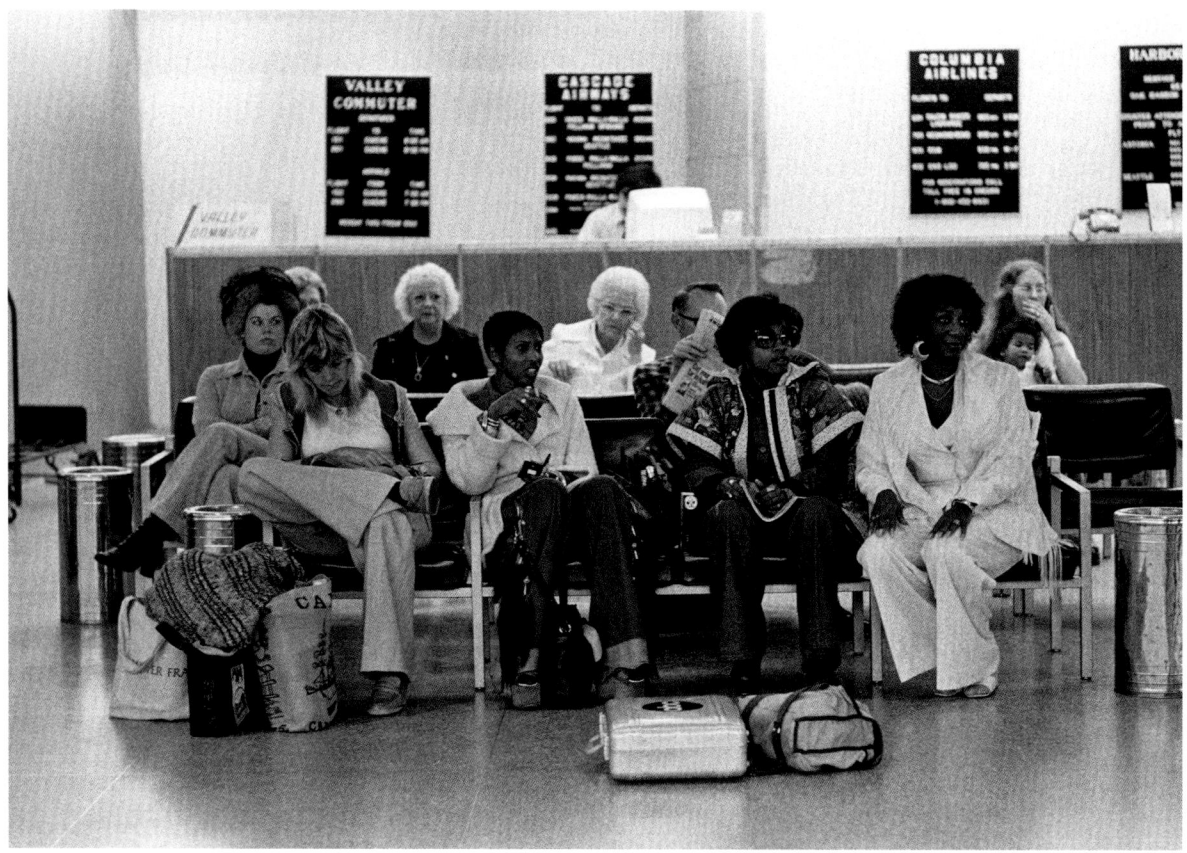

photograph of the artist," she said, adding, "They were selling the sound. There were no bios at the beginning."

"We were having to get photos, create bios to match the records that were hits that were going on," she continued. Ultimately, the magazine's linking of sound to image and biography transformed coverage of African American musicians. Mr. Talamon's work for *Soul*, which he says gave him confidence and a platform to hone his craft, made an important contribution to its visual ethos, providing readers with a vivid window into the lives of people they respected and idolized. His well-regarded work for the magazine led to other projects and commissions, including assignments from individual artists and record companies.

Mr. Talamon, sixty-nine, considers himself "a visual caretaker of Black folks' history," documenting a vital music scene that was important to Black Americans and to the nation. In their honesty and gravity, his photographs portray a world of virtuosity and struggle, where political and racial boundaries were transgressed and the direction of American popular music dynamically altered. "I've always thought of my photographs as documents that went beyond screaming into a microphone," Mr. Talamon wrote in his foreword. "My body of work has been about the whole unvarnished process, as opposed to just that portion that publicity machines and record companies want you to see."

In the 1980s, as the music business changed and record companies started

Chapter 1

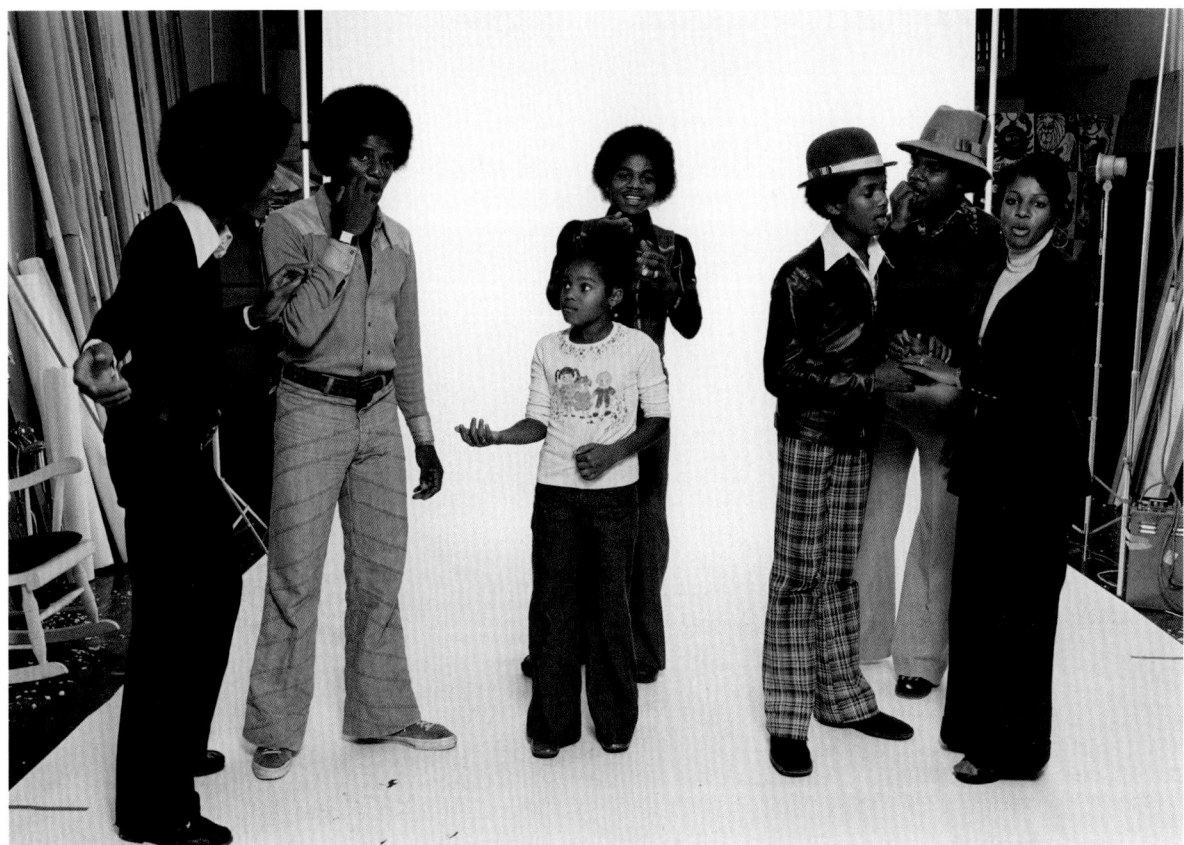

issuing work-for-hire agreements for photographers, Mr. Talamon turned his attention to other pursuits, including stills for John Singleton, Tony Scott, Steven Spielberg, and other filmmakers. Yet the extraordinary archive of music imagery he left behind continues to expand our understanding of Black entertainers and the significant role they played in popular culture. "These photographs are a celebration of the music, an aesthetic, a style that's gone," Mr. Talamon said. "But for that moment, it was magical. I would like to think that maybe I caught a little bit of that magic and was able to leave a record of what these musicians did and how good they were."

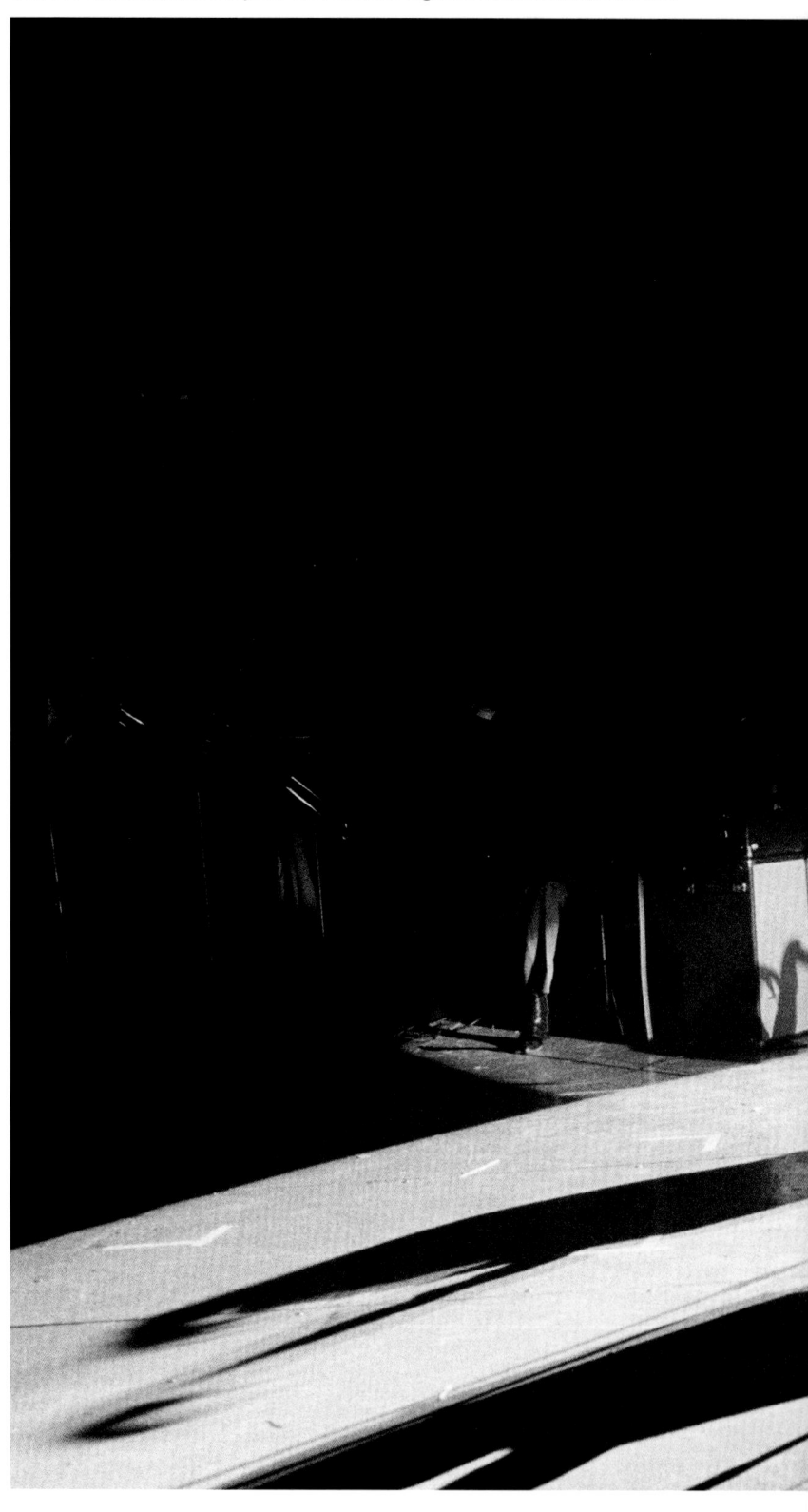

Chapter 1

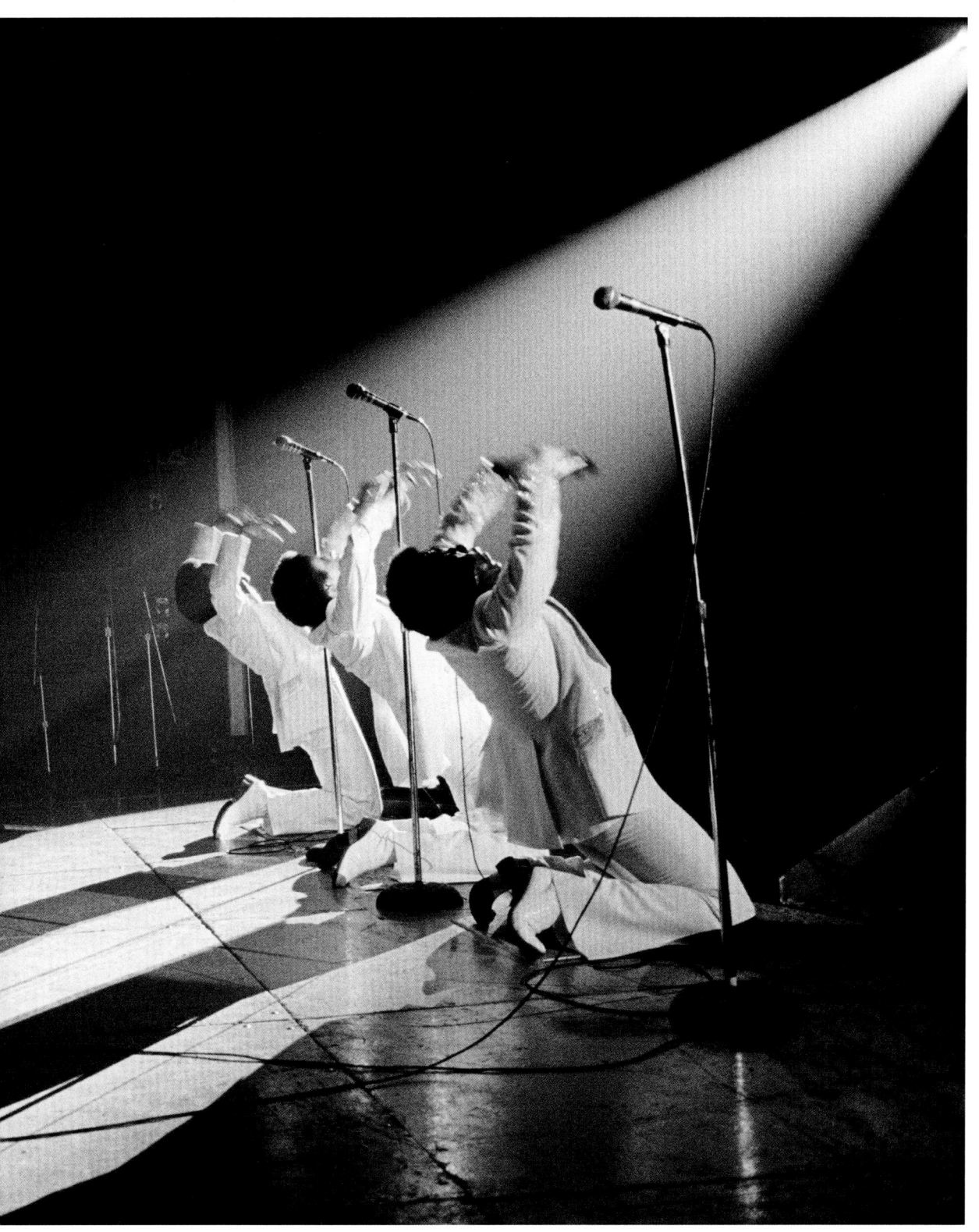

# Holding a Mirror to Race

Published March 24, 2014

The vintage images are as old as the expectations they can summon. An ambrotype from the 1860s with two men of apparently different races, squaring off, fists up. An oddly formal studio portrait of men cloaked in Ku Klux Klan robes. A pensive portrait of an abolitionist. An enslaver, clutching a whip and staring defiantly.

But instead of receiving any explanations, viewers have to plumb their own minds—and assumptions—going from each photograph's poles of black and white into the gray nuances of reality. That is the power behind a remarkable interactive website called Mirror of Race, which uses nineteenth-century photographs depicting people of various races in situations that are often ambiguous in their content and intent.

Unlike a classic museum exhibition, where wall labels provide context and analysis, Mirror of Race invites viewers to first confront its imagery free of curatorial interpretation. Viewers can then click on the picture's accompanying texts, one with information about what is known about it, the other a scholarly analysis of its subjects and their interactions. The information raises more questions and, hopefully, spurs discussion.

The project was founded by Derek Burrows, a musician and storyteller whose work draws upon the traditions of the African diaspora; Greg French, who has amassed one of most important private collections of early American photographs dealing with race; and Gregory Fried, who teaches philosophy at Suffolk University in Boston.

Mirror of Race—which also includes essays, short films, and smaller special exhibitions devoted to pictures of enslaved people, abolitionists, racial violence, and gender—addresses a drawback in dealing

Photographer unknown, Two men boxing. Staged studio scene, ca. 1860–65

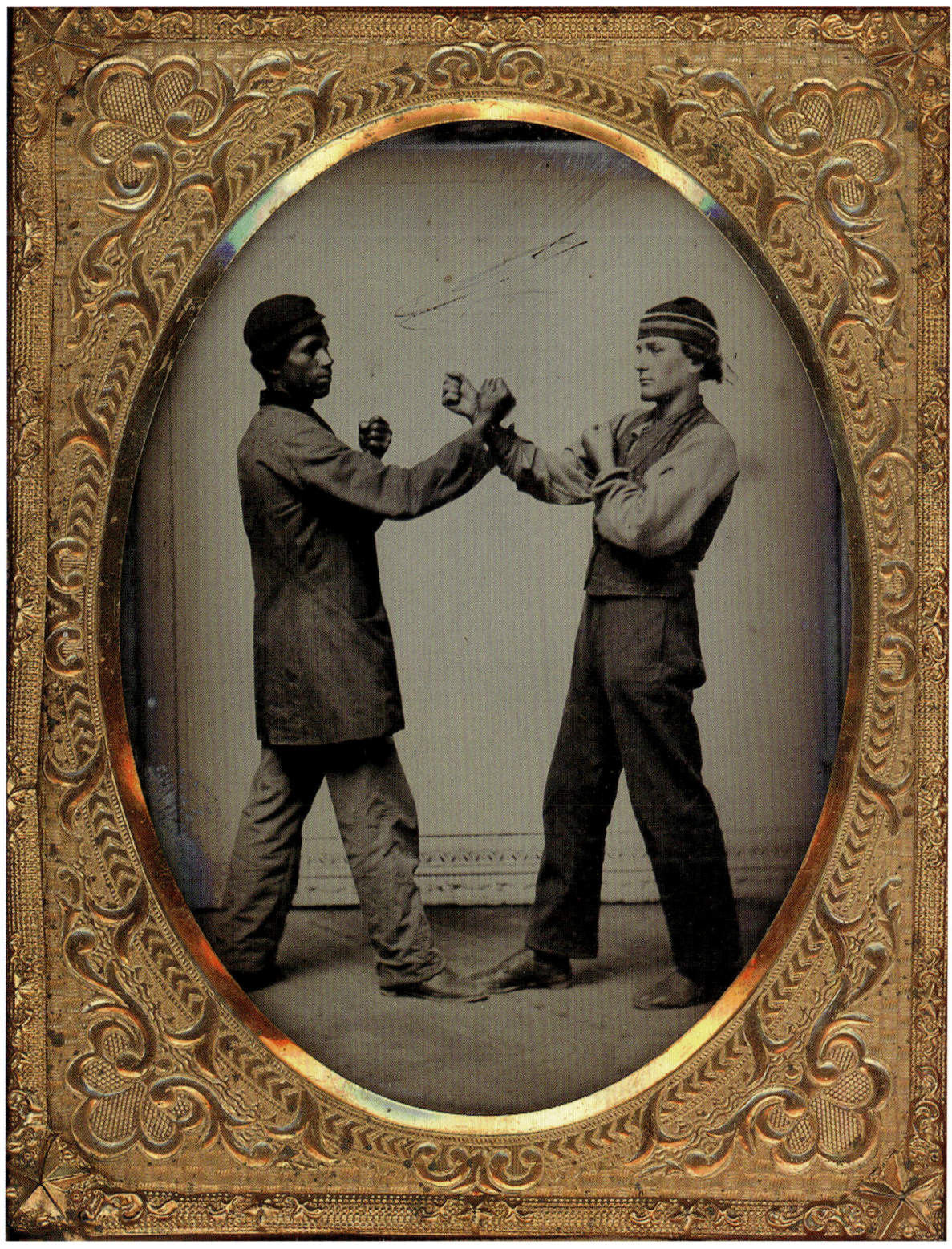

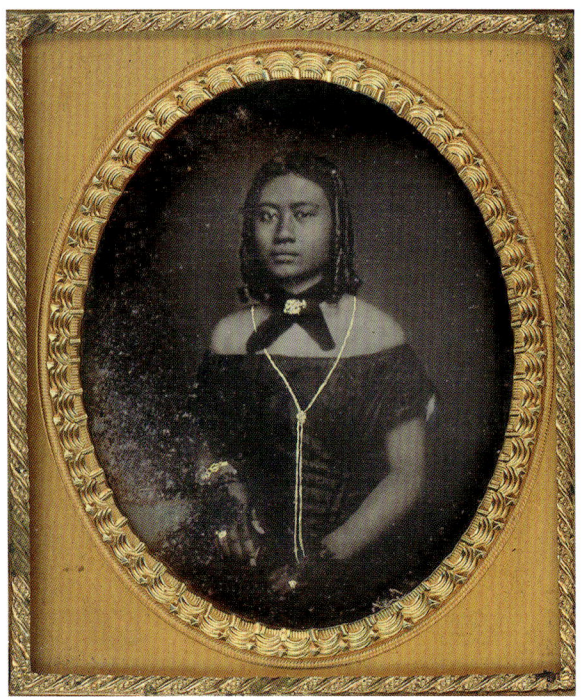

Photographer unknown, Princess Victoria Kamamalu. Studio
portrait, ca. 1855

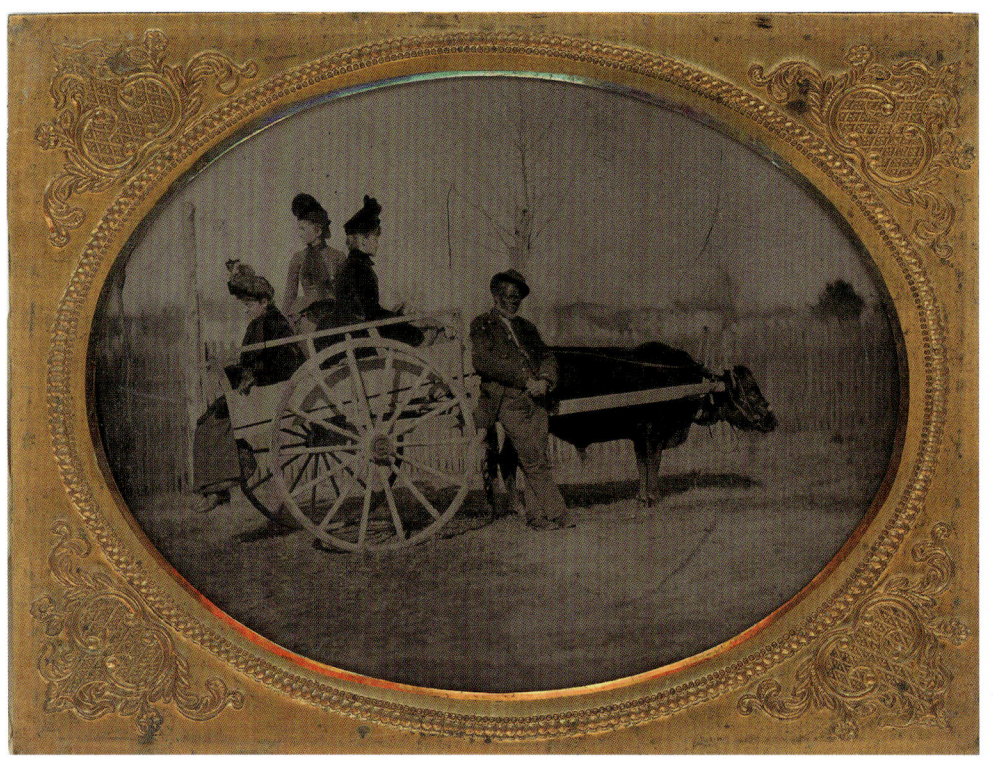

Photographer unknown, Ox cart. Outdoor scene, ca. 1875

Chapter 1

with racism: Most Americans would rather not talk about the racial anxieties, suspicions, and stereotypes that keep them apart. But the website shows that photography can be an effective way to jostle even well-intentioned people out of denial.

"Photography has the paradoxical ability to allow us to contemplate intimately from a safe distance, and so, like an anesthetic, photography can give us the opportunity to confront the historical reality of race without recoiling in anger, guilt, or fear," Mr. Fried said in an email interview. "It gives us the chance to reflect and to think without immediately turning away from what is uncomfortable."

The project's central metaphor, the mirror, derives from its most dominant artifact, the daguerreotype. The polished and reflective metal surfaces of these early photographs, when viewed at a certain angle, meld their own imagery with that of the viewer.

Though no longer reflective on the screen, the images in Mirror of Race provide a metaphorical link between the present and a safely distant past. In viewing them, participants are invited to privately self-examine racial perceptions, free of judgment or retribution, and ultimately acknowledge that racism is not just the domain of the white supremacist but is everyone's problem.

Consider a recent op-ed in which a doctor noted that African American breast cancer patients were sometimes "less likely to be recommended by physicians to receive curative cancer care," even when they had similar health insurance coverage as whites.

"I don't think this is because doctors are racist, but rather that they make assumptions about race that can be harmful," Dr. Harold P. Freeman wrote. He added that "a specialist treating a poor Black woman may doubt that she will comply with a complex treatment and recommend a simpler, but non-curative, therapy instead."

Those kinds of perceptions, which are rooted in racial stereotypes or prejudice, are not always so deadly, but they are often resistant to change. Mr. Fried observed that the Mirror of Race takes its cue from cognitive psychology. "Virtually everyone, no matter their way of self-identifying, projects implicit bias in the way they see others," he said of recent research. "The good news is that if we become aware of this implicit bias and reflect upon how we apply it, we can make progress in reducing its hold on us."

The inability to see or even name the problem—insisting, for example, that the indifference toward Black women by the medical establishment is not racist—can make it virtually impossible to resolve.

Mirror of Race insists that owning up to blind spots through honest self-inquiry is crucial to getting past them.

"While no one can overcome prejudice either in themselves or in society just by reflection, it is a step in both the internal and interpersonal dialogue that needs to happen," Mr. Fried said. "We must start somewhere, and we can always start with ourselves."

# Photographing Civil Rights, Up North and Beyond Dixie

Published October 18, 2016

An elegantly dressed African American woman kneels in the middle of a road, her knees protected by a sheet of cardboard. She is blocking dump trucks, an act of civil disobedience to protest unfair hiring practices at a hospital construction site.

The 1963 image by Bob Adelman appears to be a typical civil rights photograph. But it is not. The solitary woman's act of defiance was far from the Deep South: It took place at Brooklyn's Downstate Medical Center.

The picture appears in a new book by the historian Mark Speltz, *North of Dixie: Civil Rights Photography Beyond the South*, which provides a more expansive view of the civil rights movement, both geographically and culturally. It is a much-welcome corrective to standard histories, as well as journalistic coverage at the time, which focused on Jim Crow segregation in the South, especially as captured in some historic, disturbing, and indelible images of the day.

The most widely published and acclaimed photographs of the period typically documented extreme incidents of violence, murder, and civil disobedience in the South, events that spurred such reforms as the Supreme Court's 1954 ruling in *Brown v. Board of Education* or the passage of the Civil Rights Act a decade later. Ultimately, this narrative concentrated on harsh oppression, Black and white resistance, and political triumph.

But the story of racism and its confrontation is more complex. The discrimination African Americans experienced—especially outside of the South in supposedly more liberal Northern climes—was sometimes de facto or indirect. During the civil rights movement, some photographs helped make visible that which many Americans refused to see or acknowledge, allowing individuals and groups to demonstrate the pervasiveness of racial prejudice as well as combat stereotypes and shape their public image.

"A small, frequently reproduced selection of the era's most vivid photographs has since become iconic and is considered by many to represent the entire movement. These widely recognized images from the South tell a powerful and compelling story, but . . . it isn't the whole story," Mr. Speltz wrote. "Cast by the media at the time as sporadic and less significant than the heroic, nonviolent protests in the South, the local activism that took place in the North, West, and Midwest is all but absent in the way we characterize, teach, and remember the civil rights era."

The book surveys a range of photographers, including Ruth-Marion Baruch, Don Hogan Charles, Diana Davies, Jack Delano, Leonard Freed, and Charles "Teenie" Harris, among others, whose images remind us that the struggle took place not just in Selma, Birmingham, and Little Rock, but in cities and towns across the United States.

Although Black Americans sought safer and freer lives as they moved northward and westward during the Great Migration between 1910 and the end of the 1970s, they were followed by the prejudice they fled. Mr. Speltz documents the reality: covenants that prevented the sale, lease, or rental of houses to Black people; African American

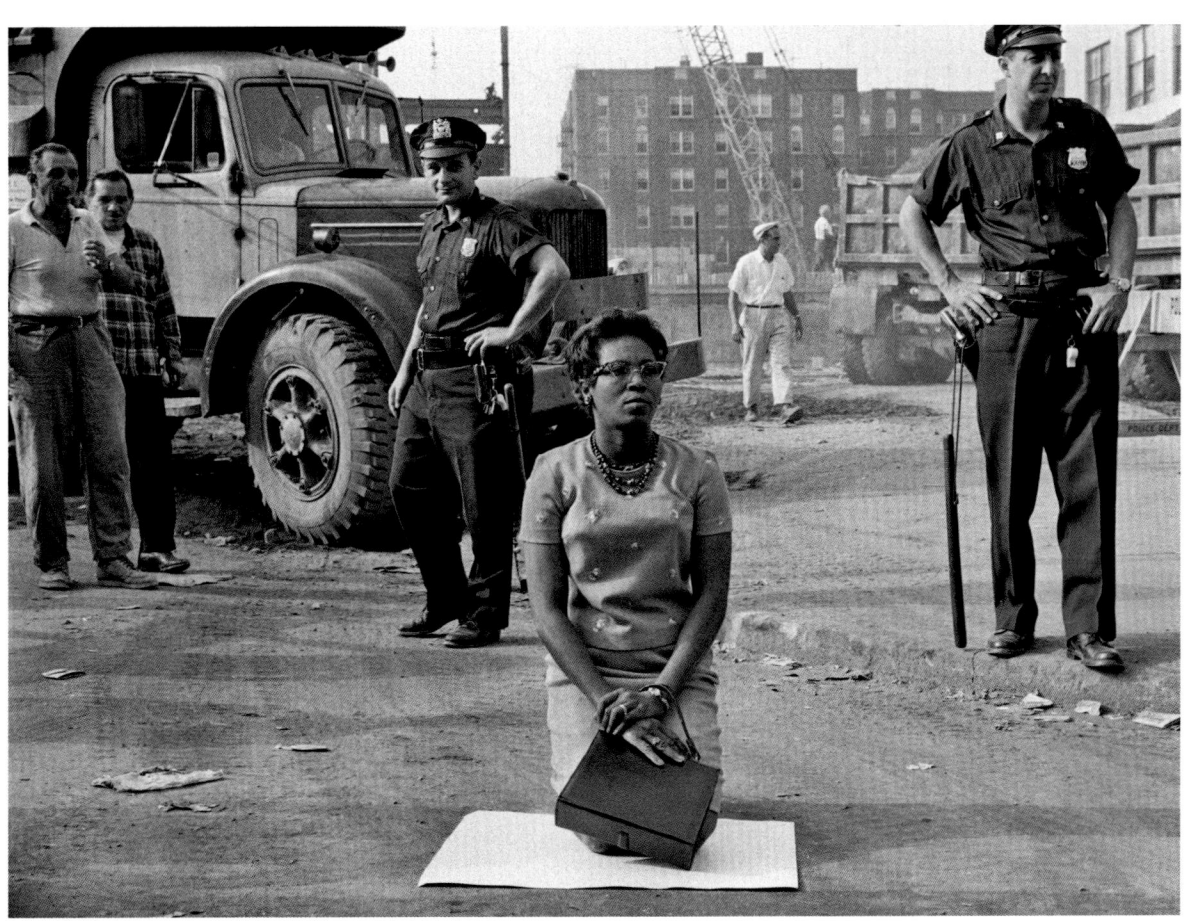

Bob Adelman, A woman blocking dump trucks, slowing construction through civil disobedience as part of a protracted battle against unfair hiring practices at the Downstate Medical Center, Brooklyn, 1963

communities bulldozed and replaced by highways and urban renewal projects; segregated and inferior schools and public accommodations, from swimming pools to restaurants; widespread employment discrimination; and police brutality, surveillance, and unrest.

The photographs in *North of Dixie* portray a range of activities and places: a demonstration in front of the segregated White City Roller Rink in Chicago; a boy with his hands in the air as National Guard troops in Newark march behind him; a portrait of the African American actress Fredi Washington wearing an anti-lynching armband; a boy trying on a coat at the Black Panthers' free clothing program in Toledo, Ohio; a Black family admiring a house in a whites-only neighborhood in Philadelphia; jeering counterprotesters in Chicago waving a Confederate flag; and activists waging a sit-in and hunger strike outside the Los Angeles Board of Education.

These photographs did more than dispute the idea of racism and segregation as a singularly Southern problem. They

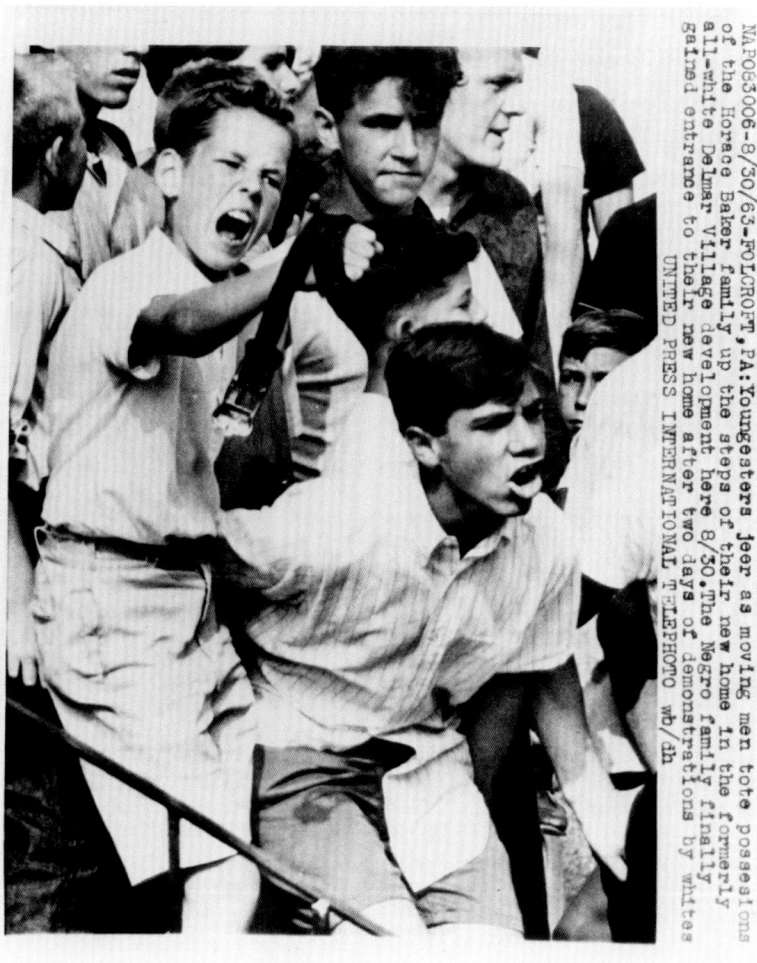

Photographer unknown, Young boys harassing the Horace Baker family, the first African American family to move into the all-white Delmar Village neighborhood of Folcroft, Pennsylvania, 1963

John Vachon, The Jackson family admiring a house that turned out to be in a whites-only neighborhood, Philadelphia, 1956

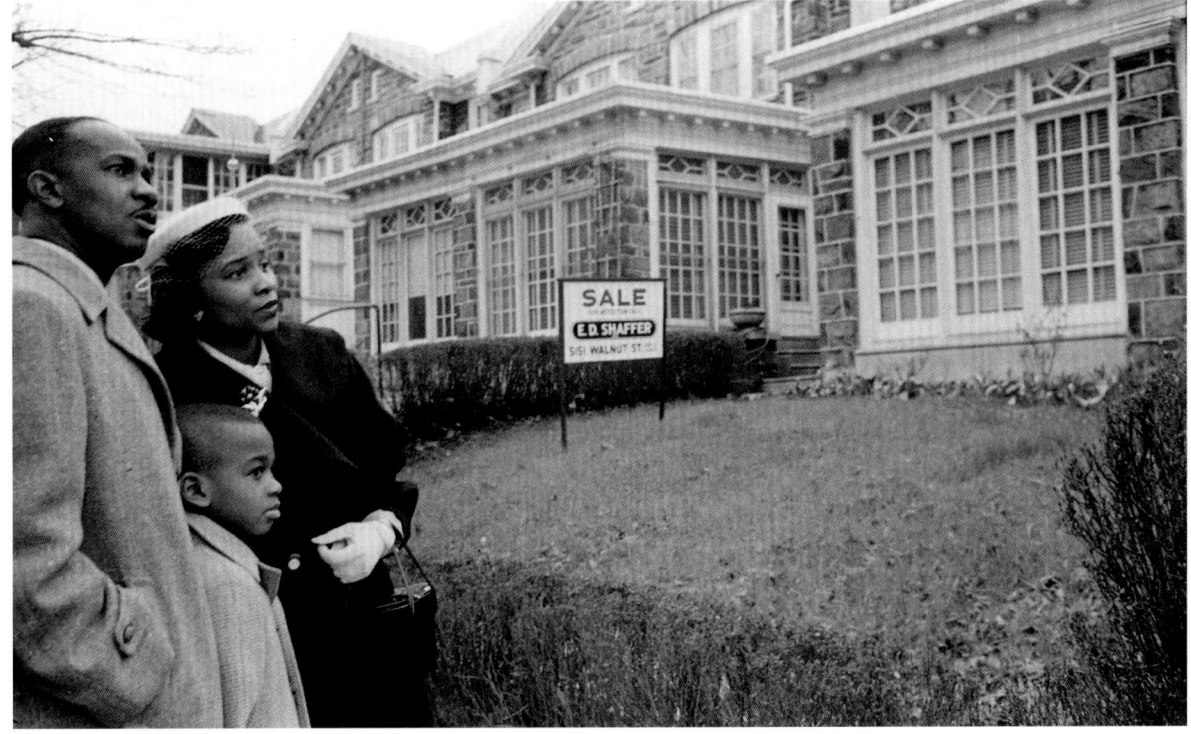

also disrupted the self-image of white Northerners as racially benevolent, in contrast to the ferocious bigotry of their Southern counterparts that was depicted in the news media.

During the period of the civil rights movement, mainstream newspapers and magazines—which earlier, in contrast with the African American press, had rarely covered issues of racism, segregation, and Black activism—usually depicted these problems through a Southern lens, relying on sensationalist images of violence and murder to arouse the interest of readers. "Historical photographs of northern struggles remain less familiar today for a variety of reasons, but primarily because the uncomfortable truths they contain complicate a celebratory civil rights narrative," Mr. Speltz wrote.

In the book's epilogue, Mr. Speltz recognizes that the struggle continues, and with it greater recognition of the geographical breadth of the problem. During a time when some question the legitimacy of the nation's first Black president and African Americans protest police shootings from Baltimore to Ferguson, Missouri, and New York to Tulsa, Oklahoma, the camera remains a reliable and powerful force.

"These resonant pictures and their recurring themes should remind us that racism and concerted efforts to roll back hard-won civil rights gains persists," Mr. Speltz wrote about the photographs in *North of Dixie*. "The ongoing and constantly evolving struggle against police brutality and militarism, entrenched poverty, institutionalized racism, and everyday microaggressions suggests that photographs will continue to play a crucial role in documenting the struggle and advancing the much-needed dialogue around it."

Revisiting Images

# Whiteness and Race, between the Storms

Published August 11, 2016

A group of photographs from the 1940s and 1950s, thought to be from an Oklahoma photo studio, show white people in a range of situations: awkward portraits, basketball teams and ballroom dancers, people at work, in church, at leisure, even a dead man in an open coffin.

These black-and-white images elicited a range of reactions when they were exhibited last year by the artist Pete Mauney at the Teaching Gallery of Hudson Valley Community College in Troy, New York. To some visitors, they elicited feelings of nostalgia. To others, their carefree racial homogeneity and lack of diversity—unremarkable at the time they were taken in Woodward, Oklahoma—were disconcerting.

Given these fraught political times, the title of Mr. Mauney's fascinating work—*Between the Storms*—today triggers a range of meanings, both meteorological and racial.

These photographs represent the calm between two actual storms: Woodward was twice devastated by tornadoes, one in 1947, another in 2012. But metaphorically, they speak to two other historic and opposing "storms": the virulent segregation that took root in much of the nation, including Oklahoma, after Reconstruction, and the rise of the modern civil rights movement. The images represent the last gasp of unregulated, rampant, and legal segregation, when white Americans were unconcerned about the lack of diversity in their lives, and when Black lives were perpetually battered by racial indifference, bigotry, and violence.

Today, the Republican presidential nominee promises to "make America great again," which some political analysts see as a code phrase for turning back the clock on the demographic shifts and multiculturalism that are drastically altering the nation. In this

Chapter 1

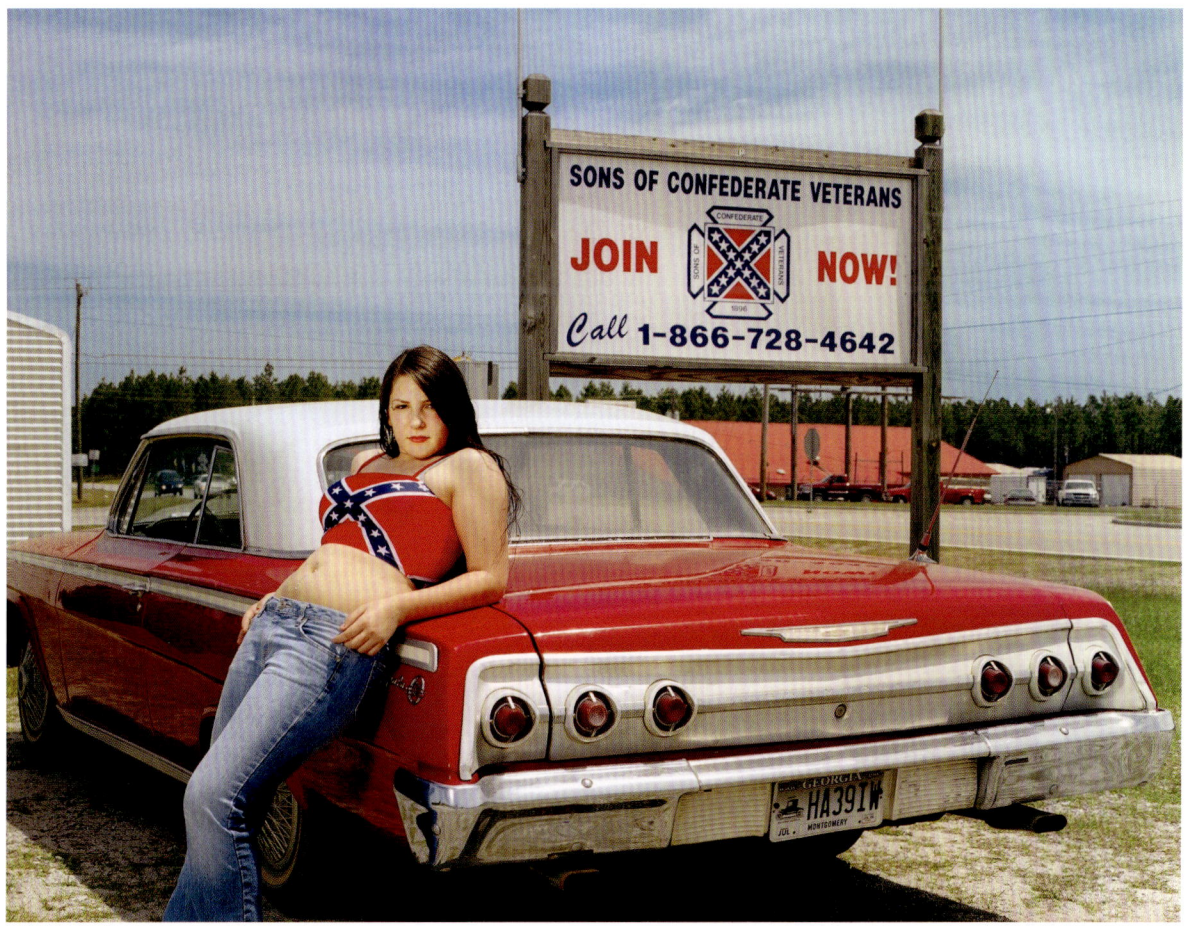

context, Mr. Mauney does something unusual for a white artist: He explores the stark reality of race relations, not through the eyes of its victims but rather through the lens of whiteness, establishing it as a race in need of examination. *Between the Storms* subtly asks its white viewers to confront what many typically refuse to even acknowledge: the lack of diversity in their lives, and the ease with which they, then and now, foster myriad forms of de facto segregation and racist attitudes and behavior.

Yet there are people who still believe that discussions about racism must be initiated by people of color. Implicit in many white liberals' idealization of Barack Obama in the Democratic presidential primaries of 2008, for example, was the notion that he could bestow upon white America racial "atonement and redemption," as the writer and political activist Barbara Ehrenreich concluded at the time.

Those expectations ignore an abiding truth: Only white people can resolve the problem of their own prejudice.

Cultural observers and scholars began to explore the idea of "whiteness" as a racial concept in the late 1980s. To be white in America was to possess a kind of default race that was so dominant and normative that it did not need to be named, let alone examined. These scholars noted that white racism would have no possibility of cure until white people themselves honestly scrutinized their own race, its attendant privileges and power, and their anxieties, fears, and biases about people of color.

As unmindful as some white people are about the social rewards of their own color, they remain guardedly aware of the presence of people of color. Vulnerable in a society that often fears and stigmatizes them, African Americans cannot help but appraise the status of their Blackness in relation to the prejudice they encounter daily. Ultimately, talking about these issues frankly—especially admitting personal biases—is, for many, confusing, difficult, self-incriminating, or embarrassing, especially for people who see themselves as being of open minds and good will, and thus incapable of harboring racist attitudes.

In this regard, the very culture that excludes people of color, perpetuates racism, and underwrites white privilege can also alter racial perceptions by demonstrating the value of white self-inquiry. Yet such examinations remain extremely rare. Indeed, in American culture, the vast majority of important work about race is created by artists of color.

Nevertheless, white artists have done powerful work about race: Lillian Smith's 1949 book, *Killers of the Dream*, which scrutinized the racism of white Southerners

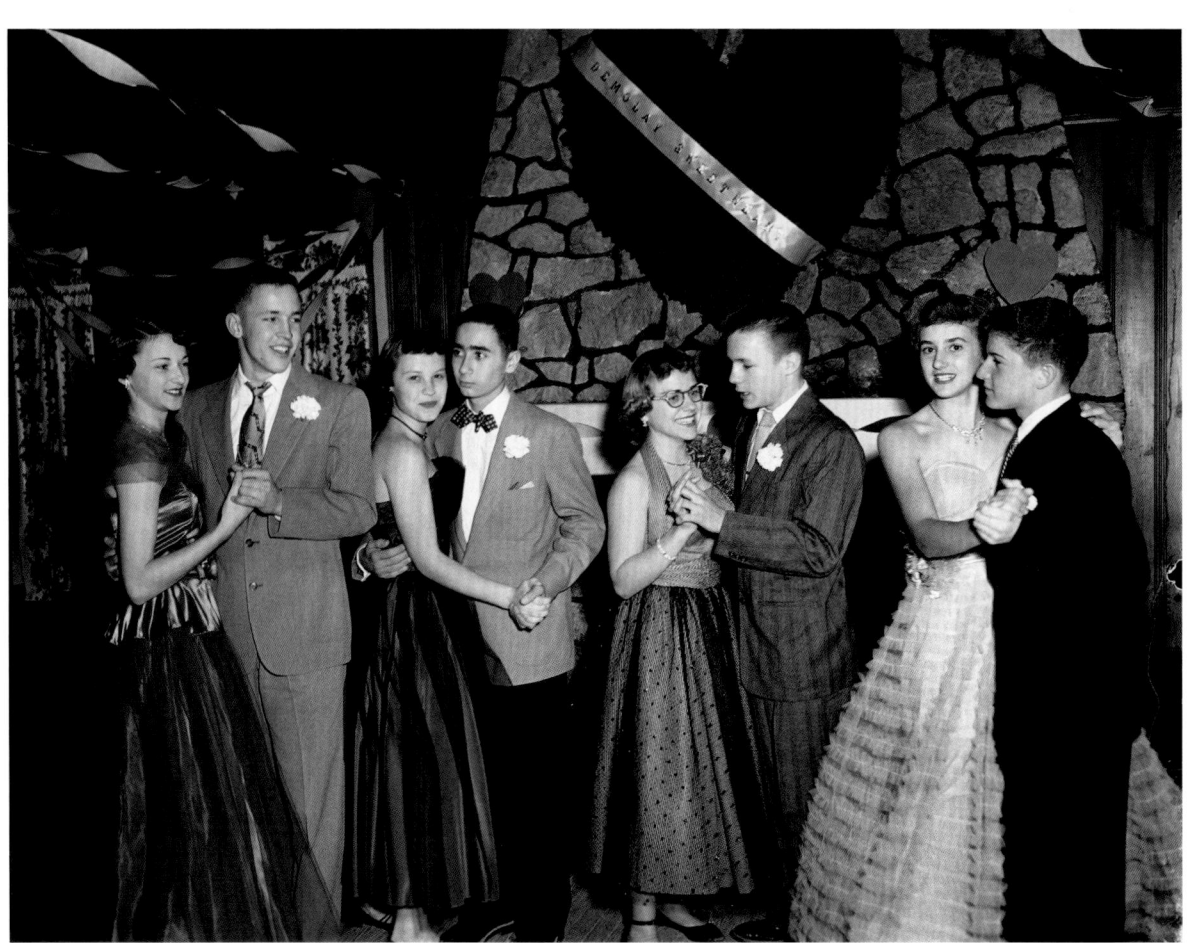

Photographer unknown, Untitled, Woodward, Oklahoma, ca. 1940s

Chapter 1

through personal recollections and meticulous analysis, established the idea of transcending bigotry through honest self-inquiry. Or *Far from Heaven*, Todd Haynes's magisterial 2002 film about an emotional affair between an upper-middle-class white housewife, betrayed by her closeted gay husband, and her Black gardener, which showed a love doomed by the passive-aggressive racial politics of a staid Connecticut town in the 1950s.

Some of the best work on the subject has been made by white photographers and photo-based visual artists: Marc Asnin's stark examination of skinhead culture and white supremacy; Wendy Ewald's collaborative portraits, including a white girls' alphabet that revealed the unconscious sense of racial superiority of some of its subjects; Gillian Laub's *Southern Rites*, photographs and a documentary film that exposed the de facto segregation of a contemporary Georgia town and its troubled and sometimes violent attempt to reintegrate; and *Memory Flash*, by the collective John-Q, a series of performances, interventions, and installations based on archival photographs, film, and ephemera that investigated the complex intersection of race and gay and lesbian sexuality in Atlanta.

Once again, we find ourselves as a nation between two cultural storms: the period, commencing in the 1970s, when ideas of pluralism, multiculturalism, and diversity took hold and the dawn of a demographically transformed America in which the nation's white majority—at times shaken by fear and resentment—is inevitably becoming a minority. This reality makes honest racial self-inquiry and analysis of whiteness even more urgent. In this regard, photographers and artists of all ethnicities—who are often at the cutting edge of new ideas about society and culture—must help us to navigate rough waters.

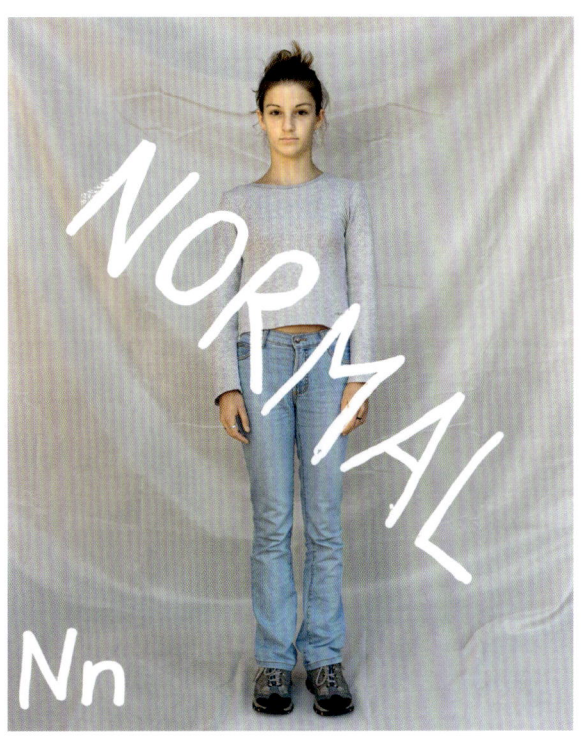

Wendy Ewald, *Normal, adj.*
*Typically describing something that is usual or conforms to the standard. Often people prefer to think of themselves and be thought of as normal. However, how does one know what is normal? Something is only normal when it has conformed to its surroundings and does not stand out. However, if moved to a different surrounding, the previously normal thing would become strange or different. Nothing is ever truly normal*, 1997–2001; from the series *American Alphabet: White Girls*

# The Heartbeat of Our Being, in Black and White

Publishec December 20, 2016

The pictures accompanying Adger Cowans's essay in a new monograph on his work are not his professional photos, but snapshots from his personal life: his childhood home, a group portrait of his mother's relatives in their Sunday best, and Mr. Cowans cradling his godchild.

These pictures affirm the importance of photography not just in Mr. Cowans's life, but also in the lives of millions of African Americans for whom it was a way to show themselves as they wanted to be seen, and in marked contrast to the negative stereotypes they often confronted. But for Mr. Cowans, these informal images also underscore his understanding of the medium as personal, humanistic, and intimate.

*Personal Vision: Photographs* is a comprehensive introduction to an important but under-known photographer with a varied career: he worked as a Navy photographer, apprentice to Gordon Parks, documentarian in 1960s Harlem, and as a Hollywood portrait and on-set photographer.

Mr. Parks was one of his most ardent admirers. "Often such talent abides by rules set by others, but Adger's individualism sets him apart, simply because he follows his own convictions," wrote Mr. Parks. "His photographs go far as imagery can go without actually speaking. Cowans has acquired the freedom to master himself."

*Personal Vision* attests to Mr. Cowans's mastery, featuring a broad range of photographic subjects: a raking overhead shot of a man protecting himself from a sudden rainstorm with a makeshift cardboard umbrella; the World Trade Center, shot with a slow shutter and transformed into a rush of tiny streaks of light; an abstract image of a contorted female model; a blissful Sarah Vaughn in song; the musician and activist

Josh White, guitar in hand and face radiating with joy; a mother in Suriname, seemingly lost in thought as she cradles her baby; and a reflective Spike Lee, taking a break from directing *School Daze*.

Mr. Parks's admiration for these photographs is not surprising. Both men's work shared an important attribute: an appeal to empathy. The impact of Mr. Cowans's photographs resides in their ability to imbue images of street life or portraits, of everyday subjects or celebrities, with powerful emotional overtones. Whether depicting the impressionistic spectacle of people barreling forward in a snowstorm or the emotive faces of his subjects, mostly Black but also white, Mr. Cowans's lyrical images portray life as resonant with feeling.

In doing so, he represents not only the parallel realities of our lives, but affirms that much of our existence, no matter our race or social standing, is inevitably the same. "He is not just documenting an event; he is literally talking to the rhythmic heartbeat of your being," the photographer and writer Anthony Barboza observed of Mr. Cowans's photographs. Pulsing with the heartbeat of their subjects, these images make visible that which is often unseen: the complex humanity that defines each of us, making us far more similar than different.

Mr. Cowans wrote that he was first moved by photography when he took pictures of poor children holding balloons. He had watched them longingly looking at a street vendor, which moved him to buy them balloons. "When I saw those images I understood the power of a photograph. The photos were not about being poor; they were about happiness," Mr. Cowans recalled in the book. "The

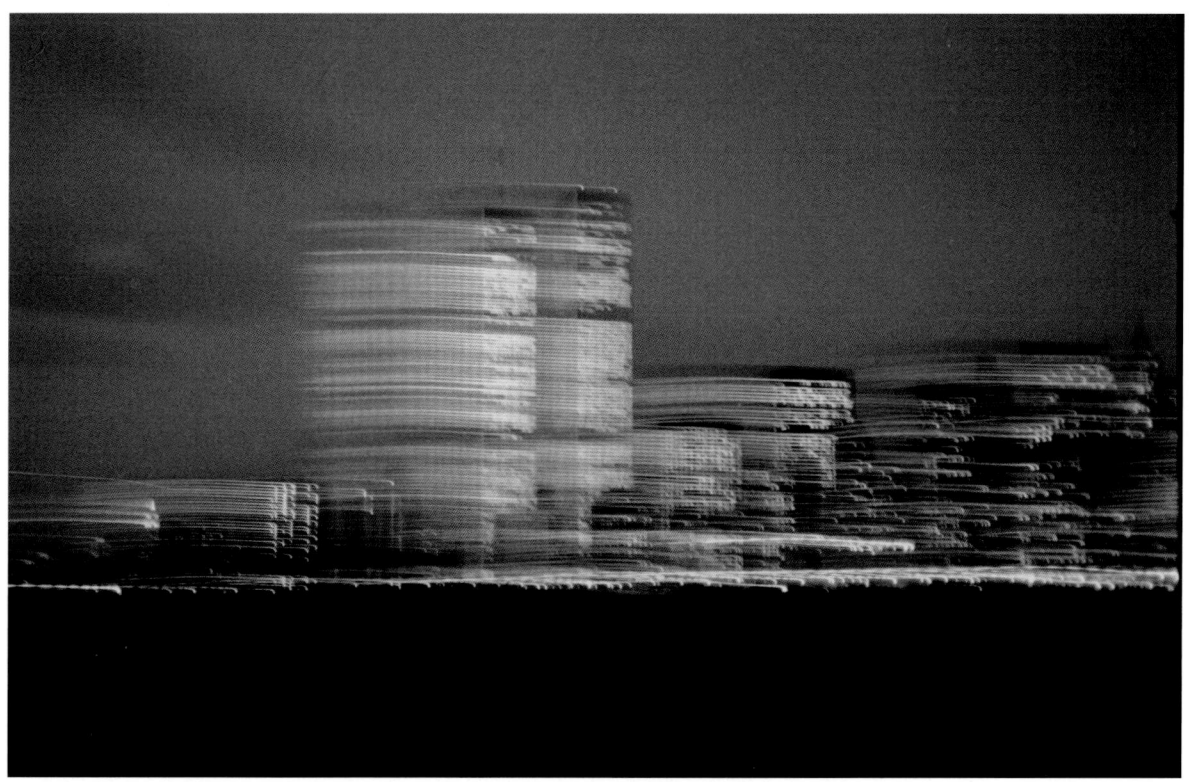

Adger Cowans, *A Slow-Shutter Shot of the World Trade Center*, New York, n.d.

smiles on those faces made me understand how a photo could move people to see, think, and feel. It is important to give emotion to your work."

Allusions to the rhythmic in Mr. Cowans's work, and his collateral interest in photographing abstract phenomenon, like ripples on the surface of water or the juxtaposition of diaphanous fabrics, not only highlight his desire to represent what is most abstract about human existence—our intangible and fleeting emotions—but also point to an earlier passion: music.

Before he was a photographer, studying at Ohio University in the 1950s, Mr. Cowans was a musician, despite his family's enthusiasm for picture-taking. "Everybody in my family had a Kodak box camera and they loved to pose," he wrote. "My mother would make beautiful albums and I would spend many hours looking at relatives who have passed on, folks that lived far way, newborn babies, travels, favorite cats, dogs, horses, and life. Still, I wasn't interested in photography. I was more into music, and I really didn't want to work—I just wanted to play music."

As Mr. Cowans's interest turned to photography, it became central to his artistic practice, which also includes painting and printmaking. In the 1960s, he played an important role in the Harlem-based African American photo collective Kamoinge, and he later joined AfriCOBRA (African Commune of Bad Relevant Artists), an influential artist collective founded in Chicago.

Mr. Cowans's production has been prodigious. In the end, through his art, he has explored the human condition, in ways both original and varied. But as Tuliza Fleming, curator at the Smithsonian National Museum of African American History and Culture, noted about him, "Although his creative style and mode of expression has undergone many phases during his career, several important components of his work and aesthetic have remained constant—his incredible sensitivity to the soul of his subjects, his ability to stay in the moment and capture that moment in his images, and his uncanny ability to simultaneously reveal the seen and the unseen."

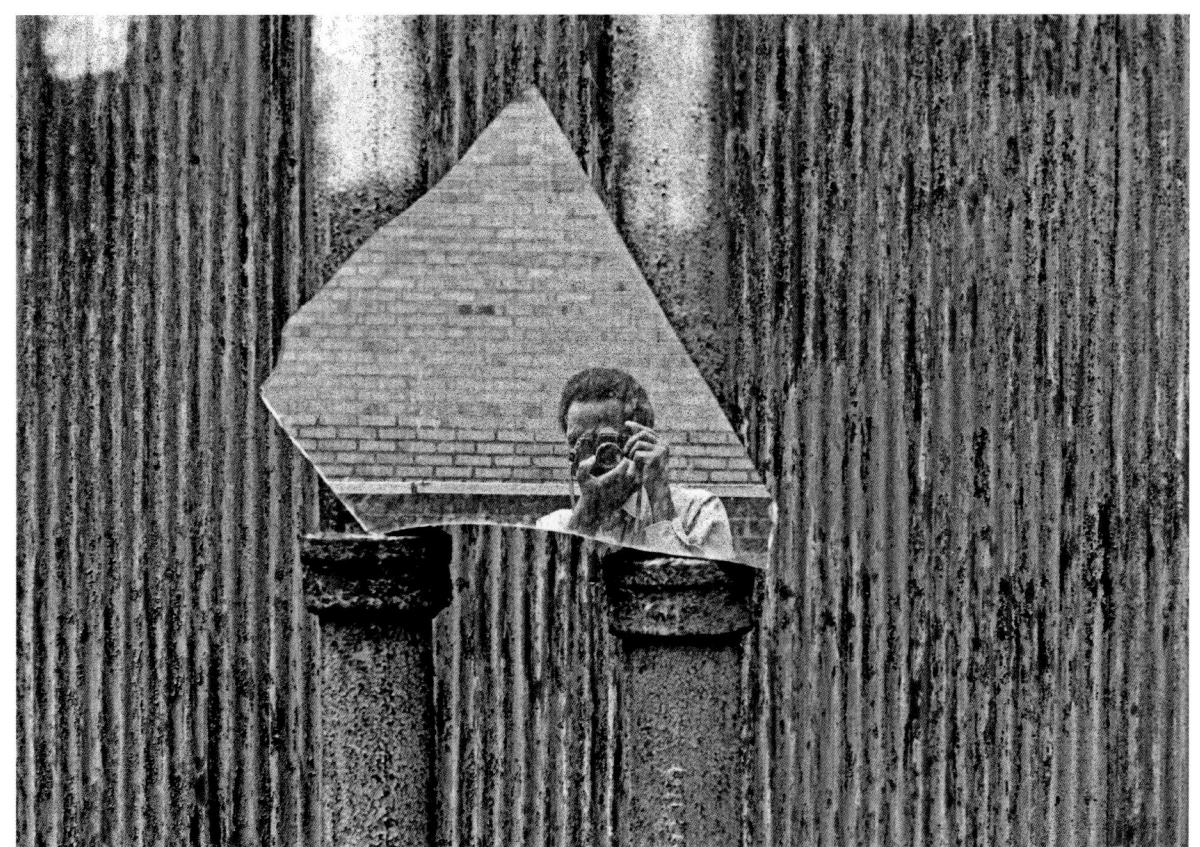

Adger Cowans, *Self-portrait*, 1975

# Black Performers, Fading from Frame, and Memory

Published January 22, 2014

The harder you look at Carrie Mae Weems's *Slow Fade to Black*—blurred, soft-focus images of mid-twentieth-century stars like Marian Anderson, Dorothy Dandridge, Billie Holiday, and Eartha Kitt—the more you see. As the title suggests, these striking, ethereal images, several of which appear in Ms. Weems's retrospective at the Guggenheim Museum in New York (on view through May 14), play on the concept of the cinematic fade, the transition of an image to or from a blank screen. The freeze-frame makes it impossible to tell whether the scenes are fading out or fading in—whether the women themselves are disappearing or materializing.

Some viewers, especially younger ones, will not recognize them. But memories may be jarred loose for older viewers as they gradually discern familiar features, postures, and gestures. For Ms. Weems, *Slow Fade to Black* is foremost about rekindling interest in path-setting African American entertainers who have vanished from our collective imagination. "I started to realize that I rarely heard mention of these women," she said. "Unless, I was playing them on CDs in my own home, I didn't hear them or see them much anymore. This saddened me. These women have given us a gift and a legacy, and yet we have forgotten them. They are disappearing, dissolving before our eyes."

This disappearance is not just a result of generational differences, but prejudice, too. While many white stars from the period, like Frank Sinatra and Marilyn Monroe, continue to be remembered, celebrated, and lucratively marketed, equally important Black performers remain largely unknown to most Americans. Ms. Weems added that the "way women are cast aside when they age" linked this vanishing to gender, too.

Chapter 1

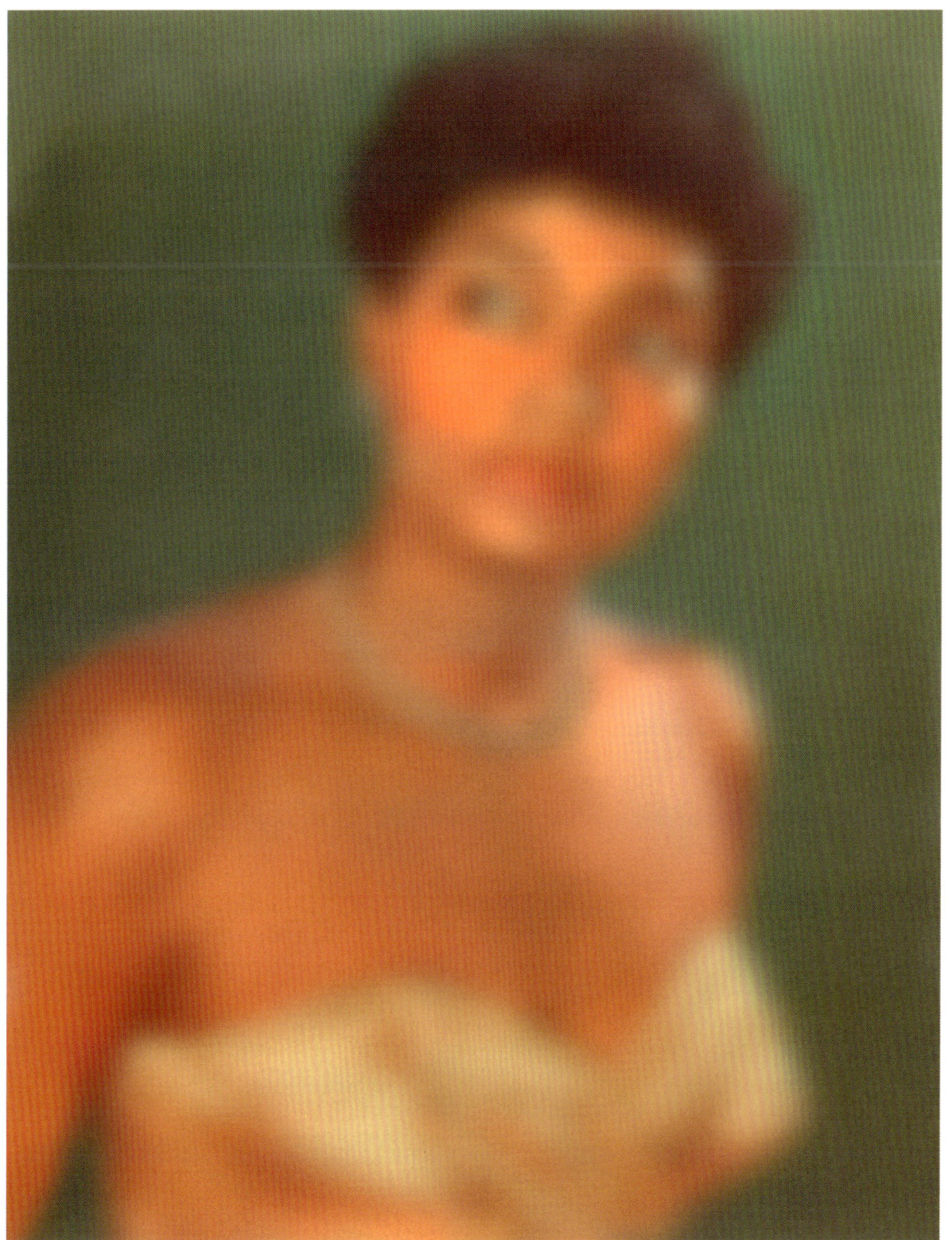

Carrie Mae Weems, *(Pearl Bailey)*, 2010; from the series *Slow Fade to Black*

"There is something very painful and poignant about this," she said.

On one level, the photographs, on the verge of dissolution, serve as metaphors of past struggles to remain visible and relevant in a culture that, at best, relegated many of these women to the sidelines. Viewed in this historical context, it is difficult to separate what we know about their subjugation—the stereotypical roles, the lack of financial reward, isolation—from their extraordinary and trailblazing work.

The meaning of these images is fluid and depends on whether viewers see the subjects as stars burning out from cultural memory or historic figures with far-reaching, and still relevant, legacies. They pose compelling questions not just about their lives but also about the incandescence and fragility of fame, the prejudices that define, limit, or make it impossible, and an obsession with youth that continues to dictate who becomes famous—and for how long. But *Slow Fade to Black* asks us to behold its subjects anew. Rather than as static icons of racial martyrdom or stereotypes of Black divas, they are represented as the consummate entertainers they were. The diaphanous and cinematic photographs give the illusion of animation as they capture the flourishes of performance—mouths open in song, hands gesturing theatrically, and hips and shoulders swaying to unheard music.

The stars are represented in decisive or memorable career moments. By basing her images on publicity stills, Ms. Weems presents the women not necessarily as they wanted to be seen but as photographers, editors, and art directors chose to represent them: Ms. Anderson singing before a bank of microphones, the Lincoln Memorial looming behind her; Mahalia Jackson, eyes closed, enraptured in song; Nina Simone at the

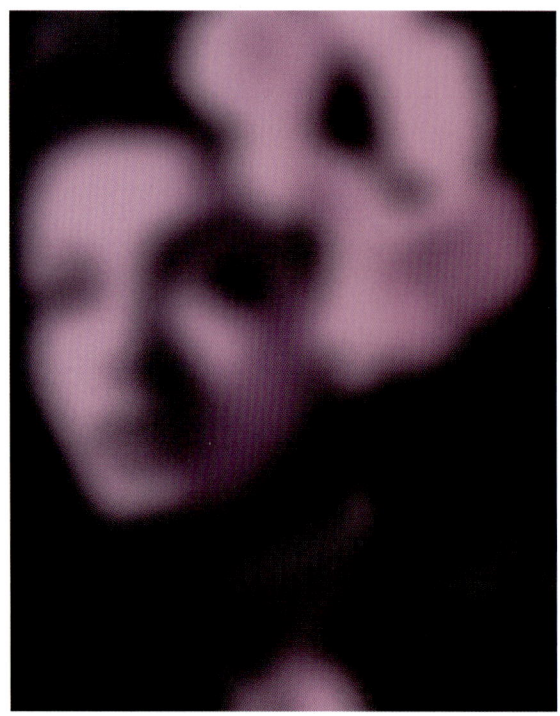

Carrie Mae Weems, *(Billie Holiday)*, 2010; from the series *Slow Fade to Black*

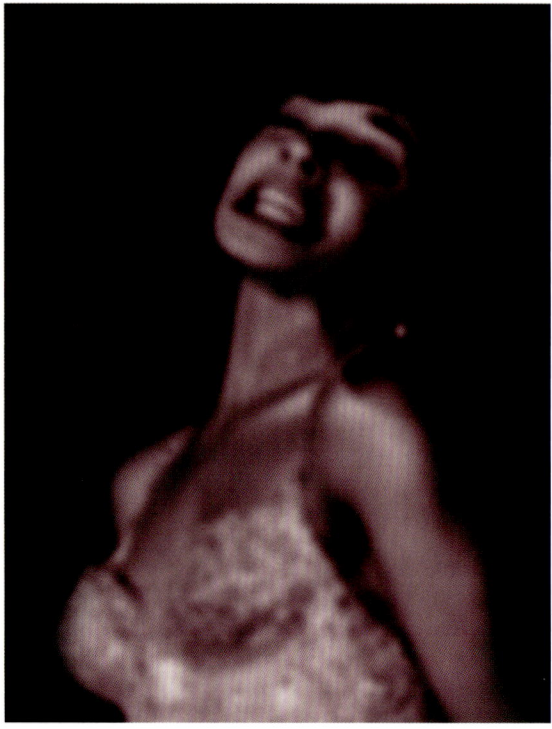

Carrie Mae Weems, *(Shirley Bassey)*, 2010; from the series *Slow Fade to Black*

Chapter 1

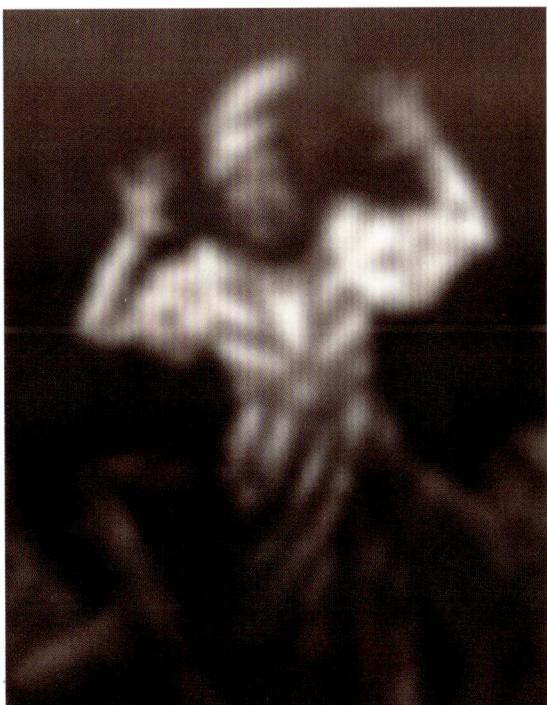

Carrie Mae Weems, *(Ethel Waters)*, 2010; from the series
*Slow Fade to Black*

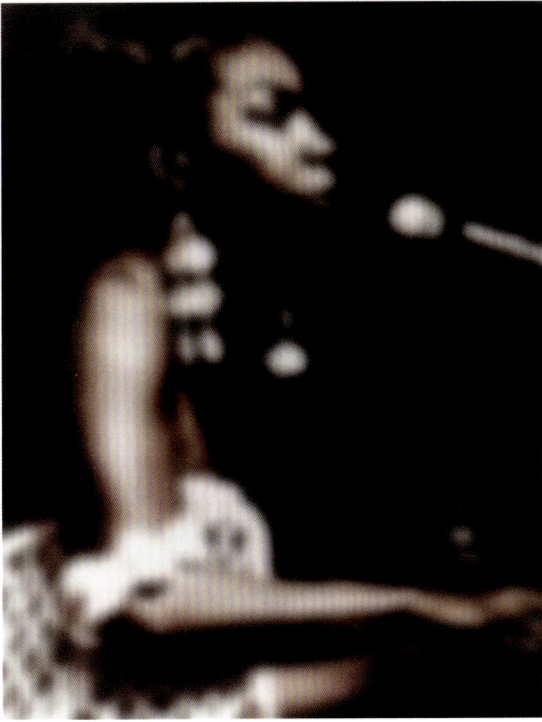

Carrie Mae Weems, *(Nina Simone)*, 2010; from the series
*Slow Fade to Black*

piano, pendulous earrings dangling; an emoting Ethel Waters, her hands waving emphatically; the face of Ms. Holiday emerging out of darkness, a huge flower in her hair; the dancer Katherine Dunham, in full headdress, striking a pose.

Ultimately, these images show how photography itself creates celebrity and how we honor and remember the famous. They remind us, too, of the potent relationship between photography and memory, not just as a vehicle through which the latter is preserved but also as a powerful and evocative medium for both making visible and restoring to history forgotten, but no less extraordinary, people.

While Ms. Weems views her photographs as fundamentally about "memory, about what we remember at various points in our lives," she acknowledges, with a sense of urgency, that for many Americans such memories do not exist. "I am of a certain generation where often I have to tell people who someone is," she said. To help remember and celebrate these women, Ms. Weems collaborated in 2012 with the pianist and composer Geri Allen in a multimedia performance at the Prospect Park summer festival *Celebrate Brooklyn!*, where projections of photographs from her series were accompanied by music by Ms. Allen and others. "I first and foremost view this as an evening of music, centered on this idea of a woman's journey, the span of a life," Ms. Weems said at the time.

She now hopes that *Slow Fade to Black* will inspire a new generation to learn about these extraordinary women. "When I speak with young people about the series, I tell them: 'Do your research. Do your homework. Pull up Spotify. You can find these voices. They are there to be heard. But now you have to dig considerably deeper to locate them.'"

# The Cinematic Images of Gordon Parks

Published August 28, 2017

When Gordon Parks photographed Duke Ellington during a television appearance in 1960, he took a series of photographs as the musician's image flickered across control room monitors. These striking pictures would mark the beginning of Mr. Parks's long, if relatively forgotten, relationship with television. Over the next twenty-five years, he directed several television documentaries and films, including a drama based on Solomon Northup's memoir, *Twelve Years a Slave*.

Although Mr. Parks's work in television and film was central to his oeuvre, it remains largely ignored by photo historians and curators. Yet, perhaps more than any mid-twentieth-century photographer, he understood how much these mediums had conditioned the contemporary eye and mind.

A new exhibition, *Gordon Parks—I Am You. Selected Works, 1942–1978*, currently on view at Foam in Amsterdam through September 6, explores how Mr. Parks not only made television and Hollywood films, but also employed cinematic techniques when taking and sequencing photographs. In addition to excerpts from his movies, the exhibition surveys a wide range of his innovative photographs, from editorial and fashion work to civil rights photos and portraits.

Deborah Willis, a photo historian who has written extensively on Mr. Parks, noted that he was never content with exploring one medium. Accordingly, she argues for the importance of looking beyond photography to better assess the impact of his work.

"As artists, photographers, scholars, and consumers, we are used to equating photographs with the emotional experience of reading photographic images," said Ms. Willis. "Gordon found other art forms to tell stories about individuals, family life, work, and injustice. Thus, he contributed to a broader conversation, exploring other media during a changing time."

The exhibition, organized by Felix Hoffmann, the head curator of the C/O Berlin Foundation, examines individual images, contact sheets, and photo-essays to show how Mr. Parks's "filmic thinking" challenged photography's imperative to "unite a plot, a situation, and a mood in a single frame." Some of his photographs attempted to transcend these decisive moments, as Henri Cartier-Bresson famously called them, by representing an event in a way that suggested its unfolding over time.

In the exhibition's catalog, Mr. Hoffmann cited several examples of this, like the linear, frame-by-frame sequencing of a fight scene in a 1948 *Life* photo-essay, "Harlem Gang Leader." Perhaps stymied by the limitations of print, Mr. Parks transformed another photo-essay, "Flavio," about a twelve-year-old boy's struggle with poverty in Brazil, into a short film, in which he included both footage and photographs. To accentuate the artist's cinematic point of view, *Gordon Parks—I Am You* includes work typically ignored by other exhibitions: excerpts from his work for film and television, including *The Learning Tree* and *Diary of a Harlem Family*. By acknowledging this work, the exhibition shows the progression of Mr. Parks's cinematic thinking and acknowledges one of his most important and enduring legacies.

During a period when the circulation of photo-heavy magazines like *Life* and *Look* was declining, film and broadcast continued to expand their reach. Mr. Hoffmann argues that Mr. Parks's multidisciplinary efforts—which besides television and five feature films included writing, music, and

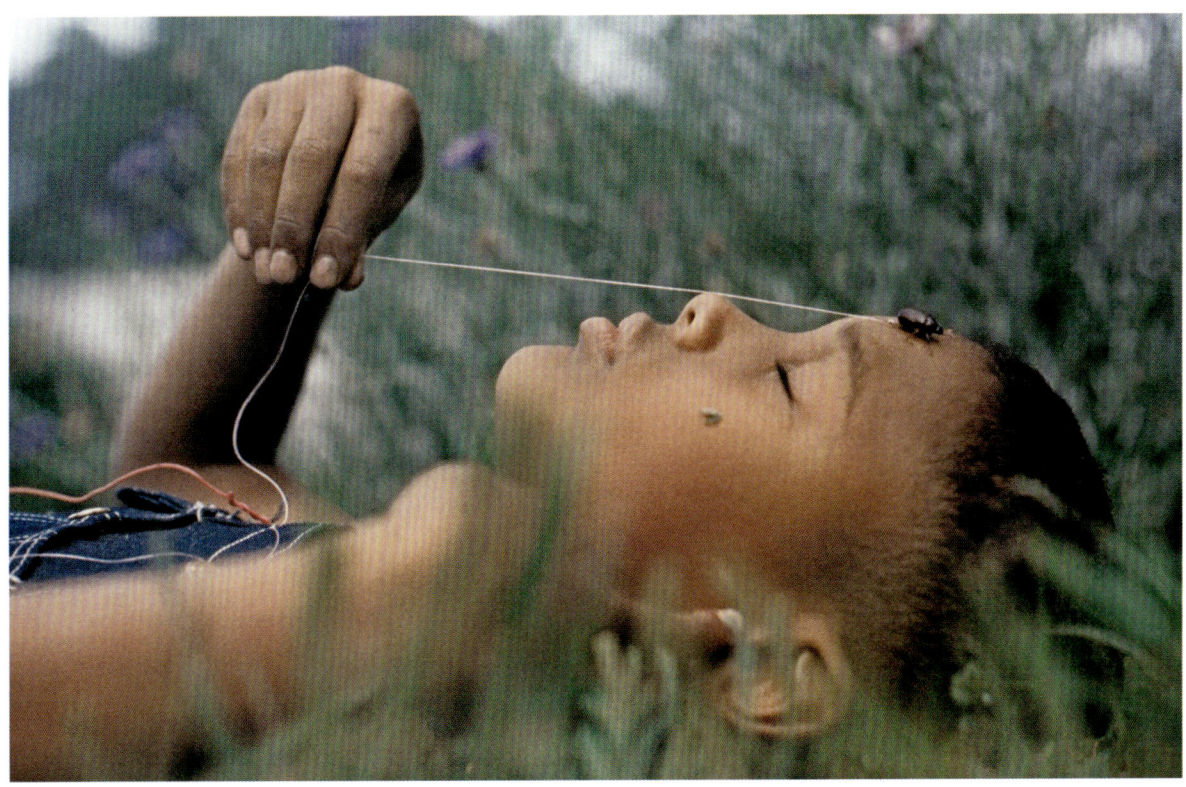

Gordon Parks, *Boy with June Bug*, Fort Scott, Kansas, 1963

choreography—were also intended to broaden his work's public and cultural reach.

Mr. Parks's debut feature film, *The Learning Tree*, the first major Hollywood studio movie directed by an African American, was a semi-autobiographical, humanistic recounting of Black life and racial prejudice in Depression-era Kansas. Released in 1969, the film was lauded for its lyricism and powerful social commentary. *Diary of a Harlem Family*, produced for public television in 1968, was similarly praised for its honest and respectful view of urban poverty through the experiences of one family.

Although not included in the exhibition, the artist's 1971 feature film, *Shaft*, was even more revolutionary. It told the story of a suave African American private investigator, John Shaft, hired by a Harlem gangster to rescue a daughter kidnapped by Italian mobsters. The film challenged Hollywood's negative and subservient view of African Americans, introducing the Black action hero into mainstream cinema. Its violent content and what some have criticized as stereotypical Black characters led some critics to dismiss *Shaft* as a "blaxploitation" film. But its empowered and confident Black protagonist, as well as its heroic storyline, were trailblazing.

The political content of these movies and programs was also consistent with that of Mr. Parks's civil rights photographs. From their themes of social justice and appeal to empathy —which the artist believed was vital to challenging negative stereotypes by reminding viewers of our shared humanity—to their focus on confident Black characters, the films

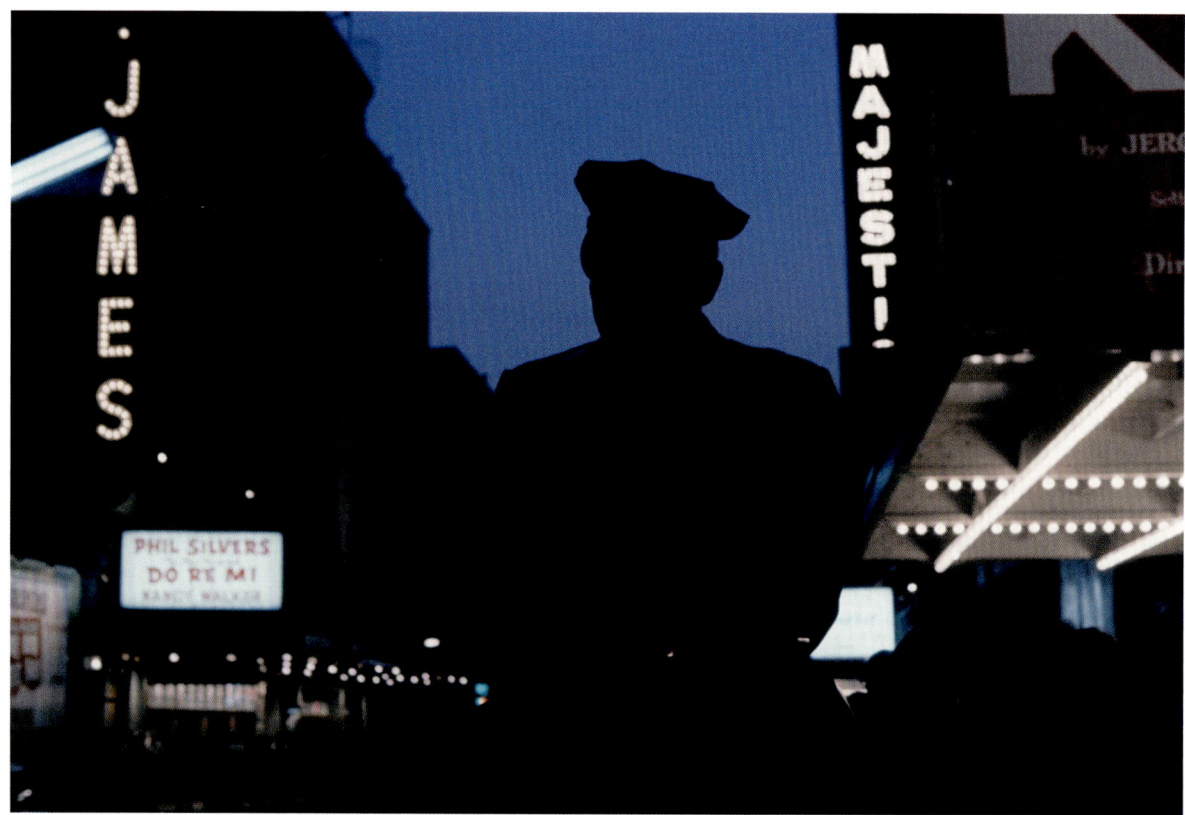

Gordon Parks, *Untitled*, New York, New York, 1960

Chapter 1

Gordon Parks, *Untitled*, Washington, DC, 1963

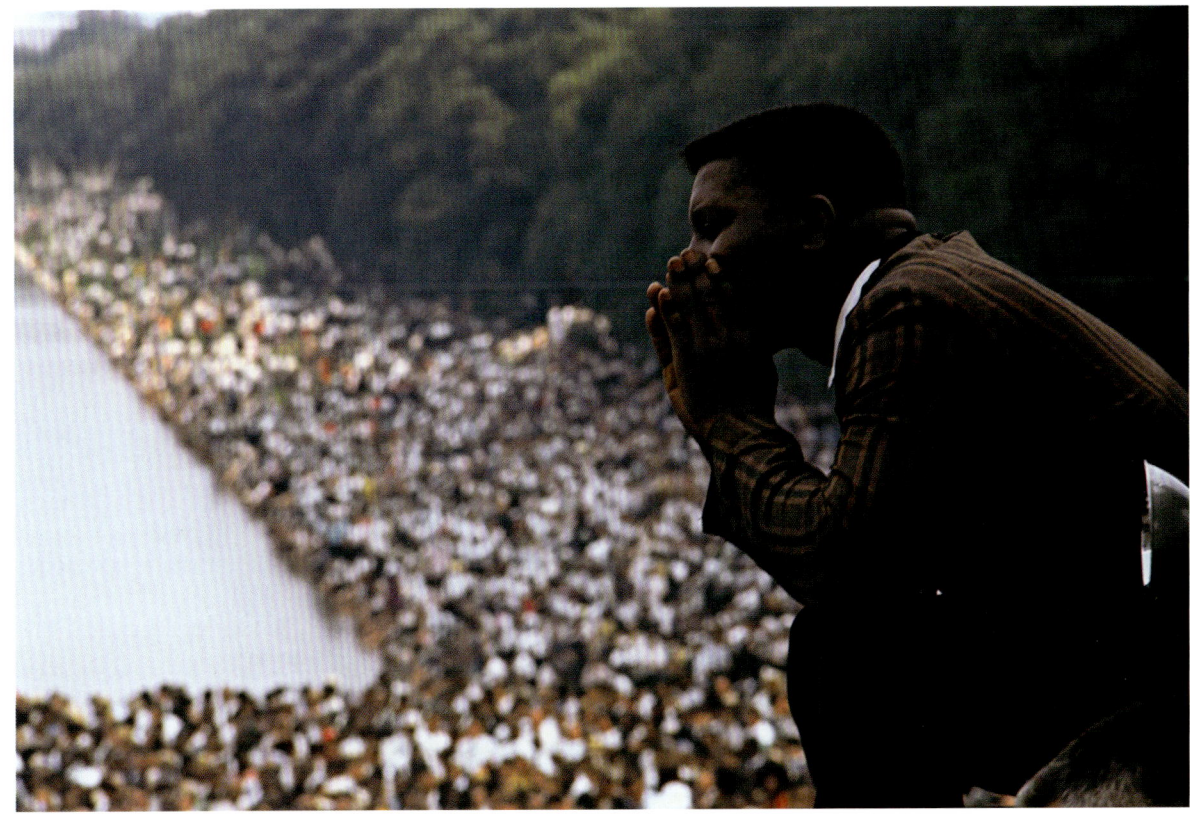

advanced the social issues explored in some of his photographs.

Peter W. Kunhardt, Jr., executive director of the Gordon Parks Foundation, welcomes this interdisciplinary approach, noting that over the next decade the organization will catalog the artist's films, television programs, music, and writing to "help shape a cohesive understanding of his many talents and work."

In the end, to understand these works in relationship to each other, as *Gordon Parks— I Am You* has done, is to grasp the collective brilliance of the artist's work—the power of his imagery, which depicts people of all races in multiple media to influence a broad national and international audience.

"Gordon's early work as a photographer developed his eye and transitioned him into film directing," said Mr. Kunhardt. "He is often called a 'Renaissance man' because he worked in so many different media, but I like to refer to him as a humanitarian artist who used whatever medium he could to have an impact."

# A Momentous Day
# Driven by
# Ordinary People

Published August 22, 2013

Hours before the March on Washington for Jobs and Freedom fifty years ago, pedestrians on their way to work scurried past the Petersen House, across the street from Ford's Theater, its conspicuous sign proclaiming it as the "house where Lincoln died." Though the passers-by were distracted, the photographer who captured the image of them, Leonard Freed, was not. He knew that soon, just blocks away, another event would inexorably alter the nation and its uneasy history of race relations.

This photograph is one of many incisive images by Mr. Freed featured in *This Is the Day: The March on Washington*, a book with essays by the civil rights leader Julian Bond, the sociologist Michael Eric Dyson, and the scholar Paul M. Farber. Rather than focusing on the immensity of the crowd or the epochal speeches, Mr. Freed aimed to capture the marchers and their range of responses and

emotions: the exuberance, intensity, determination, focus, and, inevitably, weariness that reflect the back story of a momentous day.

The march, Mr. Farber wrote, offered Mr. Freed "a spectacle—not for marveling from afar or at a fixed distance, but for exploring at ground level." The night before, the photographer and his wife, Brigitte, had slept at a campsite outside of the city. Awakening at 5 a.m., they drove into Washington a few hours before the march's official start. Once at the site, Mr. Freed wandered through the mass of demonstrators. His photographs provide one of the best records of the geographic, racial, and generational diversity of the marchers and the groups they represented.

Mr. Farber points to one "historical peculiarity" in Mr. Freed's documentation of the march: its keynote speaker, Dr. Martin Luther King Jr., appears in only one image, barely discernible as he delivers his "I Have a Dream" speech on the steps of the Lincoln Memorial, surrounded by hordes of spectators. For Mr. Dyson, the sociologist, that photograph reveals a fundamental truth: while Dr. King was a commanding leader, "he wasn't the only, and often not even the primary, vehicle" for a movement driven largely by ordinary people.

In hindsight, his absence from the images may also reflect Mr. Freed's acknowledgment of the limitations of photography. While still pictures were an undeniably powerful medium for documenting important events, they could do little to communicate the words, cadences, or inferences of a speech. In that area, television excelled.

As the *New York Times* television critic Jack Gould observed at the time, television, unlike the "frozen word or stilled picture" of magazines and newspapers, was able to capture the march's sensory and aural richness. By 1963, television cameramen could use lightweight, 16 mm cameras to navigate fluidly through fast-paced events and shoot them up close and in real time. And Telstar satellites launched the previous year allowed their images to be relayed swiftly around the globe.

Dr. King also understood the potential of television news, and its balance of spoken word and moving image, to influence public opinion.

"The march was the first organized Negro operation which was accorded respect and coverage commensurate with its importance," he said. "The millions who viewed it on television were seeing an event historic not only because of the subject but because it was being brought into their homes."

But where television sometimes fails—in that its swift pace leaves little room to dwell on the visual details of a story—the photograph excels. It demands our sustained

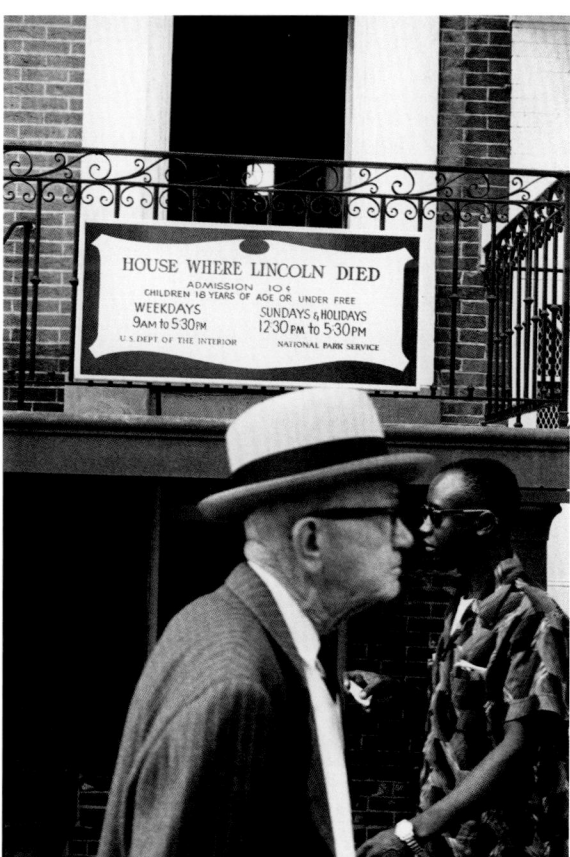

Leonard Freed, The house where Abraham Lincoln died, Washington, DC, 1963

attention, teasing out the complexities, the incongruities, and, as Mr. Freed's image of the Petersen House attests, the ironies of ostensibly straightforward circumstances. Its attention to visual nuance commands us to stare, to think, to imagine, and, ultimately, to feel.

Mr. Freed, a pioneer in the genre of socially conscious photojournalism, captured the march in ways both intimate and penetrating: the sartorial flair of demonstrators, dressed in their Sunday finery, conscious of their role as media ambassadors; sequential images of a singing woman, enraptured by her quest for equality; the middle-aged couple acknowledging the solemnity of the day by bowing their heads in prayer; and the weary marcher on her way home, lost in thought as she gazed out a bus window.

By slowing down to observe a fast-paced event, these pictures tell us much about the dynamics of race in America. For one, as Mr. Dyson points out, the panoply of African American marchers in a "rainbow" of skin colors reveals the mutability of racial categories, an insight that also challenges stereotypes. "Dark-skinned Blacks who were usually only photographed in buffoonish exaggeration," Mr. Dyson wrote, "get from Freed a forgiving realism that rescues the blackest Blacks from the wasteland of stereotype and restores them to the majestic ordinariness."

By focusing on the psychic and emotional responses of African Americans, these photographs challenge the news media's tendency to see the struggle for racial equality through the eyes and anxieties of white

people. In Mr. Freed's documentation of the march, whites are present, but Blacks are in charge. If whites were necessary for peaceful racial coexistence, as symbolized by a photograph of interracial protesters linking arms, Mr. Freed represented them "without the pretense of superiority or the burden of nobility," Mr. Dyson wrote.

In the end, the images of *This Is the Day* exemplify Mr. Freed's lifelong quest to show "the connection between things, how they relate." If coverage of the march in the news media, especially on television, was sweeping and impressionistic, these photographs unveil the intimate human connections that together produced one of the nation's most consequential events. Fifty years later, they remind us that while Dr. King's speech was justly enshrined in history, it was but one of the march's many poignant moments.

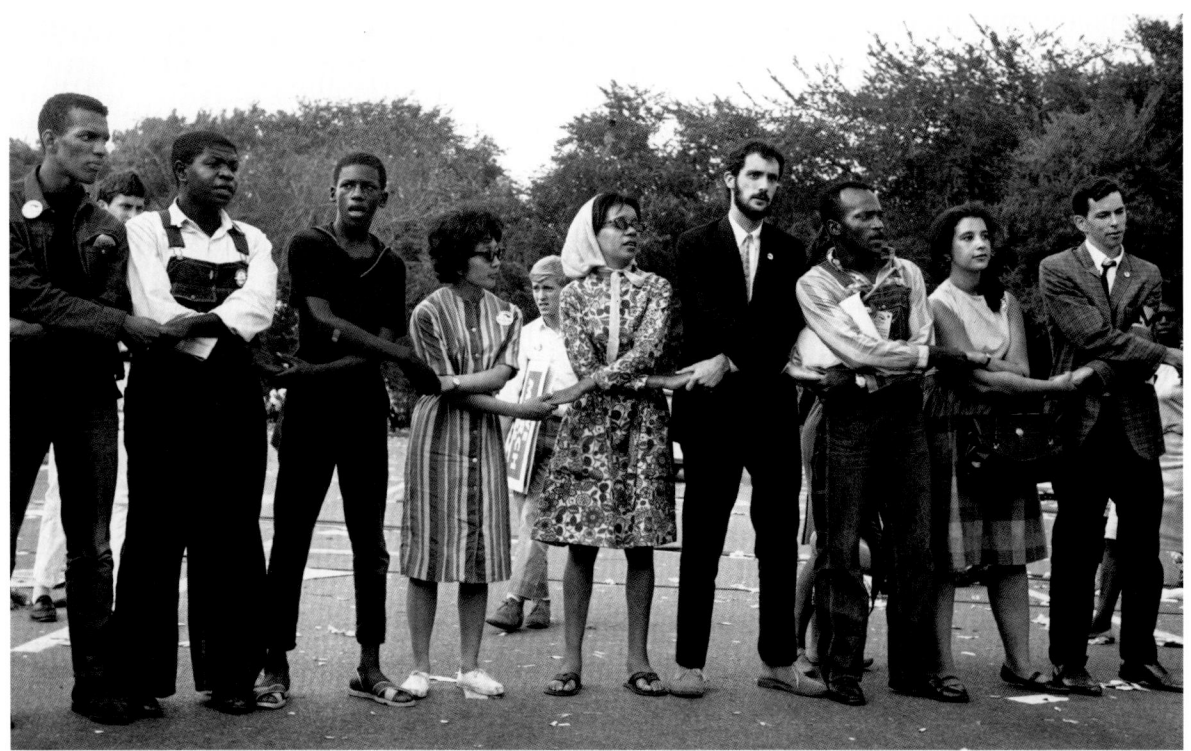

Leonard Freed, Marian Wright Edelman (center, wearing scarf) and others during the March on Washington, Washington, DC, August 28, 1963

Chapter 1

Leonard Freed, The March on Washington, Washington, DC, August 28, 1963

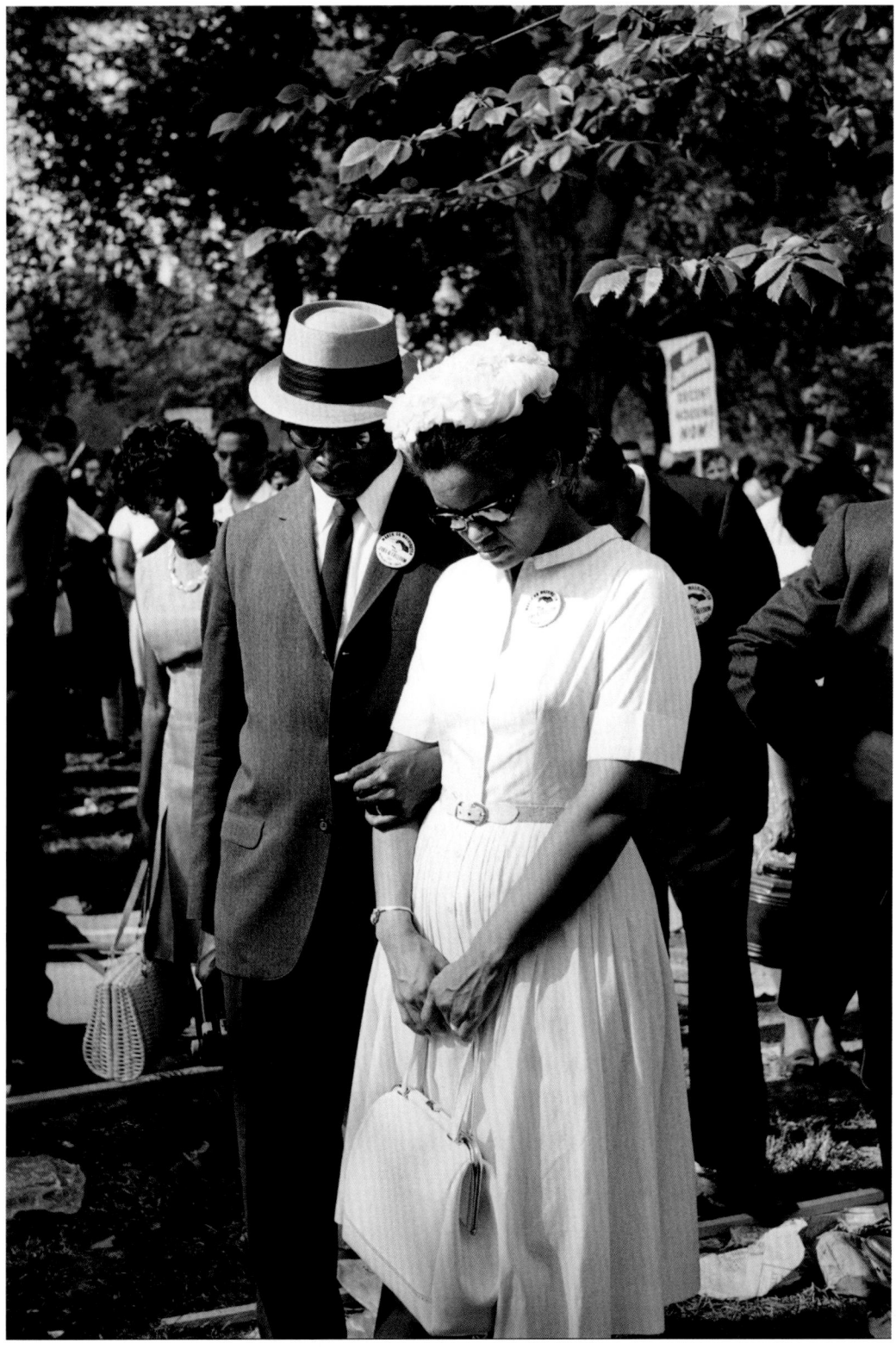

# Robert Frank, Telling It Like It Was

Published January 15, 2012

One of the most consequential images in Robert Frank's *The Americans* is a raw, cinematic photograph of a Black couple in San Francisco in 1956. Approaching them from behind as the pair relaxed on a grassy hill overlooking the city, Mr. Frank disrupted their solitude. Startled, they turned to acknowledge him. The woman was annoyed. The man crouched protectively. As his eyes locked on the photographer, his expression hardened into a scowl. The couple seemed determined to protect themselves and their dignity.

On one level, as Mr. Frank himself has said, the photo demonstrates the ease with which the camera can invade the privacy of others, portraying "how it feels to be a photographer and suddenly be confronted with that look of, 'You bastard, what are you doing!'"

But the photograph is also racially fraught. Rather than a neutral observer, Mr. Frank looms over them, an active, unseen participant—a surrogate for the intimidating whiteness that shadowed the lives of Black Americans, no matter how liberal their environment. Ultimately, the photograph implicates more than Mr. Frank. The couple's upward, incriminating gaze also meets the eyes of the viewer, who now looms over them, too, in solidarity or as a coconspirator with the unseen photographer.

Few white cultural figures of the period produced a more sobering and self-aware commentary on Northern racism. Forgoing the subject matter of typical civil rights images—it depicted neither racial violence, protest, nor the Jim Crow South—the picture was a disturbing reminder that the problem was everywhere. Confronted by the image, it is impossible not to be disturbed by it.

A contact sheet, now available for viewing via the Robert Frank Collection Guide on the National Gallery of Art's website, documents

Chapter 1

the split-second evolution of a photograph that easily could have gotten away. Of its three frames of the scene, the first depicted the couple mid-ground and from behind, quietly talking. The third is a complete blur. As Sarah Greenough, senior curator and head of the department of photographs at the National Gallery, observed, it supports Mr. Frank's assertion that he quickly turned away once he got his picture, pretending that he was focused on something else.

It was the second photo, circled in red on the contact sheet, that made it into *The Americans*. Significantly, the image was overexposed. But the photographer, undoubtedly grasping its importance, made it work in the darkroom. Mr. Frank repeatedly has cited the picture as his favorite in the book.

During the modern civil rights movement, cultural explorations of bigotry outside the South were rare and inevitably cautious. Stanley Kramer's Academy Award–winning drama from 1967, *Guess Who's Coming to Dinner*, for example, was acclaimed for taking on a subject virtually ignored by Hollywood. It centered on an affluent white San Francisco couple, complacent in their liberal attitudes

until their daughter brings home her Black fiancé, an internationally renowned physician portrayed by Sidney Poitier.

The movie was commendable for broaching a controversial subject. But it ultimately comforted its white audience by trafficking in genteel platitudes, depicting Black and white anxieties around race as equivalent, and sidestepping the underlying motivations of prejudice or its brutality.

The film lacked the direct rawness of Mr. Frank's picture. Mr. Frank, who was born in Switzerland, had immigrated to the United States a decade earlier and maintained a critical distance from his subject. His keen and skeptical eye discerned nuances that many Americans, unwilling to see themselves as prejudiced, would just as easily ignore.

"It is fair to assume that when an observant American travels abroad his eye will see freshly; and that the reverse may be true when a European eye looks at the United States," Mr. Frank wrote in his successful 1954 Guggenheim application for *The Americans*. "I speak of the things that are there, anywhere and everywhere—easily found, not easily selected and interpreted."

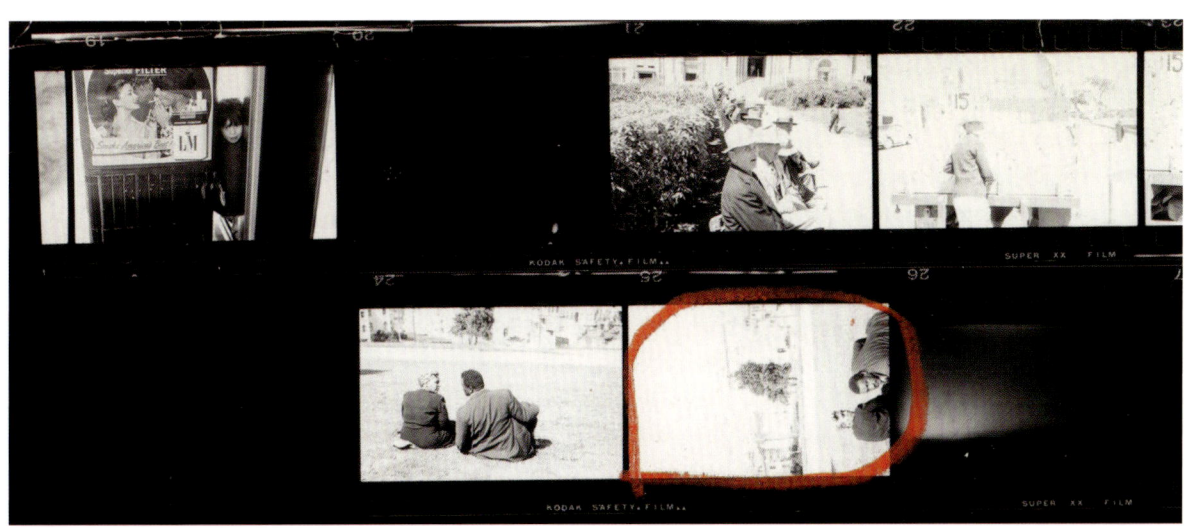

Robert Frank, Contact sheet for slide 1, 1956

Mr. Frank approached his subjects dispassionately, free of many of the era's preconceptions about the nation and its people. His point of view let him represent a vast range of people from different ethnic, racial, and socioeconomic backgrounds with nuance and complexity, rather than as stereotypes or victims.

Mr. Frank's photograph recalls another look at urban racism: *Take This Hammer*, a 1963 documentary produced by KQED, San Francisco's educational television station, and featuring the African American writer James Baldwin. The film, by Richard O. Moore, followed Mr. Baldwin visiting the city's Black neighborhoods intent on "discovering the real situation" of African Americans, "as opposed to the image that San Francisco would like to present."

The documentary detailed what Mr. Frank's photograph had earlier inferred: a city rife with racial discrimination, de facto segregation, and conflict. "This is a San Francisco Americans pretend does not exist," Mr. Baldwin ruefully observed. Through interviews with local political leaders and residents, the latter mostly young and alienated, the author documented a trenchantly divided city and a Black community beset by rampant unemployment, substandard housing, violence, and "increasing bitterness, demoralization, and despair."

Mr. Baldwin deconstructed one of the era's most abiding racial myths: that of a benevolent North that stood in contrast to a ruthless South. As white liberals strove to defend this mythic ideal—"a protection of their own consciousness," as he described it—African Americans outside the South were growing increasingly wary of living in a racial limbo, their rights suspended somewhere between legal segregation and full equality.

"There is no moral distance . . . between the facts of life in San Francisco and the facts of life in Birmingham," Mr. Baldwin insisted. "We've got to tell it like it is." From the standpoint of white commentators in the civil rights era—where liberal self-interest often precluded honest self-inquiry—it took a brilliant photographer, born and raised in another place, to tell it like it was.

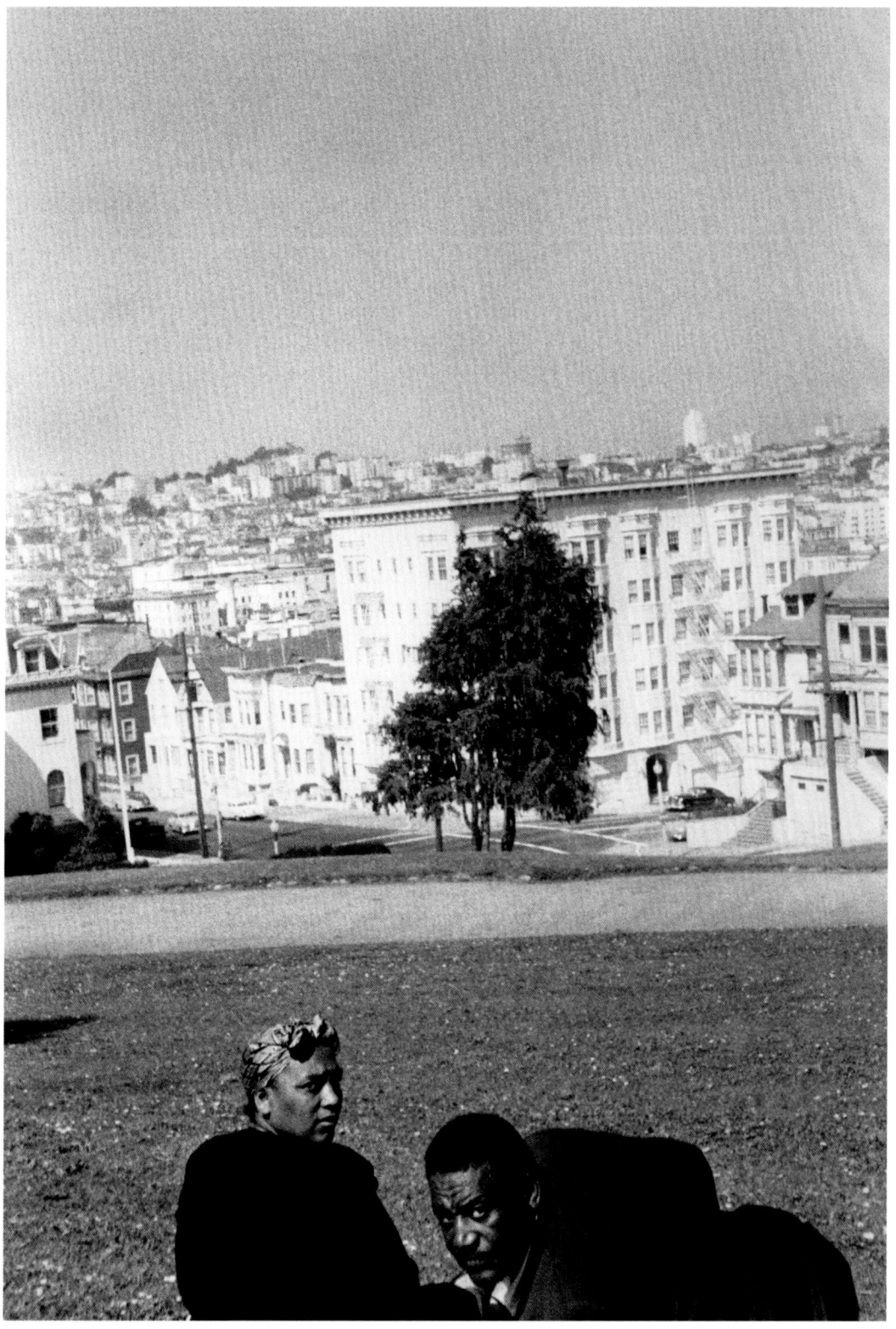

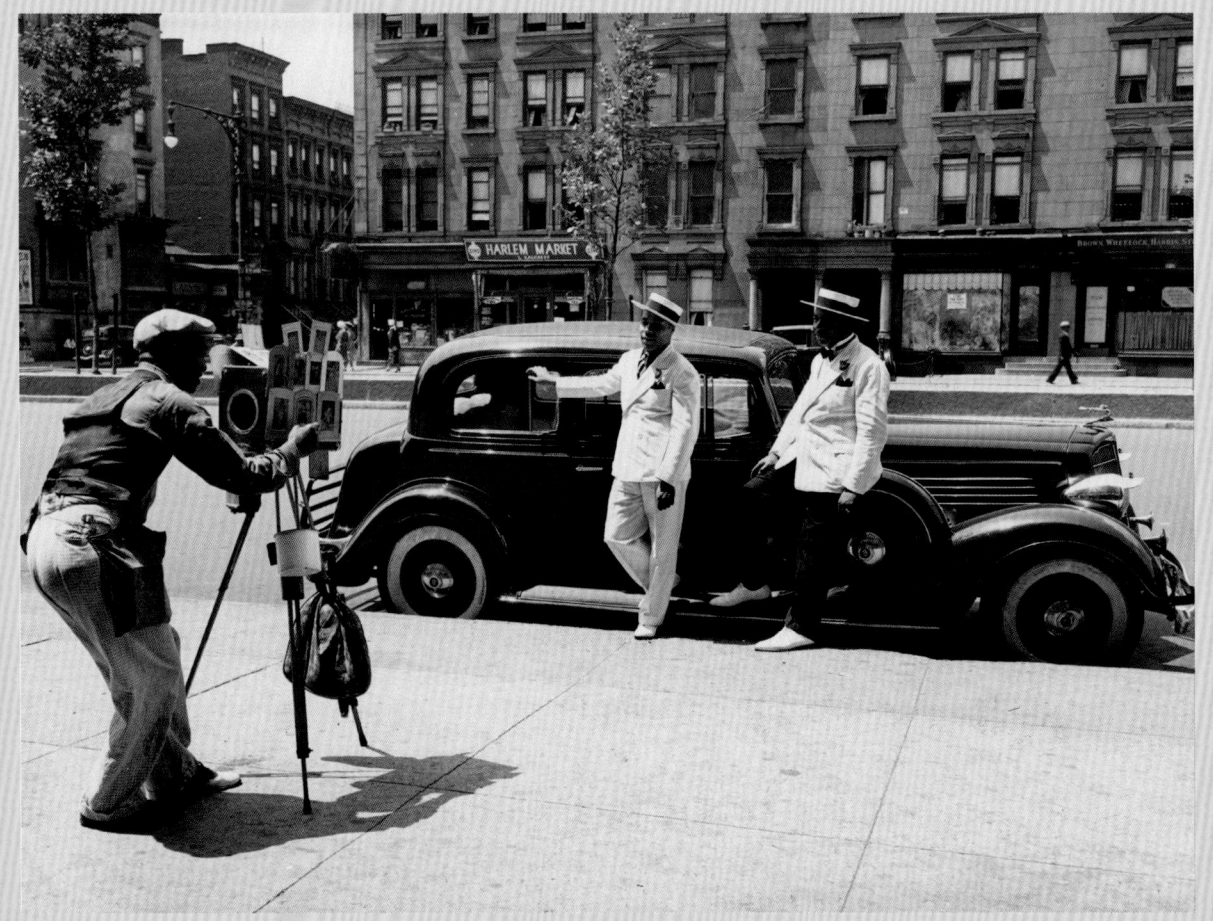

Eliot Elisofon, Photographer Zack Brown shooting dapper men, Harlem, ca. 1937

# Visibility:
# Strategies of
# Representation

# CHAPTER
# TWO

Published September 19, 2012

# Malcolm X as Visual Strategist

Robert L. Flora's black-and-white portrait of Malcolm X, the national spokesman for the Nation of Islam, stands as one of the great meta-images about photography—an astute commentary on our insatiable hunger for pictures. Taken in Los Angeles in May 1963, the photo depicts the civil rights leader and his associates as they await the verdict of an all-white jury deliberating the fate of fourteen Black Muslims accused of assaulting police officers. The pictorial magazines and tabloid newspapers they voraciously read to pass the time nearly crowd out the image.

If Flora's photograph speaks to the country's obsession with visual media, it tells another, interconnected story about Malcolm's passionate engagement with photography. The men in the picture are focused on articles about the Nation of Islam. The *Life* magazine story that engrosses Malcolm, for example, was typical of the derisive coverage of the Black Muslims in the mainstream press: "The White Devil's Day Is Almost Over: Black Muslim's Cry Grows Louder," screams its headline.

Malcolm X was one of the most media-savvy Black leaders of the period. By the time of his assassination, in 1965, he was also one of the most photographed (and televised, appearing on hundreds of local and national interview programs). Handsome, charismatic, and articulate, he provided the mainstream news media with a continuing and histrionic story that would enrapture its readers: a burgeoning Black community calling for self-determination, racial separatism, and independence to be achieved by "any means necessary," including violent insurrection. In turn, the news media afforded him a national platform for espousing a radical worldview, one that rejected the nonviolent practices and integrationist goals of the

Chapter 2

mainstream civil rights movement. (Shortly before his death, Malcolm's view of the latter grew more conciliatory.)

For more positive reporting, Malcolm X could depend only on the Nation of Islam's weekly newspaper, *Muhammad Speaks*, and, to a lesser extent, the Black press. The mainstream news media, stoked by his fierce, sometimes inflammatory rhetoric and its own anxieties around race, afforded little more than negative and sensationalistic coverage, much like the *Life* article featured in Flora's photograph. If conventional news outlets typically portrayed the Reverend Dr. Martin Luther King Jr. as the "angel of light," as the sociologist Algernon Austin wrote, Malcolm had become their villainous "angel of darkness."

While Malcolm viewed the "white press" as more or less a lost cause—its coverage remained largely negative until the day he died—he nevertheless engaged it and, at times, outsmarted it. The public's trust of and faith in visual media, and its dominant role in shaping public opinion, made it a powerful outlet for reaching his target audience: African Americans disillusioned with the mainstream civil rights movement.

Many Black people at the time rejected the Nation of Islam's religious orientation, fundamentalism, political extremism, and cultural insularity. But many were also skeptical of the mainstream movement; a 1963 poll by *Newsweek* reported that more than a third of African Americans were "resigned to the possibility that they may have to fight their way to freedom." It was the purpose of Malcolm's media campaign to motivate these people. And it was the photograph that served as one of his most effective motivators.

A keen steward of the Nation of Islam's visual representation, Malcolm X often carried a camera, his way of "collecting evidence," as Gordon Parks once observed. He relied on photographs to provide the visual proof of Black Muslim productivity and equanimity that sensationalistic headlines and verbal reporting often negated. When photojournalists visited the community, he tried to steer them toward the kinds of affirmative images—shots of contented family life, children at play and school, and thriving businesses and institutions—that might subtly ameliorate the negative texts that he knew would inevitably accompany them.

In her book *Flashback: The 1950s*, the photographer Eve Arnold writes of Malcolm's passion for getting the picture right. From 1959 through 1960, Arnold, on assignment for *Life*, shot hundreds of images for a photoessay about Malcolm and the Nation of Islam. While she won Malcolm's trust, he continually inserted himself into her process, guiding her through Black Muslim enclaves in Chicago, New York, and Washington and even, at one point, walking out ten women in traditional Black Muslim attire and posing them for a photoshoot. Arnold, a wily negotiator, acquiesced. "Malcolm set up the shots and I clicked the camera. It was hilarious," she wrote of his zeal.

But when Arnold attempted to photograph Malcolm framing a photo with his hands, "to catch him in the act," as she put it, he demurred. It was the wholesomeness of the community, and not his role as image maker, that he hoped Arnold's photographs would reveal. (*Life* pulled the photo-essay as it was going to press. Some of the photographs were published in *Esquire* the following year.)

If Malcolm was a talented visual strategist behind the camera, he was nothing less than a prodigy in front of it. Well before the rise of photo ops and *People* magazine, he endeavored, with considerable

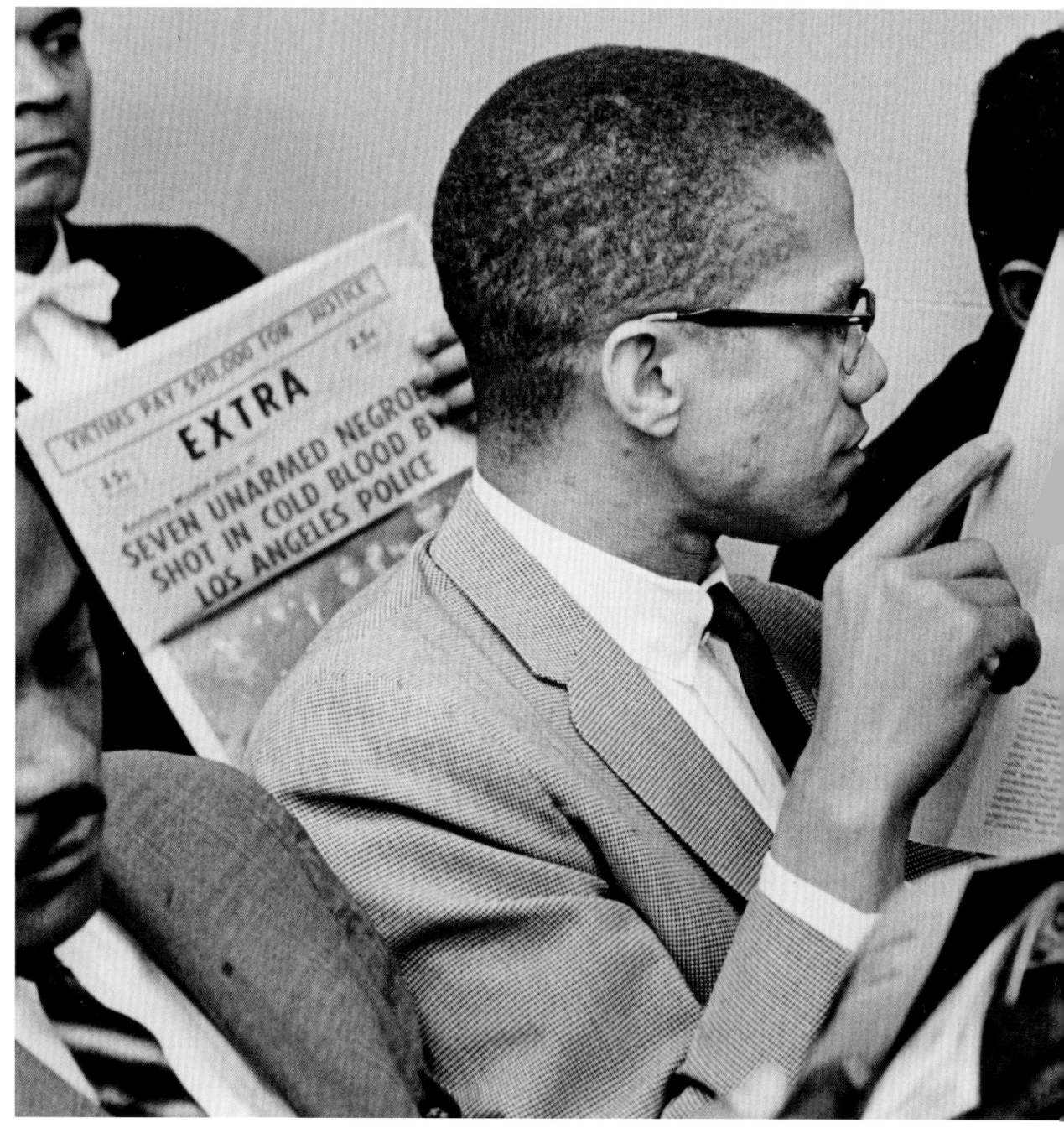

Robert L. Flora, *Malcolm X, Los Angeles*, May 28, 1963

Chapter 2

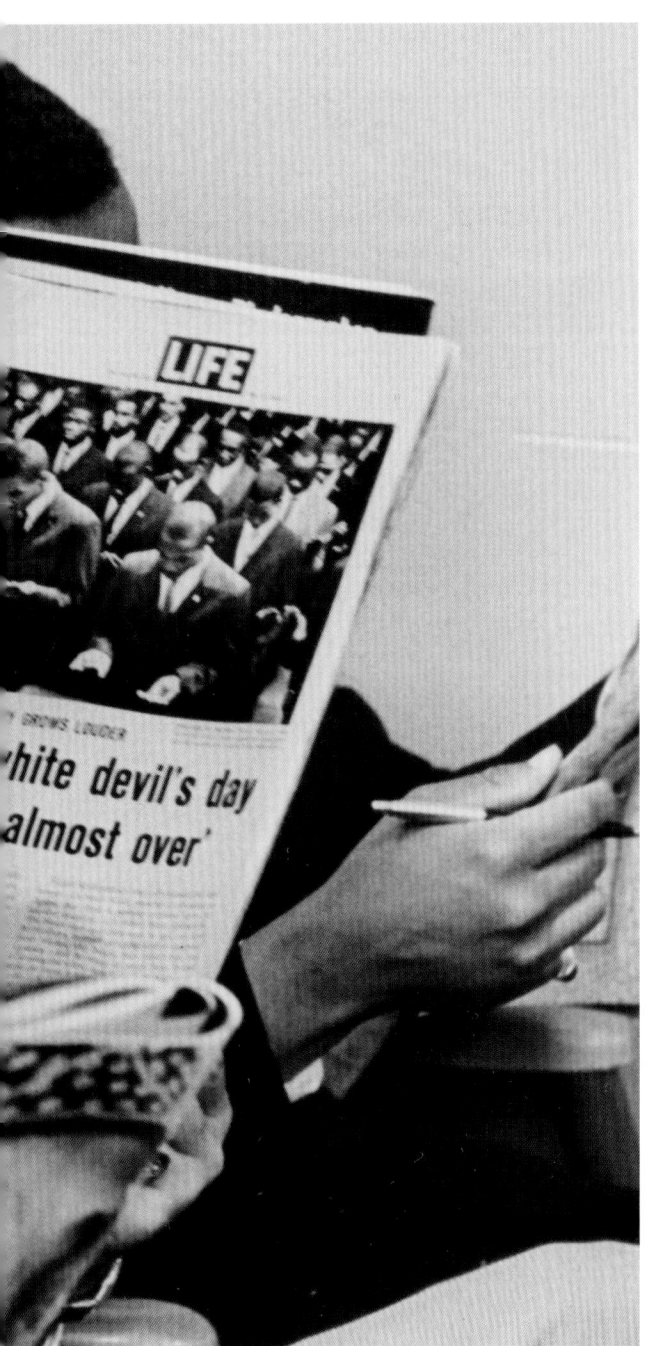

sophistication, to prepare himself—and the community he led—for the penetrating, and often unforgiving, eye of the news media. He crafted every aspect of his camera persona, from the cool self-confidence he exuded in still images to the urbane speaking style and command of ideas that were the hallmarks of his television appearances.

In *The Autobiography of Malcolm X*, he recounted the ways he altered his outward appearance, from clothing to hairstyle, to transform himself from Nebraska country kid and small-town Michigan teenager to Boston "home boy," and finally to national political and religious figure. Taking charge of his image helped Malcolm to define himself before the news media could define him. It also afforded him the opportunity, by the example he set, to reverse stereotypes and change minds.

In the end, it is the precision and sophistication of Malcolm's self-presentation that reads most vividly in Flora's photograph: the fashionable, well-tailored clothes, the chic eyeglasses, the relaxed yet formal posture, and the refined hand gesture, details meant to convey both composure and authority.

No matter Flora's motivation for taking the picture, his subject, much as always, succeeded in getting his message across. And through the myriad ideas he communicated through photographs, Malcolm X transformed the Nation of Islam—increasing its membership by tens of thousands and allowing its leaders to influence African American public opinion for decades to come.

# Zanele Muholi: Paying Homage to the History of Black Women

Published December 3, 2018

Zanele Muholi's face is luminous—and framed by a headdress of inflated latex gloves. The image is typical of the Johannesburg-based photographer's theatrical self-portraits, where hairstyles, headgear, and objects as diverse as a majestic necklace of cowrie shells or a wooden stool worn as a hat or crown suggest multiple personas and layers of historic, cultural, and political meaning.

As Muholi has said, you might look at the latex gloves "and think of balloons and play, rather than the constraints of work and domesticity or the need to breathe, to feel deflated." Characteristic of Muholi's work, that photograph is about all of these things, and much more.

The image is one of more than ninety self-portraits in *Zanele Muholi: Somnyama Ngonyama, Hail the Dark Lioness*, a monograph accompanying a traveling exhibition organized by Renée Mussai for Autograph ABP in London and now at the Spelman College Museum of Fine Art in Atlanta through December 8. In addition to photographs, the book contains essays, criticism, and poems by more than twenty curators, art historians, and writers.

The self-portraits function on various levels and pay homage to the history of Black women in Africa and beyond, the dark lionesses of the book's title. They reimagine Black identity in ways that are largely personal but inevitably political. And they challenge the stereotypes and oppressive standards of beauty that often ignore people of color. "All this stereotyping inspires a deep-seated hatred of the Black body, from head to toe: eyes, lips, everything, your features," said Muholi in a recent interview with Ms. Mussai.

Muholi, who eschews gender-specific pronouns, is cofounder of the Forum for the

Chapter 2

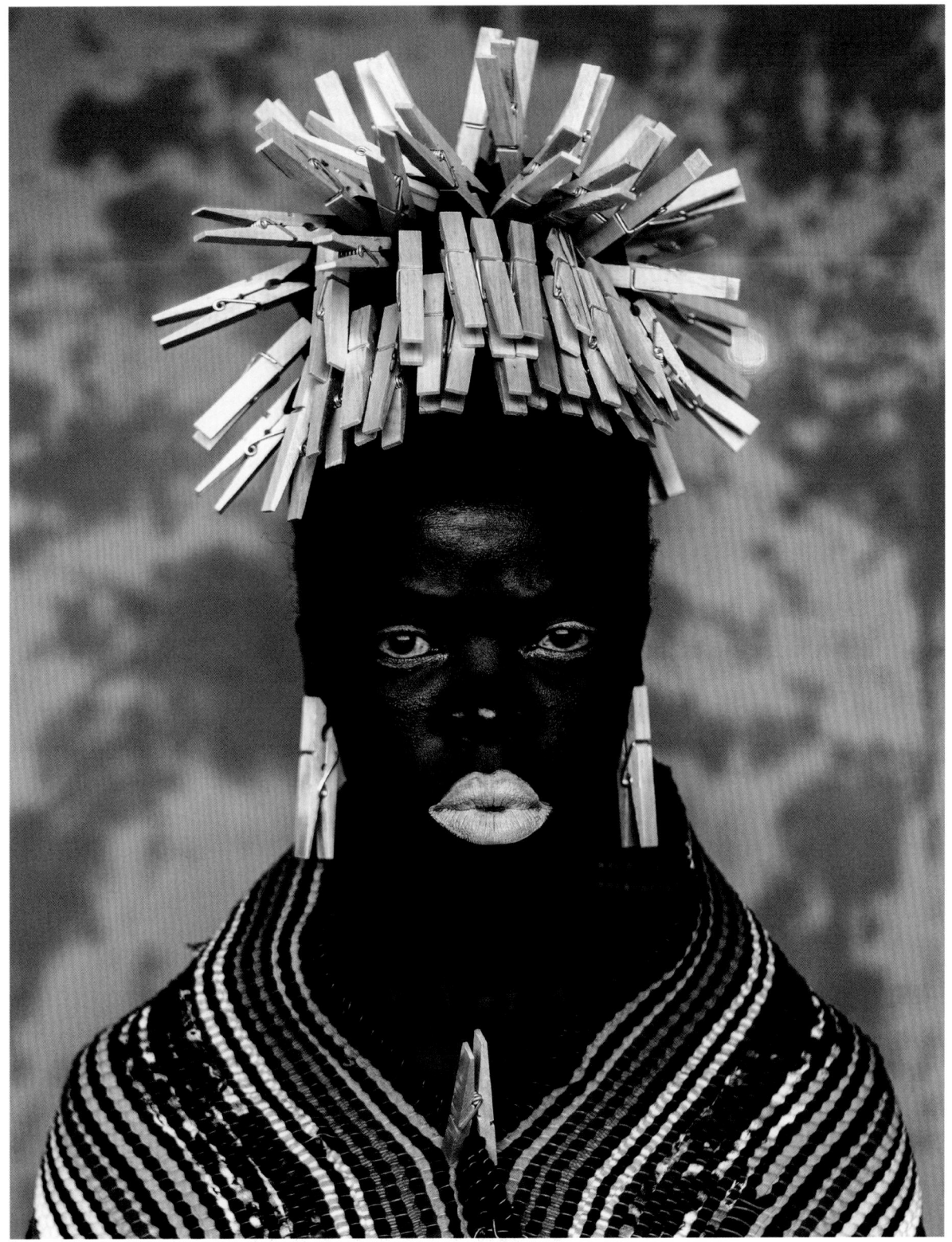

Zanele Muholi, *Bester I, Mayotte*, 2015

Visibility

Empowerment of Women, which advocates for the rights of Black lesbians in South Africa, as well as the founder of Inkanyiso, a collective for queer activism and visual media. Activism is central to Muholi's photographs, work that taps into the tradition of empowerment through Black self-representation. Since the nineteenth century, the photographic portrait has allowed Black people to represent themselves as they want to be seen, not how others pigeonhole or even dismiss them.

"I wanted to use my face so that people will always remember just how important our Black faces are when confronted by them," said Muholi, who prefers to be called a "visual activist" rather than an artist. "For this Black face to be recognized as belonging to a sensible, thinking being in their own right."

Muholi's portraits inspire by example, self-discovery, and resistance. They build on earlier series devoted to visual activism, such as *Faces and Phases*, *Innovative Women*, and *Transfigures*, which documented Black lesbian, gay, bisexual, transgender, and intersex South Africans in response to the persecution, violence, and invisibility they endured.

"Too often I find we are being mimicked, and distorted, by the privileged other," said Muholi. "We are here; we have our own voices; we have our own lives." In this regard, the photographer wants to "teach people about our history, to rethink what history is all about, to reclaim it for ourselves, to encourage people to use artistic tools such as cameras as weapons to fight back." Those words echo Gordon Parks, who more than a half-century ago called the camera his "weapon of choice" against racism, poverty, and injustice.

Using richly symbolic poses, props, and situations, Muholi's self-portraits represent African identity as nuanced and incongruous—from a stoic figure engulfed by a snakelike vacuum-cleaner hose to a series of pictures dedicated to Muholi's late sister, Basizeni, images that serve both as elegies and as "conversations with the legion of 'ancestral selves,'" as Ms. Mussai wrote.

Among the most poignant images in *Somnyama Ngonyama* are those honoring the photographer's late mother, Bester Muholi. In several pictures, Muholi wears headdresses composed of scouring pads or clothespins that allude to Bester's work as a domestic. These images push the envelope of traditional portraiture, serving as respectful homage, pointed satire, and thoughtful commentary on a difficult life made worse by apartheid.

"Bester's headdress appears like a costume that undermines the pretensions of portraiture," the art historian Tamar Garb wrote in the book. "But it also asserts the defining role that she played in an economy of subservience and spectacle. The figure is framed by her labor, haunted by pictorial precedents, captured by the gaze of her desiring daughter, for whom the love of mother was always shared, never enough, gone too soon."

When posting images online, Muholi often uses the hashtag #blackbeauty, an affirmation of how the artist is taking control of an attribute too often defined and represented by outsiders. Muholi implores viewers, like the liberated lioness of *Somnyama Ngonyama*, to question and free themselves from oppressive aesthetics.

"How is Black beauty defined? It changes over time, and it always seems to fit in with the other's consumption," said Muholi. "My point is that Black people should question this idea themselves."

Muholi hopes that *Somnyama Ngonyama* will motivate Black people facing racism, sexism, and homophobia in Africa and beyond to resist and transcend the cultural limitations imposed on them.

"The series touches on beauty, relates to historical incidents, giving affirmation to those who are doubting—whenever they speak to themselves, when they look in the mirror—to say, 'You are worthy, you count, nobody has the right to undermine you: because of your being, because of your race, because of your gender expression, because of your sexuality, because of all that you are.'"

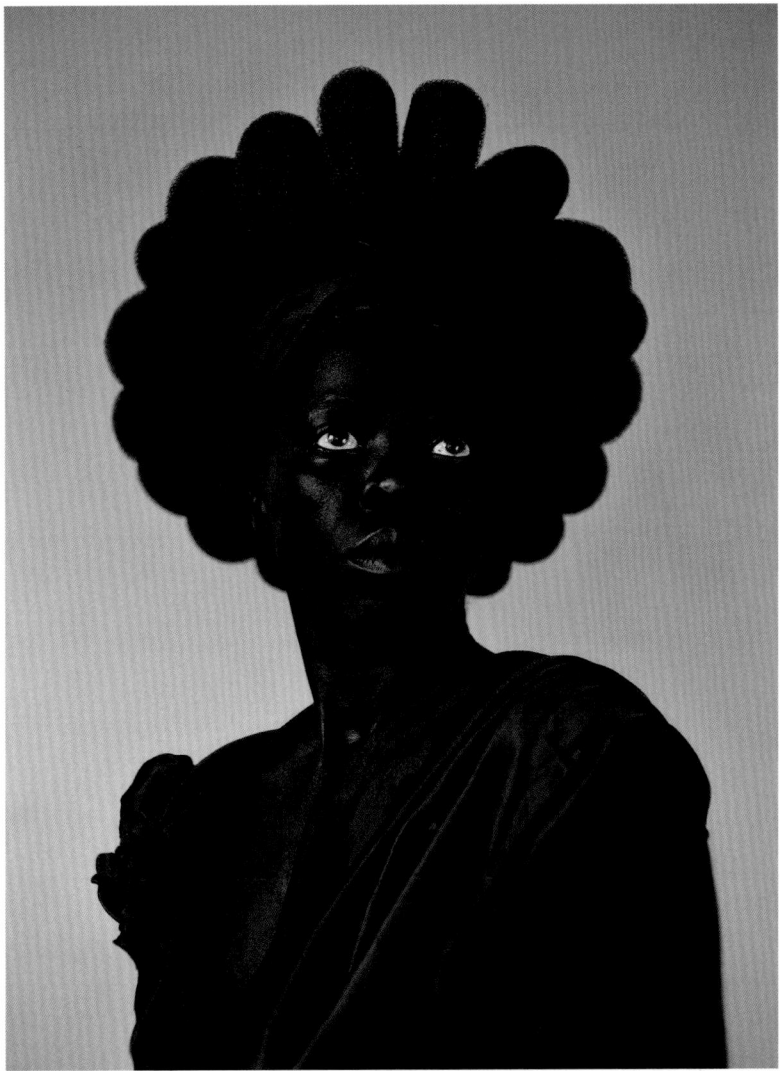

Zanele Muholi, *Ntozakhe II, Parktown, Johannesburg*, 2016

Visibility

# When Glamour Speaks Your Name

Published November 28, 2014

The 1960 publicity photo depicts a famous singer, a woman both statuesque and beautiful, smiling radiantly. A man kneels before her, adjusting her glistening gown. In the context of the image, the interaction between the two is metaphoric: a mortal kneeling before a goddess.

The picture is also a reminder of a disquieting history. Its subject, Shirley Bassey, was Black. Yet even in the 1960s, the Welsh singer's outsize talent and good looks did not guarantee her a place in the pantheon of female idols. Ultimately, no matter how brilliant or attractive, women of color historically were undervalued, and often invisible, in mainstream celebrity culture.

It is with this in mind that the writer Nichelle Gainer set out to document the visual history of Black female entertainers, businesswomen, writers, and socialites, initially in a social media project and now in an important book, *Vintage Black Glamour.*

"A Black woman in a glamorous context forty, fifty, or sixty years ago was making a statement on many different levels," Ms. Gainer said. "Wearing beautiful clothes and presenting yourself in an elegant manner was not only about personal taste and style, it was often a way to stand up for yourself and other Black people and asserting our humanity and dignity to some who were accustomed to seeing Black people in narrow ways." While conducting research at the Schomburg Center for Research in Black Culture for a novel she was writing about three friends who met as contestants in all-Black beauty pageants in the 1950s, Ms. Gainer began to track the Black press's breathless and detailed coverage of women from all professions. Her glamorous aunts, the soprano and actress Margaret Tynes

Chapter 2

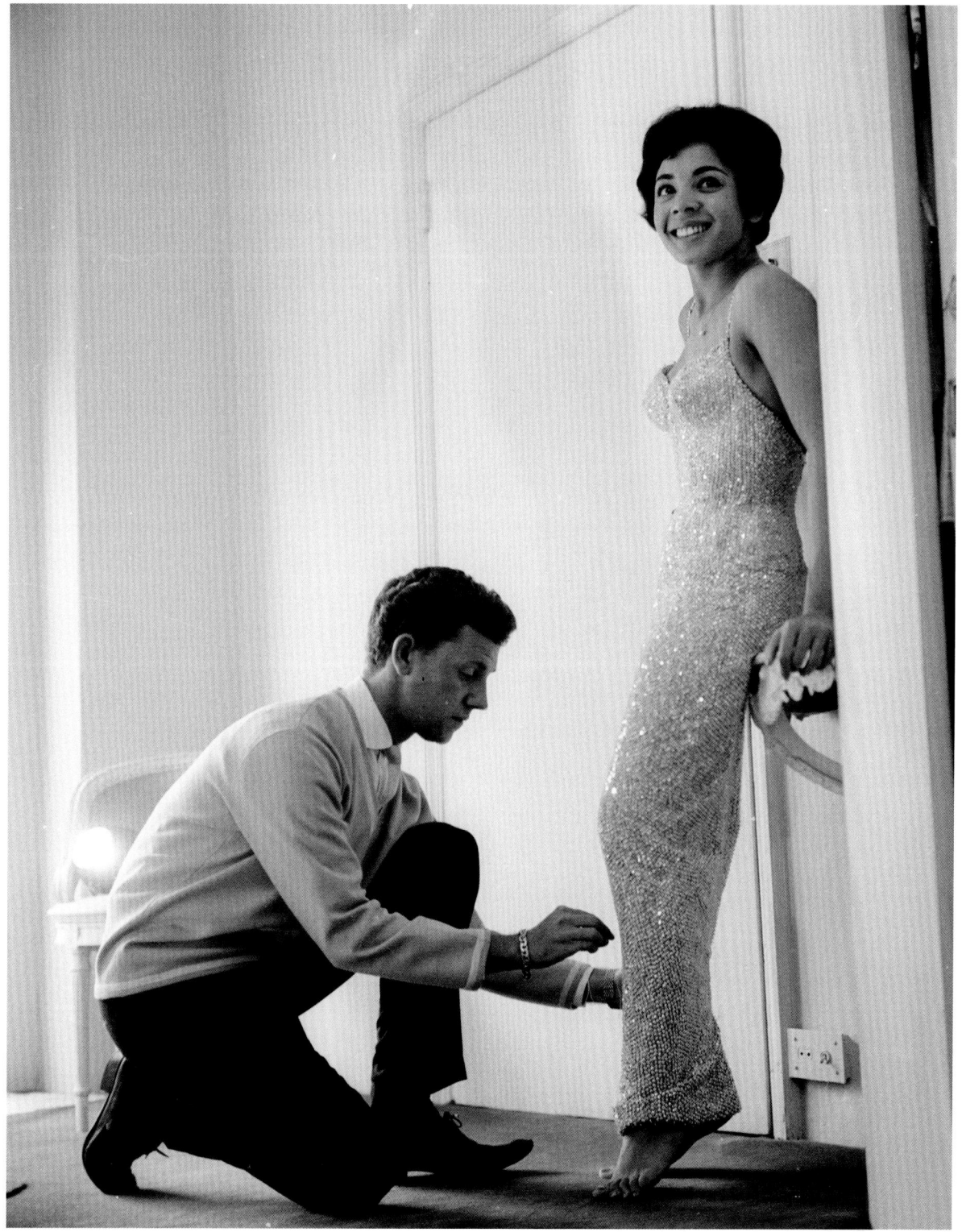

Peter Hall, Welsh singer Shirley Bassey being fitted for a new dress by designer Douglas Darnell. The sheath dress is covered with 156,000 diamante stones and weighs 28 pounds, August 30, 1960

Visibility

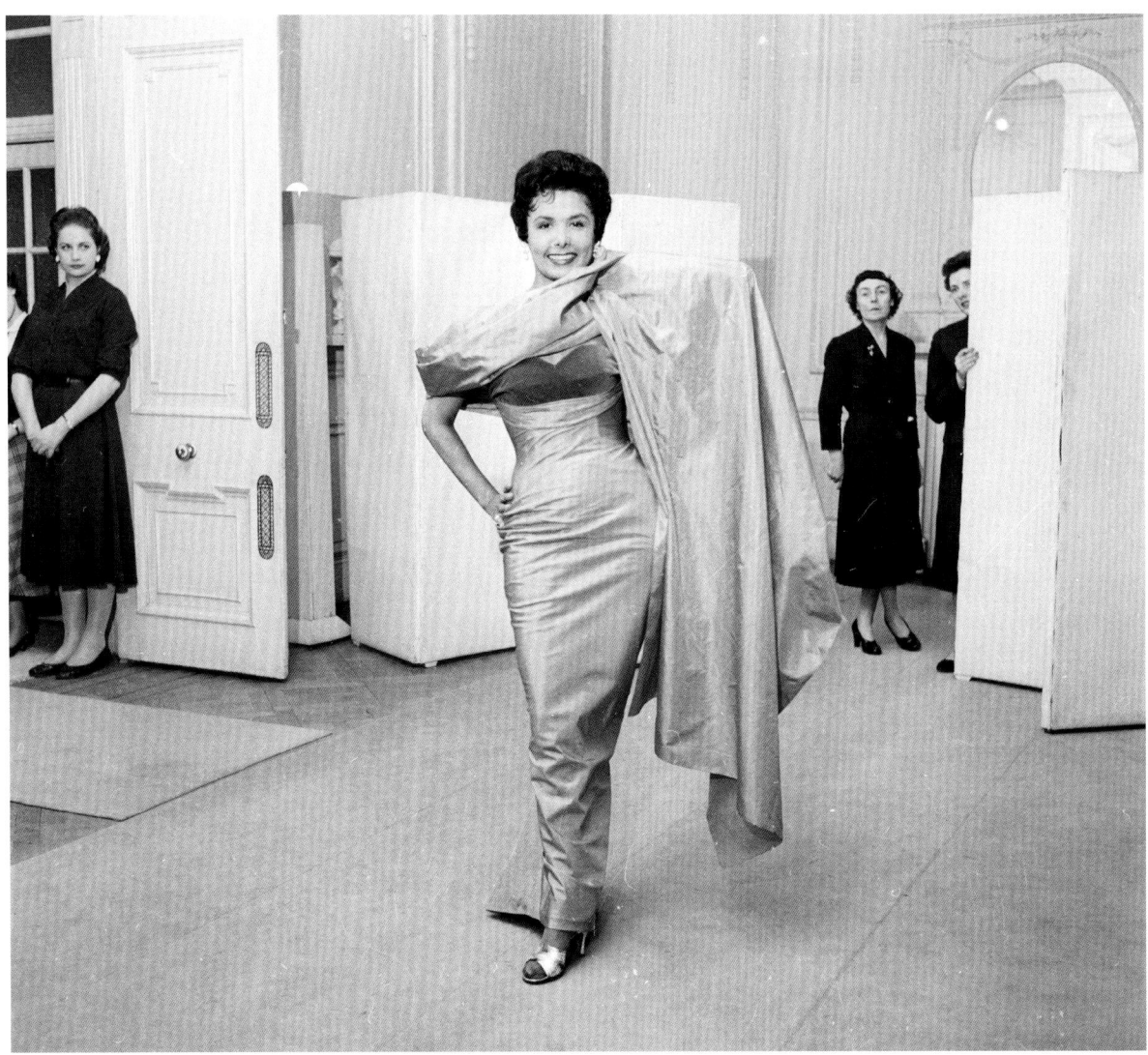

and Mildred D. Taylor, who modeled and competed in beauty pageants in the 1950s, inspired her, too.

Ms. Gainer had already been collecting images of Black female celebrities, with the idea of publishing a lavish picture book. Her research and the rise of social media intervened, and she started posting pictures and commentary, first on Tumblr and then on Facebook, Instagram, and Twitter. The project's popularity, and the desire of its

many followers to know more about these women, motivated her to complete the book. Spanning 1900 to 1980, the images in *Vintage Black Glamour* explore the many faces—and vocations—of women in the public eye: starlets, wives of famous men, well-heeled socialites, esteemed writers, beauty and fashion experts, prima donnas, movie stars, rock divas, and disco queens.

Some are famous, like Maya Angelou, Josephine Baker, Dorothy Dandridge, Ella

Chapter 2

Fitzgerald, Lena Horne, Donna Summer, and Sarah Vaughan. Others have faded—the actresses Theresa Harris and Princess Kouka of Sudan, the dancers Pearl Primus and Margot Webb, the educator Charlotte Hawkins, the hairstylist Rose Morgan, and the jazz musician Valaida Snow.

Ms. Gainer was struck by photography's ability to provide visual details and fill in the gaps in the historical record. "Words can be powerful," she wrote in the book, "but sometimes a photograph is even more so, especially when you consider that many of the subjects in this book faced obstacles that had nothing to do with their talent and ultimately excluded them from history."

The book demonstrates the complex ways celebrities construct themselves for the camera and, ultimately, for the public they want to attract. It resonates with stunning images, highlighting sumptuous clothes, meticulous makeup and hair, and seductive poses that establish these women as entertainment, business, and fashion icons.

But it is the stories behind these photographs—provided by Ms. Gainer in concise biographies and sharp observations—that remind us of the urgency of this self-construction for these women.

In the United States, for much of the twentieth century, a trenchant divide existed in the ways mainstream and African American periodicals approached Black luminaries. Magazines like *Life*, *Vogue*, and *Photoplay* routinely ignored them or represented them stereotypically. The Black press, on the other hand, affirmed their attributes and successes and reported on their life stories.

During the modern civil rights movement, for example, innovative Black pictorial magazines such as *Jet*, *Ebony*, *Sepia*, and *Our World* served as important conduits for this imagery. In these magazines, publicity photos served a political objective far beyond those of white counterparts in the mainstream press.

These images were part of a sophisticated editorial strategy which, according to the scholar Anne Elizabeth Carroll, was already evident in the first widely read African American pictorial magazine, the *Crisis*, founded in 1910 by the National Association for the Advancement of Colored People and edited by the intellectual and civil rights activist W. E. B. Du Bois.

To motivate their readers, these publications routinely juxtaposed articles about the reality and effects of racism with predominantly positive stories. In the former, pictures served as persuasive evidence, eliciting solidarity and vigilance in the face of brutal racism and segregation. In the latter, they celebrated Black achievement to counter stereotypes and instill confidence.

The extraordinary women of *Vintage Black Glamour* served as role models for countless fans who yearned for images they could identify with. Each photograph, Ms. Gainer discovered, reminded her of the title of a poem by the African American writer Pearl Cleage—*We Speak Your Names*—about the historic role of strong, talented women in representing and inspiring a community.

"A lot of people think of vintage Black pictures as either civil rights photos or Black ladies at church, or other very sober images of us," Ms. Gainer said. "I hope *Vintage Black Glamour* encourages people to look at these artists, businesswomen, and historical figures with a fresh perspective on what they accomplished and their true impact on our culture and society. I would also like people to enjoy the glamour and style of these subjects without guilt, because there is nothing wrong with enjoying style and substance."

# The Quiet Heroism of Arthur Ashe

Published August 27, 2018. This essay is excerpted from *Crossing the Line: Arthur Ashe at the 1968 US Open.*

John G. Zimmerman's modest photograph depicts a twenty-five-year-old man surrounded by commuters on the platform of a Manhattan subway station in September 1968. He is simply dressed in a short-sleeved shirt and khaki trousers. Pen in one hand, folded newspaper in the other, he is working on a crossword puzzle.

The image appears to depict an ordinary moment in America's most populous city. But its subject was far from ordinary: Arthur Ashe, the world-class tennis player, the day after he became the first Black man to win a singles title at the United States Open.

In contrast to a mainstream press that quickly transformed Mr. Ashe into an African American icon and exemplar of racial progress, Mr. Zimmerman represented the athlete as he lived, a complex and self-possessed man in the midst of a life-altering event. In time for the fiftieth anniversary of that historic victory, the photographs he took of that event are now the subject of a new book, *Crossing the Line: Arthur Ashe at the 1968 US Open*.

Mr. Zimmerman, by then a renowned sports photographer, had witnessed first-hand the nuances of race and prejudice in America. From 1952 to 1955, on assignment for *Ebony*, then the nation's most popular African American magazine, he documented the lives of Black people in the Midwest and the Jim Crow South. While these pictures sometimes documented social problems, like most civil rights photography of the period, they also celebrated the richness and breadth of African American life.

During the period of the US Open, Mr. Zimmerman photographed Mr. Ashe in a range of situations, from activities outside the West Side Tennis Club in Forest Hills, Queens, to magisterial images of him at play

Chapter 2

inside. The latter pictures, typical during major sporting events, were also politically effective—photos of Black achievement that helped to countermand the racist stereotypes that fueled white racism and undermined Black confidence.

Despite the recent passage of the Civil Rights Act, Voting Rights Act, and other reforms, the United States in 1968 remained fraught with prejudice—from the slowly dying culture of segregation in the South to more subtle, but no less harmful, forms of racism in the North and beyond. White Americans, while marginally more comfortable with racial icons, typically reserved their respect for figures who were exemplary but unthreatening: virtuous Americans, neither radical nor outspoken, who confirmed the possibility for success and served as a reminder that oppression could be overcome with hard work and the right attitude.

With his historic victory at the US Open, Mr. Ashe was quickly enlisted as a benign symbol of racial acceptance. *Life* magazine's cover story about his victory, for example, epitomized this approach. The cover photograph represented Mr. Ashe midgame, racket in hand, his face expressing fierce concentration. While the associated article briefly mentioned the racism he experienced—he was sometimes mistaken for a waiter or busboy while playing at tournaments, for example—it also tempered the social consciousness emerging in him.

Although *Life* acknowledged Mr. Ashe's nascent activism, such as his interest in working as a volunteer for the National Urban League, it strove to make it as palatable as possible to the magazine's predominantly white middle-class audience. "What I like best about myself is my demeanor," read a pull quote from Mr. Ashe, reassurance that he was neither militant nor unreasonable.

"For me, Black is beautiful, but white can be beautiful, too," he was quoted as saying, further comforting white readers.

*Life* transformed Mr. Ashe into a paradigm of emotional and physical reserve: "Detachment—the air of icy elegance—is part of Mr. Ashe's image now. It is an extra piece of identification that will enhance his celebrity," it observed, the words "icy elegance" repeated on the magazine's cover. The accompanying photographs, including several by Mr. Zimmerman, were all tennis-related, largely focused on the athlete's cool sportsmanship.

As Eric Allen Hall noted in his book, *Arthur Ashe: Tennis and Justice in the Civil Rights Era*, the tennis player fully understood the important position he held after the US Open. For African Americans, as exemplified by his coverage in the Black press, he was a role model who was also committed to advocating for racial equality and justice. For whites, he served as a nonthreatening symbol of racial progress—a benevolent sports hero ripe for corporate sponsorships and product endorsements.

Mr. Ashe also understood that his extraordinary achievement, and its attendant celebrity, provided him with a platform for advancing his political beliefs. A few days after the US Open, he became the first athlete to appear on CBS's public affairs program *Face the Nation*. Despite his momentous victory, he spoke as an activist, weighing in on subjects as diverse as civil rights legislation, the Black Power movement, and the role of the African American athlete in the civil rights struggle. Mr. Ashe's appearance was initially applauded by many. But as his activism intensified and his international tennis ranking declined, he was assailed by some in the mainstream media for squandering his formidable athletic talent on politics.

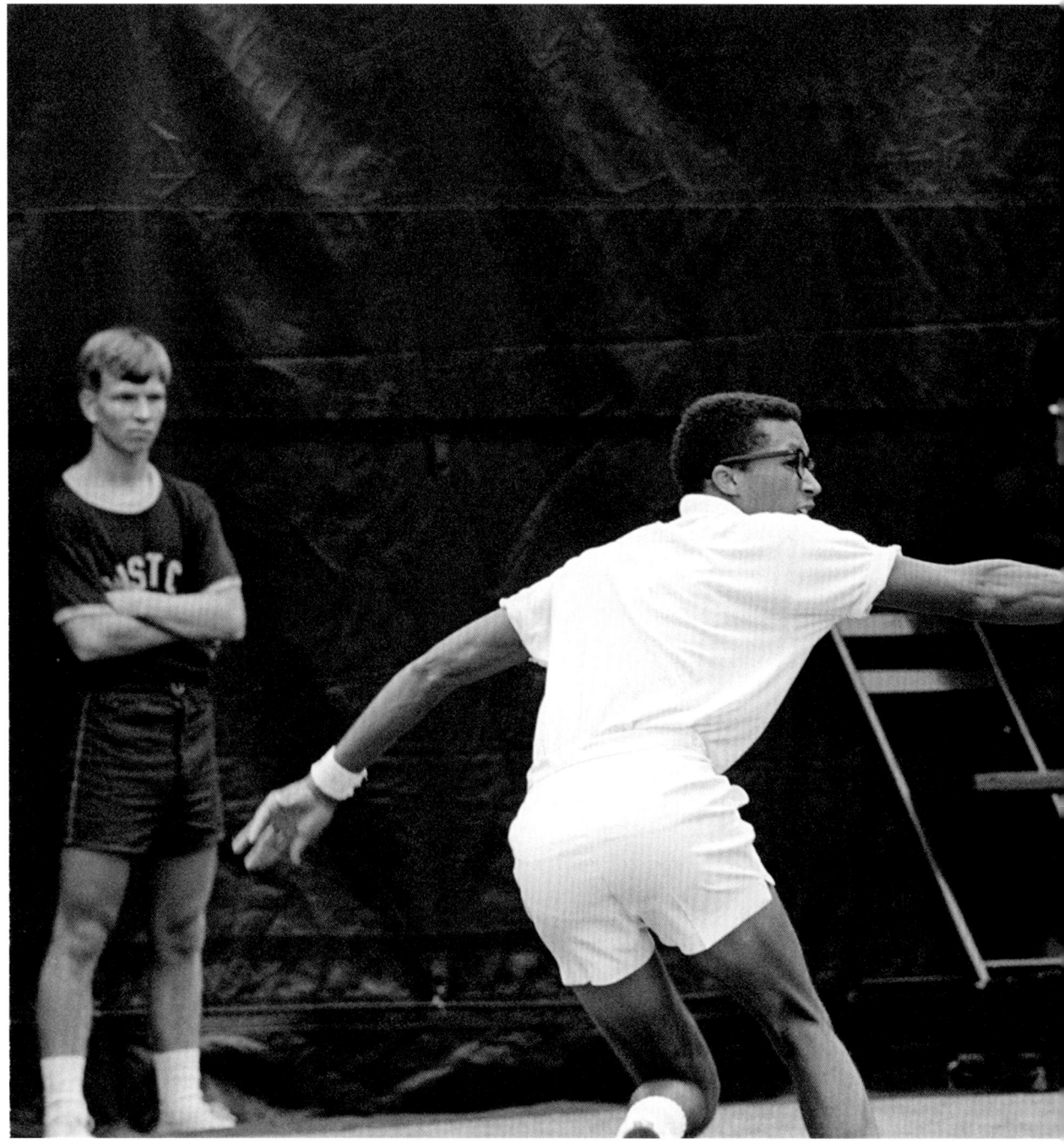

John G. Zimmerman, Arthur Ashe during the men's doubles championship. He and his partner, Andrés Gimeno, lost in the finals to Mr. Ashe's American Davis Cup teammates, Stan Smith and Bob Lutz, in three sets, 1968

Chapter 2

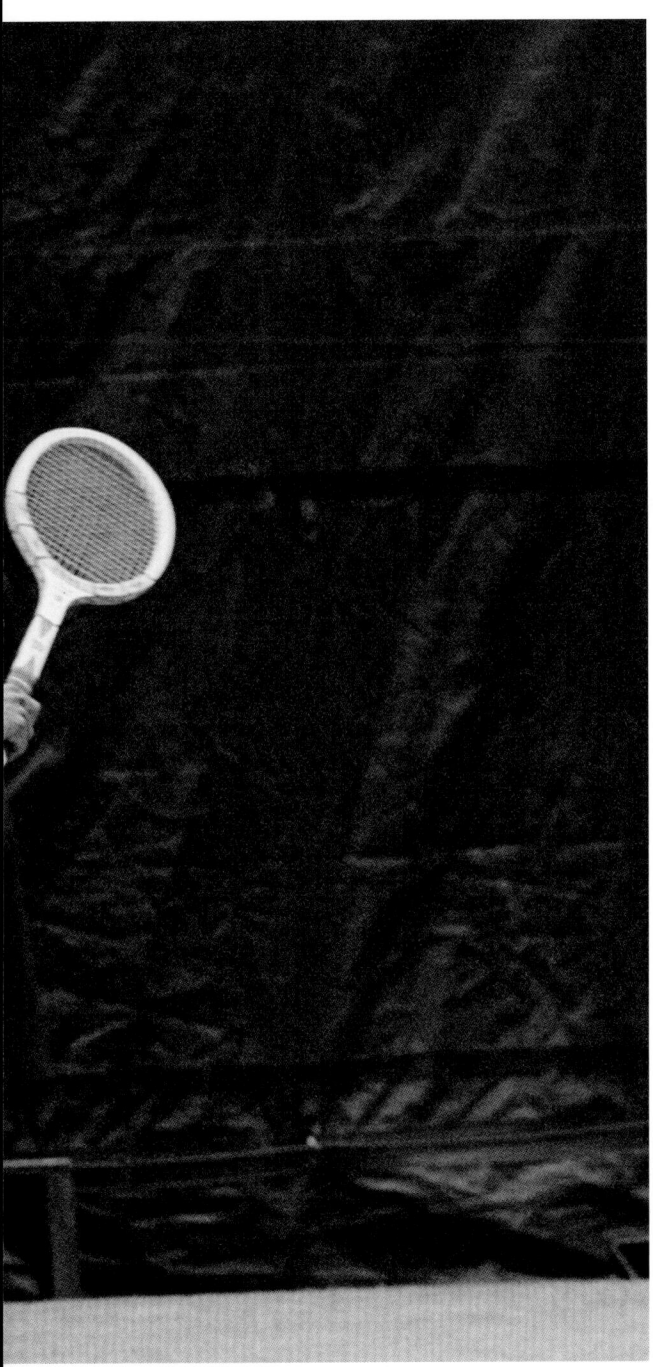

In the end, the nation found in Arthur Ashe its latest racial hero. But Mr. Zimmerman's subway photograph presented a characteristically nuanced view of his historic feat, one commensurate with Mr. Ashe's own belief that true heroism was "remarkably sober, very undramatic." Avoiding the limited representation of his subject as a consummate athlete or racial symbol, Mr. Zimmerman's photograph revealed a dimension of his life downplayed by a media intent on lionizing him: his humanity.

In an environment of rampant segregation and prejudice—when African American men and women were still reduced to dehumanizing stereotypes, caricatures, or, in more liberal quarters, magical or mythic beings—this humble image not only brought its subject down to earth, it also underscored that he was one of us. In an era when racial and ethnic differences fueled unspeakable hate and discrimination, this was nothing less than revolutionary.

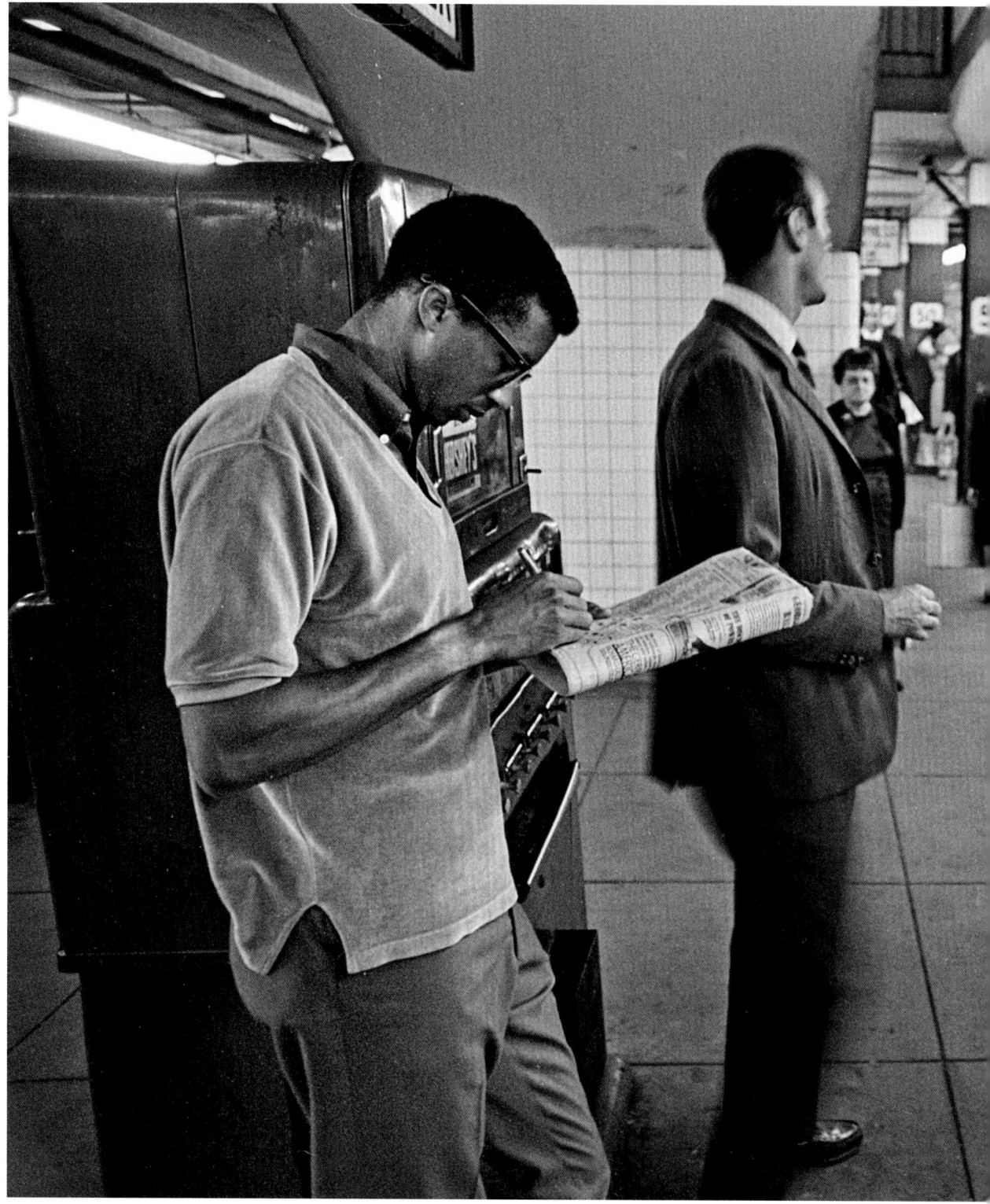

John G. Zimmerman, Arthur Ashe, left, doing a crossword puzzle while waiting for the subway, completely unrecognized the day after he won the US Open men's singles championship in New York in September, 1968

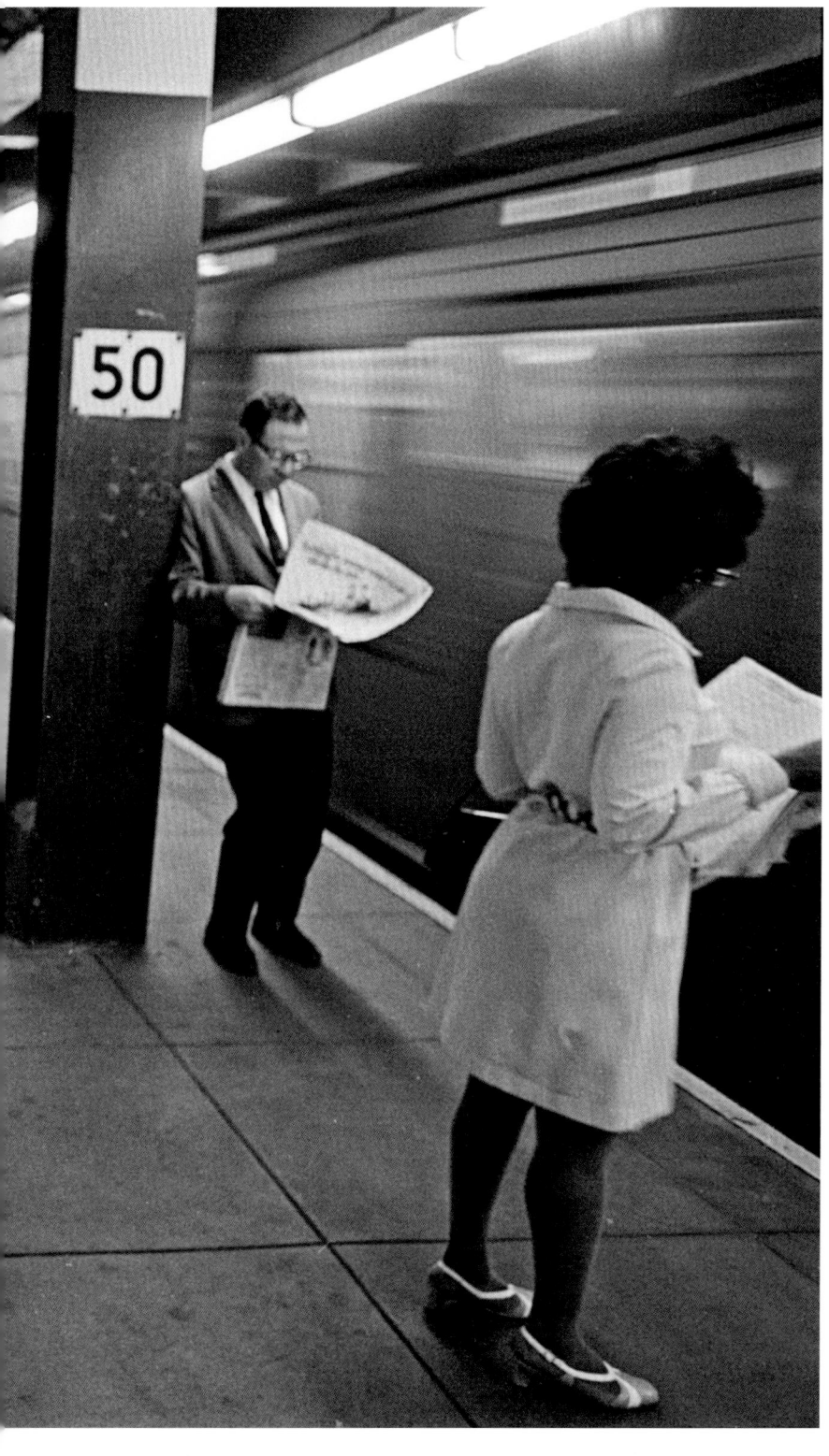

Visibility

# Making a Confederate Flag Invisible

Published June 30, 2015

The image was at once mundane and historic. In Alabama last Wednesday, on the order of Governor Robert Bentley, workers took down the Confederate battle flag on the grounds of the state capitol and were photographed as they did.

The camera, whose role it was to record a reality—and thus to make visible its compelling details of the world—now documented a symbol's imminent invisibility.

In the days since the racially motivated killings of nine African Americans in a Charleston church, conservative political leaders in the South have increasingly called for removal of the Confederate flag from government buildings and monuments. Their change of heart suggests a growing awareness, and a political calculation, that reasonable people will no longer tolerate this unrepentant and lingering signifier of white supremacy.

The Confederate battle flag was originally flown during the Civil War by Confederate Army units, most notably General Robert E. Lee's Army of Northern Virginia. During the modern civil rights movement, the flag reemerged as a contentious and violent emblem of the Ku Klux Klan and other segregationist and white-supremacist groups. The history of American photography resonates with its depiction, from its somber commemoration of Confederate war dead in the nineteenth century to its role as a weapon of intimidation during the 1950s and '60s.

"To me, naturally, the stars and bars of the Confederacy are more than insult," wrote the African American intellectual W. E. B. Du Bois in 1952. "They are threat, because they signify the slavery of four million Negro slaves whose descendants number fifteen million second class citizens today."

Chapter 2

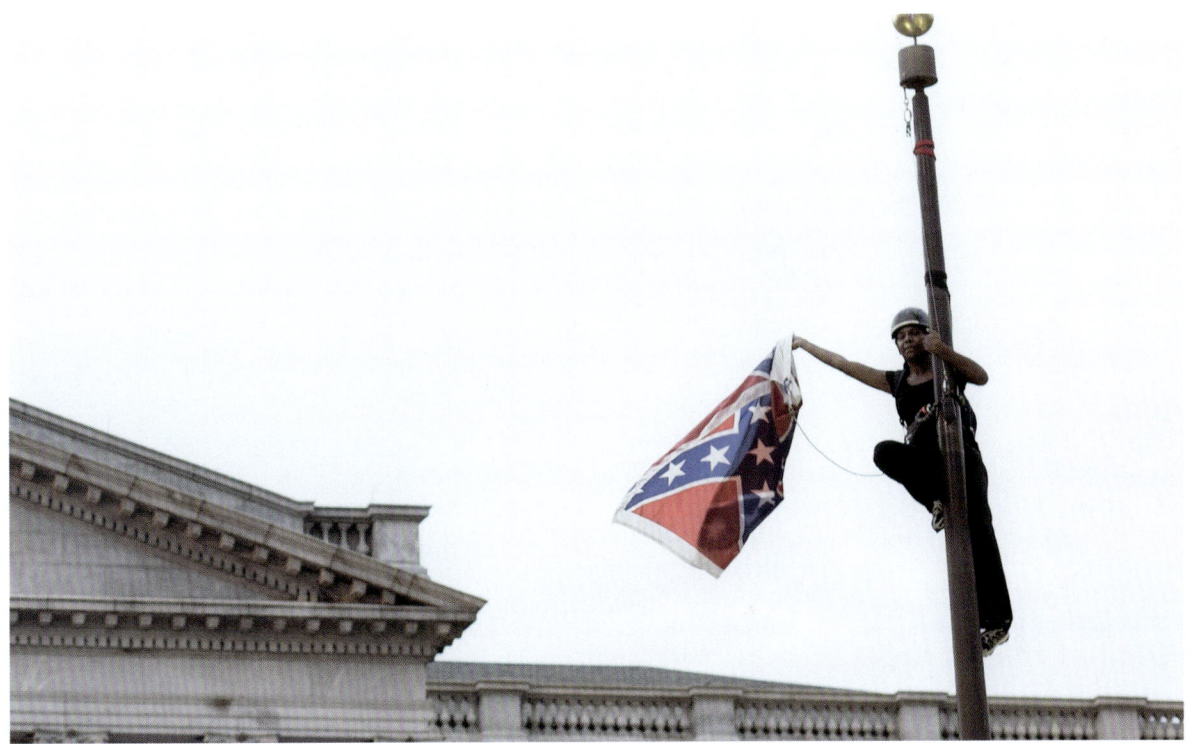

Adam Anderson, *Brittany Bree Newsome removes the Confederate flag*, June 27, 2015

The elimination of the flag from the public square is an important first step. Activists have long understood the symbolic power of its removal, as when Bree Newsome climbed a flagpole in front of South Carolina's State House last Saturday to take down the Confederate flag.

Overnight, it has become considerably more difficult to glorify one of the most daunting and hurtful symbols of racial hatred or to deny the pain it has caused. The significance of this cultural shift, and the discussion it has inspired, cannot be underestimated.

Acquiescing to the longstanding demands from multiple constituencies for the flag's removal will no doubt be difficult for many white Southerners. As Greg Stewart, the director of Beauvoir, the last home of the Confederate president Jefferson Davis, told the *New York Times* last week, "You're asking me to agree that my great-grandparent and great-great-grandparents were monsters."

Nevertheless, the self-congratulation that lurks just below the surface of white conservative support for the flag's removal is somewhat troubling. No matter how unprecedented, retiring the Confederate flag is still only a token gesture. Banishing it from government property—or from the shelves of major retail stores, as Walmart vowed to do last week—will not prevent its private use or expel it from the hearts and minds of the many who see it as an apt reflection of their heritage.

Calls for the flag's removal are typical of the way many white Americans handle the conundrum of race: It provides uplift through comforting imagery and acts, it placates by expunging offending language or symbols, and it forestalls the exceedingly difficult work necessary to resolve the deeper problem. In the end, retiring an icon is not the same as dealing with the underlying institutional, emotional, economic, and historic complications that it represents. That will require the self-inquiry, soul searching, and passion for change that white people, of all political persuasions, often avoid.

The writer James Baldwin viewed intra-racial dialogue and personal introspection as the best hope for transcending prejudice. When asked by *Esquire* after the assassination of the Reverend Dr. Martin Luther King Jr. what the "average citizen" should do to improve race relations in the United States, Mr. Baldwin replied: "If he feels he wants to save this country, he should be talking to his neighbors and talking to his children. He shouldn't, by the way, be talking to me."

But instead of questioning ourselves, we too often look to symbolic acts, milestones, and imagery to support the idea of our racial largesse. One of the dominant narratives about the election of Barack Obama in 2008, for example, concerned the status of racism itself: that the nation was at the dawn of an era of postracial benevolence.

Photographs historically have served as the noble, if unintentional, enablers of this fantasy. The camera has been there both to record and transform into feel-good moments every public step forward in mainstream institutional acceptance of African Americans. Cameras were there in 1947, when Jackie Robinson played his first game in the major leagues. Cameras were there in 1964, when President Lyndon B. Johnson signed the Civil Rights Act. Nineteen years later, cameras were there when a luminous Vanessa Williams was crowned the first Black Miss America.

And cameras were there last week, when one of the foremost symbols of intolerance was removed from the Alabama Statehouse grounds.

But as racially motivated murders abound—and are represented by a seemingly endless stream of photographic images that remind us of the pervasiveness of racial brutality and prejudice—our delusions and wishful thinking wane.

The problem of racism is not over. Not in the precincts of Southern white supremacy; not in the classrooms and shopping malls of suburban America; not in the liberal cities, whose voters were largely responsible for electing our nation's first Black president. But until we face down racism in all of its quarters, including that which lies within ourselves, it will always be the problem of other people in other places, worlds apart from the one in which we live.

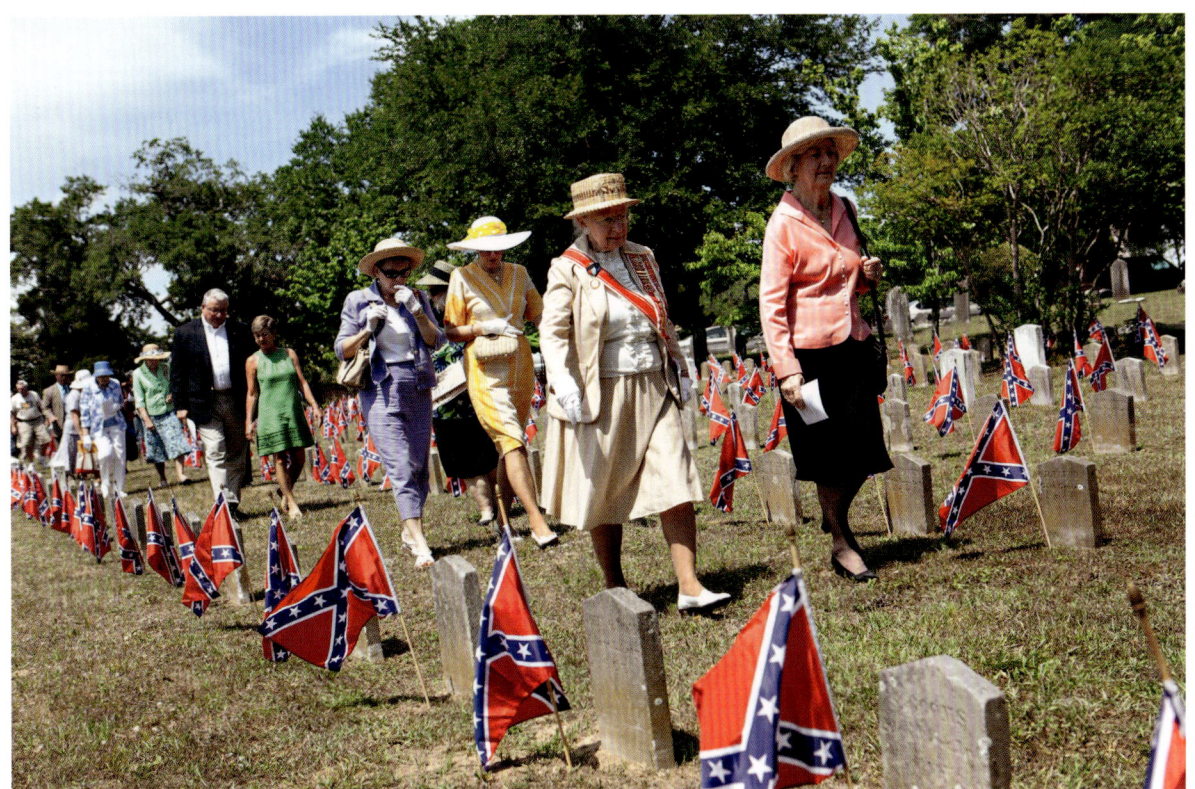

Richard Ellis, Members of the United Daughters of the Confederacy and the Sons of the Confederacy walking through Magnolia Cemetery to commemorate Confederate Memorial Day in Charleston, South Carolina. The cemetery is the resting place of more than two thousand Confederate soldiers, May 10, 2010

# Making Chicano Life Visible

Published September 14, 2017

From 1967 to 1977, *La Raza*, the Los Angeles newspaper turned magazine, provided a vital and dynamic forum for Chicano political and cultural expression. Employing a range of disciplines—including photojournalism, graphic art, satire, poetry, and political commentary—it was both chronicler and participant in the Mexican American struggle for equality and justice.

Marking the fiftieth anniversary of its founding, the publication is the subject a new exhibition at the Autry Museum of the American West that documents the relatively unknown story of photography's important role in the Chicano movement. Opening on September 16, the exhibition was organized by Luis C. Garza, a *La Raza* photographer and independent curator, and Amy Scott, the museum's chief curator, and draws from the archive of more than 25,000 images donated by *La Raza*'s photographers to the Chicano Studies Research Center at the University of California, Los Angeles.

The publication's title was originally used by the Mexican philosopher and presidential candidate José Vasconcelos in a 1925 essay, "La Raza Cósmica" ("The Cosmic Race"). In it, he argued that the uniquely interconnected identities of the Mexican people—which included European, Indigenous, and African roots—presaged a "fifth" race of the future, an agglomeration of all races. While its literal translation is "the race," the term is typically used to connote the more expansive idea of "the people."

First published in September 1967, *La Raza*—which started as a bilingual newspaper and later became a national magazine— began as an organizing tool for the Chicano movement. Mr. Garza noted that its team of activist writers and photojournalists

Chapter 2

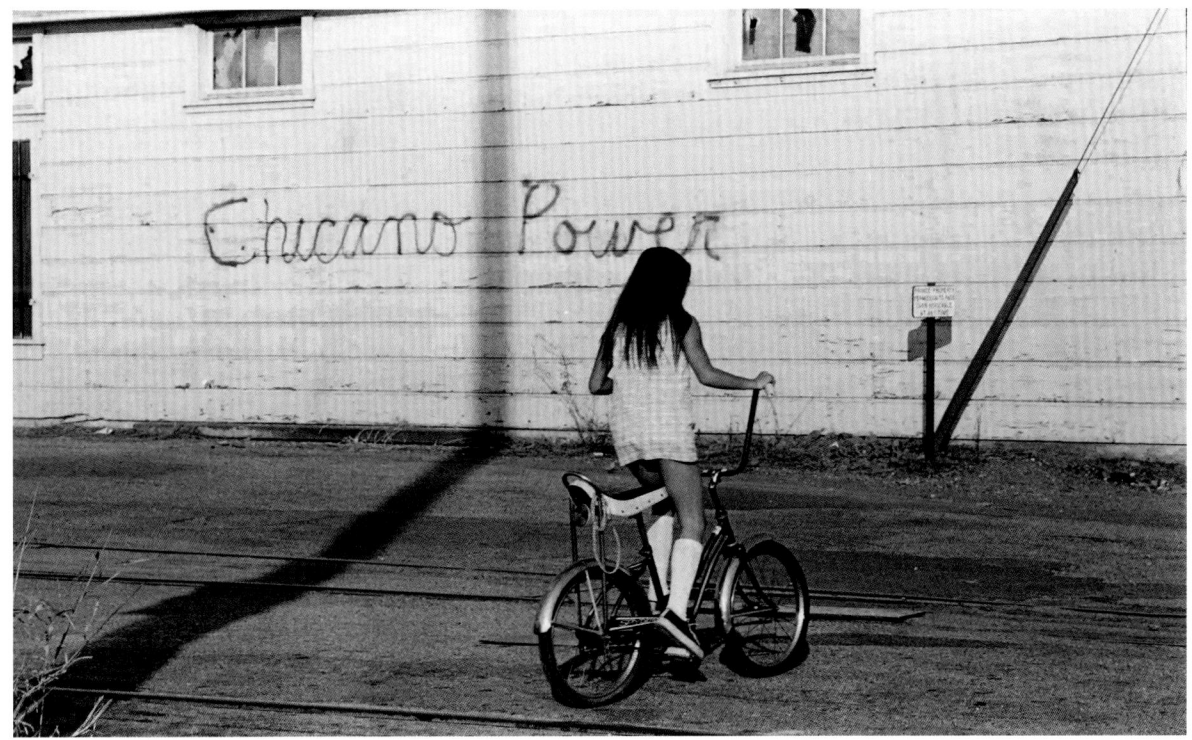

helped give "newfound voice to political, cultural, and artistic expressions."

"The success and achievement of goals, however ambitious or limited, were tied to organizing and solidifying gains while bringing attention to the grievances and demands of a systematically excluded populace," wrote Mr. Garza in the exhibition's catalog. "The intent was to make *raza* politically and culturally visible, in a way that had never been done before, as self-determining participants in local, national, and global affairs."

The exhibition is part of a broader initiative led by the Getty Foundation, *Pacific Standard Time: LA/LA*, in which collaborating arts institutions across Southern California explore aspects of Latin American and Latino art from the ancient world to the present. Karen Mary Davalos, a professor of Chicano and Latino studies at the University of Minnesota, Twin Cities, sees the *La Raza*

exhibition as an important opportunity for correcting the tendency of art historians and curators to dismiss or ignore this work.

"We have an art-historical language for folk art or objects associated with religious or spiritual experience," Ms. Davalos said. "Many art historians have dismissed photographs like this as propaganda. And while they see photojournalism as interesting visual imagery, it belongs to a category outside of art. Scholars in Chicano art history have shown how Chicano and Chicana photographers have been blurring this line for decades. They are working with imagery that is certainly aesthetic, but also documentary."

Some of the most compelling images in *La Raza* depict protest: Oscar Castillo's portrait of a proud mother and daughter marching down Whittier Boulevard in East Los Angeles during the National Chicano Moratorium against the Vietnam War, in

August 1970; Mr. Garza's photograph of Chicanas with peace sign and Mexican flag at a rally protesting police brutality; Manuel G. Barrera Jr.'s shot of a troubadour at a United Farm Workers rally; and Patricia Borjon-Lopez's photo of a march against what were criticized as anti-Latino policies of Governor Ronald Reagan of California.

Other photographs document government pushback against this activism, including police surveillance, brutality, and harassment. Some depict the activities of everyday life, from a woman styling hair in a beauty salon to a boy shining shoes. And others portray the robust cultural expression of the Mexican American community, from posters and graffiti to murals and theatrical performances.

In the end, these photographs helped shape the collective identity and political consciousness of the Chicano community. By making these images available to fellow members of the Chicano Press Association, as well as to mainstream and underground outlets, *La Raza* challenged media stereotypes by showing a self-possessed, engaged, and resilient people. "As citizen-photojournalists on the *La Raza* staff, we would arm ourselves with cameras to shoot the day's events," Mr. Garza wrote. "We were dedicated to telling our side of the story, since the mainstream media would only tell it in a negative light."

Today, when political leaders—not to mention neo-Nazis, too—appeal to xenophobia, nationalism, and white supremacy, these photographs have continued relevance. Projects like *La Raza* remind us of the complex history and nuanced identities of many Americans, a point exemplified by the newspaper's dual inaugural issue. Its two editions—dated September 4 and September 16, 1967—were meant to commemorate the founding of Los Angeles and of Mexican Independence Day, in that order. Ms. Davalos argues that the *La Raza* exhibition—and the vast archive that is its source—can help us to better understand a rich visual history that has yet to be fully recognized.

"I imagine we will find our Gordon Parks, our Manuel Álvarez Bravo, our Dorothea Lange within this archive and exhibition," Ms. Davalos said. "We will also find the ways in which Chicano photographers organically envisioned what they called community, what they called politics. We have yet to determine the trends, the themes, the visual accomplishments, and the ways these photographers were pushing boundaries."

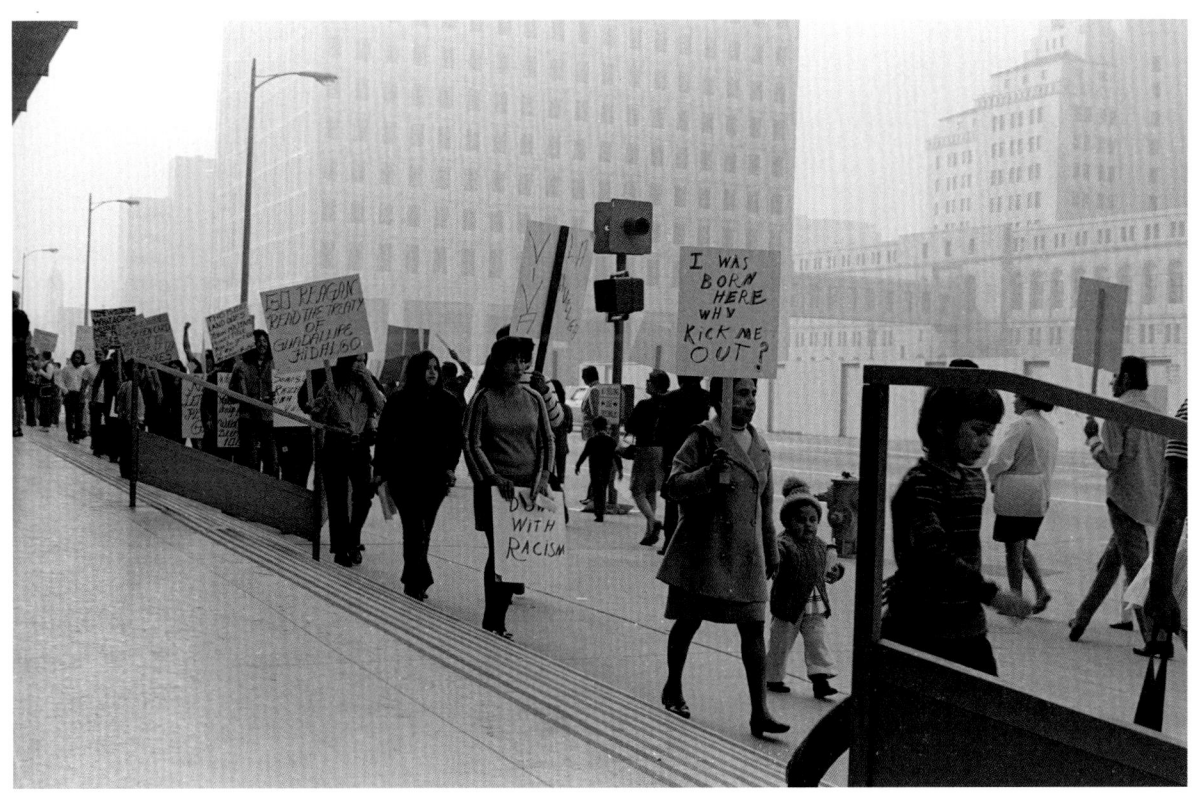

Patricia Borjon-Lopez, Protesting the policies of Governor Ronald Reagan of California, in downtown Los Angeles, ca. 1972

# Three Generations of Black Women in Family Photos

Published July 11, 2017

In an elegant room, in front of a shadowy and dramatic alcove, sits a woman dressed in a billowing red garment. Her feet are planted firmly on the ground. She stares with determination at the camera. A young girl stands next to her.

The stately photograph was taken not in a historic palace but in a contemporary Brooklyn apartment. It depicts the mother and daughter of the artist Nona Faustine, subjects of a current photo series, *Mitochondria*, which documents and celebrates the lives of three generations of African American women living under one roof.

Ms. Faustine began the series in 2008, photographing herself and some of the women close to her: her mother, Queen Elizabeth Simmons; her sister, Channon Simmons; and her daughter, Queen Ming. The women's shared living situation speaks to the strength of their familial bond and their interdependent destinies.

Formal portraits and the more candid images in *Mitochondria* portray Ms. Faustine and her relatives as they want to be seen: an attentive grandmother cuddling with her giggling granddaughter; a portrait of the child in Halloween costume; a pensive image of mother and sleeping daughter in profile; a close-up of the torso of the pregnant artist; a portrait of her stylish sister on the beach; the little girl, back to the camera, her long tresses "encoded" with the cultural meaning of hair, as Ms. Faustine observed.

Ms. Faustine's photographic projects have included the critically acclaimed *White Shoes*, in which she posed at former slave trading sites in New York, wearing only the white pumps traditionally worn by Black women in church. Another widely exhibited series, *My Country*, addresses the repressed

Chapter 2

histories of racism, segregation, and slavery through the metaphor of obstructed views of national monuments and historic buildings.

The inspiration for *Mitochondria*, however, was far more personal. "The series comes out of the family album; the images that my father, the family photographer, took of us," she said. "I wanted to give my daughter the same gift my father gave me: a visual diary. As a single mother, I wanted her to see how much she was loved." Ms. Faustine's influences for the project also include photographer Marilyn Nance's explorations of spirituality and faith in the African American community; Sally Mann's controversial photographs of her children; Roy DeCarava and Langston Hughes's epochal 1955 photo-essay about Harlem, *The Sweet Flypaper of Life*; and Rita Dove's poems about motherhood and family.

Ms. Faustine, who can trace her family lineage to pre–Civil War North Carolina, created *Mitochondria* in part as a response to the stereotypes about the Black family. As an example, she cited *The Negro Family: The Case for National Action*, the 1965 report by Daniel Patrick Moynihan that blamed a perceived decline of the African American family on destructive ghetto culture. "Black life has always been politicized in America," Ms. Faustine said. "The Moynihan Report lives in infamy as a characterization of the disarray of the Black family. There is this huge misconception of who we are, who we love, and how we raise our children."

Ms. Faustine sees *Mitochondria* preeminently as a celebration of the power of African American women to nurture family, even in the direst of circumstances. The series' title refers to the mitochondrial DNA

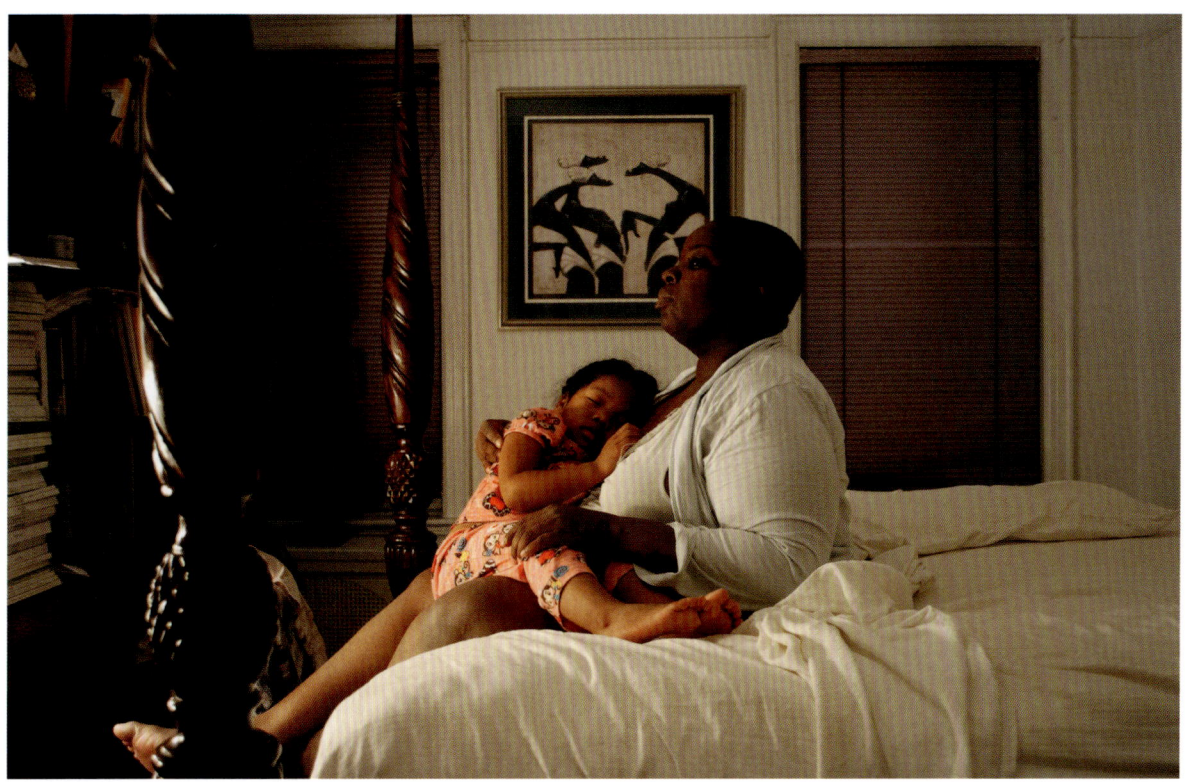

Nona Faustine, *End of the Baby Days*. A self-portrait at bed time with Queen Ming, 2012

encoded in human genes, which is inherited solely from the mother. Through this scientific metaphor, the series commemorates the continuity of African American womanhood from one generation to another. "Think of how we have mothered and sustained our families with love and richness," said Ms. Faustine. "Or the beauty of how we carry ourselves in our everyday lives. Or how we make and create out of nothing.

"Through difficult times, Black women have kept their families together," she said. "The Black mother has uplifted, sustained, and pushed her children and grandchildren forward to build something out of this life. That is where my heart lives and what I love about who we are as a people."

The series also underscores the role played by women of color in the struggle for equality and justice. Historically, African American women were marginalized within mainstream feminism. Nevertheless, they were able to turn to and embolden each other in the face of prejudice, even before the advent of the modern feminist movement. "Black women came off the slave ships as feminists. There was no one there to protect us," said Ms. Faustine, also citing Gloria Steinem's assertion that Black women "invented the feminist movement."

At a time when Black lives continue to be vulnerable to and endangered by racial prejudice, Ms. Faustine's lyrical meditations on the bonds of family serve as corrective and inspirational. In contrast to media stereotypes, *Mitochondria* celebrates the "firm families," as the poet Gwendolyn Brooks has called them, "the durable, effective, and forward youngsters; the homes regularized and rich with intelligence, affection, communication, and merriment."

If, as Ms. Brooks maintained, these "already-successes must be announced, featured, credited," then *Mitochondria* brilliantly meets the challenge, documenting the radiance, perseverance, and solidarity of one family to honor the power of family—and of motherhood—within the African American community.

"I wanted to show the quiet, normal moments of this family of African American women: our everyday life, our happy moments, our down moments," said Ms. Faustine. "*Mitochondria* is a family album, a visual diary of our intimate lives. I felt passionate about showing this because you rarely see these moments in mainstream media or museum or gallery exhibitions. We are like everyone else. And that's what I wanted to share."

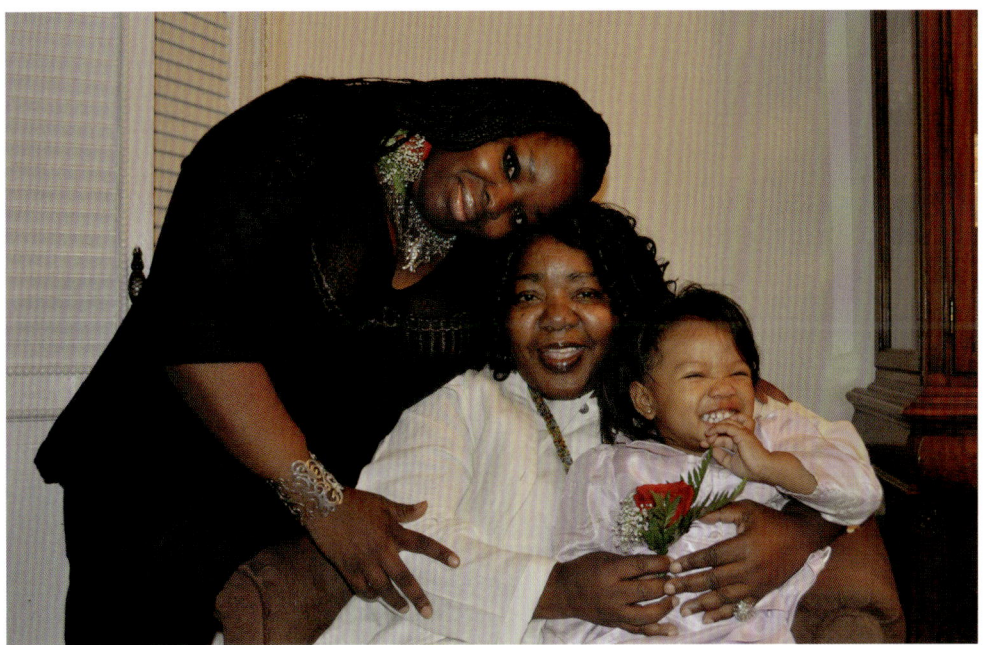

Nona Faustine, *All We Need*. On Mother's Day, the photographer and her mother took Queen Ming to her first dinner out, 2010

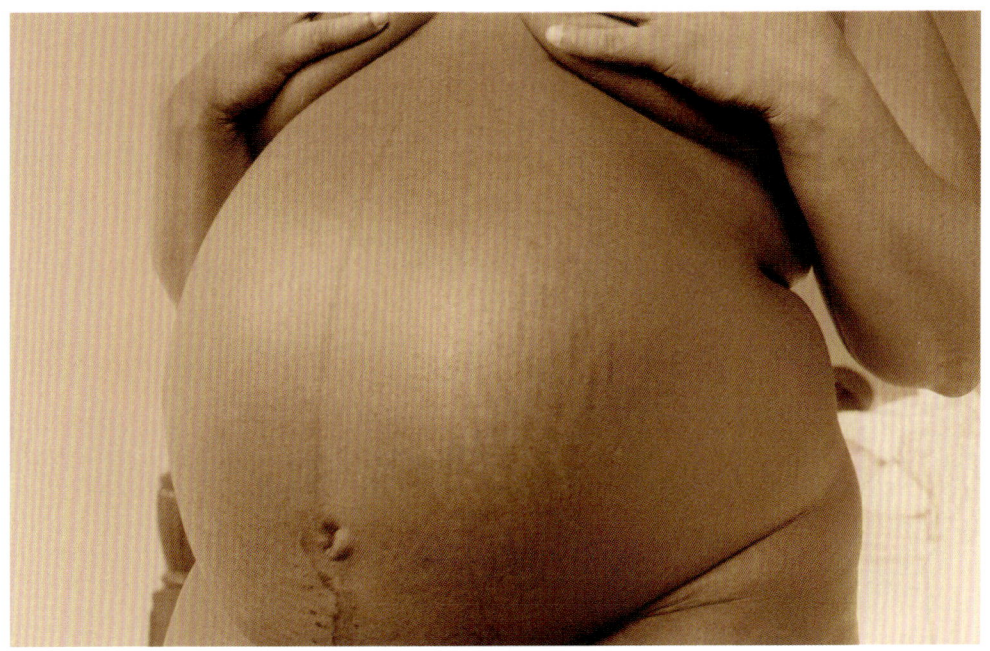

Nona Faustine, *Reborn, Self-portrait*. When the photographer became pregnant, she decided to document what she felt was the most important time in her life, 2008

# One Drop,
# but Many Views
# on Race

Published December 16, 2013

In the 2010 census—when respondents could check more than one racial group—President Obama, the son of a Black African father and a white mother, checked a single box: "Black, African American or Negro." Mr. Obama himself was unequivocal about it: "I self-identify as African American—that's how I am treated and that's how I am viewed. And I'm proud of it."

Yet the president's words are nuanced: While he opts to classify himself as Black, he implies that his racial identity is also contingent on how he is seen and treated by others in a nation prone to racial absolutes, no matter how he sees himself.

Those observations are among the provocative arguments presented by Yaba Blay in her book *(1)ne Drop: Shifting the Lens on Race*, which examines what it means to be Black. In it, she demonstrates how racial identity is not just biological or genetic but also a matter of context and even personal choice. It is revealing that the president's definitive answer came after years of being dogged by outside doubters who questioned not just his race, but also his very nationality.

*(1)ne Drop* explores the intricate and fraught issue of race through the observations of sixty contributors from twenty-five countries who self-identify, at least partly, as Black, even if they are not always seen as such because of light skin, facial features, or interracial ancestry. Their words are accompanied by portraits by Noelle Théard and a team of photographers directed by her. The book challenges narrow conceptions about Blackness, both as an identity and as an experience, and the stereotypes and rigid boundaries of color that continue to divide us.

As Blay notes, racial identity has not always been a matter of choice. In this country, well into the twentieth century, legal

Chapter 2

standards existed in much of the South to delineate the races and preserve white racial purity. In a time when one's race was solely a matter of biology and the law, as little as "one drop" of African blood would render a person Black.

The subjects in the book responded to a series of questions, among them how they identified themselves, whether assumptions were made about their race, whether their Blackness was questioned by others, and whether the light complexions that many have afforded them social privilege.

People of color have long asked these questions of themselves, and scholars and writers have explored these issues for decades. What distinguishes *(1)ne Drop* is its ability to recast a difficult and still

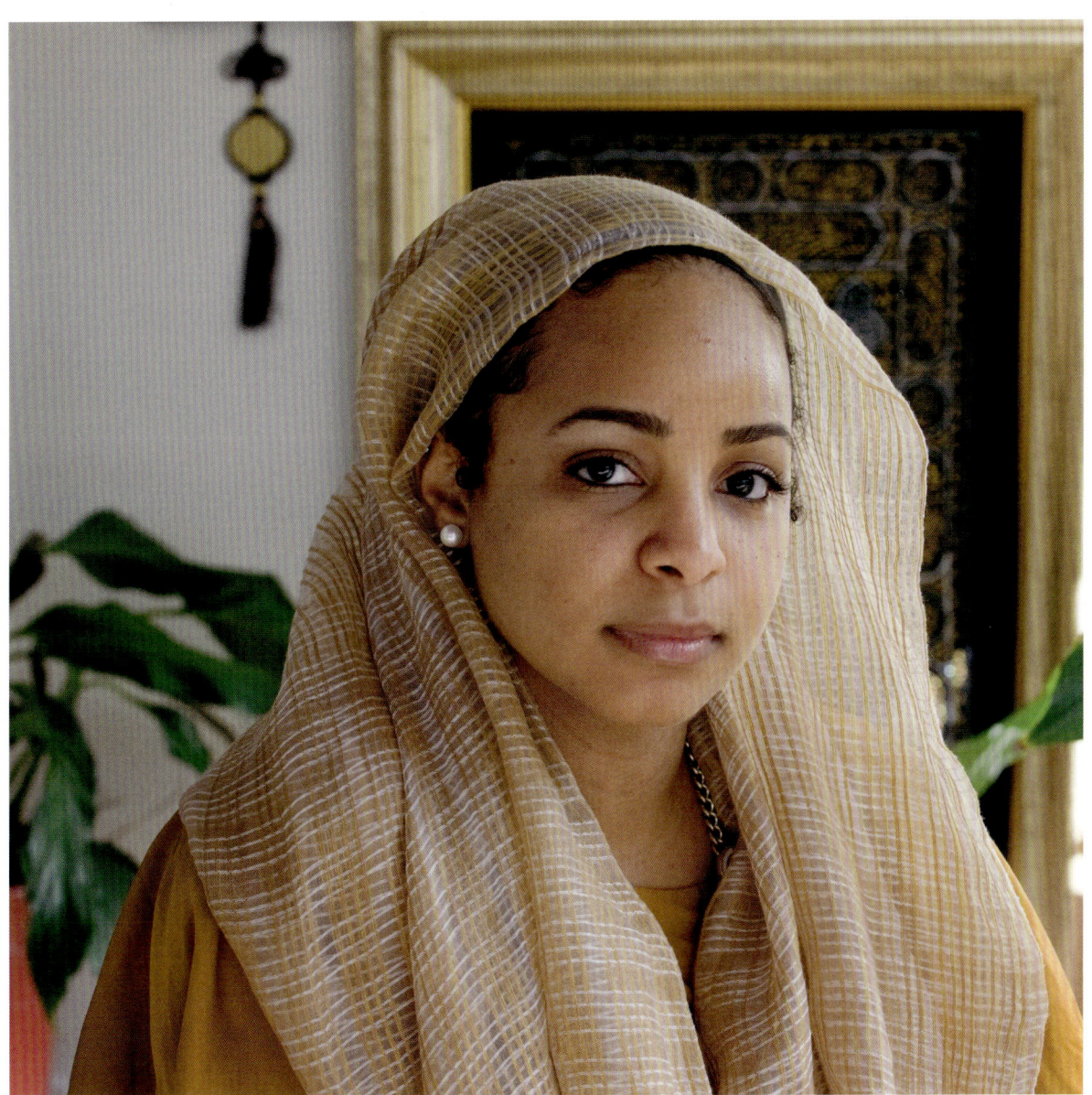

Noelle Flores Théard, *Sumaya Ellard*, 2021

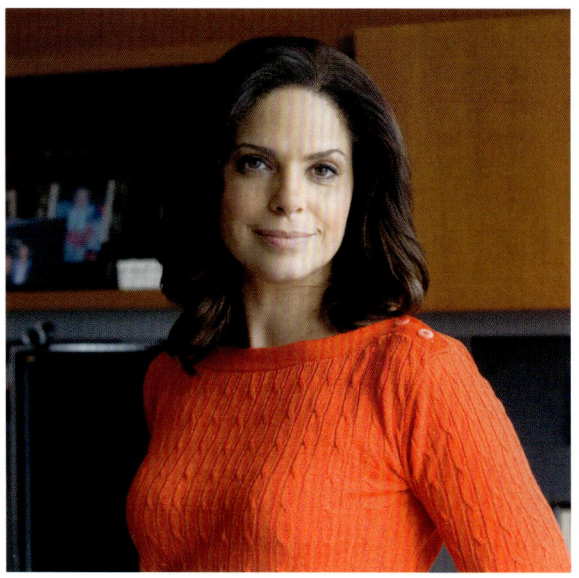

Noelle Flores Théard, *Soledad O'Brien*, 2021

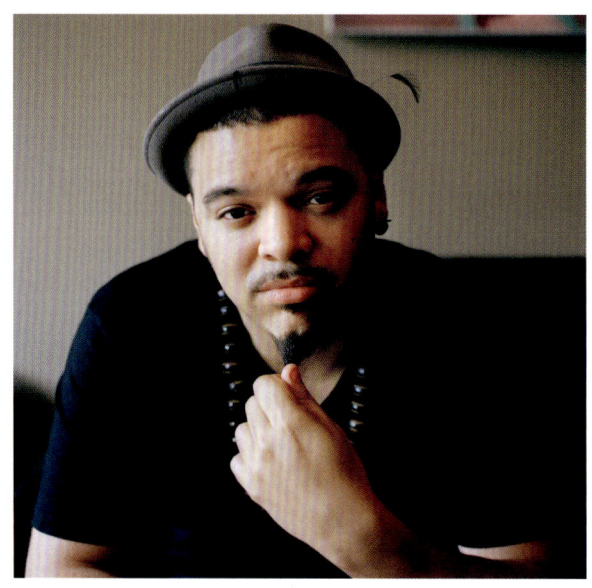

Noelle Flores Théard, *Michael Cordero*, 2021

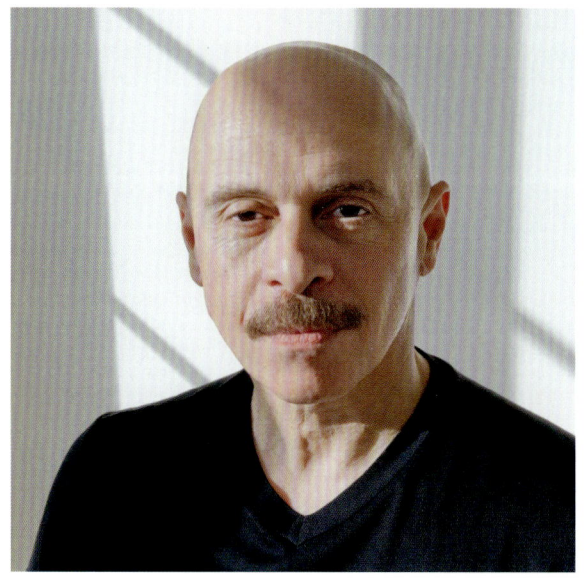

Noelle Flores Théard, *James Scott*, 2021

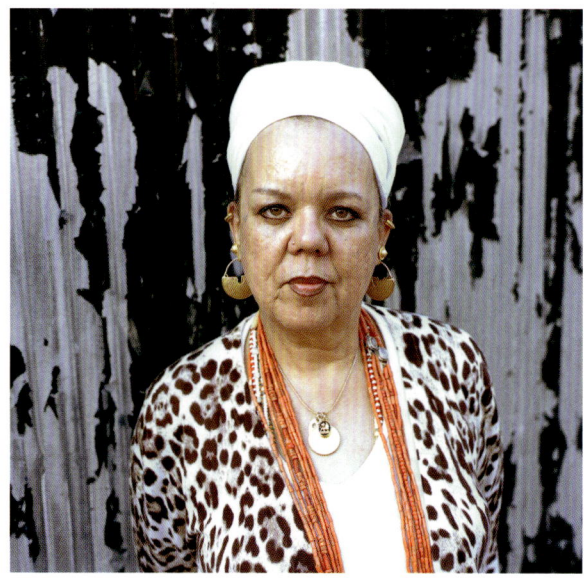

Noelle Flores Théard, *Koko Zauditu-Selassie*, 2021

Chapter 2

controversial subject in personal, visual, and lyrical terms.

The book is "descriptive, not prescriptive," wrote Dr. Blay, thirty-nine, who teaches Africana Studies at Drexel University. "It is not my goal to tell people how to identify," she continued. "I am not the Blackness-whisperer, nor am I the Blackness-hunter."

The book's nuanced view of race is enhanced by its dynamic and insightful color portraits. "Photography has become such an important part of how we come to know the world," writes Ms. Théard, thirty-four. "Portraiture in particular has a powerful pull because we as viewers are drawn into the eyes of the people photographed. Behind their eyes lives their truth. Their story."

The portraits in *(1)ne Drop* attest to the many faces, colors, and stories of Blackness: from Zun Lee, a photographer and physician of Korean and African American descent who identifies as "Black," the community most accepting of him and in which he has always felt most comfortable, to Angelina Griggs, a pale-skinned centenarian who refers to herself as "colored" and recounts the prejudice she experienced growing up in the Jim Crow South, both from whites and Blacks. It also includes the "Black/Latina" television journalist Soledad O'Brien and Liliane Braga, a writer and educator of Black, white, and Indigenous heritage from São Paulo.

The books subject's recount how their efforts to define themselves clashed with society's imperative to assign neat racial categories in order to "make something that is fluid and uncertain more certain," as a contributor, Deborah Thomas, noted. Some described the bewilderment and prying questions of acquaintances, coworkers, and strangers attempting to discern their race. Others pointed to the social stigma of having complexions that are frustratingly—

or insultingly—viewed as too dark or too light.

The quest for categories once led Louisiana to go as far as to institute a racial caste system, recognizing gradations of color, from persons of full Negro blood to *passé á blanc*, applied to those sufficiently light-skinned to pass for white.

In its multifaceted view of Blackness, *(1)ne Drop* implies that no racial category is inviolable. To identify as white, for example, is no less complicated. Although whiteness typically serves as a racial default that is rarely publicly examined or named, even today it is no more absolute than Blackness. The privileges it bestows can be mitigated by many things, from economic class to ethnicity. Like Blackness, it connotes a range of cultures and nationalities. Like Blackness, it can mean many things, manifest in many ways, and suggest many shades of pink and brown and yellow. Like Blackness, it can fracture into discordant or even contentious factions.

And, as *(1)ne Drop* eloquently reveals, Blackness and whiteness, through centuries of miscegenation, have melded together into ambiguous hues.

"All my life, people ask me: 'You white?'" Ms. Griggs, 105, observed in her vignette. "I say: 'No, I ain't white. I'm colored, just like you,' cause we all different colors."

# Black Fathers, Present and Accountable

Published September 19, 2014

An anxious little girl hugs her father as a shark swims overhead in an aquarium. A man feeds his baby as he keeps a mindful eye on his three other rambunctious children. A single father reveals the tattoo on his forearm that depicts him as his son's guardian angel. A young man poses proudly with the teacher he sees as a father figure.

While these photographs depict everyday situations, they are in one sense unusual: Their subjects are Black and counter mainstream media that typically depict African American fatherhood as a wasteland of dysfunction and irresponsibility. These images appear in a groundbreaking new book, *Father Figure: Exploring Alternate Notions of Black Fatherhood*, by Zun Lee, a photographer and physician based in Toronto. A reception and book signing to mark its release will take place Friday night at the Bronx Documentary Center.

In 2011, Mr. Lee began photographing Black men and their children from New York, Chicago, Baltimore, Toronto, Newark, New Jersey, and other cities. He relied on friends and social media to find his subjects. Intent on creating a nuanced and affirmative view of these families, Mr. Lee spent weeks at a time getting to know them.

"Out of the hundreds of fathers I came across, the ones I ended up photographing were right for this project for very simple reasons," Mr. Lee, forty-five, wrote in his book. "Not only did we develop a trust that allowed me into the inner sanctum of their private lives, but something about these fathers' interaction with their kids resonated in ways that redeemed my own story."

Mr. Lee's personal history informs the project in complex and surprising ways. When he was in his thirties, his Korean mother confessed to him that his biological

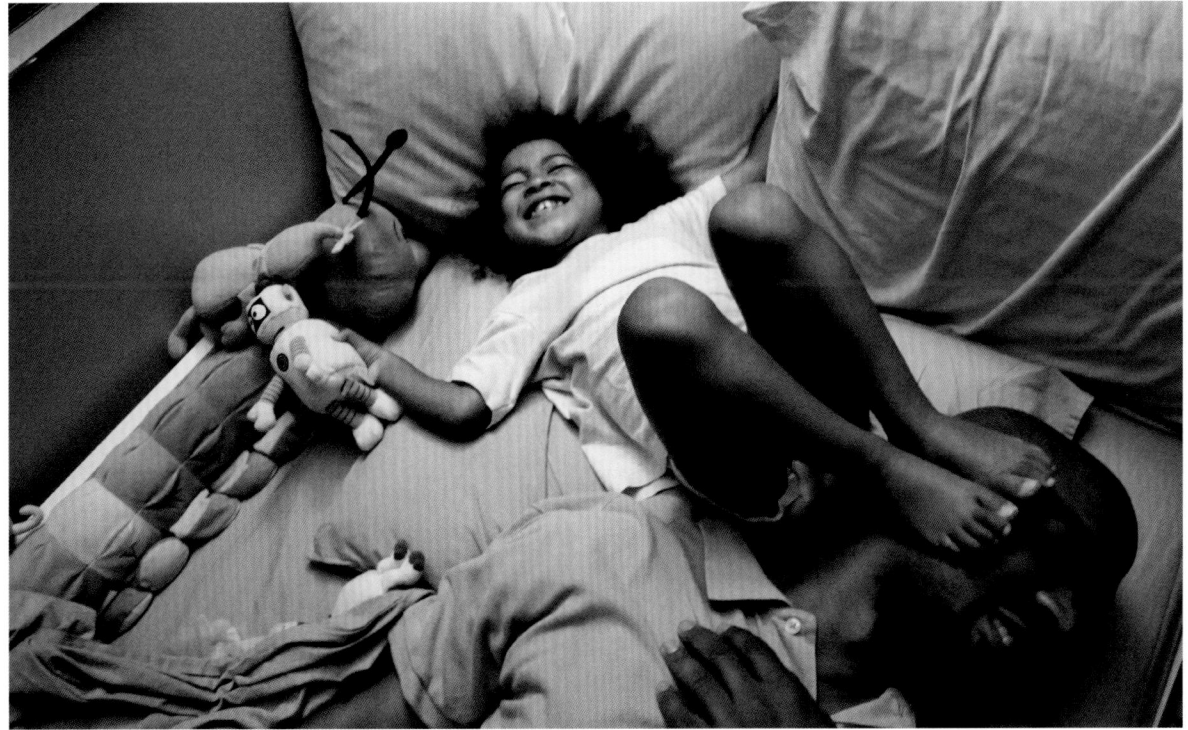

father was a Black man with whom she had a brief affair. This knowledge, combined with the physical and verbal abuse he endured from the Korean father who raised him, stoked anger and confusion. Mr. Lee wondered why his biological father abandoned his mother, why he had made no effort to reconnect with his son, and whether his childhood would have been better had he been raised by both of his biological parents.

Mr. Lee was also disheartened by the way his past echoed "the stereotypical Black absentee father narrative." This concern was tempered by the realization that he always felt supported by the African American community. In the 1970s, as a youngster, he had lived with his family adjacent to a United States Army base in Frankfurt. Rebuffed by German children his age, he sought refuge from his father's cruelty in the homes of Black friends whose parents were in the military.

"Physically, culturally, and spiritually, it was that community that provided me with the kind of love and guidance I didn't get at home," Mr. Lee said. "That socialization shaped my identity and my way of life long before I learned about my biological father."

Working on *Father Figure* allowed Mr. Lee to accept his own past. He took comfort in seeing Black parents nurturing their children in much the same way he was supported decades earlier. If the experience helped him to make sense of his childhood, it also provided a path for "quietly rebelling against mainstream perceptions of what Black fatherhood supposedly looks like."

Even as Barack Obama epitomizes African American achievement and paternal responsibility, these myths and stereotypes prevail. And despite his standing as role model in chief, Mr. Obama has helped perpetuate them. In a speech at the Hyde Park

Academy high school in Chicago in 2013, one of several similar addresses before predominantly Black audiences, he admonished the community to do more to promote marriage and encourage parenting by men.

The idea that the African American community inevitably fosters dysfunction—producing fathers who abandon "their responsibilities, acting like boys instead of men," as Mr. Obama put it in a Father's Day speech in 2008 to one of Chicago's largest Black churches—is as specious as it is persistent.

A comprehensive 2013 survey by the National Center for Health Statistics, echoing earlier studies by the Pew Research Center, revealed these stereotypes to be untrue. African American fathers were just as likely, and in many cases *more* likely, to play a hands-on role in raising their children, the report concluded. By most measures, including feeding or bathing their children or helping them with homework, Black fathers came out on top in the federal study.

The stigma of the absentee father has for decades haunted Black men, discouraging some while compelling others to challenge stereotypes by overcompensating for them. As the writer Trymaine Lee noted in the postscript to *Father Figure*, the intimacy and trust afforded Mr. Lee by his subjects allowed him to strip away "the mask that so many Black men wear to shield any sense of vulnerability from the world, a buffer between them and a society that has so often used them as a source of villainy and caricature."

The book's empathetic portraits are compelling not because they are lurid, but for the quiet way they challenge stereotypes. Like the subjects of his photographs, Mr. Lee engages in a subtle, but implicit, act of resistance—focusing on tenderness instead of violence, attentiveness instead

of distraction, accountability instead of recklessness.

"I had grown up with, and been nurtured by, African American families since I was a child. That lived experience also exposed me to another truth, that many Black men embrace their role as fathers or father figures," Mr. Lee said. "My work is not about showing the limited range of 'good' Black fathers that society tends to use as antidotes to the negativity. It became about depicting the everyday, untold stories that we collectively know exist but are not part of the media landscape."

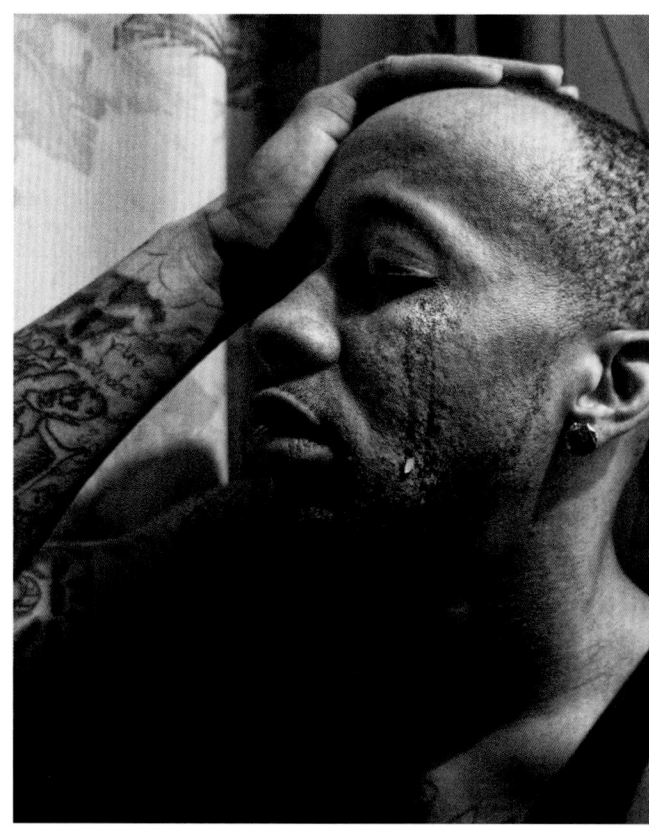

Zun Lee, *Jerell Willis, Feeling Overwhelmed, Needed Some Time Out in the Bathroom, New York*, May 2013

Chapter 2

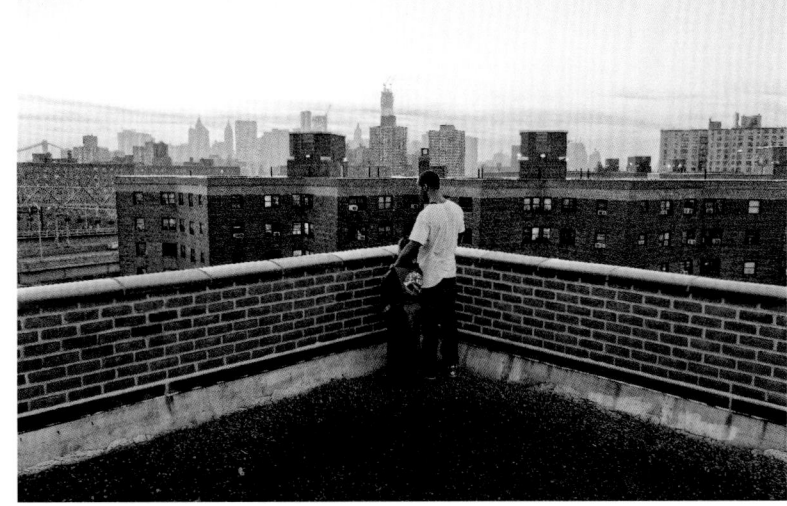

Zun Lee, *Jerell and Fidel Willis Enjoying the Sunset over Downtown New York*,
November 2012

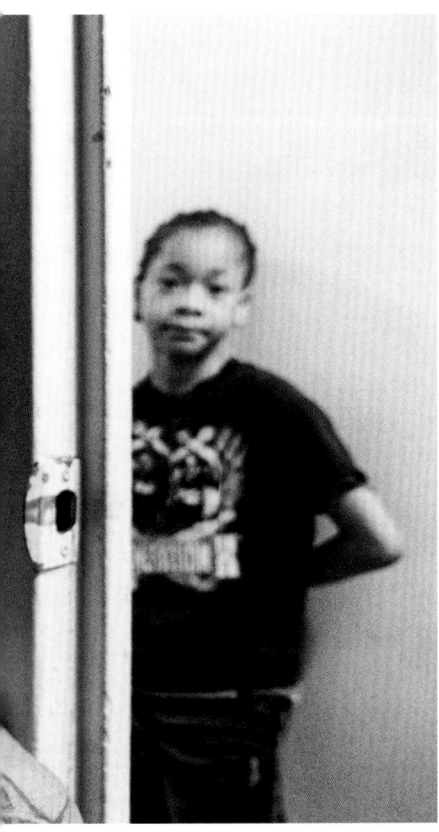

# Black Dandies, Style Rebels with a Cause

Published June 16, 2016

*The Waiting Man I*, by the American photographer Kia Chenelle, represents the epitome of male sartorial elegance. The man wears a double-breasted blazer, tweed trousers, and sleek sandals. A mass of dreadlocks issues from under his dapper hat. Sunglasses and a pocket square complete his look.

While the image could easily pass for a high-fashion photograph, it is more of a portrait and, beyond that, a meditation on Black male self-possession and power. It appears in an illuminating traveling exhibition, now at the Museum of the African Diaspora in San Francisco, *Dandy Lion: (Re)Articulating Black Masculine Identity*. Featuring the work of more than twenty photographers—and a film series—the project is the first to comprehensively explore contemporary dandyism in Black communities throughout the world, examining how men of African descent "defy stereotypes and monolithic understandings of masculinity" through clothing and style.

Organized by Shantrelle P. Lewis for the Museum of Contemporary Photography at Columbia College Chicago, the exhibition reflects a burgeoning movement among men of African descent encompassing "a manner of dress, attitude, and biting sense of humor with both historical antecedents and contemporary motivations." Ms. Lewis noted that Black dandyism integrates European menswear with a distinctly African aesthetic —a sensibility that can be traced back to fifth-century African rulers who blended the two styles as well as to the "dressing up" of enslaved Africans in Europe and America during the trans-Atlantic slave trade.

If sartorial flair combatted pervasive stereotypes of brutishness or subservience, it lives on today not just to express individuality and stylishness, but often to contest

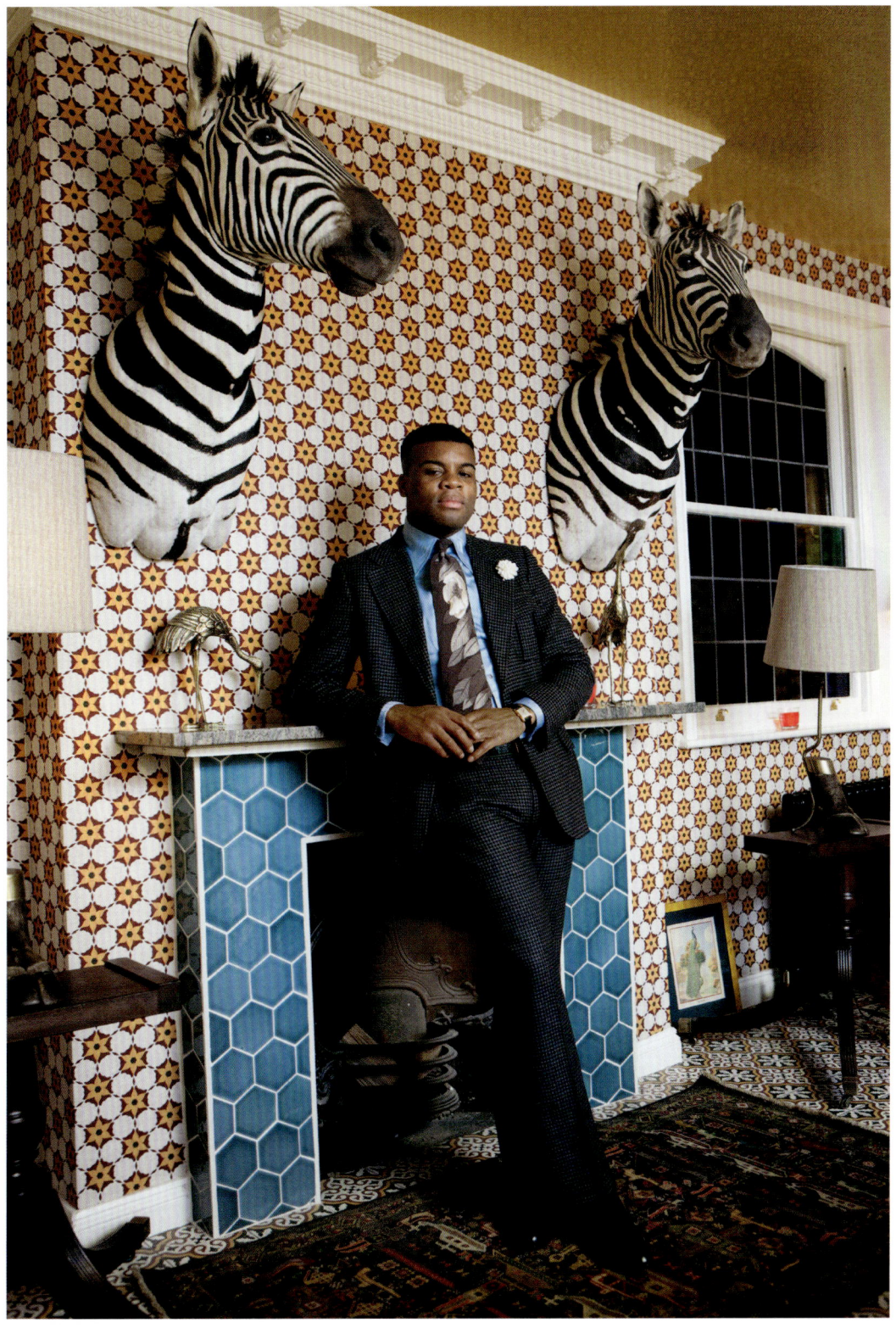

mainstream media portrayals of Black men as menacing thugs. "These trickster Dandy Lions are high-styled rebels," wrote Ms. Lewis in the exhibition's introductory text.

But as *Dandy Lion* makes clear, it is not just the dandies themselves, but photographs of them that function as rebellious surrogates, fighting stereotypes with striking counter-images. *Dandy Lion* presents a global perspective, its photographers working in diverse locations in the United States, South Africa, Congo, and Europe. Their work represents men's fashion at its boldest and most dynamic: audacious leopard prints, Dutch wax cloth suits paired with plaid ties and pocket squares, stylish straw hats and fedoras, spats, and ever-present sunglasses. These men "are not afraid of color nor of mixing and matching styles, much in the same vein as the era of hip-hop that birthed them," Ms. Lewis wrote.

Historically, within Black and white cultures across the world, the dandy has served as a transgressive figure. In nineteenth-century Europe, the French poet and critic Charles Baudelaire, drawing on the writer Jules Barbey d'Aurevilly's study of the quintessential fashionable dandy, Beau Brummell, helped popularize the dandy as the epitome of urban countercultural resistance and of the brashness of modernity. To Baudelaire, the dandy was a sartorial revolutionary. He employed clothing and style in "the passionate pursuit of an original selfhood that makes its own rules," the art historian Susan Fillin-Yeh wrote. Or as Baudelaire himself put it, "Dandyism [is] an institution beyond the laws."

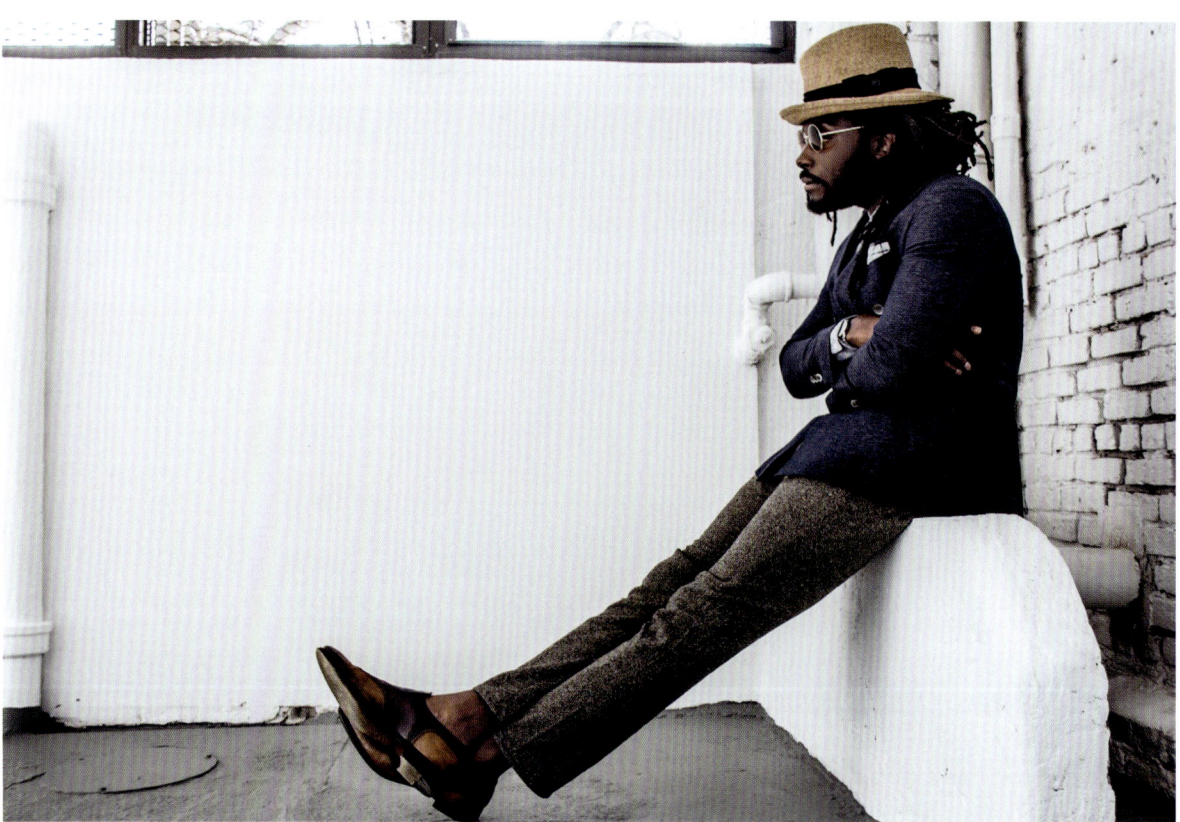

Kia Chenelle, *The Waiting Man I*, 2013

Chapter 2

The idea of dandyism as a form of personal expression and social and cultural resistance among people of color has a long history in the United States. The writer Stuart Cosgrove has examined this connection in relationship to the zoot-suiters of the mid-twentieth century—African American and Latino dandies whose richly tailored and padded clothing conveyed a distinctly political message.

"The zoot suit was a refusal . . . of subservience," Mr. Cosgrove wrote. "It was during his period as a young zoot-suiter that the Chicano union activist Cesar Chavez first came into contact with community politics, and it was through the experiences of participating in zoot-suit riots in Harlem, that the young 'Detroit Red' began a political education that transformed him into the Black radical leader Malcolm X."

As early as the nineteenth century, the appearance of the Black dandy was often cause for alarm in white America—a threatening presence, as the art historian Richard J. Powell observed, in the context of a "society where Black people (and specifically Black men) had clearly demarcated positions and identities and posed a challenge to the American body politic when they failed to conform to white expectations."

While scholars have traced the roots of the Black dandy to the West—specifically, Britain—Ms. Lewis noted that he originated in Africa. Throughout the continent, highly refined sartorial aesthetics and tailoring were the hallmark of African men's fashion for centuries. Dandyism has remained an important part of African society, advanced by such movements as la Société des Ambianceurs et des Personnes Élégantes (the Society of Ambience Makers and People of Elegance), which originated in the French-speaking Congo, as well as the Swenkas, the debonair working-class Zulu men of South Africa.

In the end, *Dandy Lion* reminds us of the extent to which the dandy has historically challenged—and continues to challenge—a limited or proscribed view of men of color.

"Whether hanging out at a gentlemen's club or attending the African Street Festival in London, there is an unspoken conversation being had between Black men globally about how they want to be seen in the world," reads an exhibition text. "The decision to defy social expectations of how they show up in the world is an exuberant act of agency and defiance in the face of a world that isn't always friendly to Black men and boys."

# Framing—and Reflecting—Beauty

Published March 11, 2013

Inside a beauty parlor in a small Florida town, Carrie is having her hair done. She is oblivious to the commotion around her. Peering intently into a mirror, she is at that quintessential moment of beautification when she must decide if the image she sees pleases her and she is ready to face the world.

Deborah Willis captured that moment in Eatonville, Florida, a small, predominantly African American town outside of Orlando. But you could argue that she first encountered that moment—many times over—as a child at her mother's Philadelphia beauty shop.

That candid portrait is part of *Framing Beauty*, Ms. Willis's exhibition at the International Visions Gallery in Washington (on view through April 13), which explores how present-day African Americans construct their identity and image. But the storied artifacts, subjects, and communities depicted in these photographs imbue them with both a sense of history and continuity with the past.

The subjects of *Framing Beauty* are the students and beneficiaries of a long history of African American vigilance and activism—a poignant insight revealed in Ms. Willis's photograph of Carrie. In Eatonville, a town known for its legacy of autonomy, Carrie grasps—and controls—the mirror that reflects her determined and attractive face, a metaphor of the personal ways African Americans have constructed their image in order to empower themselves.

The photograph, one of five beauty parlor images in *Framing Beauty*, reminds us of the powerful role of the beauty industry in African American history and culture. As the historian Tiffany M. Gill points out in her book *Beauty Shop Politics*, these businesses spurred not only Black entrepreneurship

Chapter 2

in the Jim Crow era but also political activism. Motivated by such organizations as the National Negro Business League, African American women in search of economic independence created vibrant communal spaces where women supported each other in the service of social and cultural change.

That historical allusions abound in Ms. Willis's exhibition is not surprising. In addition to her photographic work, she is a widely known historian and curator of African American photography. Influenced by her father, an amateur photographer, and her cousin, the proprietor of a photo studio, she was inspired to become an artist after reading a library copy of Roy DeCarava and Langston Hughes's *The Sweet Flypaper of Life* in the early 1960s. It was the first time Ms. Willis, sixty-five, had seen a book with photographs of Black people, which changed her life. She pursued her formal studies at the Philadelphia College of Art in the mid-1970s, later receiving an MFA from the Pratt Institute and a PhD in cultural studies from George Mason University.

*Framing Beauty* is informed by Ms. Willis's scholarship. Not just about the way contemporary African Americans shape their self-image, the work ultimately reminds of the historic ways photography allowed a people to countermand the negative image of themselves in the culture at large. The

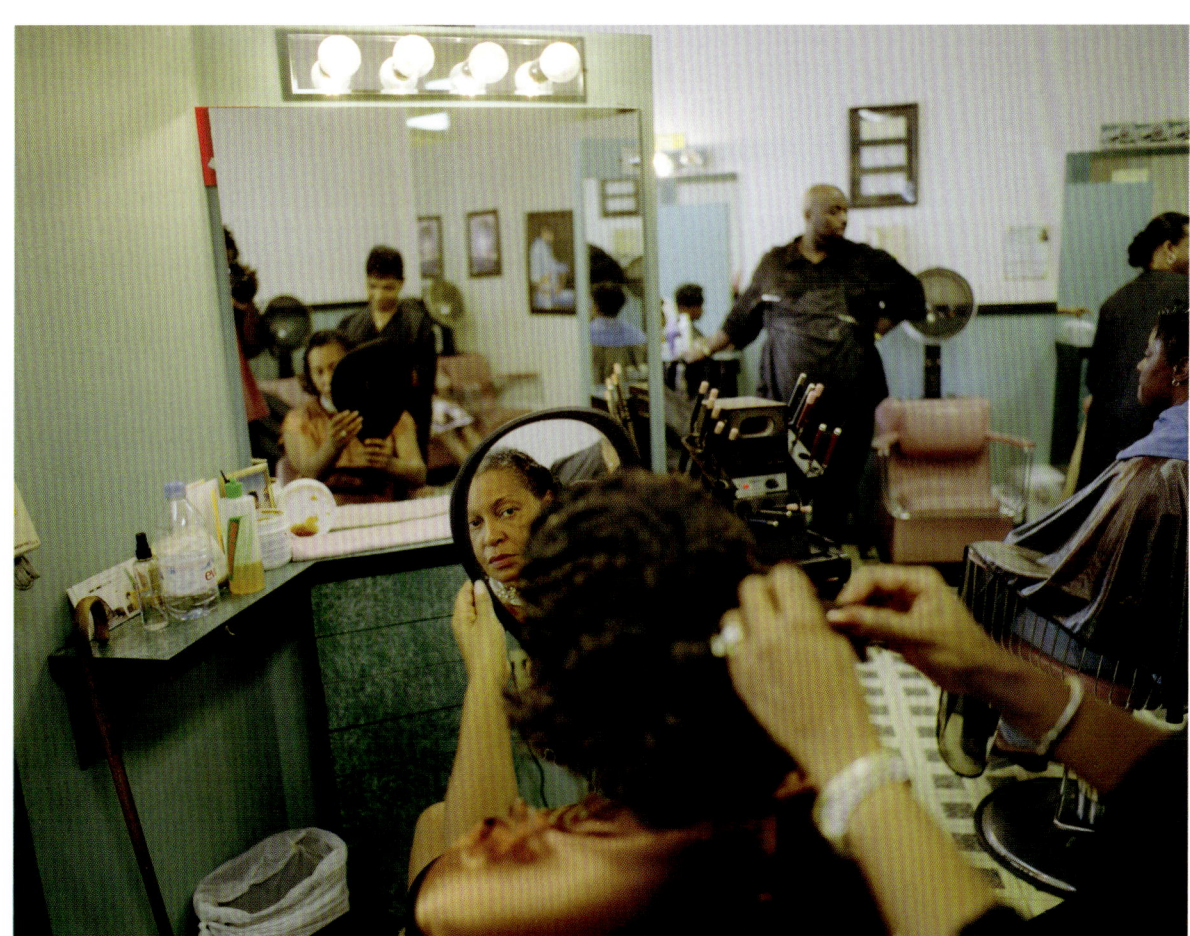

Deborah Willis, *Carrie in Euro Salon, Eatonville, Florida*, 2004

exhibition helps us to understand, as Ms. Willis observes, the extent to which the medium allowed a people, even in times of abject oppression, to "experiment with varied ideas of themselves and ultimately to honor how they saw themselves and wished to be seen by others."

Eatonville, one of a number of locations represented in *Framing Beauty*, provided Ms. Willis with a perfect environment to explore the rich connection between past and present notions of African American identity and self-presentation.

Eatonville was one of the first Black towns to incorporate after the Civil War. It soon became a Southern mecca for African American culture and the arts, popularized in the 1920s and 1930s by Zora Neale Hurston, who grew up there and became the preeminent female writer of the Harlem Renaissance and the inspiration for Ms. Willis's *Embracing Eatonville*.

By the 1930s, Eatonville emerged as a model of Black self-sufficiency, despite its continuing struggles with poverty, illiteracy, and the hostility of the segregated world around it. Questioning the idea of integration—the enduring liberal answer to segregation—the town embraced a separatism that allowed its inhabitants to go about their lives and shape their self-images in an atmosphere less burdened by interracial tension.

As Hurston observed about the empowerment she felt growing up in Eatonville, it was not until she was sent to school in Jacksonville, Florida, at the age of thirteen, that she saw herself as different and marginal: "I was now a little colored girl. I found it out in certain ways. In my heart as well as in the mirror, I became a fast brown," an anxious and tentative image of herself conditioned by the veil of apprehension and derision that enshrouded her in the outside world.

The mood of the Eatonville photographs, like that of the exhibition in general, is largely one of quiet dignity—of a people unselfconsciously celebrating their beauty and naming their style, to paraphrase Ms. Willis. Their subjects engage in updated versions of self-construction, following in the footsteps of ancestors who liberated "themselves from the legacy of caricatures that sought to define them throughout most of Western visual history."

This theme resonates in Ms. Willis's photographs: a serene and elegant Madonna and child transgressing the racial limitations and blind spots of art history; a mural on the side of a Harlem church, its heavenly imagery depicting the passage from the earthly to the sacred in the form of parishioners, dressed in their Sunday best, walking into the building below; bodybuilders, their physique obsessively sculptured, engaging in public displays of authority and prowess; and a majestic elder, her cane braced in one hand like a scepter, being tended to in an Eatonville beauty parlor.

In the end, as Ms. Willis's scholarship has confirmed, the photograph has historically served as a powerful mirror in the African American community, reflecting the achievements, triumphs, and positive imagery all too often erased from the culture at large. Her compelling photographs bring this story up to date, ever mindful of the previous generations who emerged from the shadow of whiteness, in their own image, self-possessed and beautiful.

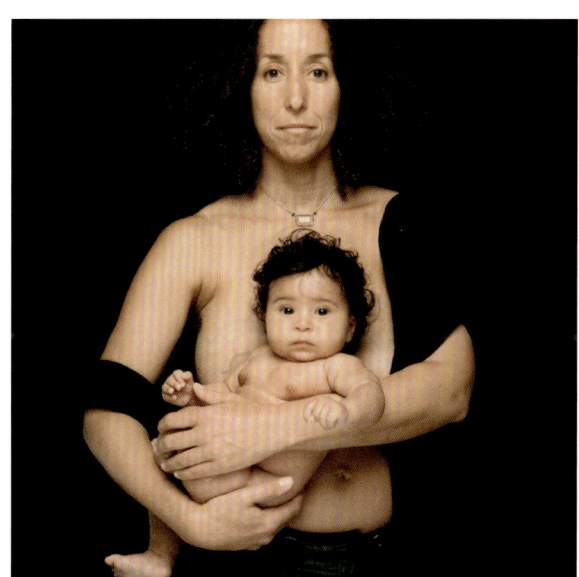

Deborah Willis, *After Madonna*, 2008

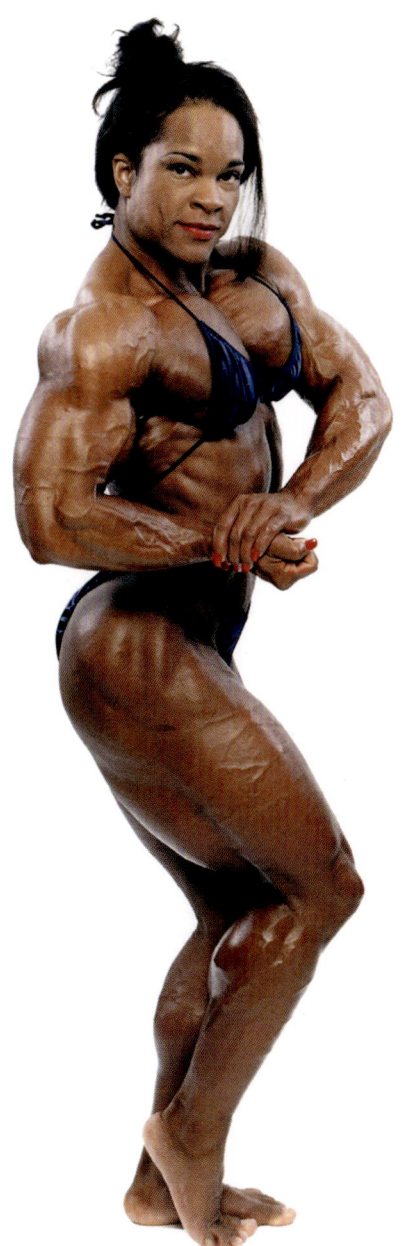

Deborah Willis, *Nancy Lewis, Bodybuilder*, 2008

# These 1970s Pageants Celebrated Black Women's Beauty

Published June 14, 2018

Raphael Albert was a successful British entrepreneur who did more than just promote beauty pageants: He photographed them. Throughout the 1970s and 1980s, he documented pageant life, his images a continuum of enthusiastic contestants strutting down runways in swimsuits, modeling the latest fashions and being crowned.

It might be easy to dismiss Mr. Albert's photographs as relics from a sexist past. Except for one significant detail: His subjects were Black. For these women, members of West London's Afro-Caribbean communities, pageants nurtured racial pride and self-expression.

These exuberant photographs are the subject of *Raphael Albert: Miss Black and Beautiful*, an exhibition organized by Autograph ABP in London and, now, at Mac Birmingham. Curated by Renée Mussai, the exhibition offers insights into

a consequential, but largely overlooked, aspect of Black culture and political expression in Britain.

Mr. Albert was born and raised on the island of Grenada and moved to London in the early 1950s. After studying photography at the Ealing Technical College & School of Art, he worked as a freelance photographer for Black British newspapers, including *West Indian World* and *Caribbean Times*. In 1970, he began promoting beauty pageants, founding a series of popular contests, including Miss Black and Beautiful, Miss West Indies in Great Britain, and Miss Grenada.

Mr. Albert's work as a photographer extended beyond pageants. Throughout his career, he documented life in the West Indian communities of London, making portraits and photographing local families and social events. But his best-known images are of beauty competitions and studio portraits

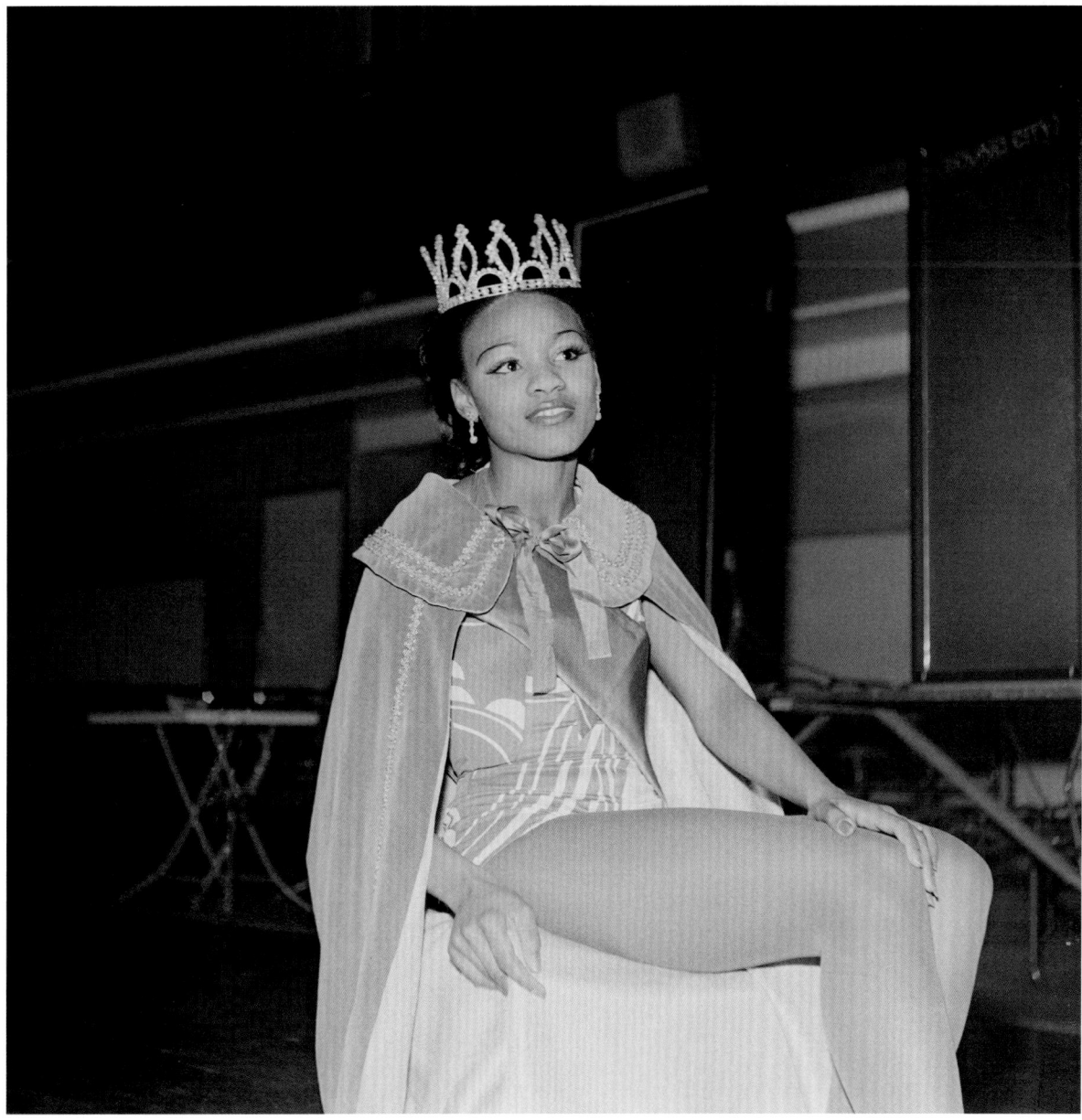

of aspiring Black models (the latter also included in the exhibition).

These photographs meticulously document the rituals of pageantry as well as the style and sensibilities of women virtually erased from the British mainstream media: radiant beauty queens, replete with crowns and scepters, posing with their vanquished competitors; a glamorous woman modeling jewelry, a ring on every finger; a model, legs crossed and staring directly into the camera, sporting a bold plaid pantsuit; and a contestant lounging in a swimsuit and wearing huge platform shoes.

While much of what Mr. Albert photographed might also be found at conventional

Visibility

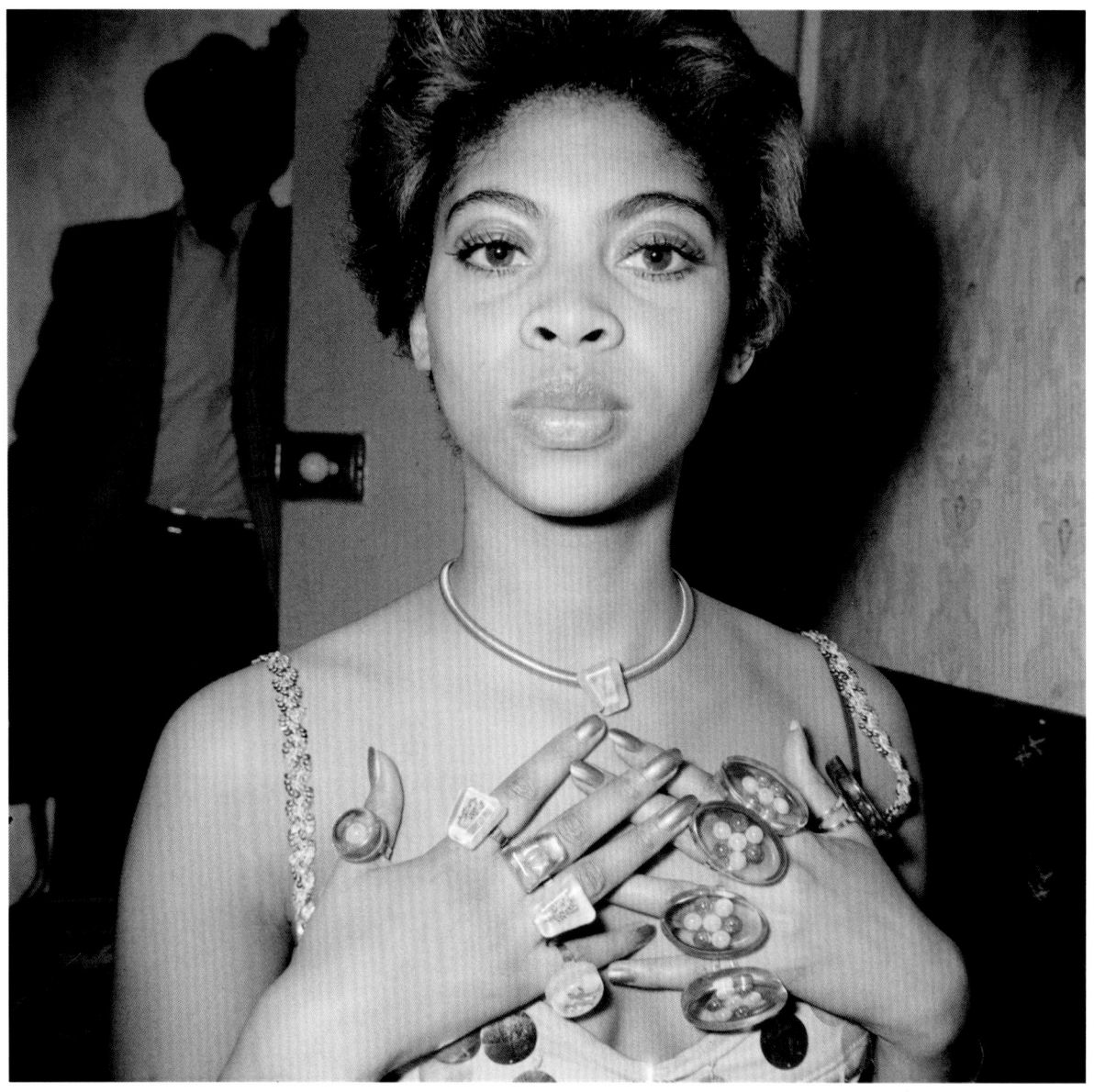

Raphael Albert, *Holly Modelling Jewelry at Blythe Road, Hammersmith, London,*
ca. 1970s; from the portfolio *Black Beauty Pageants*

beauty pageants, his subjects faced cultural and social obstacles unknown to their white counterparts. Their performances in events, and before the camera, were inevitably in relationship to a mainstream culture that routinely ignored or disparaged them as it focused almost exclusively on the beauty and concerns of white women.

Feminists typically have criticized beauty contests for objectifying their subjects and perpetuating a submissive view of women. Just last week, the Miss America pageant announced that it will end its swimsuit competition: "We are not going to judge you on your outward appearance," said its chairwoman, Gretchen Carlson, a former Fox News anchor and Miss America. Nevertheless, even mainstream pageants have sometimes been heralded by racial and religious minorities as markers of social progress.

As Black women began participating in these competitions—in certain cases only after prohibitions against their inclusion were lifted, like with the Miss America pageant—they tested the presumption that beauty was synonymous with whiteness. With victories in the Miss World, Miss Universe, and Miss America contests, Jennifer Hosten, Janelle Commissiong, and Vanessa Williams, respectively, did more than shatter glass ceilings in the 1970s and 1980s. In the eyes of some, they served as icons of racial progress and role models for young women of color.

Nevertheless, these pageants featured token Black contestants while largely continuing to perpetuate an idealized image of white beauty. "This fair image weighs most heavily on the brown shoulders of minority women who bear a special beauty burden," wrote the psychologist Rita Freedman. "They too set out in search of it, only to discover that failure is built in for those whose lips

smile too thickly, whose eyelids fold improperly, whose hair will not relax enough to toss in the wind, whose skin never glows in rosy shades."

Thus, the dedicated Black pageantry promoted and documented by Mr. Albert was fundamentally more empowering. If these contests focused on the women's physical attributes—participants had to wear swimsuits and high heels—they nevertheless allowed contestants to define themselves outside of conventional notions of attractiveness and self-presentation. Commensurate with the international Black Is Beautiful movement, which began in the United States in the 1960s, these pageants created "a distinct space where Black women were able to both occupy and own the idea of 'beauty' for themselves, and without the need of conforming to Eurocentric ideals," as Ms. Mussai noted in an interview with OkayAfrica in 2016.

In the end, Mr. Albert, who died in 2009 at the age of seventy-four, documented a consequential moment when women of color, flexing their power, explored their individuality and beauty in the face of racist stereotypes and limitations. "Imbued with an exquisite, revolutionary sensuality and a certain joie de vivre," observed Ms. Mussai about Mr. Albert's photographs, they embodied "an aura of hedonistic confidence in a new generation of Black women coming of age in Britain during the 1970s, fueled by complex cultural politics of identity, difference, and desire."

# Pictures of Men, Friends or Lovers

Published January 10, 2014

Trent Kelley wondered how he could study the history of African American gay men when so many of them had lived their lives in relative secrecy. He found his answer in vintage photographs—which he began to collect on eBay, at flea markets, and at estate sales—which depict everything from urban dandies and workers to athletes and soldiers.

Then what?

Eager to share his findings and thoughts, he set up a Flickr stream he titled *Hidden in the Open: Photographic Essay of Afro American Male Affections*, which featured some two hundred photographs from the Civil War to the present, an essay, and romantic snapshots of contemporary Black gay couples, men Mr. Kelley contrasts as being "out in the open."

The early portraits, most from the late nineteenth and early-twentieth centuries, reflect the broader African American embrace of photography as a powerful means of self-representation that defied withering stereotypes.

"Historically, the Afro American gay male and couple have largely been defined by everyone but themselves," wrote Mr. Kelley, a playwright in Texas. "Afro American gay men are ignored into nonexistence in parts of Black culture and are basically second-class citizens in gay culture."

The path to social acceptance for African American gay men has been fraught. While the Black church led the struggle for equality and justice, Mr. Kelley notes that it also often denied its gay members those very same ideals. And the wider gay rights movement, for many years dominated by middle-class whites, has harbored biases against men and women of color.

But *Hidden in the Open* testifies to the existence of a historic and thriving Black gay

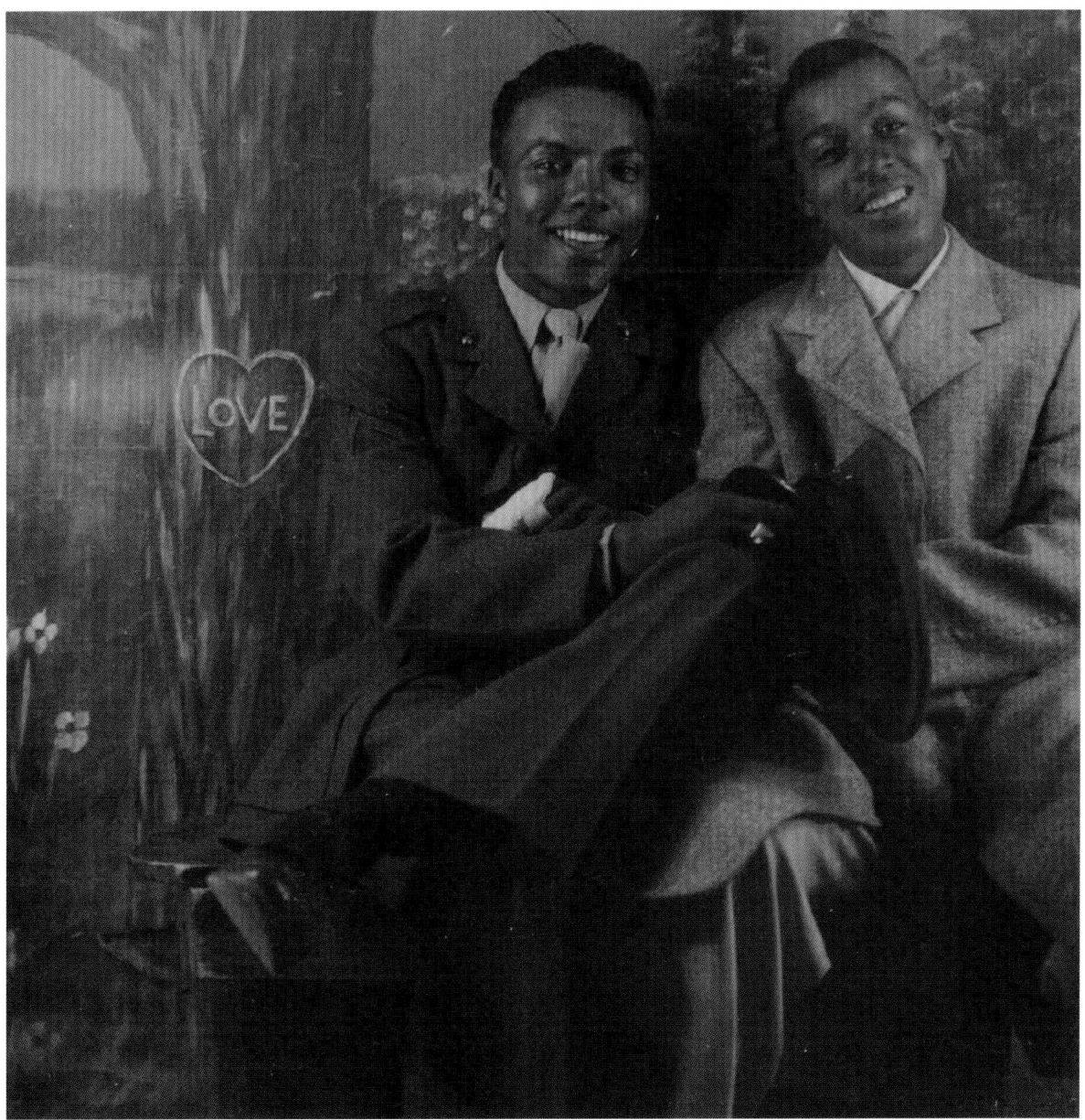

culture, one that was neither monolithic nor dependent on white people. It challenges the patronizing view of the besieged African American gay man, shunned by his own community and inevitably reliant on white men for companionship and self-expression. Such stereotypes ignore the depth of white homophobia as well as the presence of tolerated gay subcultures within the African American community.

The affectionate pairings featured in *Hidden in the Open* also challenge modern discomfort with male intimacy, sexual or otherwise. Even as American public opinion today is largely supportive of gay equality and same-sex marriage, the idea of male

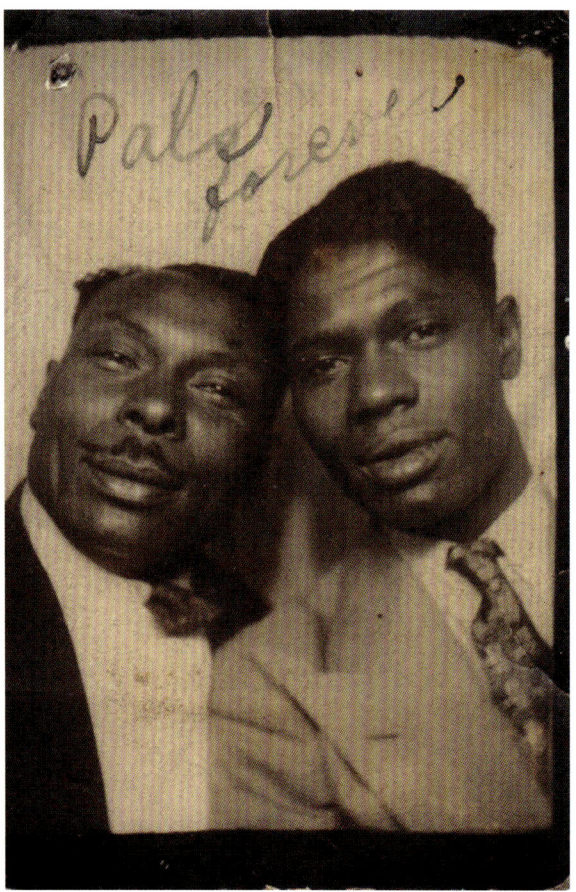

Photographer unknown, Untitled, n.d.

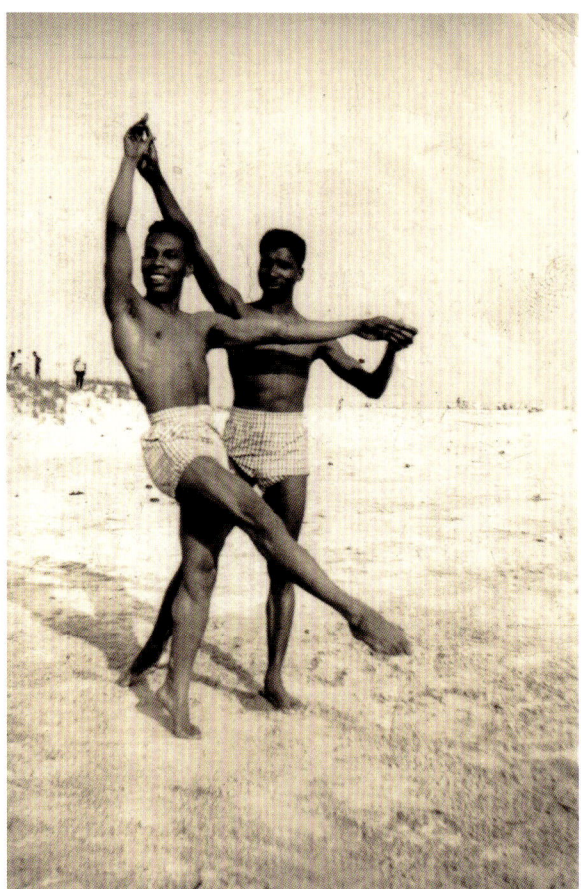

Photographer unknown, Untitled, n.d.

intimacy can still fuel uneasiness and homophobia.

This discomfort was not always the case. In his book *Dear Friends: American Photographs of Men Together, 1840 to 1918*, the art historian David Deitcher wrote that the introduction of photography in the United States in the mid-nineteenth century coincided with "a surprisingly broadminded attitude toward same-sex intimacy." Close, even passionate bonds of friendship with members of one's own sex were accepted and even encouraged.

Public displays of male closeness flourished during this time. As Mr. Deitcher observes, such intimacy was evident in all-male bastions of middle-class privilege, like universities, as well as socioeconomically diverse milieus, like the military, fraternal organizations, and big cities where millions migrated from farms and small towns in search of work.

This historical context makes the nature of some of the relationships depicted in *Hidden in the Open* uncertain and ambiguous, as Mr. Kelley acknowledges: "Not every gesture articulated between men was an indication of male-to-male intimacies. Assuredly, what all photographs in this essay have in common are signs of Afro American male friendship, affection, and love that were recorded for posterity without fear and shame."

These quiet photographs underscore a poignant irony about masculinity: While emotional intimacy can be difficult for men, the capacity for us to bond in ways fraternal and nonsexual is profound. And with attitudes about homosexuality rapidly changing, these connections are increasingly evident across sexualities, with men of different orientations sharing platonic friendships based on a common masculinity, not sexuality.

If such bonds have been important to all men, they have been crucial for men of color. The alliances between African American men—as well as with their female counterparts—were historically a matter of survival, a means of uniting against the forces of slavery, segregation, and racism.

# Gordon Parks's Harlem Argument

Published November 11, 2015

Fresh from assignments at *Vogue* and *Glamour* in 1948, Gordon Parks appeared one morning at *Life*'s New York headquarters, determined to show his portfolio to Wilson Hicks, the magazine's esteemed picture editor. Mr. Hicks was initially reluctant, but he warmed to Mr. Parks's work and the story he pitched about the gang warfare then plaguing Harlem.

That meeting resulted in two milestones: The photo-essay Mr. Hicks commissioned, "Harlem Gang Leader," would be *Life*'s first by a Black photographer and the first of many for the magazine by Mr. Parks. The project is the subject of an exhibition, *Gordon Parks: The Making of an Argument*, at the Frances Lehman Loeb Art Center at Vassar College in Poughkeepsie, New York.

Organized by Russell Lord for the New Orleans Museum of Art, the exhibition tracks the conception, execution, and editing of that photo-essay. It examines the published article in relation to the hundreds of negatives, proof prints, contact sheets, and editorial notes from the archives of the Gordon Parks Foundation. Documenting complex editorial decisions and practices, it exposes the usually private negotiations between photographer and photo-editors and art directors.

*The Making of an Argument* is an illuminating exercise in visual and racial literacy, investigating how words and images communicate multifaceted realities, convey points of view and biases, and sway or manipulate meaning. As the hundreds of photographs taken for the story were whittled down to the few published in *Life*, the editorial selection process, as Mr. Lord noted in his catalog essay, raised questions about authorship and meaning: "What was the intended argument? And whose argument was it?"

To get his story, Mr. Parks gained the trust of the Midtowners gang and its seventeen-year-old leader, Leonard Jackson, who was known as Red. In the time he spent with Mr. Jackson, Mr. Parks became "a welcome companion in all of [his] activities, including diplomatic sessions with other gangs, fights, quiet moments at home, even a visit to a funeral chapel to examine the wounds of a deceased member of a friendly gang."

Mr. Parks hoped that the photo-essay, by drawing attention to a serious social problem, might encourage programs to help endangered youth. But the range of images he took for the article, in contrast to those that made it into the magazine, suggest that his conception of the project differed considerably from his editors'. While Mr. Parks would become an important and influential staff photographer at *Life*, "Harlem Gang Leader" was his pilot project. Thus, as Mr. Lord wrote, "the decisions made in producing the photo-essay were most likely exclusively those of editors and staff at *Life*."

If the magazine's aim in publishing it was to inform its readers about a pressing social dilemma—and boost sales through dramatic and controversial images—it did so by perpetuating stereotypes. While the photo-essay focused on a community beset by racism and poverty, its view of Harlem was narrow, a foreboding and stifling cityscape shrouded in mist and shadows.

During the editorial process, photographs were aggressively cropped and manipulated, often to complement the article's graphic layout. In one photograph, *Life*'s editors, intent on creating a dramatic picture of Mr. Jackson and a friend viewing the open coffin of a fallen gang member, cropped out a third teenager and darkened the distracting background.

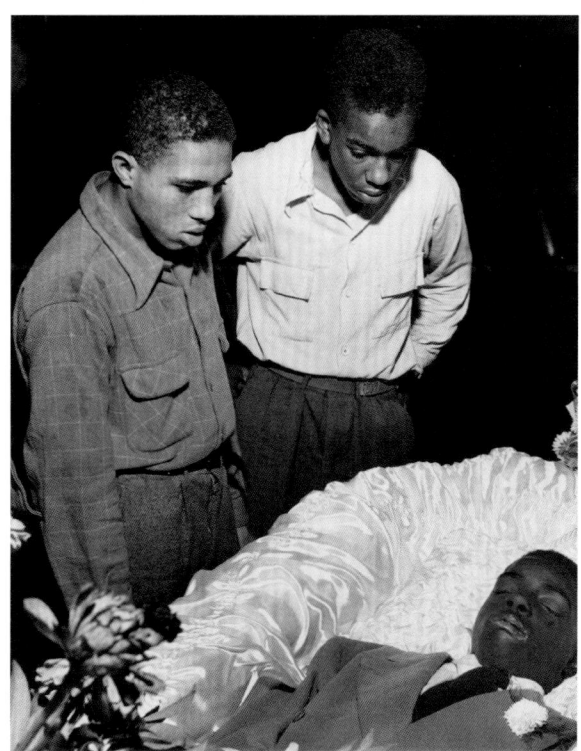

Gordon Parks, *Red and Herbie Levi at the Funeral of Maurice Gaines*, Harlem, New York, 1948

*Life*'s editors largely dismissed many photographs that focused on the more affirmative events and rituals of everyday life. While he recorded the violence and aggression of the Midtowners, Mr. Lord said, Mr. Parks "made just as many pictures of intimate moments of quiet domesticity and boisterous, carefree Harlem street life."

Photographs of Mr. Jackson's brother reading, for example, were rejected for publication, and the words "Red's young brother / not gangster" were bluntly scrawled on their contact sheet. Images of children frolicking around an open fire hydrant or of Mr. Jackson attending to domestic chores were similarly excluded.

For Mr. Parks, such images would have portrayed the complexity and subtleties of Mr. Jackson's story, and of Harlem, a neighborhood typically depicted in the mainstream press as lurid and dangerous. Rather than one-dimensional characters, the photo-essay's subjects were multifaceted human beings, capable of responsibility, love and generosity, but also driven to violence, an understandable, if self-destructive, response to poverty and racism.

By demonstrating the fullness and complexity of its subjects' existence, the photo-essay could have helped the magazine's white readers to make connections to their own lives, an empathetic response that Mr. Parks believed was vital to challenging stereotypes and misconceptions about people they saw as fundamentally different from themselves.

In the end, Mr. Jackson was dismayed by the photo-essay's portrayal of him as a slick gangster, living a fundamentally unhappy and lawless life. "Damn, Mr. Parks, you made a criminal out of me," the photographer recalled him saying after the essay was published. "I look like Bogart and Cagney all mixed up together."

In the exhibition's moving coda, photographs by Lyric Cabral depict Mr. Jackson, stooped and frail, fifty-nine years later. In one image, a great-nephew steadies him as he enters an emergency room. In another, a barber trims his now-gray hair. Ms. Cabral's poignant images of Mr. Jackson, who died in 2010, bear little resemblance to the teenager depicted in *Life*.

"They remind us of the other Red Jackson," wrote Mr. Lord, "not the one so prominently displayed in the pages of *Life*, but the one who scrubbed the floor, washed the dishes, carried and entertained neighborhood children at parades, and cracked open the fire hydrant on hot days. This was the Red Jackson *Life*'s readers would not have a chance to know. This was the Red Jackson Gordon Parks knew."

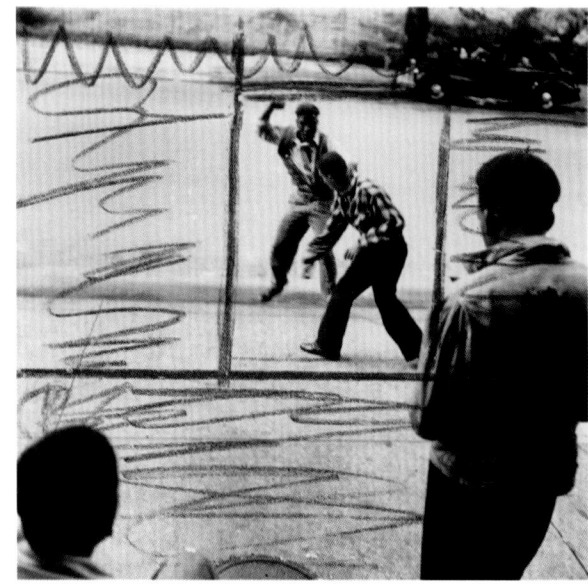

Gordon Parks, *Untitled*, Harlem, New York, 1948

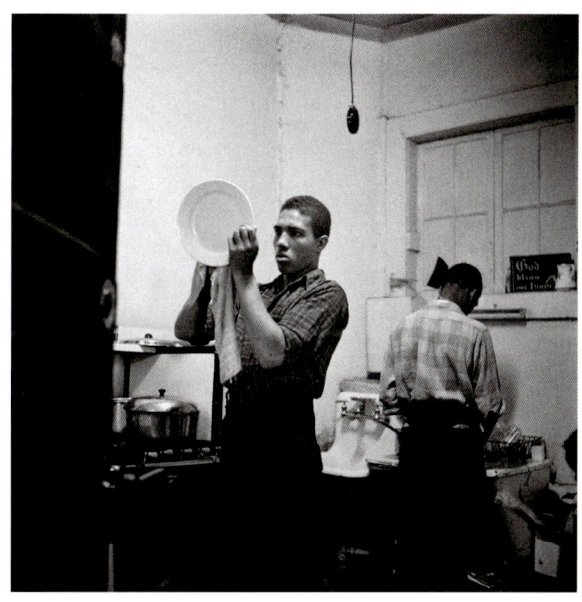

Gordon Parks, *Untitled*, Harlem, New York, 1948

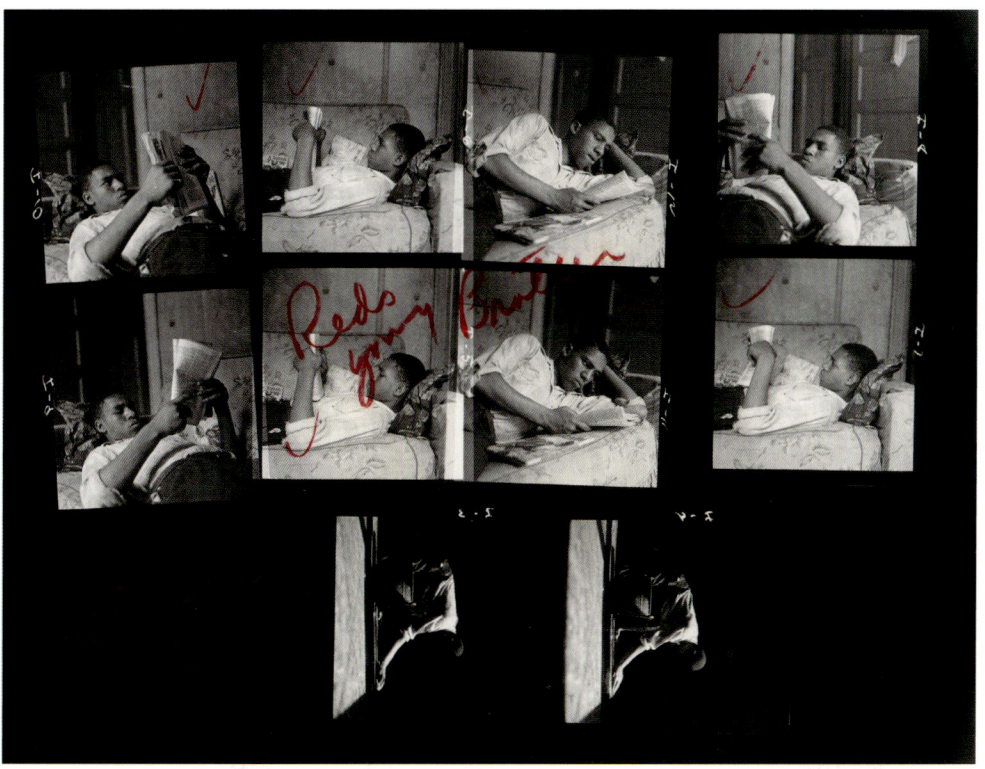

Gordon Parks, Untitled (Contact Sheet), Harlem, New York, 1948

# Dr. King's Complex Relationship with the Camera

Published March 30, 2018

The images of the Reverend Dr. Martin Luther King Jr. delivering his "I Have a Dream" speech before a spellbound crowd on the National Mall in August 1963 are etched into history—and the American consciousness—as the defining moment in the struggle for civil rights. But that reading distorts the movement's complex history, reinforcing the perception of Dr. King as an almost divine leader who was solely responsible for healing the nation's troubled race relations.

Historical images frame our understanding of history, and photographs defined Dr. King in the public imagination, for better or worse. His enemies manipulated photos or gave false captions to discredit him, from accusing him of communist ties to purporting that he encouraged violence during peaceful demonstrations.

African American newspapers and magazines routinely reported on the details of his life and activism through pictures, years before mainstream publications. And those mass media outlets—though at first circumspect and, in Dr. King's final years, increasingly critical as he turned his attention to poverty, war, and racism outside the South—nevertheless produced a visual narrative that helped transform a regional movement into a national one.

If the news media sometimes vilified Dr. King, it also contributed to the mythic view of him as the charismatic leader "who single-handedly directed the course of the civil rights movement through the force of his oratory," as the historian Clayborne Carson wrote of his distorted legacy. In that, photos became as powerful as words as Dr. King was transformed from a human being into a visual symbol of courage, fortitude, or benevolence: the stoic cleric posing for a mug shot after being arrested during the Montgomery bus

Chapter 2

boycott, or the consummate family man to whom white Americans could better relate.

The idealization of Dr. King in his lifetime was set against a backdrop of white distrust and anxiety. While support for him remained high among Black Americans, he was largely unpopular with white Americans. In a 1963 survey by the Gallup organization that gauged national sentiment of public figures, only the Soviet leader, Nikita Khrushchev, was more disliked. By 1966, nearly two-thirds of Americans held an unfavorable opinion of Dr. King.

If he was for many white people the standard-bearer of a Black America that was otherwise unknown to them, the news media's mythic imagery rendered Dr. King enigmatic. He had become, in contexts both positive and negative, the preeminent but two-dimensional icon of a political struggle that involved thousands of organizers, activists, and sympathizers. By contrast, the most compelling photographs of him were neither idealized nor simplistic, but endeavored to portray his complexity and humanity.

James Karales's candid picture of Dr. King at the kitchen table (p. 247), talking with his young daughter Yolanda, for example, reminds us that the lives of Black Americans, no matter how famous, were inevitably fraught. Disappointment registering on his face, he was explaining to the child, for the first time, the perils of segregation and why she could not visit a restricted amusement park. A photograph of the civil rights leader in intense conversation with President Lyndon B. Johnson affirmed that he was not simply an activist clergyman, but also a tough negotiator adept at politics.

What is perhaps most extraordinary about Dr. King and photography is not how the medium defined him, but how skillfully he used it to define the story of civil rights. He was a visual tactician who, along with his advisers, understood the power of the camera to expose the brutality and injustice of segregation.

The historic Children's Crusade in Birmingham, Alabama, in May 1963, for example, was largely organized for the camera. Dr. King and his strategists recognized the need for pictures that would demonstrate the depravity of Jim Crow segregation to a skeptical public. Anticipating a fierce response from Bull Connor, the city's segregationist commissioner of public safety, and aware of the media's hunger for provocative images, they planned a nonviolent demonstration of more than a thousand schoolchildren. The pictures that came out of

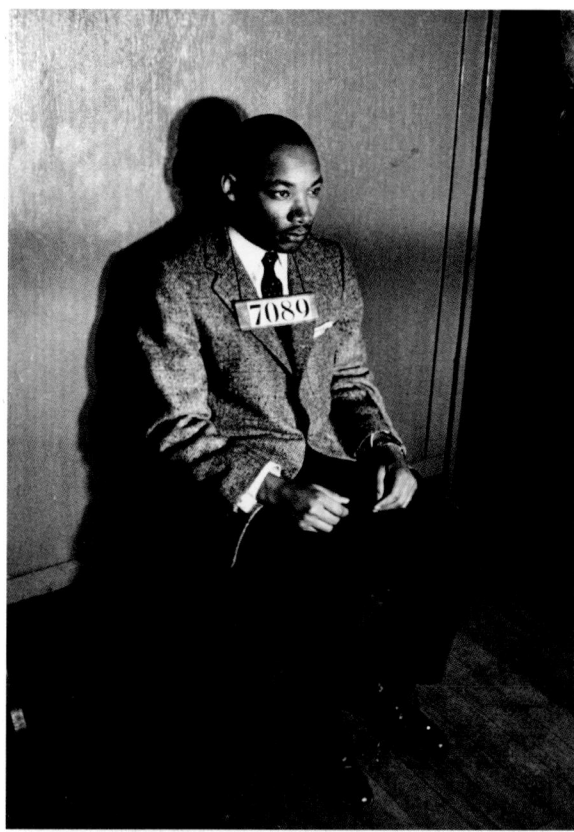

Don Cravens, The Rev. Dr. Martin Luther King Jr. sitting for a police mug shot. He was arrested after directing a boycott of segregated buses, 1956

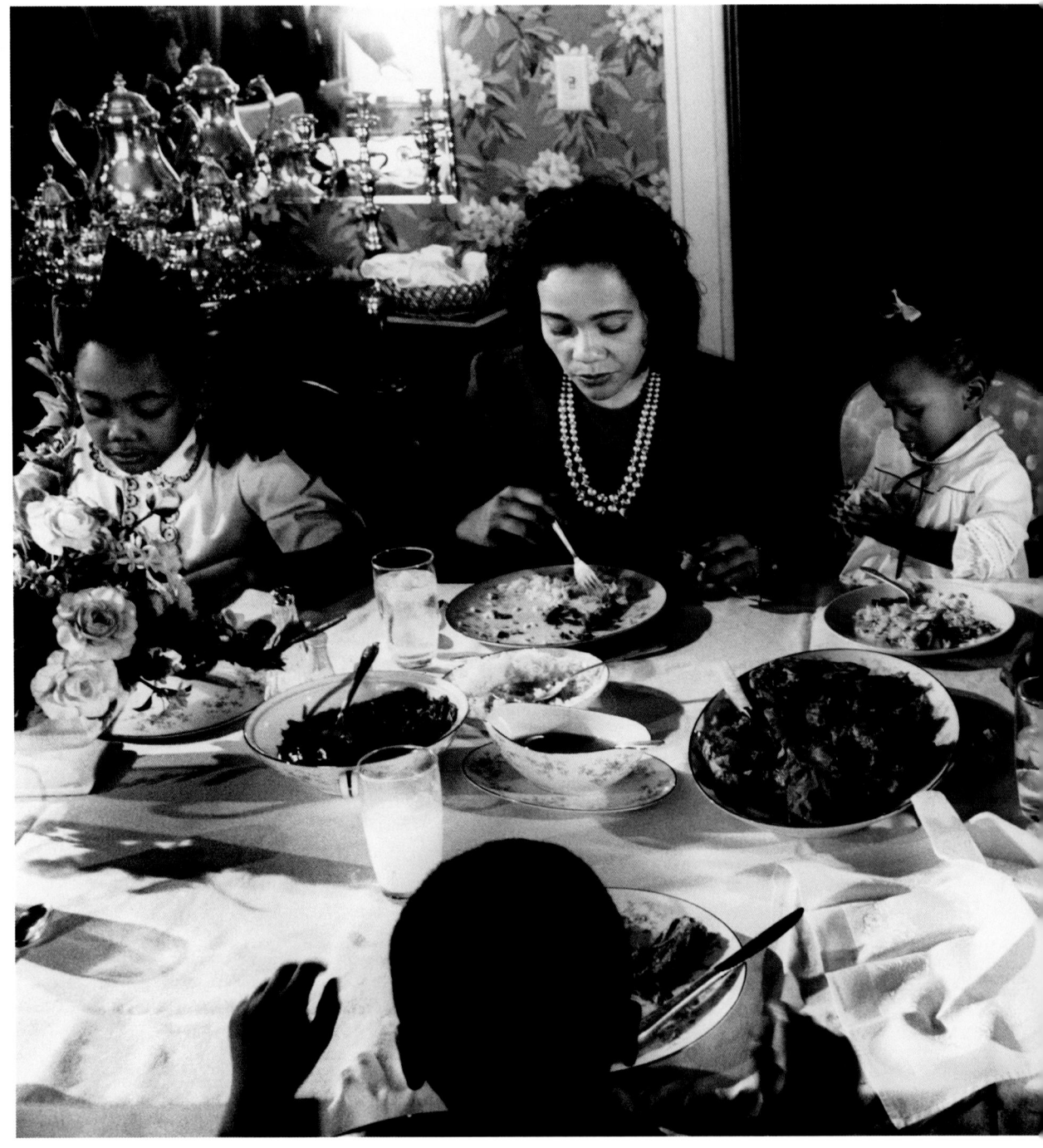

Flip Schulke, Martin Luther King Jr. eats Sunday dinner with his wife Coretta and their young children at home in Atlanta, 1965

Chapter 2

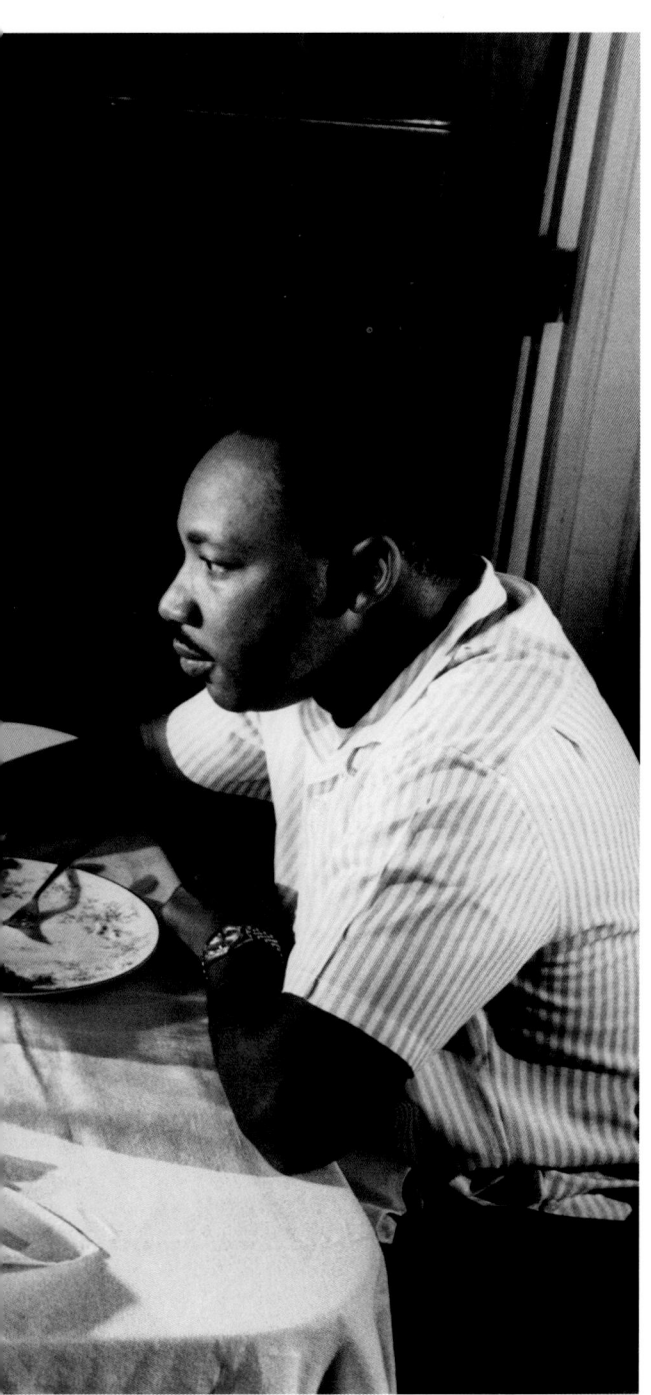

Birmingham—youngsters attacked by police dogs or knocked to the ground by fire hoses— were devastating. Seen around the world, these images broke through skepticism and complacency, providing unassailable evidence of the evil of segregation and how it imperiled democracy. A year later, Congress passed the landmark Civil Rights Act, legislation partly spurred by the shocking photographs and television news footage from Birmingham.

But it was another widely seen photograph, taken fifty years ago next week, that most dramatically challenged the myth of Dr. King: that of him lying mortally wounded on a balcony at the Lorraine Motel in Memphis. Rather than an icon of the heavenly orator, imprisoned martyr, or revered prophet, the stark image transformed the civil rights leader into a human being destroyed by racial hatred. If photographs of Dr. King in life served as a kind of Rorschach test—teasing out our capacity for acceptance, identification, or prejudice—that image of him in death is a sobering reminder of the extent to which myths are built on fantasy and projection, erasing the individuality of the people they enshrine. "I always saw Martin Luther King Jr. as this incredible spiritual leader, who spoke in a way that inspired people in emotional tones," said the photographer Steve Schapiro of his famous subject. "What you don't realize is that people are human at the same time. You can be a leader and still have your own particular worries."

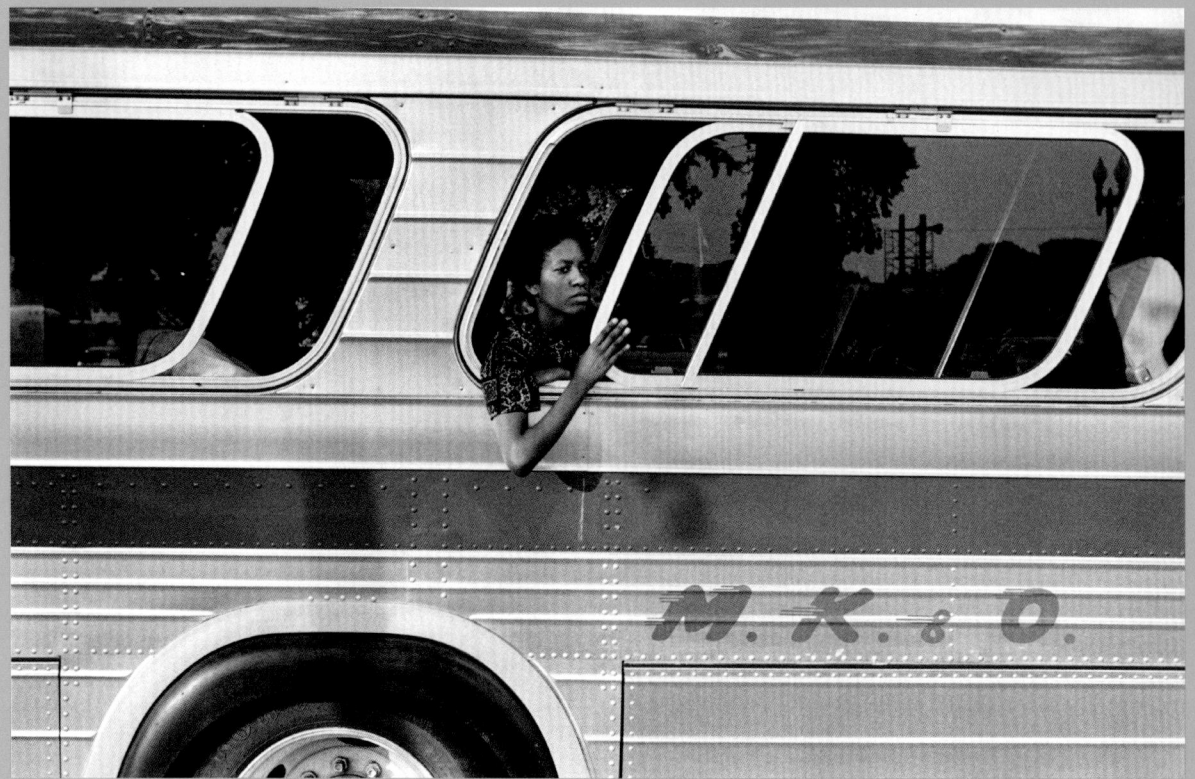

Leonard Freed, The March on Washington, Washington, DC, August 28, 1963

# History and Memory:
# Engaging the
# Past to Understand
# the Present

# CHAPTER
# THREE

# Reimagining a Tragedy, Fifty Years Later

Published September 13, 2013

As a youngster living in Queens, the photographer Dawoud Bey was traumatized by a picture he encountered in a civil rights photography book. In the stark black-and-white image, a twelve-year-old African American girl, Sarah Jean Collins, lies severely wounded in a hospital bed, her eyes covered by bandages. Blinded in one eye, Ms. Collins was one of the survivors of the deadly bombing by white supremacists of the Sixteenth Street Baptist Church in Birmingham, Alabama, on September 15, 1963.

The photograph has gripped Mr. Bey for the nearly five decades since he first saw it. It has taken him that long to create a response to it. With *The Birmingham Project*, an exhibition of large-scale diptychs and a video at the Birmingham Museum of Art, his response has found its form, in time to commemorate the fiftieth anniversary of the bombing on Sunday.

Six children died on that day, including four girls in the blast, which occurred as they prepared for Sunday school: Denise McNair, eleven, and Addie Mae Collins (Sarah Jean's sister), Carole Robertson, and Cynthia Wesley, all fourteen. Two boys were killed in related incidents: Virgil Ware, thirteen, gunned down by a white teenager as he rode his bicycle, and Johnny Robinson, sixteen, shot by the police, reportedly as he fled after throwing stones at a car where white teenagers hurled taunts and waved a Confederate flag.

Mr. Bey's diptychs pair a present-day youngster the same age as one of the murdered children with men and women the ages the boys and girls would be if they were alive today. "I wanted to give tangible and palpable physical presence to the young people martyred that day," he said. "While the horror of the day is clear, the actual identities of the

Chapter 3

young people have become abstracted in a fuzzy and mythic kind of way."

The five-month process of finding his subjects was arduous. They not only had to be the right age but also live in Birmingham. Mr. Bey reached out widely in the Black community, soliciting volunteers on Craigslist, through word of mouth, fliers, and school visits, and by enlisting the aid of local ministers. At the invitation of Birmingham's mayor, William A. Bell, Mr. Bey spoke about the project and the need for subjects at a meeting of the City Council.

"The specificity of the ages made it that much more difficult," he said. "The outreach continued even while I was making the photographs."

Typical of his process, Mr. Bey, who teaches photography at Columbia College Chicago, maintained full control over the aesthetics of his images but worked collaboratively with his subjects, talking with them, ensuring that they were comfortable, and allowing them to choose their clothes, hairstyles, and accessories.

The portraits are set in two locations: the Birmingham Museum of Art and the Bethel Baptist Church. During the 1960s, African American admission to the museum was restricted to one day a week—"Negro Day," as it was called. The church, headquarters for the Alabama Christian Movement for Human Rights, played a central role in the civil rights movement.

The unrelated sitters, paired only after all of the portraits were completed, share uncannily similar expressions and body language. "The decisions about which individual photographs to place together," Mr. Bey said, "had to do with how they related in a number of different ways, whether gestural or expressive, through disposition or some other personal

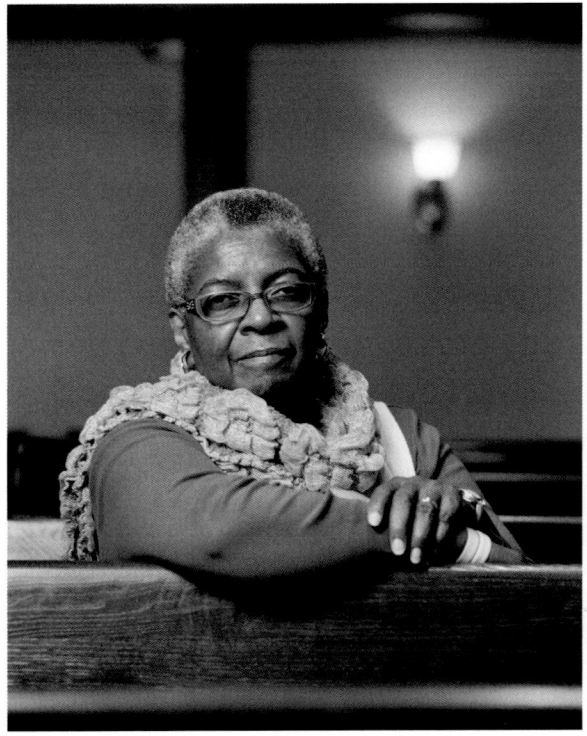
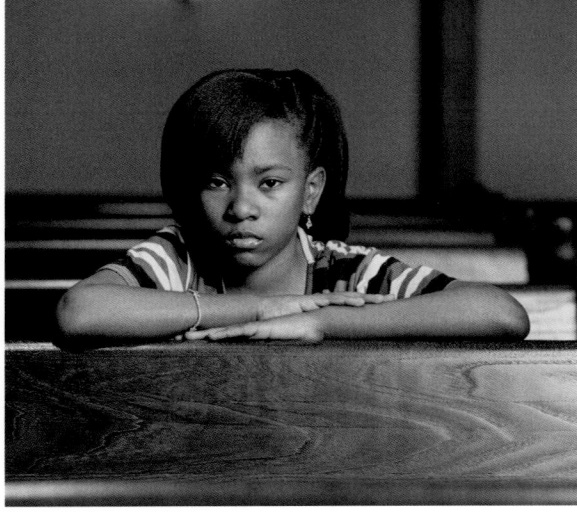

Dawoud Bey, *Mary Parker and Caela Cowan*, 2012

aspect that would make each resonate more forcefully in relation to the other."

This resonance intensifies the poignancy and emotional impact of the diptychs. Despite the half-century that separates them, the paired subjects speak to intermingled histories and shared destinies: adults who helped forge a path of acceptance and stability for African Americans and the young beneficiaries of their bravery and largesse who may well do the same for future generations.

This is but one of the legacies lost to the children who died, and one of the heartbreaking implications of the tragedy that Mr. Bey helps us grasp. His imagery transcends the limitations of social history, which usually ignores the human dimension of its nonfamous victims. *The Birmingham Project* aims to restore their humanity and to underscore what has been lost.

Mr. Bey's video, *9.15.63*, further humanizes this story. Filmed in Birmingham, it evokes a quiet Sunday morning. In split screen, it juxtaposes a slow-motion pan of trees, the tops of buildings, lampposts, and electrical poles, shot from below and framed by blue sky, with the interior details of businesses, like hair dryer hoods, a row of razors and clippers, or stools.

These placid spaces, devoid of people, resonate with history, alluding to the beauty parlors, barbershops, and lunch counters that facilitated African American activism and resistance. As the video concludes, with children's drawings hanging in a classroom counterpoised with the exterior of the Sixteenth Street Baptist Church, it brings us back to the tragedy. We realize that its outdoor footage is shot from the perspective of the four girls as they made their way to church that day.

The power of *The Birmingham Project*, and Mr. Bey's work in general, resides in its ability to draw us into the issues it raises through work that is beautiful and visually compelling. It is in this sense that he collaborates not just with his subjects but also with the viewer.

By transforming an epochal story into a flesh-and-blood reality, *The Birmingham Project* invites us to reflect on the consequences of a historic crime, and, through images of contemporary Americans who are no different from us, to examine our personal relationship to it. Identifying with the surrogates of six martyrs—young and old—we better comprehend, and feel, the magnitude of their loss: innocent childhoods obliterated in a violent flash, a half-century of wisdom learned and milestones achieved that would never be.

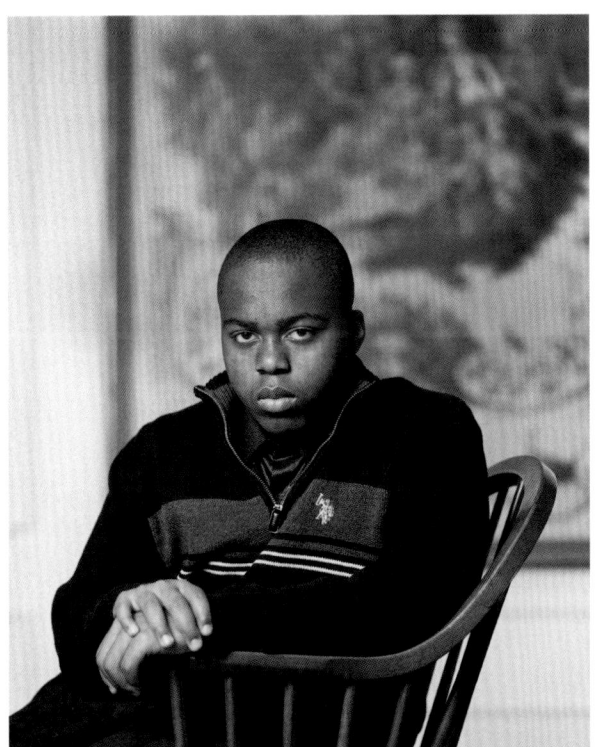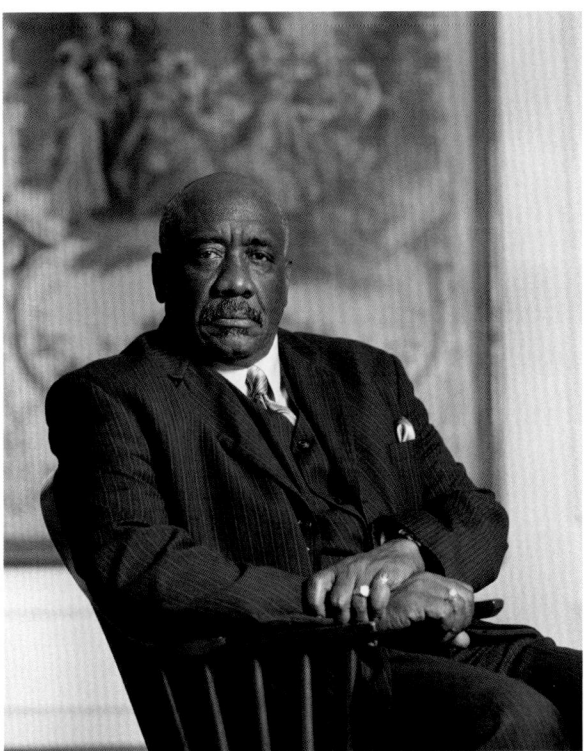

Dawoud Bey, *Timothy Huffman and Ira Sims*, 2012

# Rarely Seen Photos of Japanese Internment

Published February 8, 2017

At first glance, Dorothea Lange's photographs of Japanese Americans, taken in the early 1940s, appear to show ordinary activities. People wait patiently in lines. Children play. A woman makes artificial flowers. Storefront signs proudly proclaim, "I am an American."

But these quiet images document something sinister: the racially motivated relocation and internment during World War II of more than 110,000 people of Japanese ancestry who lived on the West Coast, more than sixty percent of whom were American citizens.

Anchor Editions recently began selling prints of twenty of Ms. Lange's Japanese internment photographs. Half of the proceeds are earmarked for the American Civil Liberties Union, which sued to stop the government's mass incarceration of Japanese Americans and continues to protect immigrant rights.

Although Ms. Lange's photographs were commissioned by the federal government as part of its documentary programs, they were suppressed for the duration of the war. Never actively distributed, her prints were sometimes defaced by military personnel, the word *impounded* scrawled across them. After the war ended, the photographs were discreetly deposited in the National Archives, where they remained, largely unseen and unpublished, for decades.

"These photographs exemplify Lange's mastery of composition and of visual condensation of human feelings and relationships," the historian Linda Gordon wrote in the 2006 anthology *Impounded: Dorothea Lange and the Censored Images of Japanese American Internment*, which brought many of the photographs to light. "They also unequivocally denounce an unjustified, unnecessary and racist policy. Ms. Lange's critique

Dorothea Lange, Third generation of American children of Japanese ancestry in crowd awaiting the arrival of the next bus which will take them from their homes to the Assembly center, Byron, California, May 2, 1942

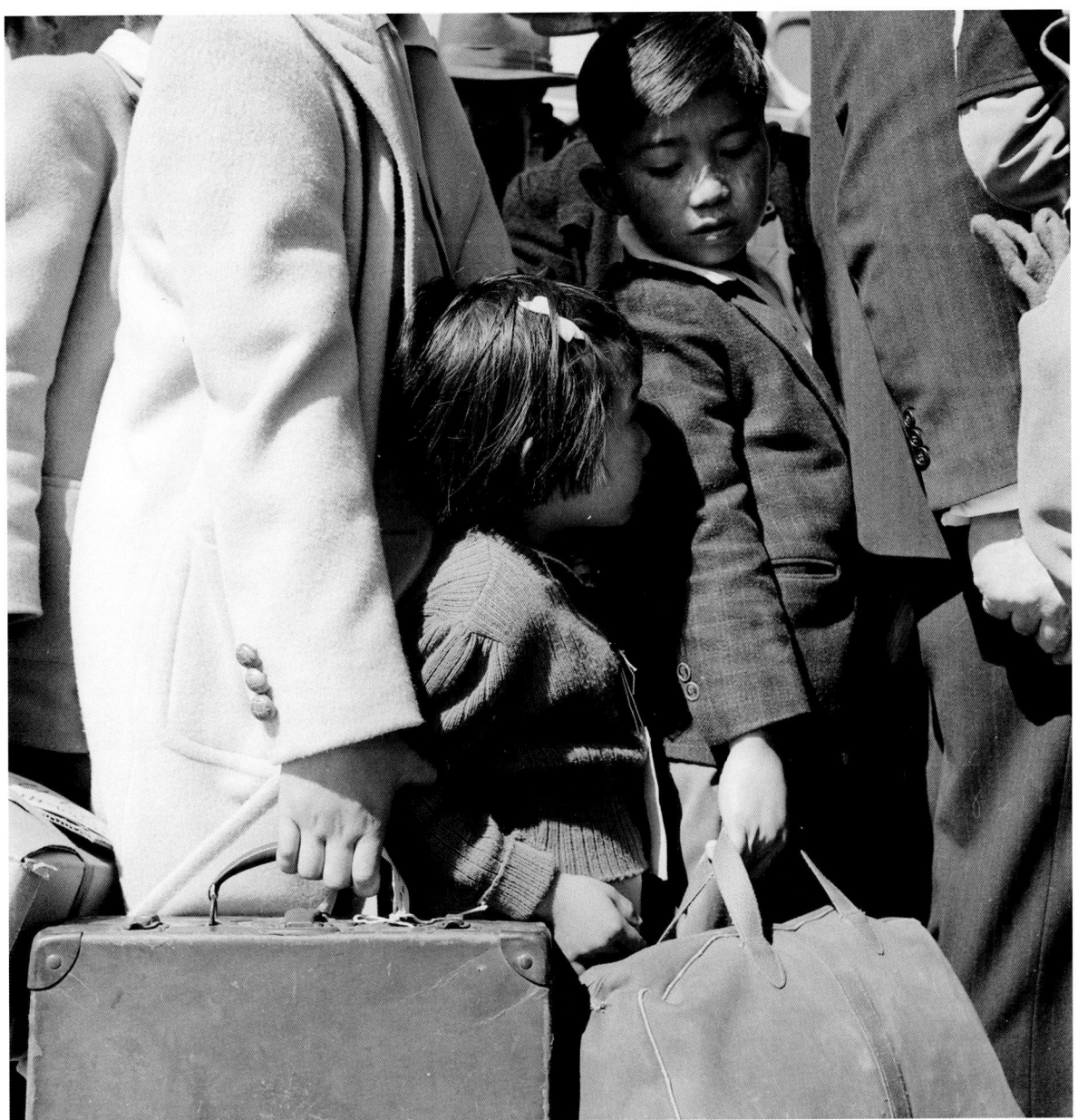

is especially impressive given the political mood of the time," an era when even liberal public figures, such as the celebrated writer and illustrator Dr. Seuss, gave in to fear about Japanese Americans.

Ms. Lange's photographs capture not only the oppression of a people but also their struggle to retain their dignity: neatly dressed families huddled together, awaiting transportation to detention camps; a slouching girl, her eyes cast downward, guarding her family's meager possessions; a group of children raising an American flag, affirming their loyalty to a nation that viewed them as alien and dangerous; a relocation center in Manzanar, California, in stark contrast to the majestic mountains beyond it.

At the time, the internment was hailed by some and condemned by others. Activists warned that the incarceration of loyal and patriotic Americans would do little to protect the nation, and would serve instead as grist for enemy propaganda. In retrospect, some have compared the internment centers to concentration camps. Nevertheless, in February 1942, two months after Japan attacked Pearl Harbor, President Franklin D. Roosevelt issued an executive order that authorized the exclusion of all people of Japanese descent, both citizens and immigrants, from the West Coast.

The order, which presumed that Japanese Americans were disloyal and potentially traitorous, was meant to protect the country's most vulnerable assets, including airports, power plants, railroads, shipyards, and military installations, from sabotage and spying. As enacted, the order was unambiguously racist: While it also applied to German and Italian nationals, they were spared the indignity of mass incarceration and were instead evaluated on a case-by-case basis.

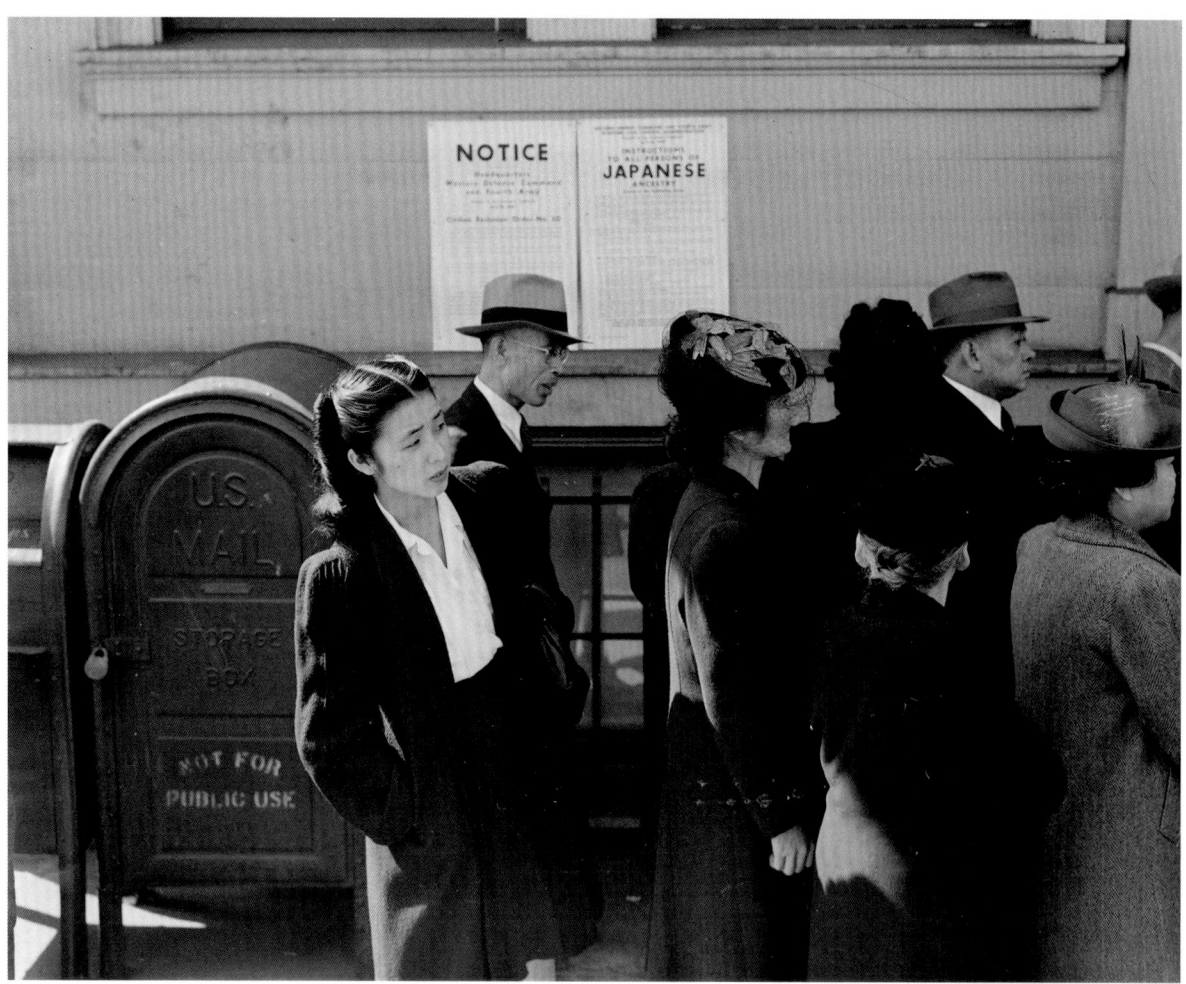

Dorothea Lange, Residents of Japanese ancestry appear for registration prior to evacuation. Evacuees will be housed in War Relocation Authority centers for the duration, San Francisco, California, April 25, 1942

Chapter 3

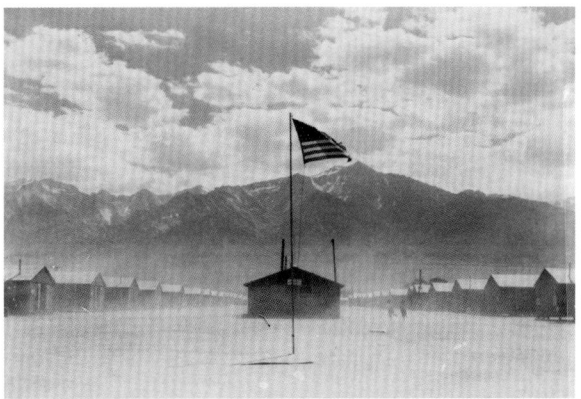

Within weeks of the executive order, Japanese Americans were ordered to secure or sell their houses, liquidate their businesses, and abandon their work or studies. They were told to report to "assembly centers" with only the basic necessities—clothes, bed linens, toiletries, and essential personal effects—they could carry. Pets were forbidden. Major household items were stored by the federal government, but at the owners' risk.

Conditions in the assembly centers, typically off-season racetracks, unused fairgrounds, or stockyards, were abysmal. Families lived in tiny, often windowless stalls that were invaded by insects and smelled of urine and horse manure. The detainees were eventually relocated to newly built camps in remote areas, where they remained—beset by illness and depression, and surrounded by barbed wire and armed guards—for the war's duration.

Photographing such conditions was not new to Ms. Lange. As a member of the documentary project of the Farm Security Administration in the 1930s, she chronicled the lives of the rural poor. She was a masterful portrait photographer, affording her underprivileged subjects, of all races, the same respect as she did her more affluent clients and subjects. Like her FSA photographs, her images of incarcerated Japanese Americans are notable for their compassion and empathy, capturing the self-possession, complexity, and struggles of Americans victimized by stereotypes and viewed by many as criminals.

According to Ms. Gordon, Ms. Lange was angry at what she encountered in the camps: "The documentary style she had developed in the 1930s was inherently critical, and viscerally, emotionally so." Yet, interestingly, she provided no images of resistance. "Of course the Army would not let her near any evidence of it, and she did her work so early in the development of the camps that resistance may not yet have developed," Ms. Gordon surmised.

Ms. Lange's photographs remain as relevant as ever. Anti-immigrant, racist, and nationalist fervor are again on the rise. And some are championing the censoring, limiting, or discrediting of reporting in order to manipulate news and information.

"Despite the yawning gap between prewar generations and those born after the war," the historian and artist Patricia Wakida wrote in the preface to the groundbreaking anthology *Only What We Could Carry: The Japanese American Internment Experience*, "there is nevertheless an unnerving familiarity to many of the dark themes running through this book. The neighbor who watches from a safe distance, the church employee who tries to make the best of a horrible situation, the racist politician whose vitriol fires up others with hated, the anguished apologist who accepts egregious injustice as necessity, the victim who blames himself—such voices are still heard today . . . The targets have changed, but the themes have remained constant."

# An Elegy to India's Vanishing Cinemas

Published February 8, 2018

Movies fascinated Nandita Raman growing up in Varanasi, India, an interest fostered while hanging out in the movie theater owned by her mother's family, the first in the city to show talkies. She visited often, watching films and exploring behind the scenes, captivated by the visual environment, from the movies themselves to watching her uncle select vivid posters for coming attractions.

"It felt like a miniature world within a world," Ms. Raman recalled. "More than a dozen people were on staff. Because I came from the owner's family, I had access. I really loved to go up into the projection room. I would hang out in the ticket booth."

But when Ms. Raman visited the theater in 2006, she encountered the empty shell of what had once been a flourishing business, with the seats and projection room gone and dust covering everything. The sight inspired her to spend the next three years photographing India's vanishing single-screen movie houses for the resulting series *Cinema Play House*. Now on view at the George Eastman Museum in Rochester, New York, the photographs tell a story that is both deeply personal and acutely aware of greater culture issues.

Her search for movie houses in Varanasi, Delhi, Kolkata, and Chennai led her to discover that some of these theaters, once packed with boisterous crowds, were shuttered or struggling to stay open. Built largely during the first half of the twentieth century, their popularity began to wane as home video emerged in the 1990s and multiplexes became popular a decade later.

Ms. Raman's photographs show spaces that are paradoxically majestic and intimate: Once luxurious interiors replete with towering screens, grand staircases, and opulent lobbies were designed to

Chapter 3

Nandita Raman, *Untitled #5 (Natraj)*, 2009

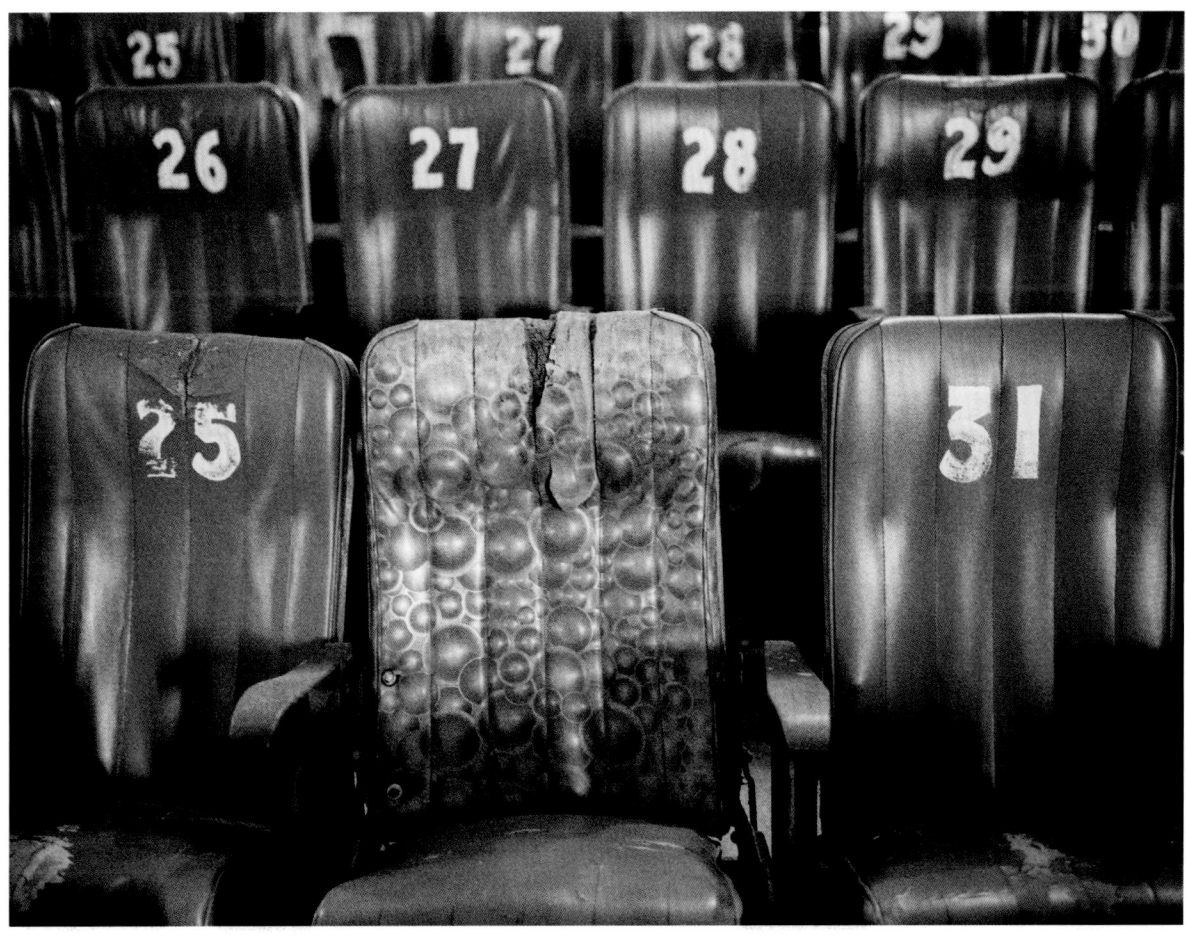

make going to the movies both personal and fleeting.

"There was a grandness to the cinema making and going experience in India," Ms. Raman said. "These theaters were huge. They had capacities of 600, even 1,200 people. The screens were really big. But the nature of films and their subject matter invited you to escape into darkness, into a make-believe world." Immensely popular both at home and eventually globally, the Indian cinema supported a range of genres and subject matter, from romantic musicals and social realist explorations of urban working-class life to period dramas and coming-of-age films.

*Cinema Play House* chronicles a slowly dying culture known for its eccentricity and originality. The photographs underscore the grandeur, individuality, and decline of these movie palaces: the huge screen and cavernous interior of a now-crumbling building; the lush carpeting in an abandoned theater lobby; a mammoth film projector surrounded by detritus; tall stacks of film cans in a makeshift storage area; the shattered glass of a ticket booth; or the elaborate murals of a once palatial movie hall.

Ms. Raman's elegiac pictures may be largely devoid of people, but they resonate with the evocative ghostlike traces of that once-vibrant community of passionate

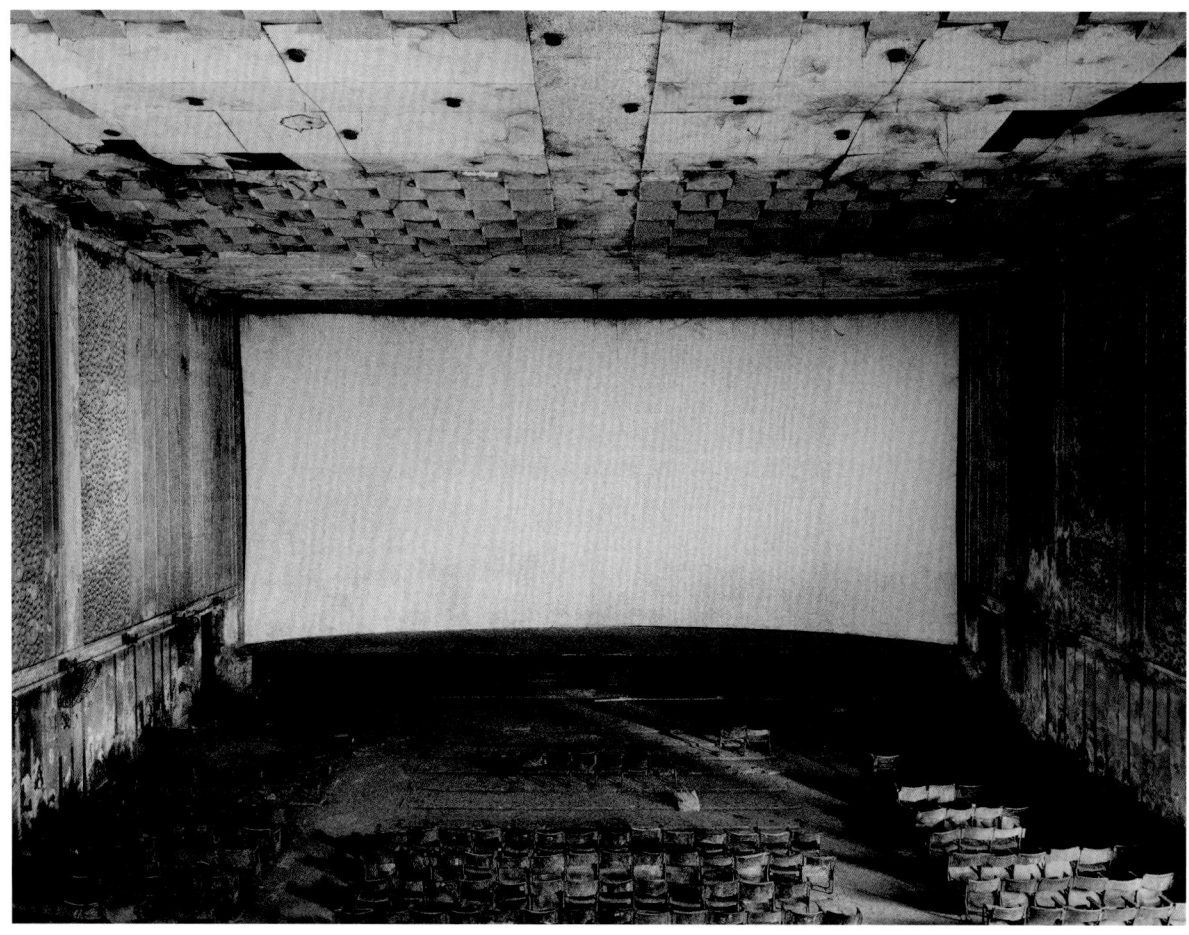

moviegoers entranced by these idiosyncratic buildings. While she photographed workers and a few audience members, she edited out most of these images from the series, resulting in pictures that are stilled and silent but also pulsing with life and history. Ms. Raman sees these photographs as a window into the inner lives of theater owners, too, who often helped to design their own buildings, in contrast to today's cookie-cutter corporate multiplexes.

"They didn't follow a template and each cinema was unique," she noted in an artist statement. "These theaters seemed to contain cues to the psyche of the people who built it and who occupy it." Her images show

those quirks: a row of mismatched seats, a huge circular window that mirrors the shape of the film reels in front of it, a portrait of Vladimir Lenin adjacent to a fire extinguisher, and the marble parquetry of a palatial lobby.

Ms. Raman's photographs also speak to the central role that movies have played in the life of a nation that is home to the world's most prolific film industry. The decline of single-screen theaters coincided with the passing of the era when film emerged as a dominant creative force in India, culminating in what is widely regarded as the golden age of popular cinema in the 1950s. During this time, filmmakers offered eager audiences a popular visual art that sometimes

Chapter 3

Nandita Raman, *Untitled #4 (Orient)*, 2009

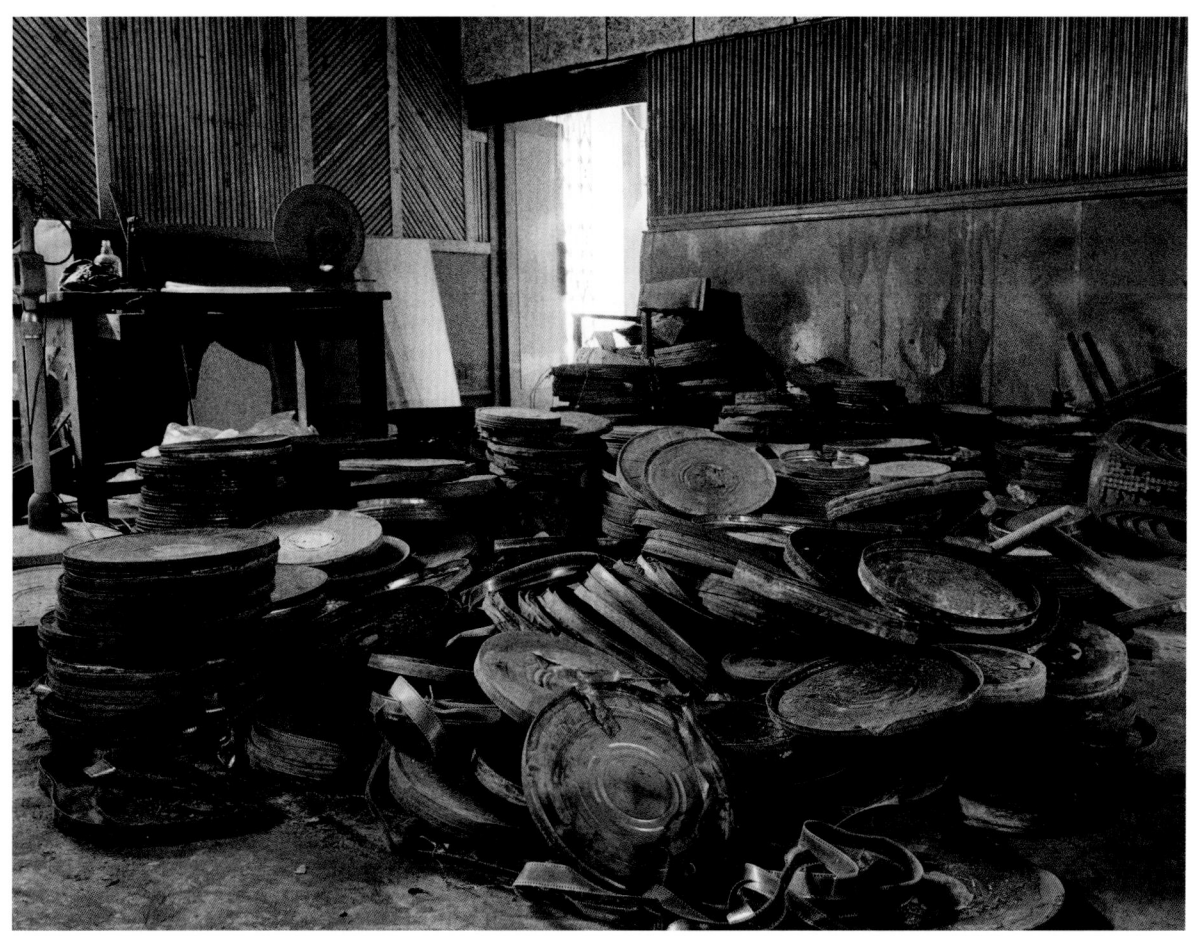

also addressed the social realities of a nation, from the caste system to the role of women.

In the end, the film industry inspired Indian society as much as it reflected it—from sparking trends in popular culture and fashion to influencing public attitudes about spirituality, relationships, social mores, and politics. Commenting on its broad impact, then Prime Minister Jawaharlal Nehru observed in 1955 that "the influence of the films in India is greater than the influence of newspapers and books combined."

Ms. Raman, who now lives in New York, laments the fading of this vital and distinctive culture, acknowledging the global forces and corporate interests that have transformed the Indian film industry.

"When I went into the more modern multiplexes in these cities, I could not find anything to hold on to," she said. "The single-screen theaters were much more generous in telling their age and story to me."

# The Modern Spirits of Ebony and Jet

Published December 3, 2015

Since February 2013, Barbara Karant has holed up for six hours at a time inside the former Chicago headquarters of the Johnson Publishing Company. Armed with lunch, lights, a tripod, and her camera, she was there to photograph the building's abandoned interiors.

The resulting series of images—*820 Ebony/Jet*, a reference to the company's most popular magazines as well as the building's street number on South Michigan Avenue in Chicago's Loop—uncannily embodies the spirit of the legendary African American company that occupied the building for forty years.

The series celebrates the visual dynamism of early-1970s architectural and interior design: boldly patterned carpeting and wallpaper, some influenced by African textiles; elegantly curved and lacquered built-in lounges; discreet cabinets and shiny glass shelves; Lucite screens with polka-dot cutouts; long, dramatically lighted hallways; huge picture windows; shadows cast by venetian blinds; and phantom rectangles where paintings and photographs once hung.

The eleven-story structure, completed in 1972, was the brainchild of John H. Johnson, chairman and founder of the company that revolutionized African American magazine publishing. The first building on the Chicago Loop conceived and commissioned by a Black corporation, it was designed by the African American architect John Moutoussamy. Its interiors, styled by the Palm Springs–based designers William Raiser and Arthur Elrod, complemented Mr. Moutoussamy's austere and light-filled rooms.

To capture the "core essence" of the historic structure, Ms. Karant set out to document its "semi-skeletal state" before the final traces of its architectural and interior

Chapter 3

design vanished. The building was sold to Columbia College Chicago in 2010. For Ms. Karant, an adjunct professor at the college, the absence of furniture and personal artifacts did not detract from the building's historic vitality.

Seeing the structure as a time capsule, Ms. Karant wrote that "the textures, colors, residual structures, and remnants from the Johnson workplace all combine to create a unique, altered environment . . . Outside of the influence of human intervention, time has been mark-making within the Johnson Building for over forty years."

If Ms. Karant's photographs document a particular midcentury aesthetic, they also implicitly address an issue typically ignored in mainstream cultural history: the complex relationship between African Americans and modernism. In the period when Mr. Johnson conceived his vanguard building, Black cultural figures were more or less erased from mainstream discussions of modernism, despite the fact that they were often committed and trailblazing modernists.

Between the end of World War I and the mid-1930s, the writers and artists of the Harlem Renaissance, for example, typically explored modernist ideas, styles, and politics —from the challenging of literary conventions and notions of subjectivity in the writing of Countee Cullen, Langston Hughes, and Zora Neale Hurston to the vivid abstraction and social purpose of the painters Aaron Douglas, Lois Mailou Jones, and Jacob Lawrence. As a patron of modern architecture and design, Mr. Johnson assumed his place in a path-setting history, in which Black cultural figures, well beyond appropriating the avant-garde, were vital to its emergence.

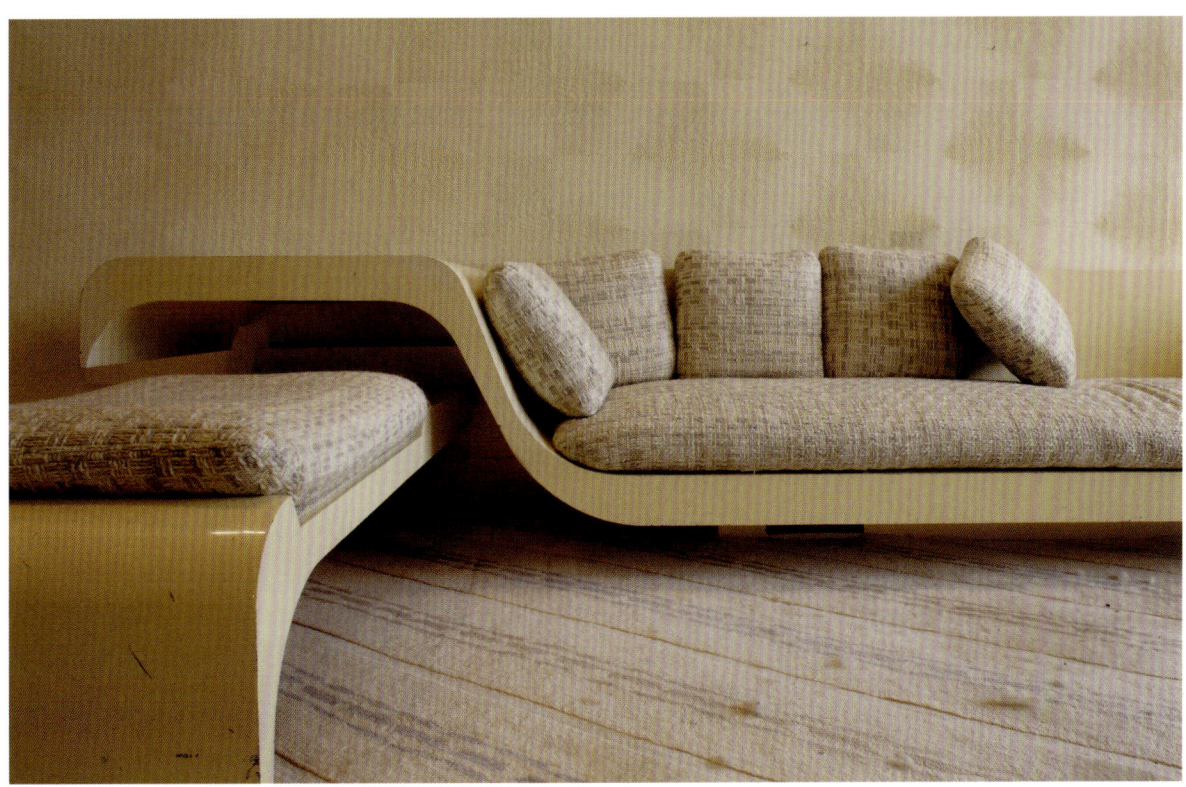

Barbara Karant, *Floor 7 #2*, 2013

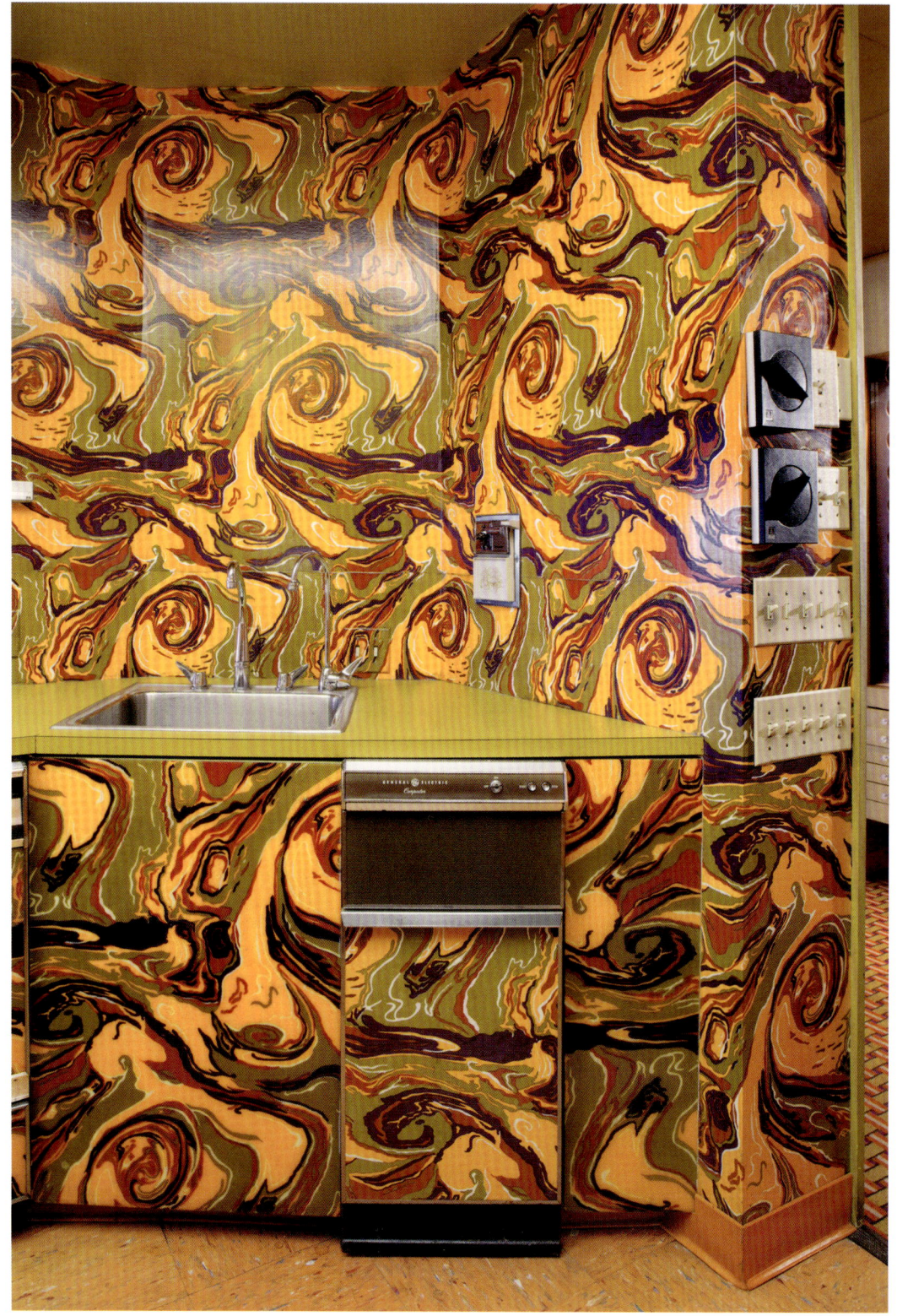

Barbara Karant, *Floor 10 #9*, 2013

Chapter 3

As James Smethurst wrote in his ground-breaking book, *The African American Roots of Modernism*, Black writers, as early as the Reconstruction period in the nineteenth century, were pioneering in their exploration of the "fragmented subjectivity and urban alienation that became a hallmark of modernism in the United States." They were also "among the very first to imagine, represent, and promote a US artistic bohemia linked to an 'American' new literature."

That much of this art was created in the spirit of resistance—as a way of transcending and defying prejudice and stereotypes—was not lost on Mr. Johnson. His determination to erect an important building in Chicago's central business district was intensified by the resistance he endured from real estate agents and bankers.

One area of contention was Mr. Moutoussamy, whom bankers perceived as inexperienced, even though he had built schools, apartment buildings, and other significant structures. "Most of the people building office buildings are White, and none of them have been willing to let him build their building," Mr. Johnson wrote in his autobiography. "And if a Black man doesn't let him build *his* office building, he will never get the experience."

Beginning with *Negro Digest* in 1942, Mr. Johnson created distinctly modern and sophisticated magazines committed to altering how African Americans were represented, and represented themselves, in the culture at large. His new headquarters, which would become a source of pride for many in the Black community, was another way to visualize this mission.

In this context, Ms. Karant's photographs depict more than just the desolate remains of a once vital building: They make visible, in ways both compelling and poignant, an important aspect of the company's self-image. So significant were the ideals communicated by the building that Mr. Johnson insisted that its architecture and interior design be preserved, a policy that continued even after his death in 2005.

Ultimately, the Johnson Publishing Company building was a daring social statement, a monument to the ingenuity and determination of Mr. Johnson and the people his publications represented. It was also an important showcase for Black cultural expression, from Mr. Moutoussamy's vibrant architecture to the corporate collection of African and African American artists displayed throughout its offices.

"The horizontals, the glass, the marble, the fabrics, the warm colors," Mr. Johnson wrote. "All these elements integrated into one grand design express the essential meaning of our firm . . . openness: openness to truth, openness to light, openness to all the currents swirling in all the Black communities of this land."

# The Lasting Power of Emmett Till's Image

Published April 5, 2017

There are few photographs more consequential in African American history—and our nation's—than those of Emmett Till's mutilated corpse. The images from 1955 are gruesome and emotionally devastating, coming as they did after the fourteen-year-old was beaten and shot by two white men. And while authorities in Mississippi tried to bury the teenager as quickly as possible, his mother, Mamie Till Mobley, insisted otherwise, allowing photographers to commemorate the ghastly scene. "Let the world see what I have seen," was her brave retort.

Once again, this image has sparked controversy after its appropriation in a painting by the white artist Dana Schutz in *Open Casket*, on view at the Whitney Biennial, has stirred up heated protest and debate.

Understanding the painting's historic source, a shocking black-and-white photograph evidencing the depth and depravity of white supremacy, provides a point of perspective. The murder of Emmett Till took place in August 1955 in Mississippi, where Emmett was visiting family. The teenager, from Chicago, was said to have either flirted with or whistled at a white woman in a store. Three days later, the woman's husband and his half-brother abducted him in the middle of the night. They brutally beat him, shot him in the head, and shoved his body in the Tallahatchie River.

The killers' trial was a sham. An all-white, male jury acquitted both men of kidnapping and murder. In 2007, the woman at the center of the case, Carolyn Bryant Donham, recanted her original testimony in an interview with the historian Timothy Tyson, admitting that Mr. Till never made advances toward her.

Mrs. Till Mobley fought efforts to conceal her son's mangled corpse. The Tallahatchie

Chapter 3

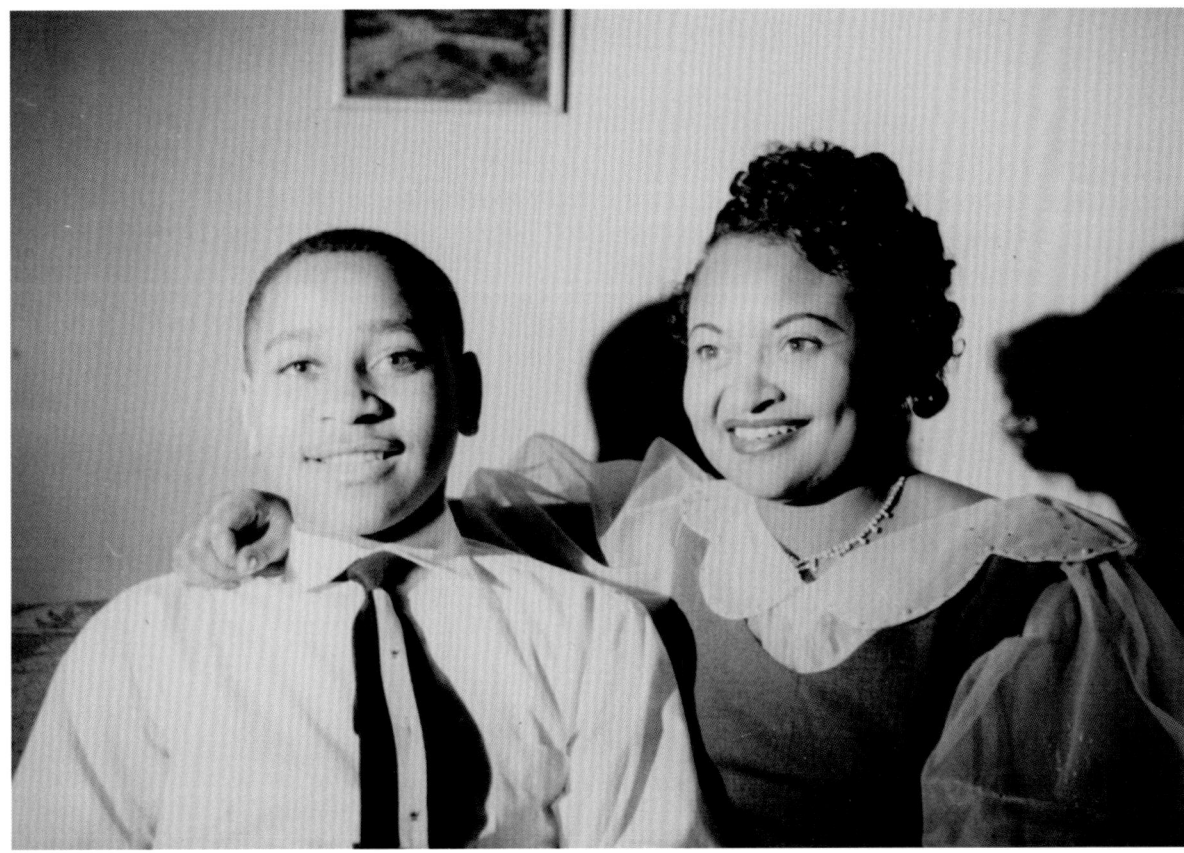

sheriff ordered the body's immediate burial in Mississippi, arguing that it was badly decomposed. His mother demanded that her son's remains be returned to Chicago. "The main thing [the police wanted] to do was to get that body in the ground so nobody else could see it," she later recalled. Although the body was eventually released by the sheriff's office, it was on the condition that the coffin remain sealed.

Mrs. Till Mobley disobeyed the order. The coffin stayed open at his funeral so mourners could witness how Emmett's face was disfigured beyond recognition. His right eyeball rested in a mass on his cheek. His left eye was missing. The bridge of his nose was crushed and his right ear was severed in half. His temple was shattered by a bullet.

But it was another of his mother's actions that changed the course of history: She permitted several photographers to take pictures of her son's disfigured corpse and urged the publication of the gruesome images. "[People] would not be able to visualize what had happened, unless they were allowed to see the results of what had happened," she later said. "They had to see what I had seen. The whole nation had to bear witness to this."

Mrs. Till Mobley's entreaties went only so far. No mainstream magazine or newspaper would publish the photograph, deeming its graphic imagery inappropriate. But she was able to turn to the far more receptive editors of widely circulated Black magazines like *Jet*, the *American*

*Negro: A Magazine of Protest*, and the *Chicago Defender*.

The publication of this image incited a revolution, rousing thousands of young African American men and women—many who lived in parts of the country far removed from the de jure segregation of the South— into actively joining the civil rights move- ment. A single photograph was so powerful that it inspired what the sociologist and activist Joyce Ladner has called the "Emmett Till Generation" of Black activists.

It is against this vivid historical back- drop that we should view the controversy around Ms. Schutz's 2016 painting. It depicts Emmett in his coffin, but it does so abstractly and in ways that are confusing, contradic- tory, and hurtful to many viewers. Mrs. Till

Mobley loved her son, and it took immense courage to allow his disfigured body to be photographed, let alone circulated around the world. But she did so out of urgency and with a specific objective: to capitalize on the authority of photography to provide millions of readers with irrefutable confirmation of the gravity of the war against racism and segregation in 1950s America.

Unlike the original photograph, *Open Casket* is inscrutable and even grotesquely decorative. It lives outside of historical context. We live in another wrenching time, when young Black men continue to be endan- gered. But insensitively appropriating a complicated photograph with multiple layers of meaning from another era does justice to neither the image nor its historic role.

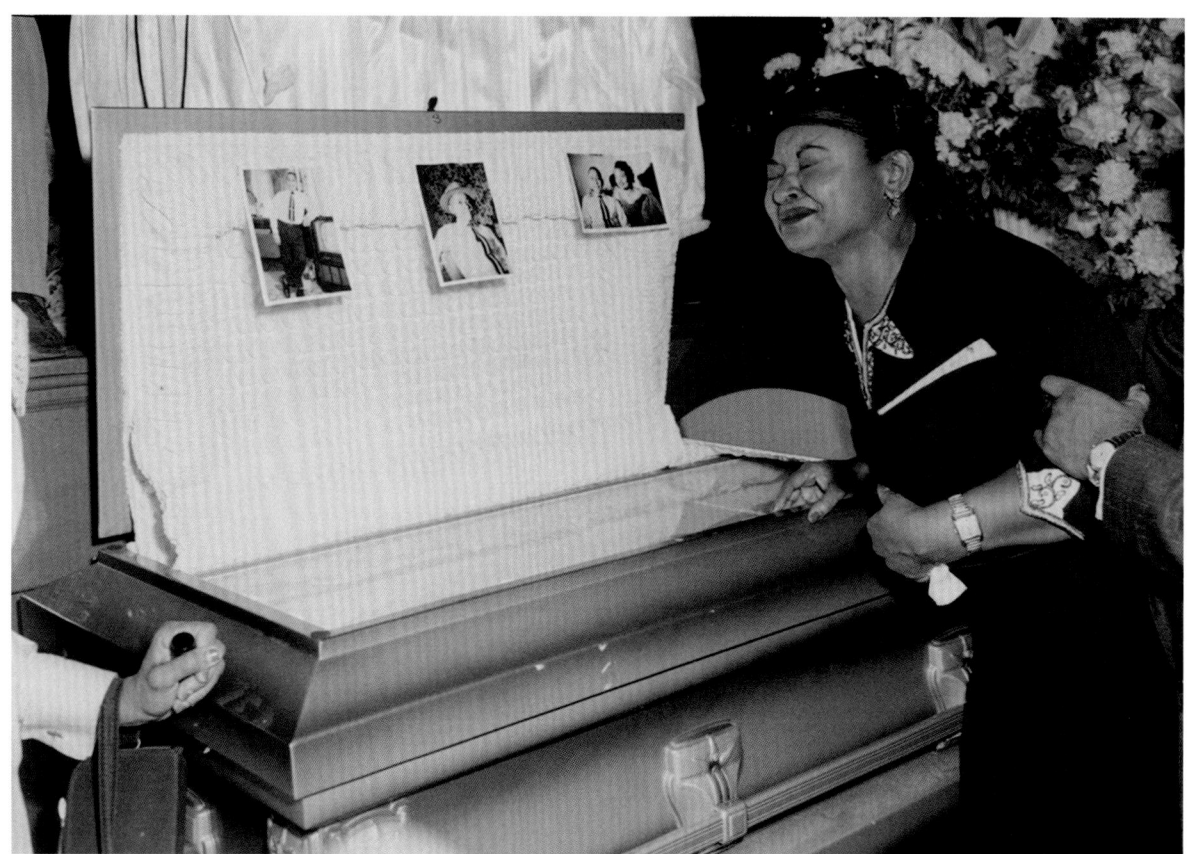

Photographer unknown, Mamie Till Mobley weeping at her son's funeral, Chicago, September 6, 1955

Chapter 3

Photographer unknown, United States Representative Charles Diggs, left, and Mrs. Till Mobley conferred over a paper at the murder trial, 1955

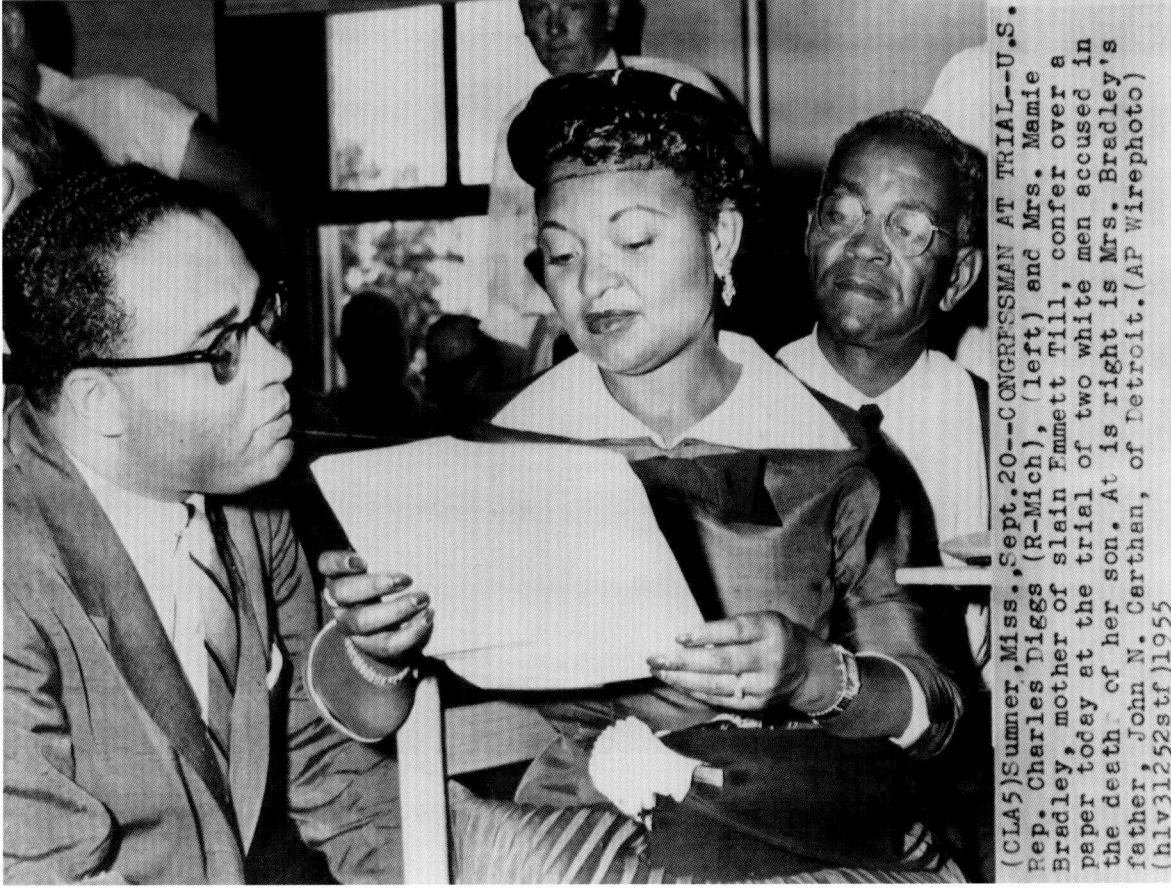

Ultimately, the white artist who chooses to explore issues of race has a responsibility to the history and content of work they appropriate. And while some critics have made Ms. Schutz's race the overarching issue—that a white artist should not traffic in Black pain—the problem is not about her race. White artists should, and indeed have a responsibility to, examine the most vexing and intransigent issue of our time: white racism in all of its forms, from that of the complacent liberal to the neo-Nazi supremacist.

But cross-cultural work demands insight, respect, sensitivity, and rigor. It also requires honesty about and self-inquiry into one's own racial attitudes. To be an artist, no matter how expressive or interpretive, does not give anyone license—or cover—to casually appropriate African American history and culture.

But Ms. Schutz's enigmatic painting reads like it was made in a historical and cultural vacuum. It's missing the diligence necessary to grasp the original photo's cultural and social meaning. Instead, we are left with a painted approximation of it: blurred features, frenzied brushstrokes, and painterly slashes that feel like another violation of Emmett Till's body.

# This Photo of a Seven-Year-Old Girl Transformed the Abolition Movement

Published March 7, 2019

The daguerreotype shows a seven-year-old girl. Her face is pale, her expression somber. Her elegant plaid dress, trimmed in lace, and the notebook on the cloth-covered table behind her, suggest that she comes from a prosperous family.

Though modest, the photograph, taken in Boston in 1855, is actually historic. It shows not a white child but a Black girl—Mary Mildred Williams—who was born into slavery. It was an image so compelling to white Americans at the time that it helped transform the abolition movement. Housed in relative obscurity at the Massachusetts Historical Society, the daguerreotype was recently rediscovered by the photographer and scholar Jessie Morgan-Owens while researching her dissertation. "Mary's daguerreotype was one of the first images of photographic propaganda and one of the first portraits made solely to prove a political

point," Ms. Morgan-Owens wrote. "It marks a forgotten moment in media history: when photography, introduced to the United States in 1839, first began to make its tenacious claim on our sympathies and on our political points of view."

Mary is now the subject of Ms. Morgan-Owens's groundbreaking book, *Girl in Black and White: The Story of Mary Mildred Williams and the Abolition Movement*. Mary and her family had been enslaved in Virginia. Her father, Henry Williams, escaped to Boston and worked with members of the Vigilance Committee, which provided legal and financial help for fugitive slaves, to free his family in the South. Senator Charles Sumner of Massachusetts, a prominent ally, saw an opportunity in the family's story.

After helping to secure her freedom, Mr. Sumner enlisted Mary—whose light skin

Chapter 3

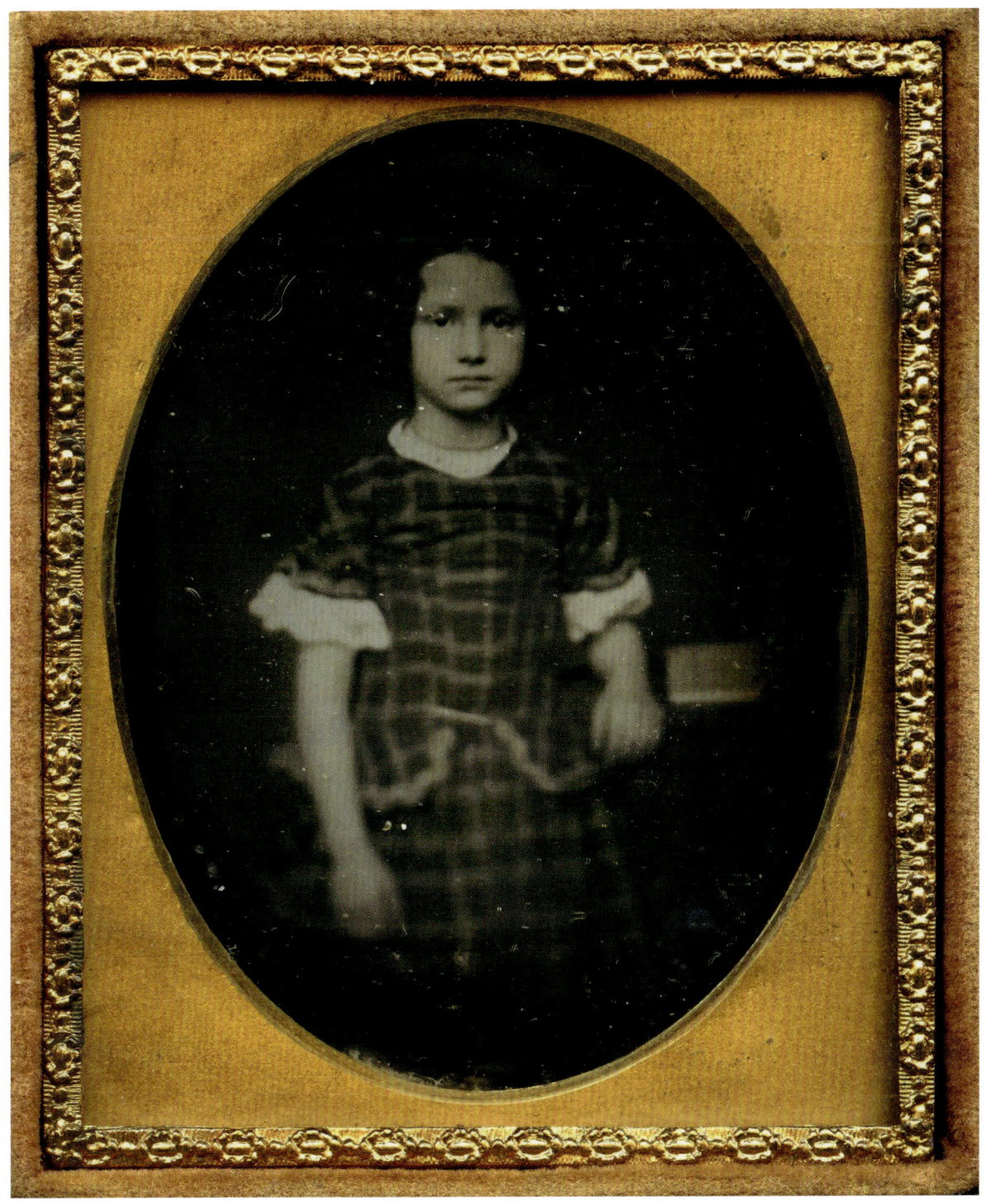

reflected the legacy of generations of sexual violence against enslaved women—as a poster child for the movement. He saw in her experience a parallel with Mary Hayden Green Pike's popular abolitionist novel, *Ida May: A Story of Things Actual and Possible*, in which a white girl is kidnapped, her skin dyed brown, and sold into slavery. Ms. Pike's fictional portrayal presumably motivated white Northerners to turn against slavery and the Fugitive Slave Act, which required that runaway slaves be returned to their masters, by stoking the fear that even their children could be vulnerable.

By emphasizing Mary's light complexion, Mr. Sumner similarly appealed to the empathy and self-interest of white Americans. Calling the child "Little Ida May," he arranged for a daguerreotype to be taken of her, distributed a paper copy of it, and embarked on a sold-out lecture series in which she appeared. On several occasions, the program included Solomon Northup, a freeborn Black man whose best-selling memoir, *Twelve Years a Slave*, recounted his kidnapping and enslavement in the Deep South.

"Mary's story provided the evidence I needed to make the argument that abolitionists were using photography in innovative ways, and that photography was political from day one," Ms. Morgan-Owens said. "I wrote it up and moved on, but Mary's story haunted me. I wanted to know more about who she was, what she looked like, why her presence had the power to persuade."

The photograph's release was itself significant, as the story of the "white slave from Virginia" captivated the press. "The little girl has no feature which indicates any Negro origin," noted one newspaper about her appearance at the Massachusetts State House. "Her eyes sparkled just like those of any other little girl when she saw the big cod-fish hanging in the hall." Another journalist noted with scarcely concealed racism that "she is a good looking child, with a pale face a very little freckled, chestnut colored hair, and has no characteristics of the Negro race in her features."

In retrospect, Mary's story and the photograph that turned her into an abolitionist icon speak to a long tradition of white Americans relating to racial heroes who look like them, no matter how tangential to the story of African American protagonists. Even today, some Hollywood films about racism and segregation—*Django Unchained*, *The Help*, or *Green Book*, for example—focus on white saviors rather than the Black Americans at the forefront of the struggle.

By highlighting the light-skinned Mary, Mr. Sumner appealed to the prejudices of white Americans who were potentially sympathetic to the abolitionist cause. Employing her image to suggest that slavery was not bound by skin color, he transformed it into a benign icon: a symbol of an institution so malevolent that even innocent children who were practically white were swept up in it; a rallying cry against slavery through the lens of white self-interest and an excuse to feel virtuous without committing to absolute racial equality.

Despite its historical importance, Mary's daguerreotype was but one example of transformative imagery in the antislavery movement. A gruesome photograph published in *Harper's Weekly* in 1863, for example, of a shirtless enslaved Black man, a pattern of welts across his back, confirmed for many Northerners the barbarism of plantation life. Prominent Black abolitionists Frederick Douglass and Harriet Tubman were among the most photographed Americans of the nineteenth century.

Mary Mildred Williams's fame was fleeting. For many years, she worked as a clerk in the registry of deeds in Boston, and died in New York in 1921. But in retrospect her remarkable story is no less important, with implications not only for the past, but for the present. "To use a twenty-first century metaphor, I believe stories like Mary's offer a patch in the virulent social programming about white girlhood that American society has inherited from that time," Ms. Morgan-Owens said. "She complicates the visual language of antislavery. Meanwhile, the ignorance and nearsightedness that occasioned this story can still be found in activist communities today, as evidenced in narratives of pity, savior complexes, and colorism, in who gets chosen to be a poster child."

# Anonymous Men, Made Real

Published October 7, 2013

On Memorial Day in 1897, a magisterial bronze sculpture by Augustus Saint-Gaudens was unveiled on the Boston Common. It commemorated the storming of Fort Wagner in South Carolina on July 18, 1863, by Colonel Robert Gould Shaw and the 54th Massachusetts Volunteer Infantry, the first Black regiment raised in the North during the Civil War.

The battle was bloody and costly. Colonel Shaw was killed and nearly a third of the infantry's one thousand members were dead, missing, or wounded. Despite its defeat at Fort Wagner, the 54th's fortitude in battle was a turning point in the war, paving the way for greater African American participation.

The Shaw Memorial, one of the finest examples of nineteenth-century public art, was noteworthy for its celebration of Black achievement in an era when such recognition was rare. But this acknowledgment only went so far: While the likeness of Colonel Shaw, who was white, was based on photographs of him, the depictions of the Black soldiers were based not on them but on the faces of models hired by Mr. Saint-Gaudens.

Sarah Greenough and Nancy K. Anderson, curators at the National Gallery of Art in Washington, were determined to make real the monument's anonymous soldiers. To this end, they have organized an exhibition: *Tell It with Pride: The 54th Massachusetts Regiment and Augustus Saint-Gaudens' Shaw Memorial*. The show includes the Saint-Gaudens full-scale patinated plaster model of the sculpture, on long-term loan to the National Gallery. It also has studies, vintage photographs, letters, ephemera, as well as the work of contemporary artists who explore the legacy of the 54th Regiment.

The story of the 54th Regiment, unfolding against the backdrop of slavery and segregation in the South, also reflected the North's racial contradictions and ambivalence. Its Black soldiers received a rousing send-off as they marched through the streets of Boston on their way to war. But coursing beneath the air of celebration and good will was an undertow of doubt and prejudice. Skeptics questioned their fitness for combat. Federal restrictions limited their service to noncommissioned status and their pay to a rate significantly lower than that of their white counterparts.

The Shaw Memorial reflects this paradox. On one level, the men are ancillary to the monument's eponymous white hero: the regiment leader Colonel Shaw, a twenty-five-year-old, Harvard-educated son of prominent Boston abolitionists. The colonel and his majestic horse dominate the composition, freestanding and towering over the troops who march behind them in high relief.

But as the art historian Richard J. Powell points out in the exhibition's catalog, Mr. Saint-Gaudens depicted his African American subjects discerningly and with emotional nuance. In spite of their limited visibility, the Black infantrymen, in their distinct physiognomies and ages, provided a respectful alternative to buffoons and blackface minstrels—figures then pervasive in the culture.

Yet even in their own time, the trailblazing soldiers of the 54th Regiment were keenly aware of how easily the erasure of their individuality could devolve into the obliteration of their humanity. To underscore this awareness, *Tell It with Pride* turns to the extraordinary portraits they had made of themselves by local photo studios.

These images tell us much about the consequential role played by photography in the lives of nineteenth-century Black people and the extent to which it empowered the

Photographer unknown, A wounded William H. Carney holding the tattered flag, ca. 1860s

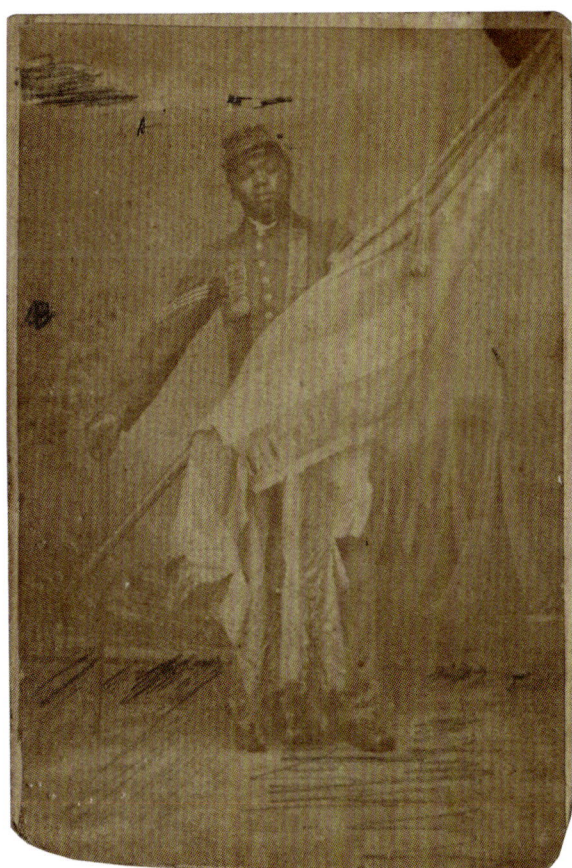

regiment's courageous volunteers. While the use of photography was extensive in the Civil War, in both civilian and military contexts, it was "also intimately woven into the fabric of the 54th," as Ms. Greenough notes.

Photographs served as a promotional tool for the regiment's abolitionist recruiters—including Frederick Douglass, Lewis Hayden, Robert Purvis, Charles Lenox Remond, John Stewart Rock, and Sojourner Truth—whose own charismatic portraits inspired African Americans to enlist. Photographs were also talismanic, providing soldiers with likenesses of their loved ones, and vice versa, as they went off to war. And they helped these men articulate "new identities for the lives they

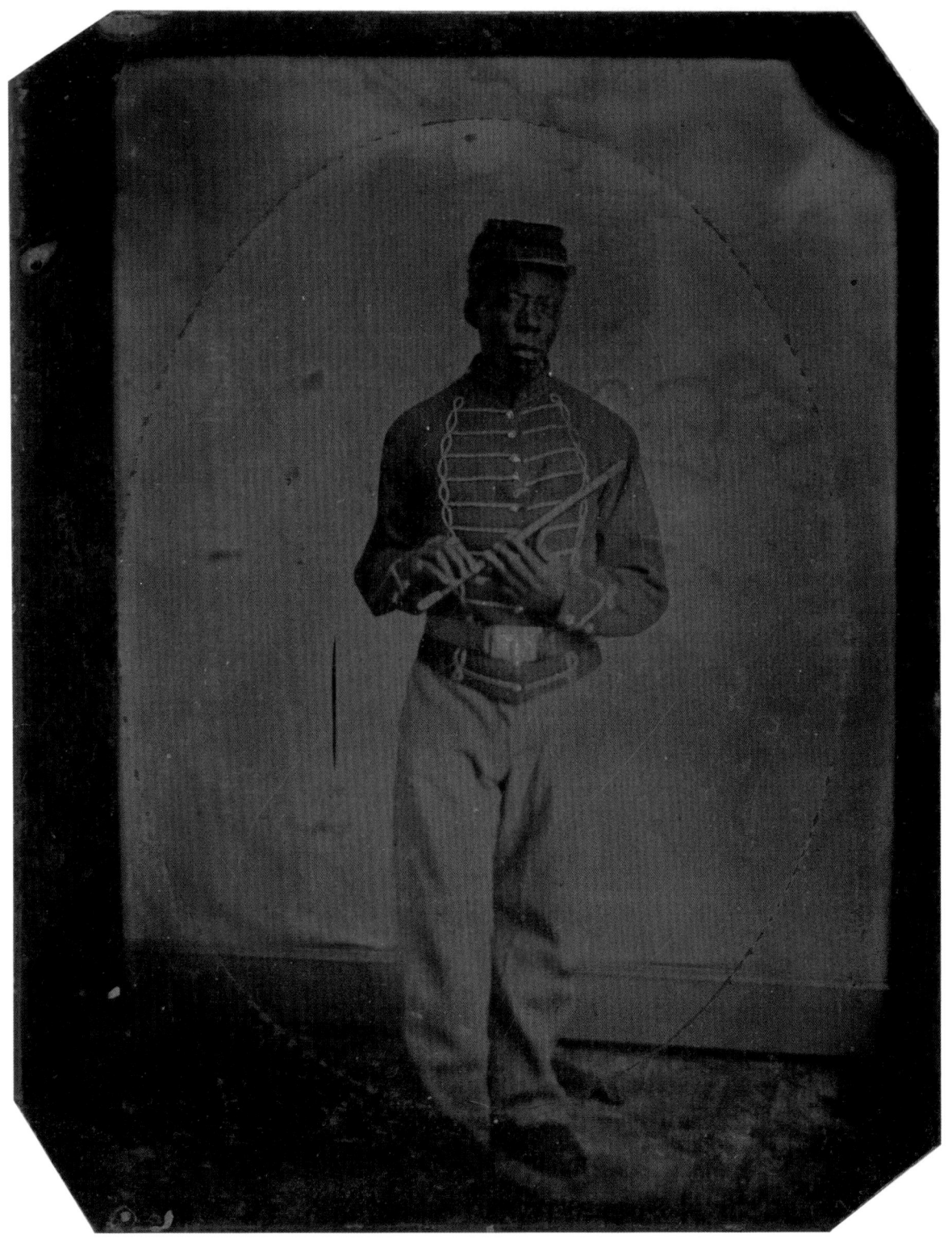

Photographer unknown, Pvt. William J. Netson, musician, ca. mid-1860s

hoped to live," to quote Ms. Greenough, in the wake of the Emancipation Proclamation, the executive order that cleared the way for their service.

This embrace of photography as a catalyst for personal and social change was widespread in the Black community. It had become, for many African Americans, a means of self-assessment and self-definition, a vehicle through which they could take control of their own image.

Frederick Douglass extolled the medium's virtues, for example, arguing that the act of being photographed was a performance that demanded as much from the sitter as from the photographer. *Tell It with Pride* scrutinizes portraits of the soldiers, the abolitionists who recruited them, and the women who nursed, taught, and guided them, elucidating the types of enactments before the camera that allowed Blacks to present themselves as they wanted to be seen.

There is no more poignant example than the photograph of a twenty-three-year-old sergeant, William H. Carney, a picture so worn and fragile that it appears in the exhibition only as a reproduction. Severely wounded in the massacre at Fort Wagner and under heavy assault, Sergeant Carney saved the United States flag from desecration.

A year later, he had his portrait taken as an artful image dense with symbolism: the sergeant's stripes on his uniform that affirm his exemplary service, the cane that speaks to his injuries in war, and, most important, the national flag, the symbol of freedom that he so intrepidly fought to protect. While the liberal press focused on Colonel Shaw's heroism, Sergeant Carney's valor, though widely recognized, was far less celebrated. It would take a changed nation—and thirty-seven years—for him to be awarded the Medal of Honor for his valor at Fort Wagner.

In the end, a modest photograph enabled a brave soldier, faced with a society that continued to degrade and dismiss him because of his race, to mark his achievement for posterity. A century and a half later, such acts of self-representation allow *Tell It with Pride* to restore to a grand monument the likenesses and stories of exceptional men once rendered invisible by prejudice.

# Images of Emancipation

Published December 20, 2012

The portrait for the carte de visite of Sojourner Truth, the African American abolitionist and women's rights advocate, was taken in Battle Creek, Michigan, in the 1860s. She wears an elegant silk dress and shawl. With one hand resting on her hip, the other on the arm of the chair, her pose is majestic and determined. She stares resolutely into the camera.

But it is the object in her lap that remains one of the image's most revelatory details: an open daguerreotype of her grandson James Caldwell, a soldier during the Civil War.

The daguerreotype's pride of place speaks not only to Truth's love for her grandchild but also to her passionate engagement with photography. As Deborah Willis and Barbara Krauthamer write in their groundbreaking new book, *Envisioning Emancipation: Black Americans and the End of Slavery*, Truth was probably the first Black woman to actively distribute photographs of herself. Those pictures were meant to affirm her status as a sophisticated and respectable "free woman and as a woman in control of her image." The public's fascination with cartes de visite, small and collectible card-mounted photographs, allowed her to advance her abolitionist cause to a huge audience and earn a living through their sale. "I Sell the Shadow to Support the Substance," proclaimed the famous slogan for these pictures.

Truth was not alone in her understanding of the power of photography. A host of other African Americans, both eminent and ordinary, employed the medium as an instrument of political engagement and inspiration. *Envisioning Emancipation* argues that photography was not incidental but central to the war against slavery, racism, and segregation in the antebellum period of the 1850s through the New Deal era of the 1930s.

The book explores how Blacks "positioned themselves and were posed by others" in order to advance, question, or alter prevailing ideas about race. It examines the ways the national debate about slavery was played out in photographs, for example, from the standpoint of abolitionists, who published them as proof of the brutality and immorality of slavery, and its supporters, who engaged photographs as visual evidence of its "natural order and orderliness."

Pseudoscientists like Louis Agassiz, the Swiss-born and Harvard-trained zoologist, adapted the medium to further notions of Black aberrance and inferiority. Agassiz employed invasive daguerreotypes of naked slaved people—the "pornography of forced labor," as they have been aptly described—to verify his theory of polygenesis, the separate human origins of Africans and Europeans, and emphasize the relative lowliness of the former.

Abolitionists used photographs to convince Northern whites—for whom the prospect of emancipation elicited responses ranging from skepticism to violence—of the unjustness of slavery. They stirred public sentiment by offering visual evidence of slavery's abuses as well as of the wholesomeness of an emerging class of freed Blacks. Juxtaposing pictures of hapless children, posed barefoot and dressed in ragged clothes, with images of the same children wearing neatly pressed and undamaged garments, for example, abolitionists were able to convey the idea that a formerly enslaved people, now rendered as attractive and healthy, were worthy of liberation.

As Ms. Willis and Ms. Krauthamer note, freedom for African Americans was not instantly achieved with the implementation of the Emancipation Proclamation in 1863; it evolved fitfully, over many decades. During that time, it was photographs created largely by and for African Americans that helped an oppressed people to imagine their own freedom. Prominent Black leaders, including Frederick Douglass and Harriet Tubman, routinely turned to the medium, much as Sojourner Truth did, to further their abolitionist campaigns.

Soon, increasingly inexpensive imaging technology, coupled with a growing national network of Black-owned photo studios, permitted African Americans of all economic classes, even "the servant girl," as Douglass observed, to construct their own versions of themselves. This affirmative imagery served to countermand destructive and pervasive stereotypes, steeling African Americans against the ruthless forces of intolerance while simultaneously convincing white people of their shared humanity.

In the end, *Envisioning Emancipation* recounts a dynamic history of Black self-possession and self-determination, one that challenges the abiding myth of the crusade against slavery and segregation: that of passive Black victims who obtained freedom mostly through the benevolence and generosity of their white saviors.

That myth does not die easily. It haunts popular culture, no more so than in Steven Spielberg's just-released film about the sixteenth president's epic battle against slavery, *Lincoln*. Despite the nuanced portrayal of its protagonist, *Lincoln* is almost devoid of images of active Black resistance and protest, ignoring a wealth of research "demonstrating that slaves were crucial agents in their emancipation," as the historian Kate Masur wrote last month in the *New York Times*.

"For my community, the message has been clear," the writer Ta-Nehisi Coates recently observed. "The Civil War is a story for white people—acted out by white people, and on white people's terms—in which Blacks feature strictly as stock characters and props." *Envisioning Emancipation* brilliantly rewrites this story, insisting that we acknowledge the names and faces of people who have been invisible for too long.

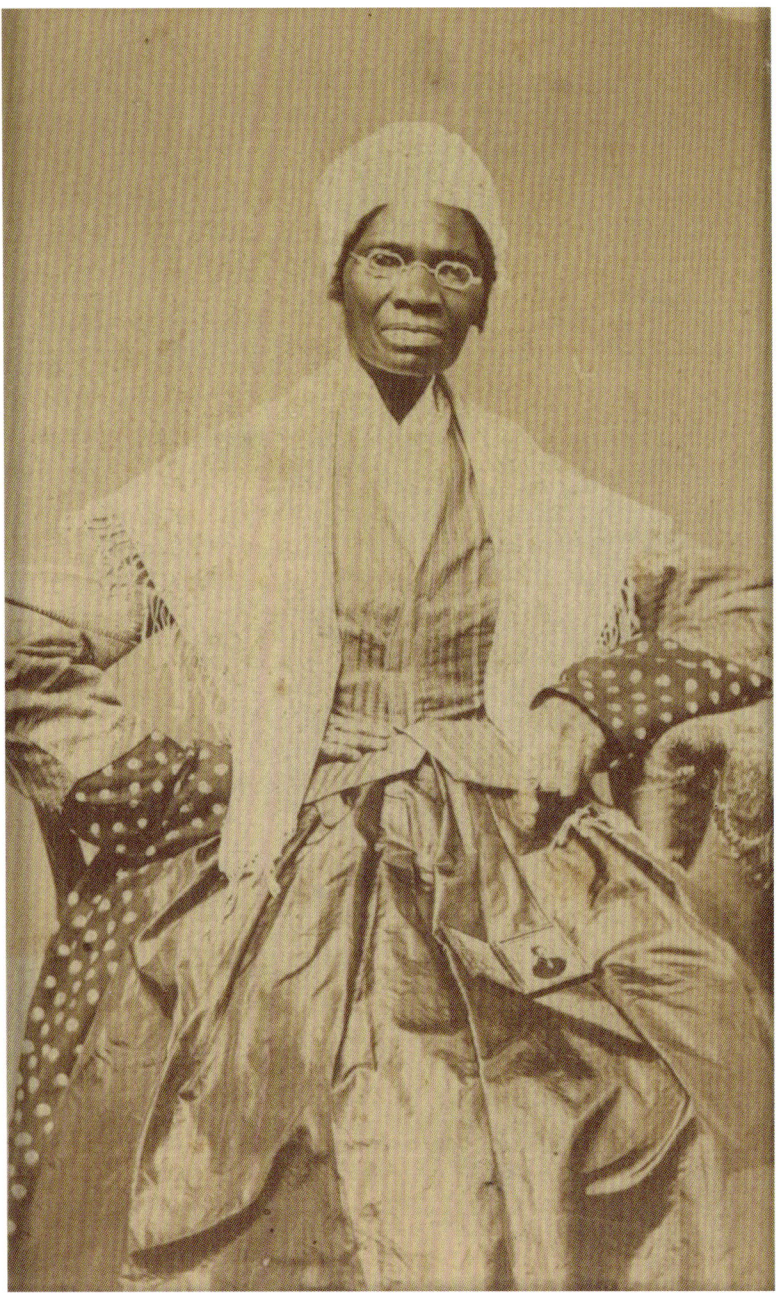

Photographer unknown, Carte de visite of Sojourner Truth, 1863

Chapter 3

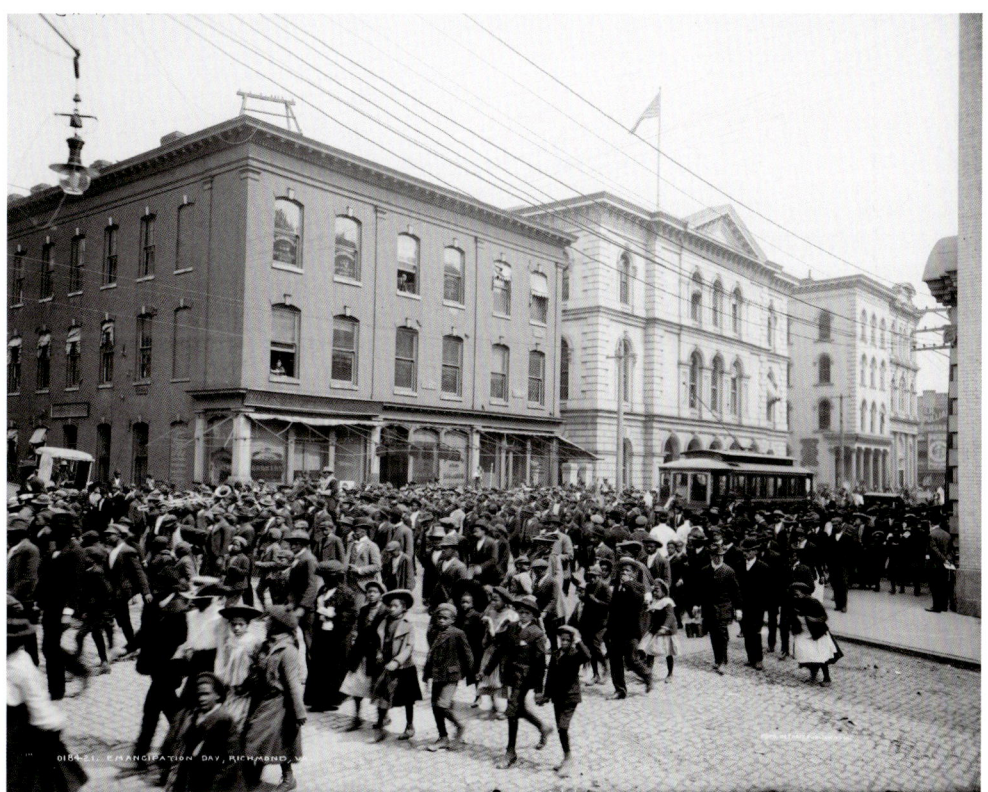

Photographer unknown, Emancipation Day, Richmond, Virginia, 1905

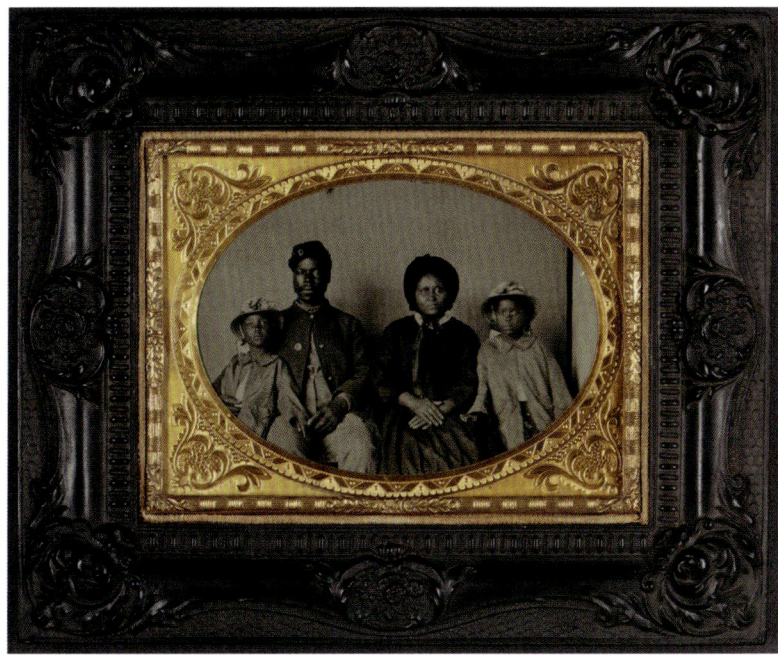

Photographer unknown, Unidentified African American soldier in
Union uniform with wife and two daughters, ca. 1863–65

History and Memory

# A Civil Rights Photographer, and a Struggle, Are Remembered

Published November 14, 2013

Jon Lewis shot thousands of archetypical civil rights photographs in the late 1960s: a picket line snaking along the horizon, children playing in squalor, activists huddled in a strategy session. What makes these photographs different is their location and the subjects. Taken in central California and not in the Jim Crow South, they depict farm laborers of Mexican and Filipino descent, the vanguard of the historic Delano grape strike.

Photographers had been documenting farmworkers since the 1850s, as Richard Steven Street, who teaches American studies at Princeton University, notes in his new book, *Jon Lewis: Photographs of the California Grape Strike*. But Mr. Lewis was the first to document, in its totality, a farm labor strike.

Mr. Lewis, who died virtually unknown in 2009 at the age of seventy-one, engaged the farmworker movement both as chronicler and active participant in some of its marches and meetings. Precise and carefully studied, his photographs exposed the harrowing backstory of the fruits and vegetables that Americans consumed daily without hesitation or thought. They made real "the human price paid by a transnational class of landless peasants, excluded from the social and legal privileges enjoyed by most Americans," Mr. Street writes. But they also revealed a wholesome and self-motivated community: farmworkers enjoying actors, the one-act political plays of Luis Valdez's El Teatro Campesino, for example, or strikers engaging in the family life or religious rituals that gave them the strength to endure.

A Marine Corps veteran and military photographer who studied photojournalism in college and graduate school, Mr. Lewis arrived in Delano in January 1966, intending to stay briefly. He remained on and off until

Chapter 3

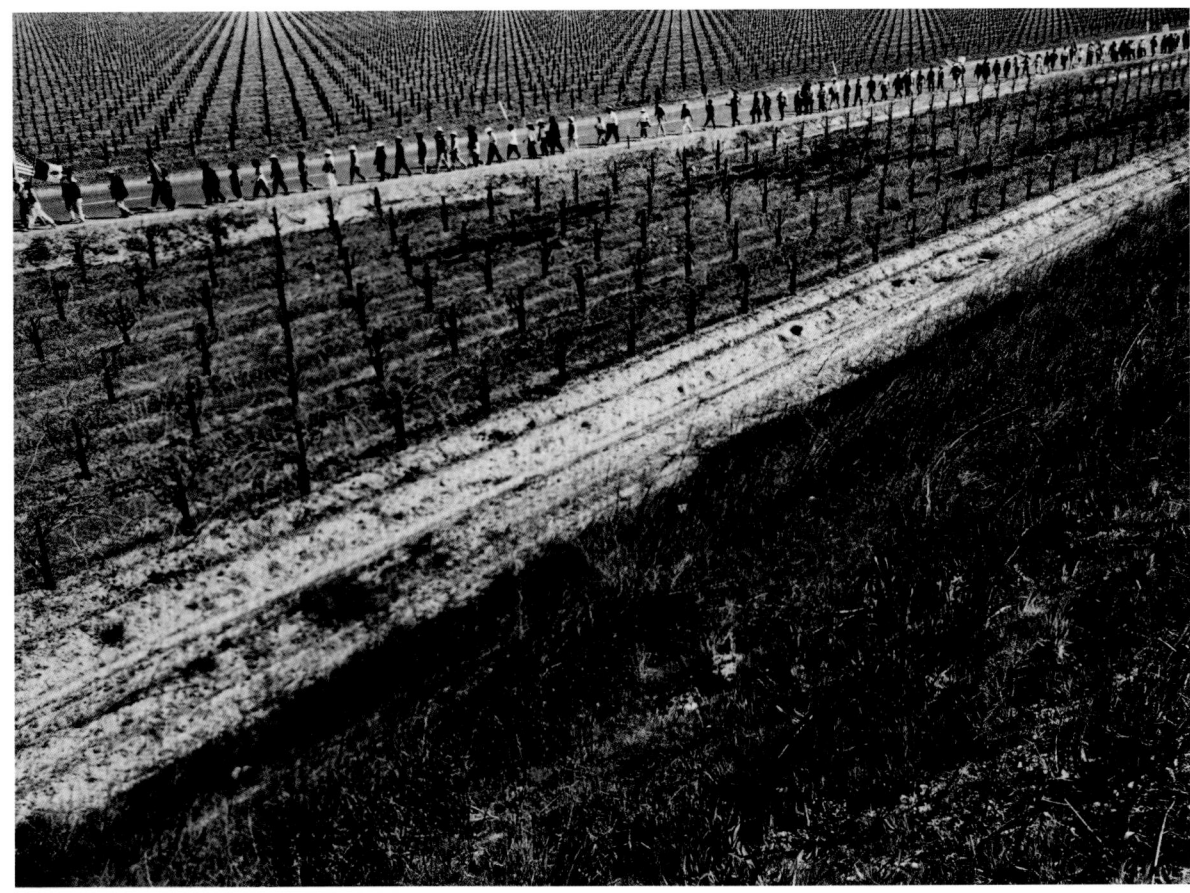

1970, when the striking farmworkers signed union contracts with the California grape industry.

Conditions for farm laborers were dire. Growers routinely ignored state labor laws. Wages were below the poverty level. Work was backbreaking. Laborers were sickened by pesticides. They lived in derelict labor camps, in unheated shacks without indoor plumbing. Child labor was rampant. Life expectancy was twenty years below the national average.

In September 1965, advocacy groups joined together to organize a strike against growers, which eventually included a national boycott of table grapes. Six months later, the Mexican American farm labor activist Cesar Chavez led a three-hundred-mile pilgrimage from Delano to Sacramento in an attempt to compel growers and the state to address the grievances of farmworkers and to bring public attention to their cause.

Mr. Chavez, a founder of the United Farm Workers and the union's most prominent advocate, could rely on Mr. Lewis, the son of struggling Nebraska corn farmers, for compelling, useful, and ultimately influential images. Such photographs demonstrated the plight of the farmworker without resorting to the kind of photographic clichés— the stoic laborer as a symbol of a nation's indomitable spirit, for example—that would have detracted from the troubling reality of their situation.

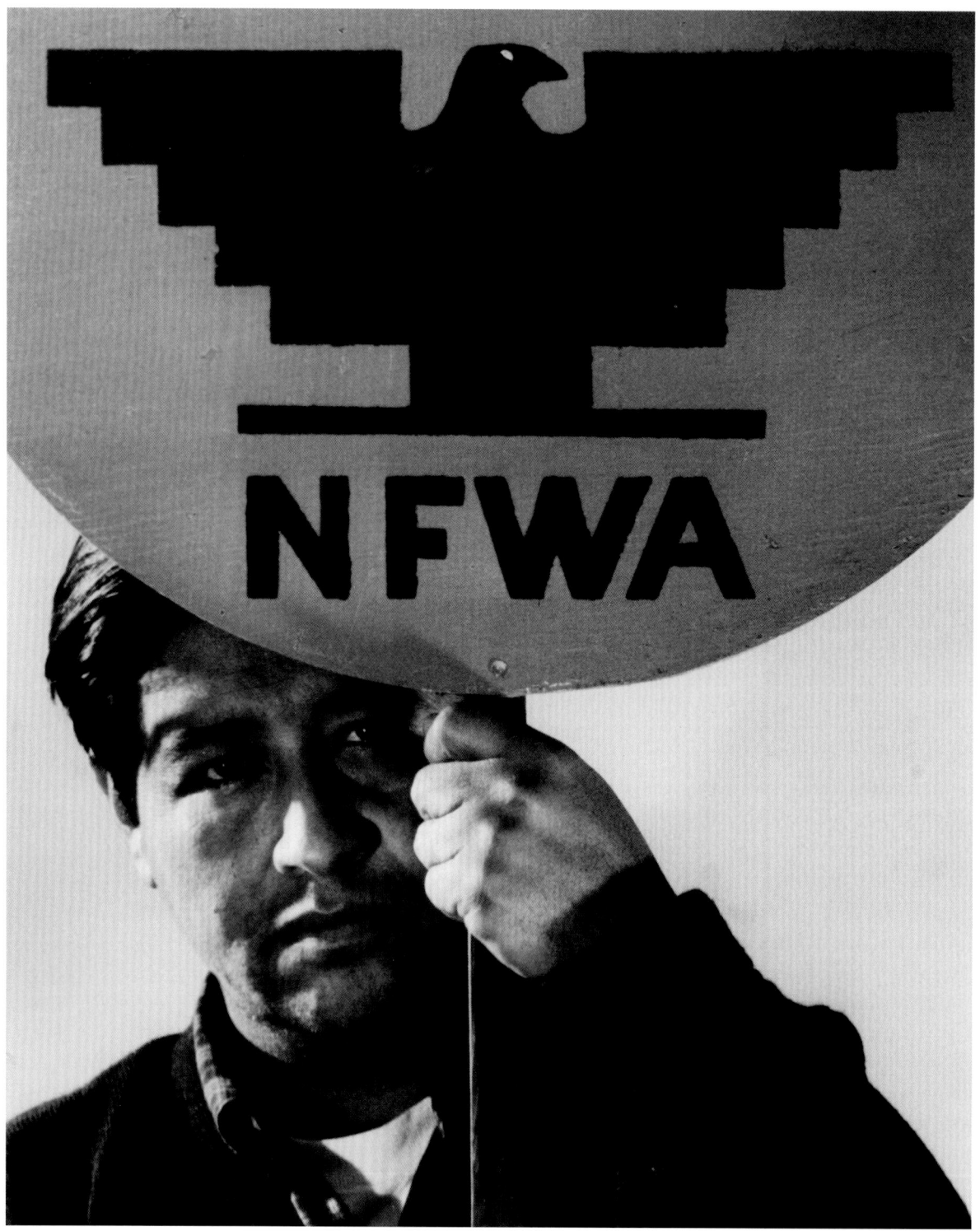

Jon Lewis, Cesar Chávez, Winter, 1966

Chapter 3

Mr. Lewis's imagery falls principally into two categories: long establishing shots that provide an overview of his subjects' lives and nuanced portraits. The former includes a haunting picture of a stooped worker, a tiny figure engulfed by a massive field of lettuce; a striker waving a sign at workers taking a break, admonishing them to join; and workers kneeling in front of a makeshift shrine set up in a battered Mercury station wagon.

The portraits are equally compelling: a pensive Chavez, shot from below, the United Farm Workers thunderbird logo soaring above him; an aging worker carrying a massive crate of grapes on his shoulder; children listening in rapt attention to speakers at a rally; a lyrical photograph of a strike supporter, Senator Robert F. Kennedy, his face dramatically lit by television lights.

The book's other significant revelation, beyond the photographs, concerns Mr. Chavez's confidence in the ability of pictures to move a skeptical or indifferent nation. "We took every photograph of violence and used it to publicize what they were doing to us," Mr. Chavez later recalled. "We wanted those and other images to be seen by the public."

Mr. Lewis provided Mr. Chavez with a powerful arsenal of images. He endured the wrath of growers, professional isolation, and indigence to create, as Mr. Street writes, "an extraordinarily intimate and comprehensive photographic record not only of Cesar Chavez but also of field hands, activists, clergy, nuns, radicals, Mexicans, Anglos, Filipinos, politicians, actors and professional activists who forged the modern farmworker movement." In the process, he amassed a commanding and eloquent body of work—culminating in an elegiac book, *From This Earth*, self-published in 1969—that helps restore to history the details of a consequential, but less remembered, struggle for equality and freedom.

Like Malcolm X, who mastered both photography and the media in the service of the Nation of Islam, Mr. Chavez carried a camera to document the strike. And like the Reverend Dr. Martin Luther King Jr., he engineered the kinds of events and images that he believed could alter public opinion, from those that emphasized religious symbols and ritual affirming farmworkers' faith and commitment to nonviolence to shots of arrests and harassment, some strategically provoked when photojournalists were present.

As Mr. Lewis recalls in the book, Mr. Chavez's trust in photography was inspired by the African American civil rights movement. He proposed a cross-country pilgrimage based on the bloody 1965 Selma to Montgomery march in Alabama, for example, because it generated media images, both still and televised, that transformed public opinion.

"People don't understand how attuned he was to the civil rights movement," Mr. Lewis said of Mr. Chavez. "He thought that he could rekindle interest, generate new imagery, and create what amounted to a massive photo opportunity that projected the kind of picture that he wanted the public to see."

# Finding Inspiration in the Struggle at Resurrection City

Published October 24, 2017

Devastated by the assassination of the Reverend Dr. Martin Luther King Jr., Jill Freedman quit her copywriting job at a New York advertising agency and headed to Washington, DC, to protest poverty and live among shacks and tents on the National Mall. Little more than an amateur photographer at the time, her commitment to racial and economic justice made her the only photographer who stayed and documented the entire six-week encampment known as Resurrection City.

Her striking photographs are on exhibit at Steven Kasher Gallery in New York and featured in a book, *Resurrection City, 1968*, published with photographs and texts by Ms. Freedman and essays by John Edwin Mason and Aaron Bryant. These photographs document, and invite us to reconsider, one of the most controversial episodes in civil rights history.

Resurrection City was the centerpiece of the Poor People's Campaign, organized by the Southern Christian Leadership Conference (SCLC) and, initially, by Dr. King. The campaign departed from earlier demonstrations—which had touched on economic issues but emphasized racial discrimination—to focus on jobs, education, and a fair minimum wage. Its expanded platform helped attract a wide range of participants, including poor whites, Mexican Americans, Puerto Ricans, and Native Americans.

It was initially conceived as a series of nonviolent demonstrations, marches, and meetings with government officials in Washington and other cities. But after the King assassination, and under the direction of the Reverend Ralph Abernathy, SCLC's new president, the campaign focused on Resurrection City, a temporary settlement

Chapter 3

built of plywood and canvas near the mall's reflecting pool.

Construction began on May 13, 1968. Soon, several thousand people were living in a settlement that buzzed with activity. Rallies were held. Celebrities visited. Speeches were delivered. Demonstrators made daily pilgrimages to federal agencies. And Ms. Freedman photographed what she witnessed. "I knew I had to shoot the Poor People's Campaign when they murdered Martin Luther King Jr.," she later recalled. "I had to see what was happening, to record it and be part of it. I felt so bad."

Gaining the trust of its residents, Ms. Freedman intimately documented life in the settlement: people congregating outside their makeshift shelters; demonstrators walking past a line of grim-faced policemen; a dapper man selling copies of *Muhammad Speaks*, the official newspaper of the Nation of Islam; children in rain boots frolicking in the mud; a kneeling man, his back to the camera, playing the flute; litter scattered on the marble steps of a building; and numerous portraits of residents—dignified, resolute, and sometimes weary.

These photographs present a measured view of a historical event that has been more typically labeled a failure by journalists and scholars. The campaign resulted in little substantive change in federal policy. And the encampment itself was beset by problems: fragile structures endangered by intermittent rain and flooding, sanitation and health issues, petty theft, and rifts between organizers. On June 24, more than a thousand police officers cleared the encampment and evicted its remaining five hundred residents.

But Ms. Freedman's photographs affirm it was also a place of quiet defiance. These images depict solidarity among activists of all races. They reveal the dignity and courage of parents determined to provide their children with a better life. They portray a range of faces—beautiful, radiant, serious, laughing, or animated in song and protest. They remind us that, for some, the settlement provided a respite from the unremitting poverty of home. "I'm living better here than I ever did there," was the way one resident then described it to the *New York Times*.

Ms. Freedman's images underscore the vital role played by photography in the movement. Dr. King conceived the Poor People's Campaign as a "new kind of Selma or Birmingham"—an event that might serve as a catalyst for change. He was keenly aware of the power of visual media, whether in print or on television, to spur change, commenting on several occasions about the authority of pictures to shift public opinion. His own popularity, and that of the movement he led, waning, Dr. King viewed the campaign as a way of reinvigorating support for the movement, given its broad platform of economic justice.

But the images of Resurrection City had the opposite effect. Seen in its time as a fiasco, the event was generally represented by images of desolation, filth, and decay. Ms. Freedman's photographs of Resurrection City are neither idealized nor derisive. Instead, they offer a compassionate and candid view of a historic event shrouded in myths and stereotypes.

"If you forget about things like traffic lights, dress shops, and cops, Resurrection City was pretty much just another city. Crowded. Hungry. Dirty. Gossipy. Beautiful," Ms. Freedman wrote. "It was the world, squeezed between flimsy snow fences and stinking humanity. There were people there who'd give you the shirt off their backs, and others who'd kill you for yours. And every type in between. Just a city."

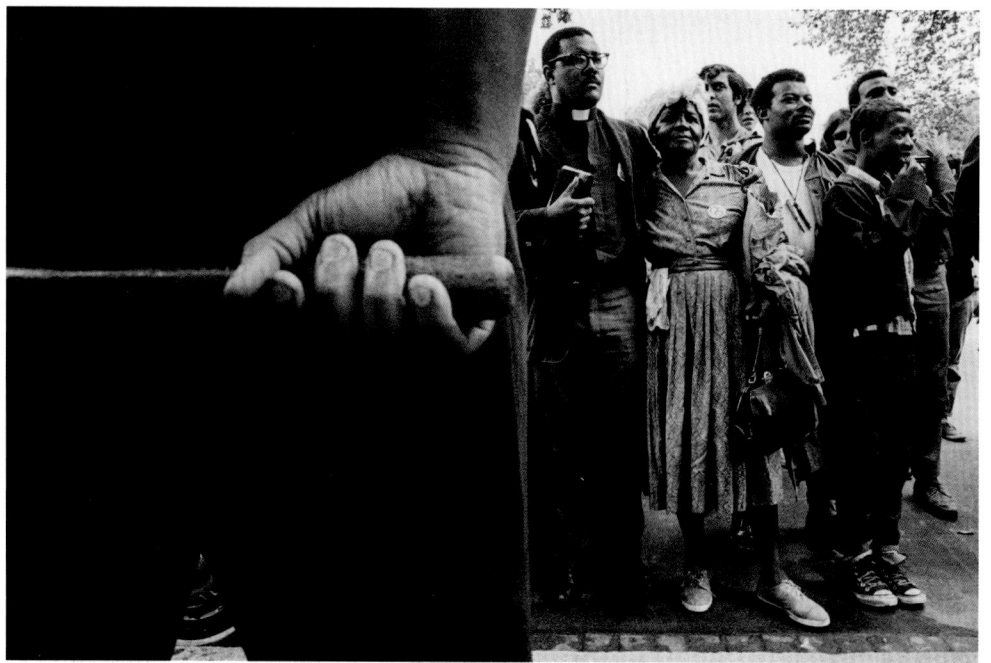

Jill Freedman, A policeman faces demonstrators, Washington, DC, 1968

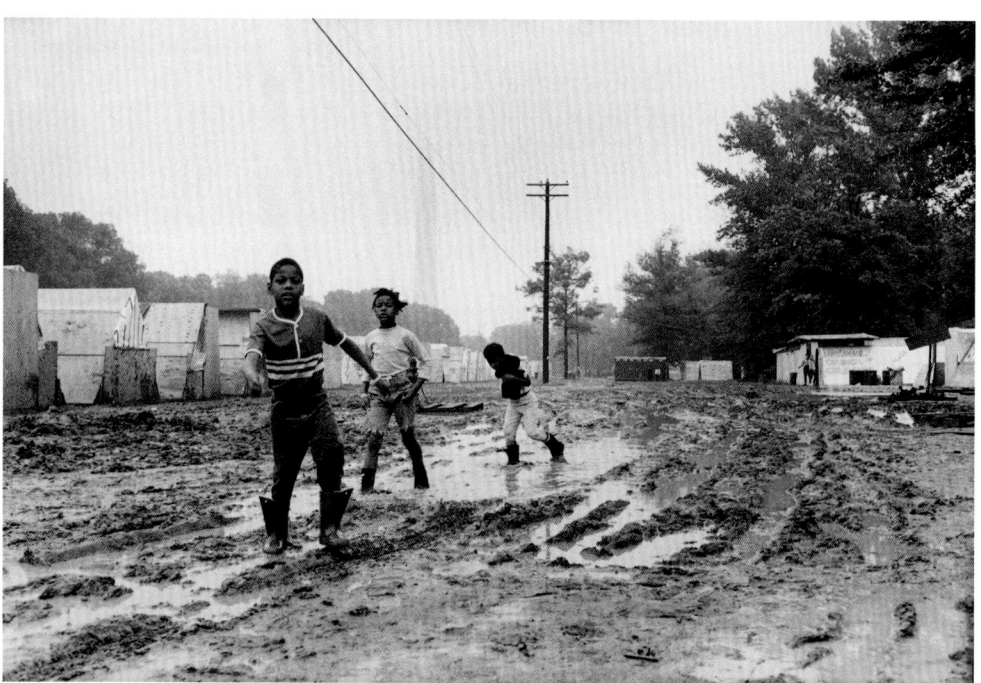

Jill Freedman, Boys playing in the mud after days of rain, Washington, DC, 1968

Chapter 3

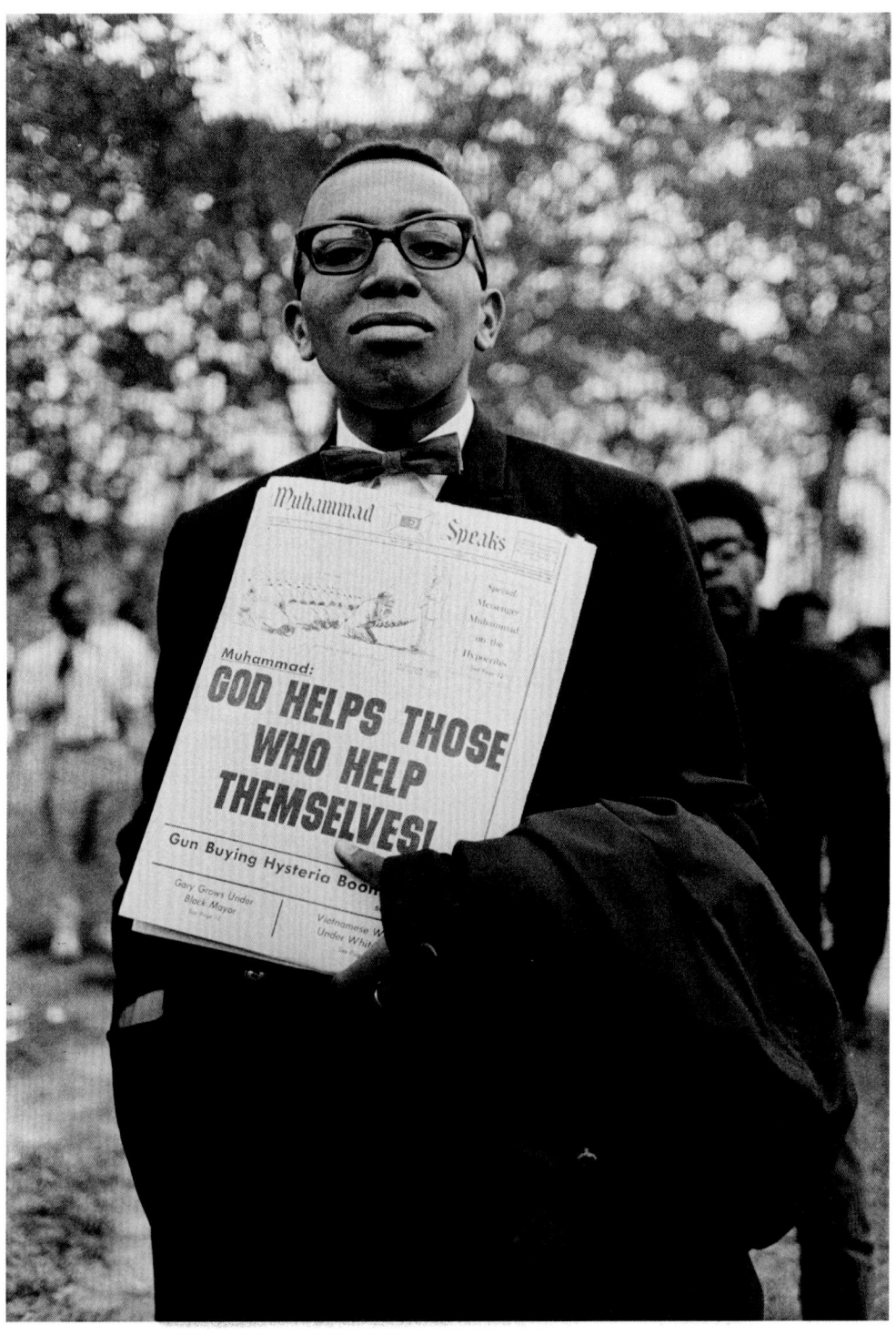

# A Cultural History of Civil Rights

Published May 9, 2014

Two men sit inside a rural Mississippi community center. One of them, a Black civil rights activist, has a shotgun at the ready. Their vigil—in a town where the Ku Klux Klan could strike at any moment—is in a makeshift library whose walls are covered with books.

This compelling photograph, taken during the historic 1964 Freedom Summer, is a reminder of the multiple and sometimes conflicting tactics of the civil rights movement. It is also a hopeful metaphor for the power of knowledge to combat prejudice and oppression.

With this idea in mind, thousands of volunteers, many of them college students from the North, descended on Mississippi in June 1964. Their purpose was to work with local activists to register African American voters in a state that often denied them that right. To address the racial inequalities in Mississippi's education system, they set up thirty Freedom Schools in small towns, as well as meeting houses and community centers.

Matt Herron had relocated from the North to Jackson, Mississippi, with his wife, Jeannine, and two small children a year earlier to work as a freelance photojournalist, pitching stories to *Life*, *Look*, and the *Saturday Evening Post*, and to participate in the movement. He assembled a group of photographers—the Southern Documentary Project, he called it—to document the Freedom Summer. Although often overlooked by historians, the project is the subject of an insightful new book by Mr. Herron, *Mississippi Eyes: The Story and Photography of the Southern Documentary Project*.

While the era's documentary photography was dominated by images that provoked shock, anger, or defiance, the project told a different story. Concentrating on educational

Chapter 3

Matt Herron, *Community Center Construction, Freedom summer*, Mileston, Mississippi. Mileston summer volunteer carpenter, Jim Boebel, and a local resident post a shotgun watch at the community center against a fire bomb threat by local whites. Threats were common that summer and local men took turns guarding the community every night. Library books were donated by friends of Student Nonviolent Coordinating Committee groups in the North, June 1964

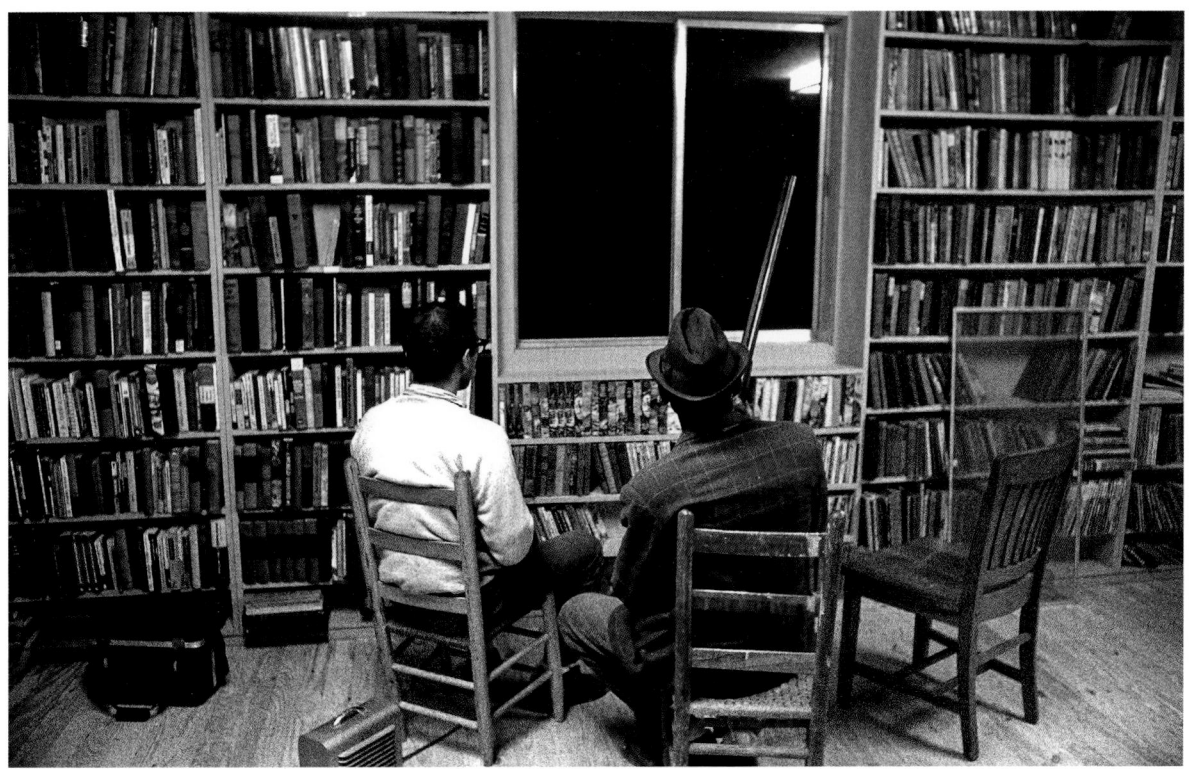

and artistic activities, it reminds us that the civil rights movement was as much cultural as sociological.

The project's other photographers included George Ballis, Nick Lawrence, Danny Lyon, Norris McNamara, and David Prince. Fred DeVan was its sole Black participant. It was financed with $10,000 raised by Howard Chapnick, director of the Black Star photo agency. Mr. Herron was also able to secure the cooperation of the photography unit of the Student Nonviolent Coordinating Committee in Atlanta, where his wife organized the darkroom that developed and printed film for the two groups.

*Mississippi Eyes* contains many noteworthy works: Mr. Prince's photographs of the memorial service, held in the charred

ruins of the Mount Zion Church, for the activists James Chaney, Michael Schwerner, and Andrew Goodman, who were murdered because of their investigation of the arson; Mr. Lawrence's study of workers in a cotton factory; and Mr. Ballis's record of the Mississippi Freedom Democratic Party's challenge to the state's all-white delegation to the 1964 Democratic Convention.

But it is Mr. Herron's images that are among the most compelling, both for their powerful observations and for their technical skill. Not content with the usual transient reporting on civil rights, he observed the movement over time, at close range and in considerable detail. "I often thought of myself as wearing three different hats: photojournalist, photographer as civil rights propagandist, and social documentarian," Mr. Herron wrote of his time in Mississippi.

Dorothea Lange, his mentor and informal adviser to the project, taught him the aesthetic and political values of rigor and emotional sensitivity.

"The visual person has to sweat off all the self-indulgent fat in his personality," she warned him, "the mental laziness, personal vanity, material desires, the good times and easy company that waste his energy and hold him below the level of spiritual and visual awareness at which great photographs are made."

Mr. Herron's evocative photographs meet this challenge: the Black orator Hartman Turnbow captured in an electrifying blur; the visual syncopation of carpenters perched on the wooden frame of a community center; an image of young men dressed in their Sunday best, their clothing an essay on patterns, silhouettes, and styles of dress; and an oblique, cinematic shot of a teacher and students at the Milestone Freedom School joining hands to sing "We Shall Overcome."

While civil rights photographers typically depicted boycotts, demonstrations, and conflagrations, others, such as Gordon Parks and James Karales, realized the value of prosaic imagery: of people going about their lives and persevering in a hostile atmosphere. If such images appealed to the empathy of whites, affirming that Americans perceived as alien, undeserving, or inferior were no different from them, they empowered Black people by countering the destructive stereotypes then prevalent in the culture at large.

The images selected by Mr. Herron for *Mississippi Eyes* represent African Americans mostly through the lens of personal and artistic expression—the dances, political theater, protest songs, makeshift posters, displays of spirituality and devotion, and individual dress and style that allowed them to endure and to be seen as empowered and self-possessed.

Mr. Herron's work also documented the ways culture abetted and perpetuated white supremacy in the South: an artful Ku Klux Klan recruiting poster; police officers decked out in opulent helmets; and a pursed-lipped George Wallace, then governor of Alabama, seated imperially on a dais covered in silk bunting. Mr. Herron's photograph of two elderly supporters of Mr. Wallace is a stunning treatise on the banality of evil, their lively summer dresses and matronly manner barely concealing the vitriol that seethes within them.

In his 1964 proposal to SNCC for support for the Southern Documentary Project, Mr. Herron envisioned a team of photographers "who have the insight to interpret and understand the events that unfold before their cameras, and who possess the visual sensitivity to translate these events into superb images—photographs of great pith and strength that will endure long after the civil rights struggle has passed into our history books."

A half-century later, *Mississippi Eyes* testifies to the success of his vision.

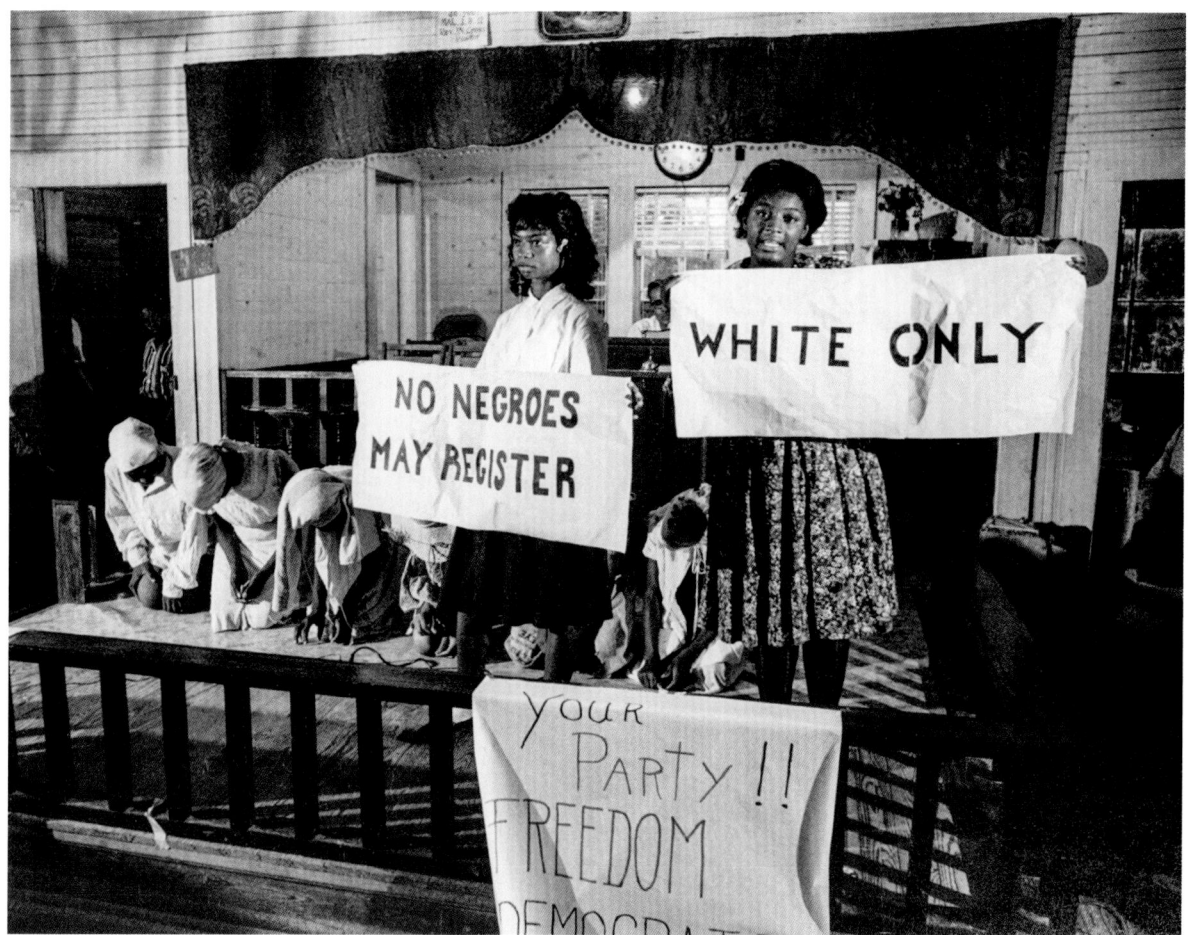

Matt Herron, *Mississippi Freedom Democratic Party*, Mileston, Mississippi. Holmes County election of freedom delegates. Students from Mileston Freedom School perform play they wrote about slavery, civil rights for MFDP delegates meeting. Holding No Negroes sign: Yvonne Pitchford, White Only: Geraldine Smith, August 1, 1964

# Black Soldiers: Fighting America's Enemies Abroad and Racism at Home

Published June 5, 2017

After visiting Fort Hood Army base in Texas, the journalist Ray Suarez observed that as much as it represented a separate military culture, with distinct rules and protocols, it was also a microcosm of the nation. "One of the most attractive aspects of the people I met at Fort Hood was their very ordinariness," Mr. Suarez wrote in 2010. "They are tall, short, men, women, rural, urban, skinny, buffed, chubby, provincial, worldly, with accents and life experience from every corner of the country."

And for much of its existence, the US military mirrored the nation in another, less auspicious way: its sanctioning of racial segregation. *Double Exposure: Fighting for Freedom*, published in association with the Smithsonian National Museum of African American History and Culture, documents the complex history of Black soldiers, illuminating their triumphs and challenges.

The fifth volume in the museum's *Double Exposure* series, *Fighting for Freedom* presents more than fifty works from its photography collection that exemplify the bravery, patriotism, and dignity of African American men and women in uniform. While Black participation in the military dates back to the Revolutionary War, the book spans the history of African American service from the Civil War to Iraq. In addition to the short texts that accompany many photographs, the book includes essays by the museum's director, Lonnie G. Bunch III, the retired Marine Maj. Gen. Charles F. Bolden Jr., and the journalist Gail Lumet Buckley.

"The images in this volume offer an insightful view into the long history of African Americans who served our country through the military," Mr. Bolden wrote. "They demonstrate the willingness of a people to stand up and be counted, even when they were not fully recognized in the legal and social systems of their day. They give us a window from which to see a small sample of the hard work and sacrifice that African Americans continue to pour into the greater life of the United States."

The book documents a proud—but contradictory—history: a cabinet card of the Medal of Honor recipient Sgt. William Carney holding an American flag during the Civil War; a stereograph from the 1870s of the headstones of Black troops at Arlington National Cemetery; a panoramic group portrait of an all-Black unit recently returned from World War I; an elegant photograph of a member of the famed Tuskegee Airmen in World War II, the first Black servicemen to become military aviators; Leonard Freed's contemplative image of a Black soldier in Berlin in 1962; and a photograph of a racially diverse group of officers discussing troop progress in east Baghdad in 2007.

Desegregating the armed forces in the last century was slow. While the US military was the largest minority employer during World War II, it remained segregated. Black enlistees were assigned to racially separate units and were typically relegated to combat support roles, like gravediggers, truck drivers, cooks, and quartermasters. The few that made it into combat served with distinction, though in largely segregated platoons under the command of white lieutenants.

When African American soldiers returned home, they encountered more racism and segregation. Rather than honor veterans who risked their lives protecting freedom and democracy, an ungrateful nation often rejected and ostracized them. Returning soldiers were routinely blocked from white neighborhoods, not only in the Jim Crow South but in sprawling northern developments like Levittown on Long Island.

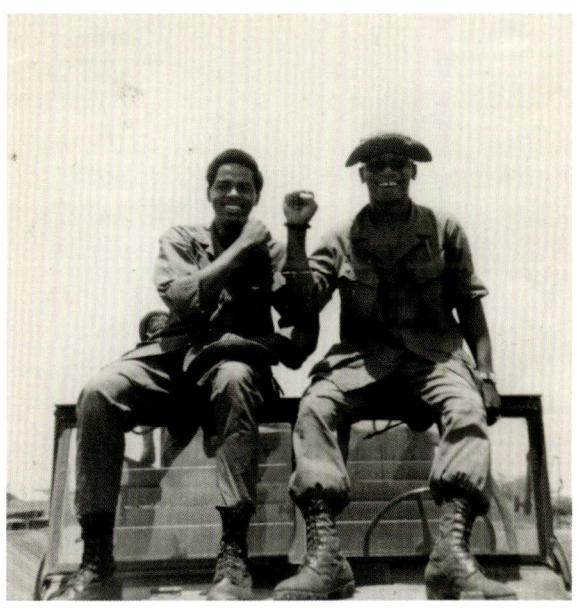

James Edward Brown III, Photograph of Spc. James E. Brown II and another soldier, Vietnam, August–December 1970

They encountered similar discrimination at universities and professional schools. In the end, Black soldiers were fighting a double war—against America's external enemies and the enemy within.

A 1948 executive order by President Harry S. Truman began the process of desegregation, establishing "equality of treatment and opportunity for all persons in the armed forces without regard to race, color, religion, or national origin." Because of considerable resistance from white military personnel, it took many years to meet the order's objectives.

The last all-Black unit was eliminated in September 1954. Nine years later, Defense Secretary Robert McNamara issued a directive instructing commanders to protect military personnel and their dependents by opposing discriminatory practices and fostering equal opportunity in the communities that surrounded bases. While the Vietnam War was the first US war to "begin with Blacks and whites serving as equals under the American flag," as Ms. Buckley noted, it was marked by racial tensions and demands by African American soldiers to use controversial Black Power symbols, like the Dignity and Pride handshake and soul power fist, to express cultural pride and solidarity.

Ultimately, the portraits of African American heroes in *Fighting for Freedom* speak to an evolving military, one that has reflected society's racial limitations as well as its capacity to change. From the celebration of Black heroes in the eighteenth and nineteenth centuries to the abject segregation of the twentieth century, the US military has revealed much about the state of race relations in the United States.

"Wartime creates some of the most trying circumstances a human being can endure and its crucible strips away all but the true essence of those who endure the heat of battle," Mr. Bolden wrote. "Perhaps in the greater scheme of things, that experience of men and women of all races fighting side by side, suffering injury and loss and also achieving great things, has advanced the necessary cause of racial equality so essential to our future and the outcomes of the battles that lie ahead."

Robert Scurlock, Photograph of Tuskegee Airman Major Lee Rayford in front of a P-47 Thunderbolt, ca. 1944–45

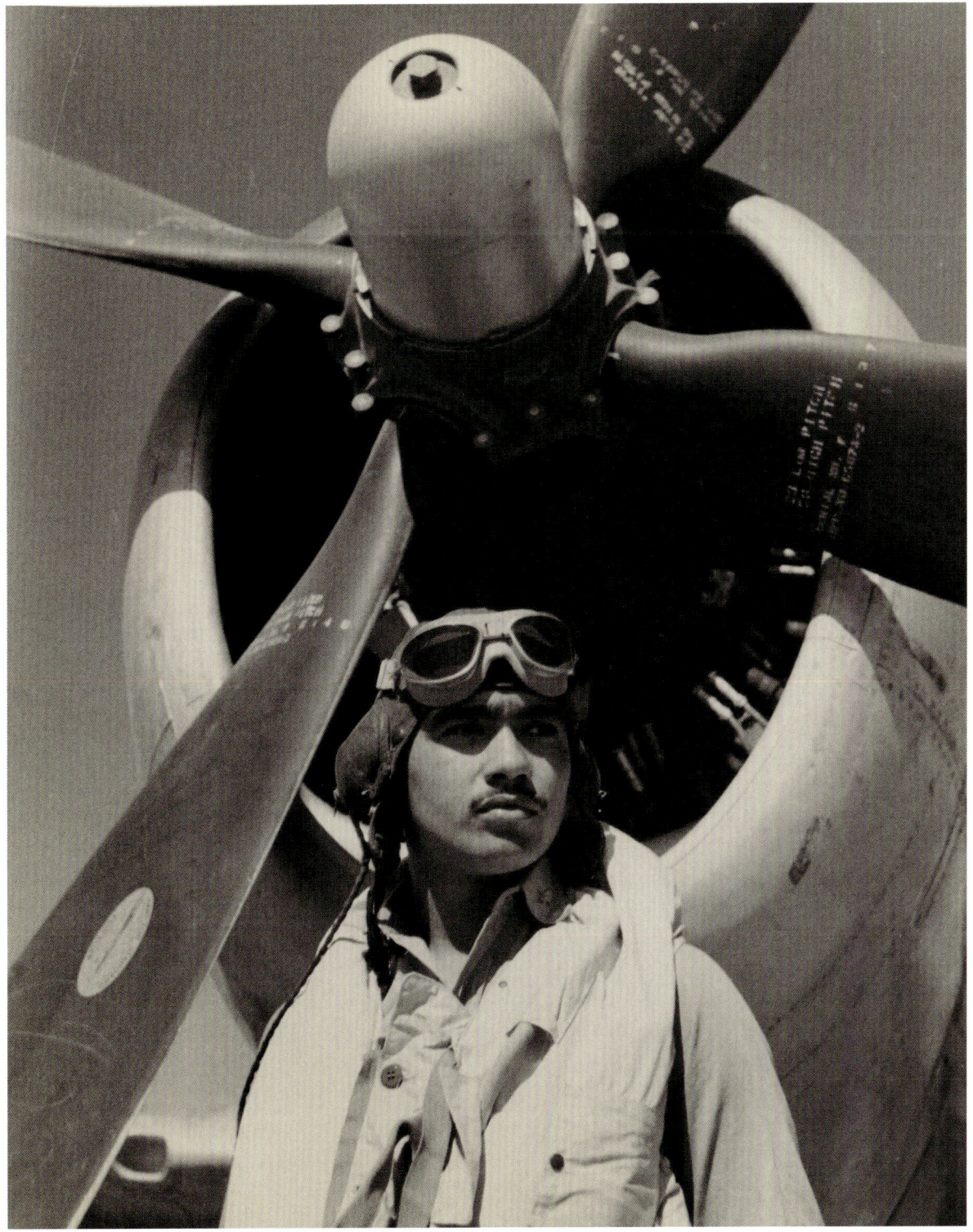

# Lynchings in the West, Erased from History and Photos

Published December 6, 2012

At first, *Disguised Bandit*—a life-size reproduction of a century-old postcard by Ken Gonzales-Day—does not suggest anything out of the ordinary. A sparse tree cuts the center of the photograph. A group of white American soldiers flanks the tree. One man grins. The others stare passively into the camera.

But the meaning—and the power—of the image resides not in what's visible, but in what's not: the "disguised bandit" suggested by the inscription at the bottom of the postcard. In the context of Mr. Gonzales-Day's art, the word *disguised* is fraught with irony: The artist has altered the photograph, digitally erasing the "criminal," who in the original scene is a brutalized corpse dangling from the tree.

*Disguised Bandit* is part of Mr. Gonzales-Day's *Erased Lynching* series, which also includes similarly altered photomurals based on postcards, souvenir cards, and published photographs of mob violence that were widely circulated and collected in the United States from the late nineteenth century through the 1930s. *Disguised Bandit*, like the other works in the series, upends expectations about the geography and targets of lynching: Its location is the American West, not the Deep South, and its victims are Mexican, not African American.

The missing bodies in these photographs serve as a metaphor for the expunging of Latinos, Native Americans, and Asians from the history of lynching in America. There are various reasons for this historical erasure, Mr. Gonzales-Day says in *Lynching in the West: 1850–1935*, a scholarly study in which he documents and analyzes the 352 recorded lynchings and summary executions of victims of all races in California.

For one, the anti-lynching movement that reached its height in the United States from

Chapter 3

Ken Gonzales-Day, *East First Street (St. James Park), Lynching of Thomas Thurmond and John Holmes, San Jose, California, 1933*; from *Erased Lynching Series I*, 2006

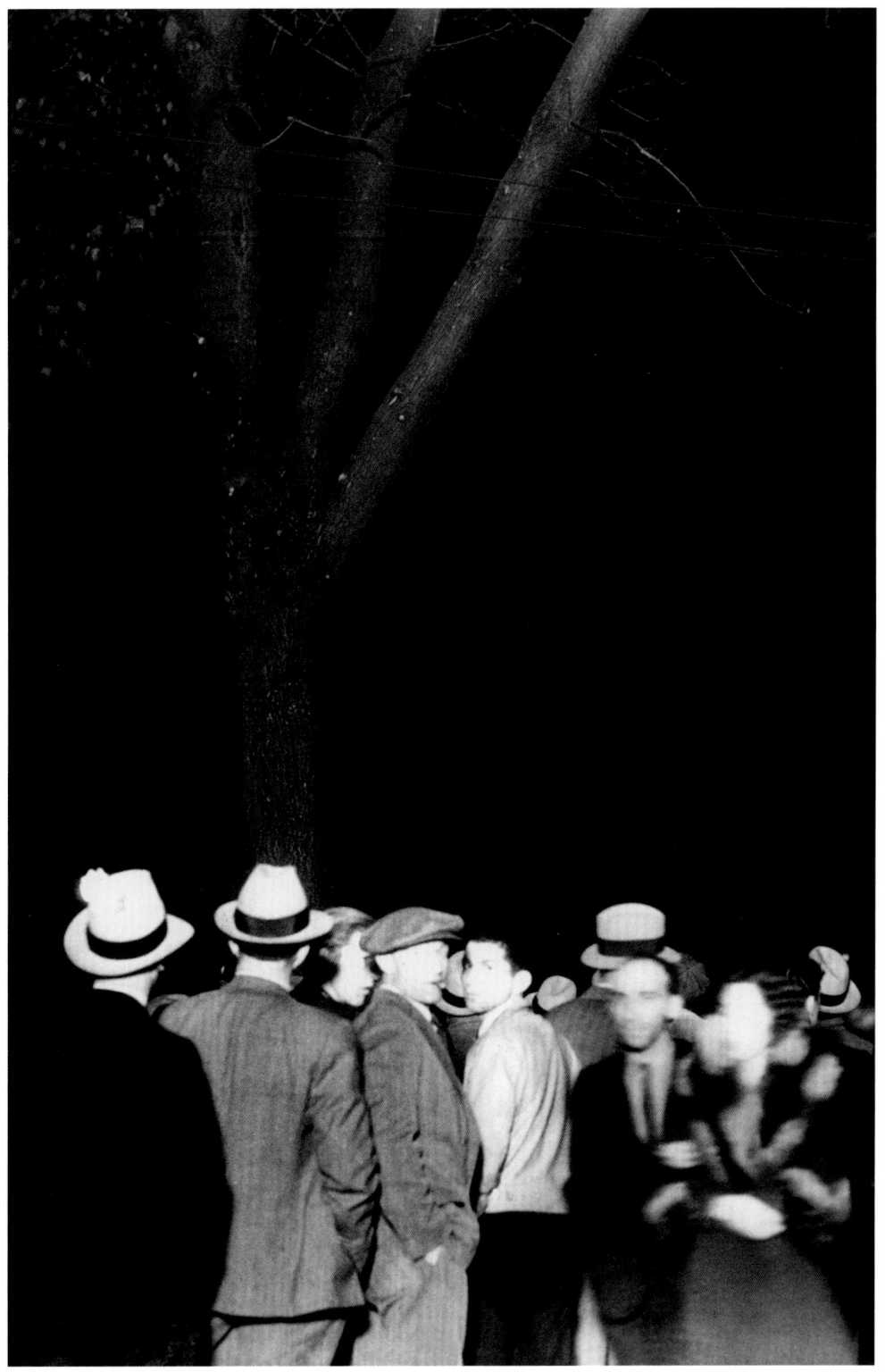

History and Memory                                185

the 1890s to the 1930s tended to focus on the widespread murder of Black Americans in the context of the Civil War, Reconstruction, and its aftermath, a history that preoccupied the entire nation rather than the more regional concerns of race relations in the West.

While lynchings of African Americans in the South and elsewhere were often defined by scholars and within popular culture as illegal acts of vigilantism and murder, the killing of Latinos, Native Americans, and Asians in the West was often romanticized and idealized. In countless history books, novels, comics, television programs, and motion pictures, these murders qualified as examples of frontier justice, a supposedly necessary means of maintaining order during the tumultuous western expansion into uncharted territories.

As Mr. Gonzales-Day's research revealed, however, vigilante hangings in California, like those in the Jim Crow South, had a powerful racial dimension: Native Americans, African Americans, Chinese immigrants, and Latinos fell victim to the mob's anger far more often than people of European descent.

The artist's intention is not to diminish the story of African American lynching, but to correct the historical record and broaden our understanding. Mr. Gonzales-Day, forty-eight, a widely exhibited artist, photographer, and researcher who teaches at Scripps

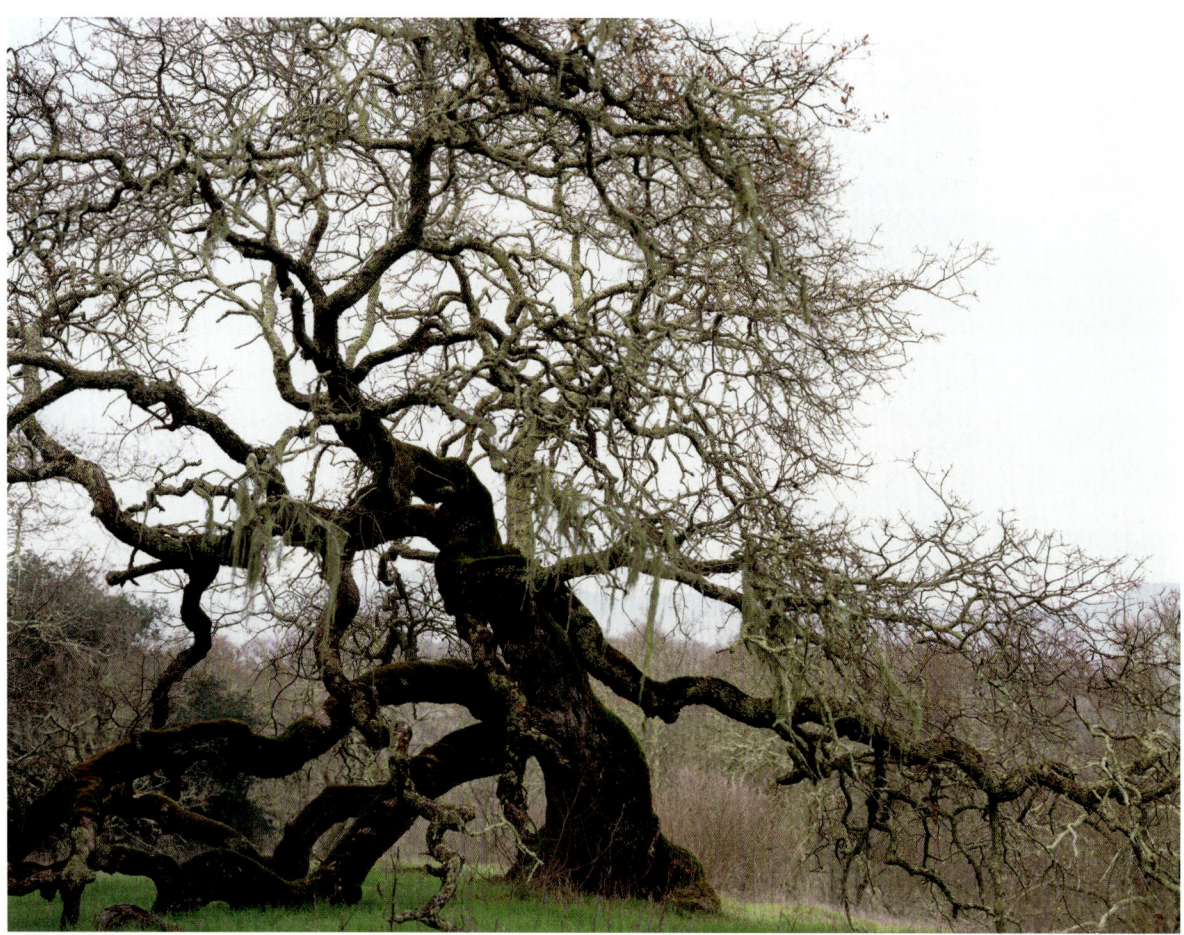

Ken Gonzales-Day, *Run Up*, 2002

Chapter 3

College, is committed to narrowing the psychic distance between the viewer and the photographs of violence and death.

As the Belgian critic and curator Thierry de Duve observes, pictures of atrocities, shocking and disquieting as they may be, result in a "vanishing of the present tense." Distilling a complex, morally troubling event into an instant, they suspend viewers in a limbo in which they are inevitably "too early to witness the uncoiling of the tragedy" and "too late, in real life," to do anything to prevent it. For Mr. de Duve, this renders pictures of bloodshed particularly disconcerting— almost unbearably—by intensifying our sense of helplessness before history.

Mr. Gonzales-Day slows down the viewing process by introducing a degree of interactivity into the experience of his work. His obliteration of the brutalized corpse shifts the focus of his imagery from the victim to the perpetrator, and summons us to complete the picture in our imagination. His photographs are routinely exhibited with brief explanatory texts about their history and absences.

As if to underscore this idea, Mr. Gonzales-Day has also produced a self-guided walking tour of lynching sites in downtown Los Angeles that allows participants "to revisit places and events made infamous" in the context of their present-day lives. The tour is an extension of the artist's own six-year pilgrimage to nearly every county in California, culminating in another series, *Searching for California's Hang Trees*, which features large-scale color photographs and billboards of lynching sites, particularly the trees that possibly served as hanging posts.

"I retraced the steps of the lynch mob and vigilance committee," he writes of his expedition. "Standing at these sites, even the most beautiful landscape is undone . . .

I have documented the empty space that lies between the historically unseen body of the lynch victim with my own unseen body."

This walking tour, along with the missing bodies of *Erased Lynching* and *Hang Trees* reminds us, too, of the power of time to erase history, in part because it is our instinct to forget the events that expose our intolerance, indifference, or depravity. But it also urges us to put our own history into a story that few of us know. More than anything, it makes us think where our ancestors—or our own bodies —might belong: as a victim dangling above or a perpetrator grinning below.

# Fifty Years after Their Mug Shots, Portraits of Mississippi's Freedom Riders

Published May 15, 2018

For seven months in 1961, hundreds of Black and white volunteers descended on Southern bus and train stations. These Freedom Riders, as they were called, occupied segregated waiting areas, lunch counters, and restrooms in an attempt to compel the federal government to do what local authorities would not: enforce a US Supreme Court ruling that declared discrimination in interstate public transportation illegal.

During their first incursion into the Deep South, as they rode buses through Alabama, the Freedom Riders were met by angry mobs of white people. Many were savagely beaten. Later that month, in Jackson, Mississippi, hundreds of protesters were arrested and hastily convicted of breach of peace. Most endured six weeks of imprisonment in sweltering, filthy, and vermin-infested cells.

Among the important artifacts of this historic campaign are more than three hundred mug shots taken of the Freedom Riders in Jackson, now the subject of *Breach of Peace: Portraits of the 1961 Mississippi Freedom Riders*. In it, the journalist and photographer Eric Etheridge provides visual and oral histories of these courageous men and women, juxtaposing vintage mug shots with short biographies, interviews, and contemporary portraits. Originally published in 2008, this expanded edition, with updated profiles and additional portraits, includes essays by the writer Diane McWhorter and Roger Wilkins, the journalist and official in the Kennedy and Johnson administrations who died last year.

Mr. Etheridge, who grew up in Mississippi, first saw the mug shots after the state's department of archives and history published them online. "I was captivated by these images and wanted to bring them to a wider audience," he recalled. "I wanted to find the Riders today, to look into their faces, to make new portraits to set against the earlier photographs." Since he began working on the project in 2005, Mr. Etheridge has tracked down nearly a hundred Riders, visiting them in their homes, conducting interviews and making new portraits.

If these mug shots inadvertently captured the humanity and special qualities of their principled subjects, as Mr. Etheridge observed, their intention was nefarious: to publicly impugn and humiliate people whose only crime was to advocate equality through peaceful protest. No matter their purpose, mug shots inevitably imply aberrance or delinquency, whether or not the people they depict are eventually found to be guilty. With this in mind, the current mayor of Jackson, Chokwe Antar Lumumba, issued an executive order in February prohibiting their release in cases involving people killed by the police.

"Mug shots and sensationalized news narratives create lasting impressions that adversely impact communities and widen the historical divides between police and community," stated Mr. Lumumba's directive. "A mug shot is just one snapshot in time, and cannot be presumed to represent the sum total of any individual's existence."

By pairing mug shots with contemporary portraits—and providing stories about individual Freedom Riders—Mr. Etheridge undoes some of the psychic and social damage perpetrated by these symbols of police malfeasance. *Breach of Peace* corrects the historical record, representing its subjects not as dehumanized icons of criminality but as exemplary citizens and complex human beings.

The Freedom Riders were a diverse group. Largely college students at the time, they came from thirty-nine states, were of different races and economic classes, and went on to varied careers: Hank Thomas, then a sophomore at Howard University, now owns fast food and hotel franchises; Peter Stoner, who studied at the University of Chicago, earned a PhD in chemistry and later worked as an auto mechanic; Margaret Leonard, who attended Newcomb College, became a journalist; Hezekiah Watkins, who was a ninth-grade student in Jackson, ran a small grocery store; and Helen O'Neal McCray, a sophomore at Jackson State University, taught elementary school and later writing and literature at Wilberforce University, a historically Black institution in Ohio.

The diversity of the Freedom Riders affirms the importance of allies in the struggle for racial equality and justice, acknowledging that the support of some in the white majority was necessary to achieve legal and political rights. In the early 1960s, these demonstrators motivated and inspired Americans of all races. "The courage and tenacity of the Riders electrified large segments of the American public and drew them into the midcentury civil rights movement as no activity had done before," Mr. Wilkins wrote. "People began asking themselves: 'What can I do?'"

The solidarity of these activists stands in contrast to the complacency and social and cultural divisions that impede progress today. The period between the initial publication of *Breach of Peace* in 2008 and its reissue in 2018 attests to the volatile and continually shifting fortunes of the struggle for racial equality and justice. A decade ago, the nation made history as a coalition of voters of all colors elected the nation's first Black president. Today, an administration routinely exploits racial anxiety and resentment.

There is much to learn from the unity, courage, and passion of the Freedom Riders, whose efforts resulted in federal regulations prohibiting segregation in interstate transit terminals. During the fiftieth anniversary of their demonstrations, many came forward to tell their stories, work that continues to the present day.

"They did not waste their golden anniversary press," Mr. Etheridge wrote. "The good news is that since 2011 the Riders have become much more frequent speakers in classrooms, libraries, and auditoriums across the country. Once more they are putting their bodies on the road, this time to share their histories, to tell how they resisted, to spread the practice of 'good trouble,' as John Lewis calls it . . . The good news is that the Freedom Riders are still overreaching."

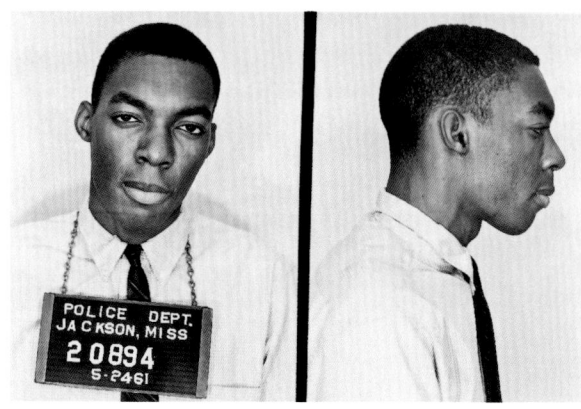

Hank Thomas, from St. Augustine, Florida, at age nineteen, 1961

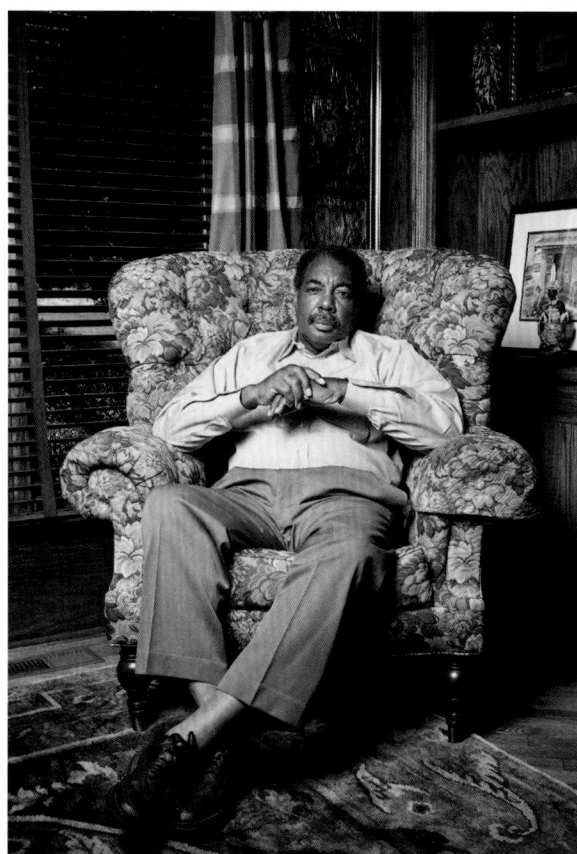

Eric Etheridge, Hank Thomas at age sixty-five. A sophomore at Howard University and one of the original thirteen Freedom Riders who left Washington, DC, on May 4. He later became a field secretary for CORE, and served as an Army medic in Vietnam. He moved to Atlanta after serving in the Army and went into the franchise business, 2007

Chapter 3

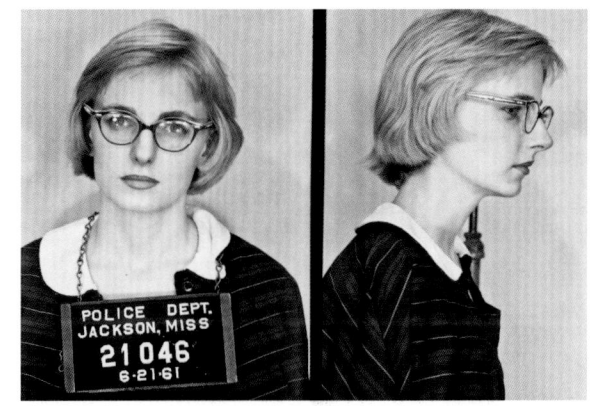

Margaret Leonard, from Atlanta, at age nineteen, 1961

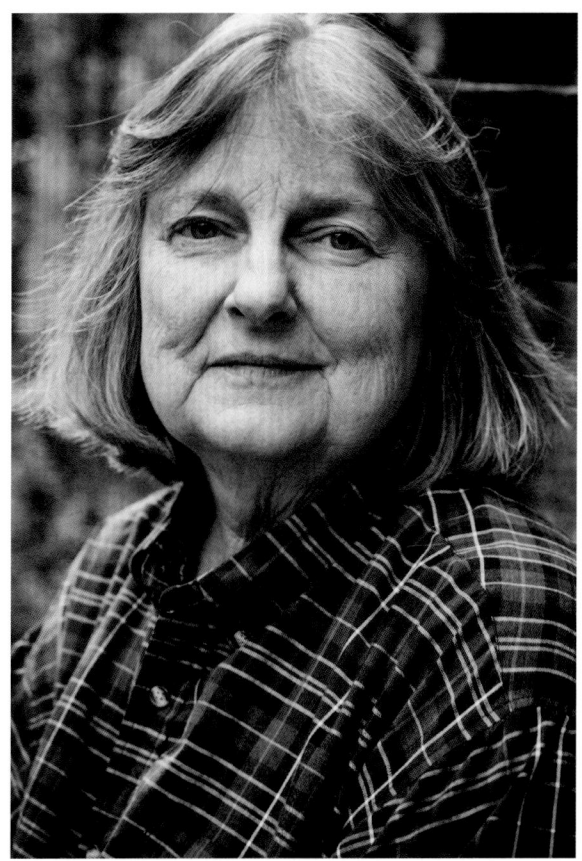

Eric Etheridge, Margaret Leonard at age sixty-five in 2007.
A sophomore at Sophie Newcomb College in New Orleans,
where she participated in CORE demonstrations. She later
became a newspaper reporter and editor. Leonard died
in 2022.

# Lee Friedlander's Overlooked Civil Rights Photos

Published February 22, 2016

The photographs in Lee Friedlander's book *Prayer Pilgrimage for Freedom* are of a subject not usually associated with him: the civil rights movement. Among his earliest and least typical images—the photographer was only twenty-two when he made them—they document a historic, if lesser known, event in the struggle for racial equality and justice.

On May 17, 1957, nearly 25,000 demonstrators gathered at the steps of the Lincoln Memorial in Washington to commemorate the third anniversary of *Brown v. Board of Education*, the landmark United States Supreme Court ruling that struck down state laws establishing separate public schools for Black and white students.

Organized by the civil right activists A. Philip Randolph and Bayard Rustin and others, the nonviolent Prayer Pilgrimage for Freedom endeavored not only to celebrate the gains made in light of that decision, but also to publicize the failure of many Southern states to follow through on the court-ordered desegregation of public schools, among other antidiscrimination practices. The three-hour event featured speeches, prayers, songs, and the recitation of scripture by such prominent Americans as the gospel singer Mahalia Jackson, the activist Roy Wilkins, the educator and pastor Mordecai Wyatt Johnson, and the Reverend Dr. Martin Luther King Jr.

"As the Founding Americans prayed for strength and wisdom in the wilderness of a new land, as the slaves and their descendants prayed for emancipation and human dignity, as men of every color and clime in time of crisis have sought Divine guidance," wrote Mr. Randolph, Dr. King, and Mr. Wilkins in their call for a pilgrimage, "so now in these troubled and momentous years, call upon all who love justice, and dignity, liberty . . . to join in a Prayer Pilgrimage to Washington . . . where

Chapter 3

we shall renew our strength, communicate our unity, and rededicate our efforts, firmly but peaceably, to the attainment of freedom."

Although the gathering failed to reach its goal of 50,000 attendees, it was the largest organized demonstration for civil rights up to that time. Although modest in comparison with the 1963 March on Washington, which attracted about 250,000 people, it would prove to be historically significant, laying the groundwork for future demonstrations. Significantly, it was also where Dr. King delivered his "Give Us the Ballot" speech, in which he implored the president and members of Congress to ensure voting rights for African Americans, a speech that helped establish him as the preeminent leader of the civil rights movement.

Mr. Friedlander's book, which includes facsimiles of the pilgrimage's call, its program, and the typed manuscript of Dr. King's speech, documents its subject in ways both dynamic and unusual. Mr. Friedlander's layout, rather than a traditional and straightforward juxtaposition of discrete photographs and texts, animates the photobook. Its images appear to blend together into the typographical equivalent of a cinematic long take—a seemingly unbroken stream of frames revealing its unfolding events, circumstances, and actions.

As the eye glides across Mr. Friedlander's syncopated photographs, it observes not only the totality and grandeur of the demonstration, but also the individual participants as well as their shared actions and unified

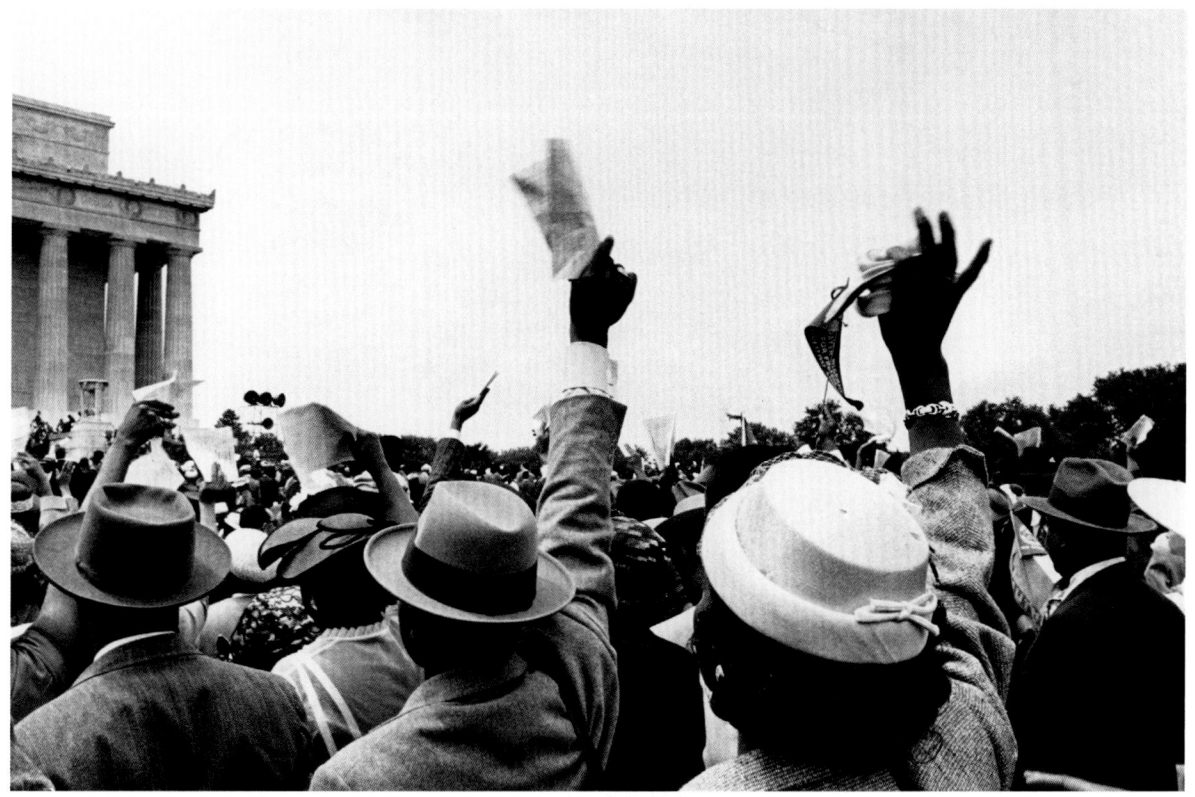

Lee Friedlander, Demonstrators gathered at the steps of the Lincoln Memorial to commemorate the third anniversary of *Brown v. Board of Education*, the landmark Supreme Court ruling that struck down state laws establishing separate public schools for Black and white students, Washington, DC, May 17, 1957

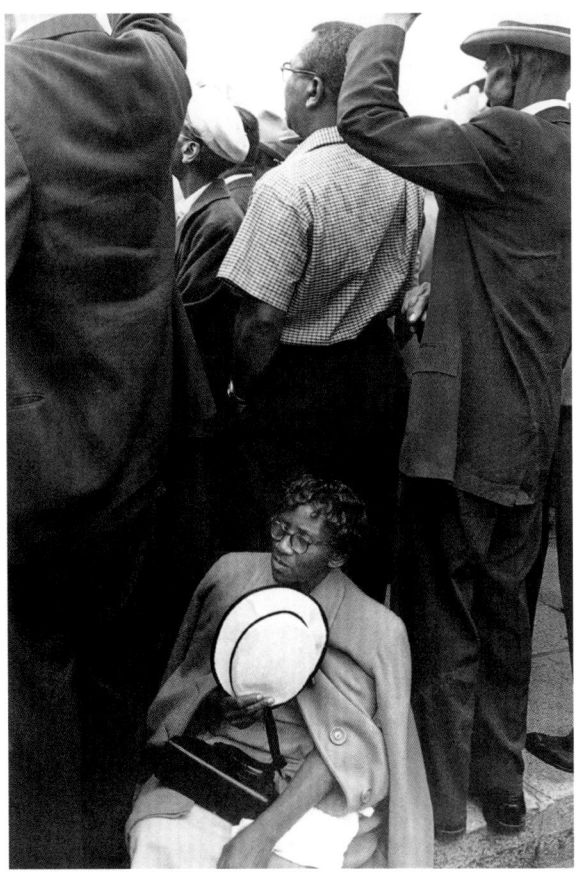

Lee Friedlander, An attendee taking a rest during the three-hour event, Washington, DC, May 17, 1957

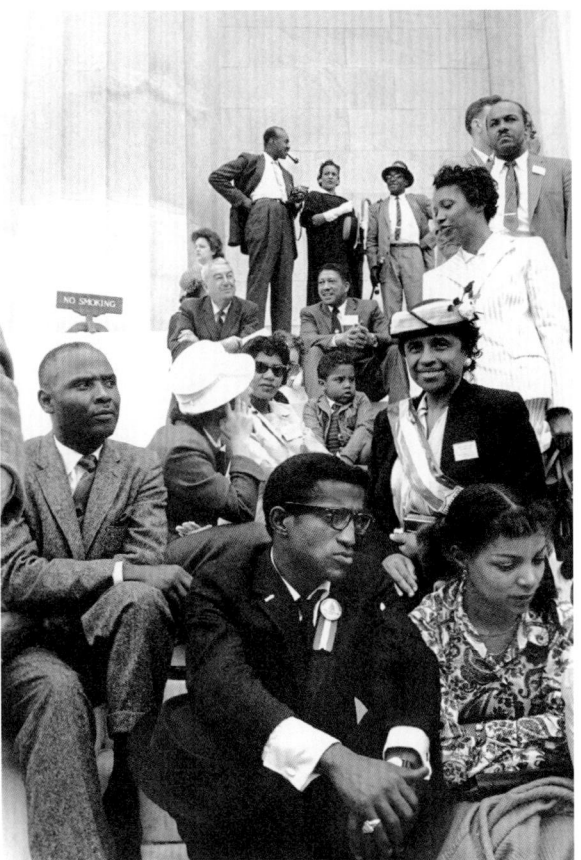

Lee Friedlander, The singer and entertainer Sammy Davis Jr., front center, with the actress Ruby Dee on the steps of the Lincoln Memorial, Washington, DC, May 17, 1957

activities: masses of people, sitting on folding chairs, standing or marching, their faces a study in solemnity and determination; the elegantly dressed father who hugs his young son protectively as they listen to a speech; groups of demonstrators huddled in conversation; a woman, exhausted after hours of demonstrating, reclining on the grass; thousands of hands raised in solidarity; Mr. Johnson, at the podium, delivering a fiery speech; and the unassuming presence of famous entertainers and activists, including the Reverend Ralph Abernathy, Harry Belafonte, Sammy Davis Jr., Ruby Dee, and Rosa Parks.

Despite the fame of some demonstrators, the mood of the event—and its representation by Mr. Friedlander—was egalitarian. Thus, the power of these images resides not only in their sweeping cinematic quality, but also in their ability to capture the intimacy, dignity, and individuality of their subjects without minimizing the magnitude of a significant historical event. And like all effective long shots, whether literal or, in this case, suggested, the totality of the big picture invariably gives way to its telling details.

Mr. Friedlander's attention to detail underscores one of the central objectives of the pilgrimage: to highlight the individual humanity of its participants and their endurance, voice, and visibility in an unjust society.

"In the words of Abraham Lincoln," the call for the pilgrimage reads, "this is a nation 'conceived in liberty and dedicated to the proposition that all men are created equal.' We believe its people treasure the heritage of equality before the law. They uphold this principle because they know that every man, whatever his race, religion or station, must be free if our nation is to remain strong."

Ultimately, rather than seeming anachronistic, the photographs of the *Prayer Pilgrimage for Freedom* prefigure the psychological depth, humanity, visual sophistication, and critical distance that later came to characterize Mr. Friedlander's better-known street photographs, urban landscapes, and portraits. As he famously said of his process: "It fascinates me that there is a variety of feeling about what I do. I'm not a premeditative photographer. I see a picture and I make it. If I had a chance, I'd be out shooting all the time. You don't have to go looking for pictures. The material is generous. You go out and the pictures are staring at you."

The lesson to be learned from *Prayer Pilgrimage for Freedom* is that in the process of photographing and being photographed, generosity can go both ways. By this standard, Mr. Friedlander's prodigious and graceful images are eminently generous to their subjects, representing them in their full humanity and self-possession, in a world too often committed to their silence and invisibility.

# Escaping to Freedom, in the Shadows of the Night

Published June 5, 2018

In his poem "Dream Variations," published in 1926, Langston Hughes yearned for a time when the African American worker, exhausted by the daily grind of hard labor and discrimination, might be truly free. This liberation, he imagined, would be achieved not in the glare of daylight, but rather under the brooding, protective cover of night. Inverting a dominant literary conceit, Blackness and not whiteness functioned as a metaphor for hope and transcendence—a "Night coming tenderly / Black like me," as Mr. Hughes wrote, that abetted the struggle for racial equality and justice.

This metaphor is central to a new series by the photographer Dawoud Bey, *Night Coming Tenderly, Black*, which draws on Mr. Hughes's lyrical poem. The project, Mr. Bey's contribution to the *Front International: Cleveland Triennial for Contemporary Art* (July 14 to September 30), is site-specific.

Installed in St. John's Episcopal Church, a stop on the Underground Railroad known as Station Hope, it summons a time in African American history when the journey to freedom was made largely through the shadows of the night.

Today, little visual evidence remains of the Underground Railroad, an antebellum network of secret routes and safe houses, maintained by brave Black and white "conductors," which facilitated the escape of the enslaved to free states and Canada. For Mr. Bey, whose work has often focused on urban environments, the challenge was to create images that evoke the history of largely rural areas. While he photographed sites in Cleveland, he sometimes found the city's urban character inconsistent with the historical past. His research led him to the more rustic town of Hudson, Ohio, thirty miles southeast of the city, with areas of landscape

Chapter 3

Dawoud Bey, *Untitled #1 (Picket Fence and Farmhouse)*, 2017

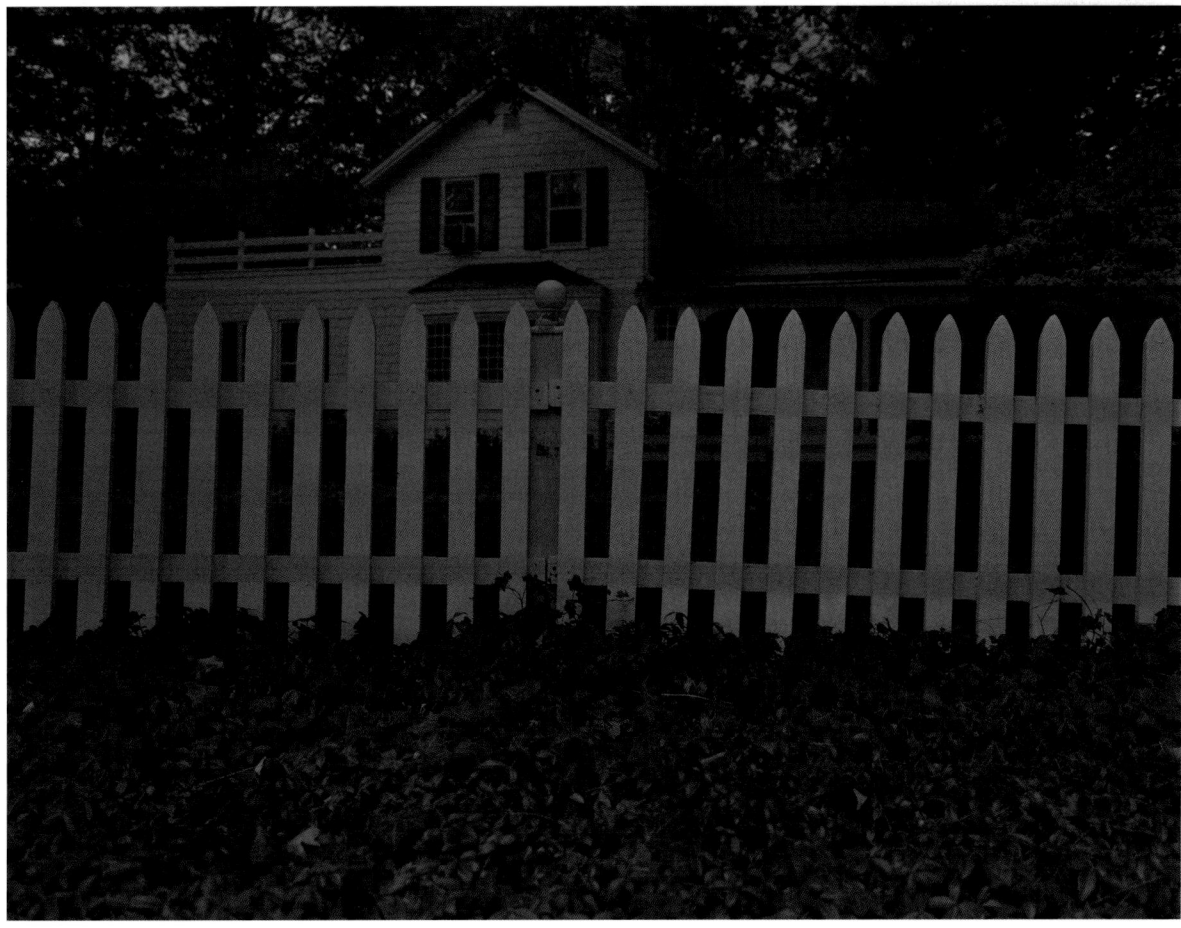

that are little changed from the years before the Civil War and where several Underground Railroad stations remain.

"I wanted the photographs to almost involuntarily pull you back to the experience of the landscape through which those fugitive Black bodies were moving in the nineteenth century to escape slavery," Mr. Bey said. "So I had to learn, for the first time, how to make photographs in that kind of space."

The photographs of *Night Coming Tenderly, Black* are among Mr. Bey's most sensual and layered. In their splendor and mystery, they transform fields, bodies of water, and houses shrouded in darkness into symbols of hope: a pristine picket fence and

farmhouse seen through the haze of night; a marsh glistening in twilight; a forest thick with small trees, a scene that is at first claustrophobic then liberating when understood through the lens of history; and an image of Lake Erie, its expansive sky and horizon foreshadowing the independence that lies beyond.

The project continues Mr. Bey's exploration of history and its relationship and relevance to the present. In 2013, *The Birmingham Project* examined the implications, then and now, of the bombing of the Sixteenth Street Baptist Church by white supremacists in Birmingham, Alabama, on September 15, 1963, which killed four African

American girls and whose aftermath resulted in the deaths of two young men. *Harlem Redux*, which the artist completed in 2016, took a nuanced look at the erasure of history and community through the rampant gentrification of a neighborhood long synonymous with Black culture in the United States.

Mr. Bey was at first skeptical when the artistic director of the Front International, Michelle Grabner, suggested that he consider installing *Night Coming Tenderly, Black* in St. John's Episcopal Church. "I'm a white box artist who makes works about nonwhite box things," he recalled saying to her at the time. He had come to see exhibitions of his photographs as enlivening, engaging, and challenging traditional art institutions through imagery typically overlooked by them.

But the historical significance of the site led to a change of heart. "St. John's was the final Underground Railroad station that fugitive slaves who had made their way to Cleveland would take refuge before making their way to Lake Erie and then on to freedom in Canada," Mr. Bey said. "To have the work shown in a space that had once been inhabited by fugitive slaves was deeply meaningful."

Mr. Bey, who was named a MacArthur fellow last year, credits another important influence for *Night Coming Tenderly, Black*: Roy DeCarava. Mr. DeCarava, who died in 2009 at eighty-nine, was one of the most influential photographers of his generation. His images, visually rich and evocative, pushed the aesthetic boundaries of photography. A founder of the Kamoinge Workshop, a collective formed in Harlem in 1963 to support the work of African American artists ignored by mainstream institutions and media, Mr. DeCarava often focused on Black subjects in his work.

Mr. Bey noted that Mr. DeCarava's photographs were typically printed in a dark and rich tonal range. In this context, the photographic print served as a metaphor for the Black subject and experience. "DeCarava used Blackness as an affirmative value, as a kind of beautiful Blackness through which his subjects both moved and emerged," Mr. Bey said. "His work was formative to my own thinking early on, and these dark landscapes are a kind of material conversation with his work, using the darkness of the landscape, and the photographic print as an evocative space of Blackness through which the unseen and imaginary Black fugitive subject is moving."

Ultimately, *Night Coming Tenderly, Black* envisions a historic struggle for freedom not in stark black and white or vivid color but in luminous shades of gray. Like the work of Mr. Hughes and Mr. DeCarava, Mr. Bey's images refuse to represent the darkness of night as a space of intimidation.

"It is a tender one, through which one moves," he observes. "That is the space I imagined the fugitive Black subjects moving through as they sought their own self-liberation, moving through the dark landscape of America and Ohio toward freedom under cover of a munificent and blessed Blackness."

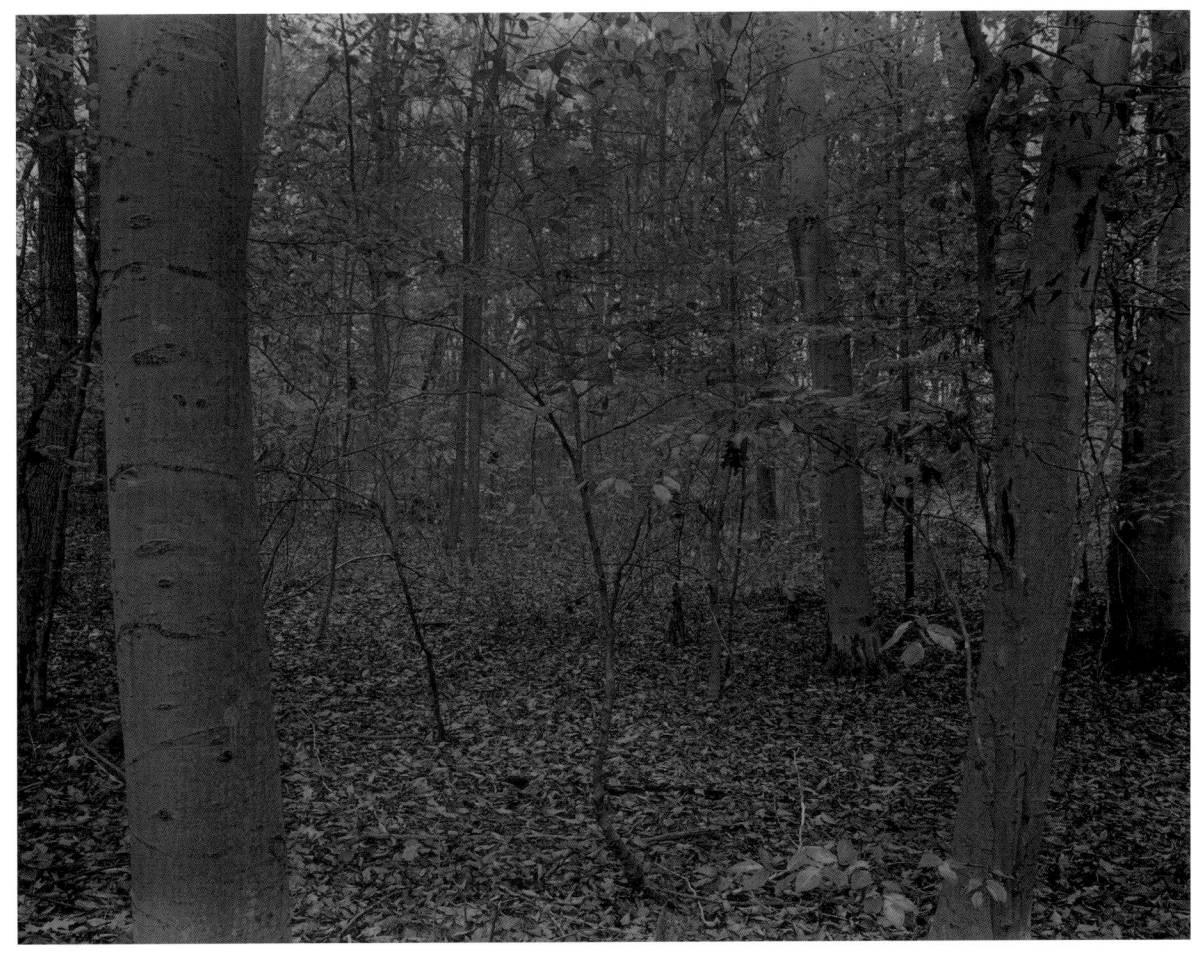

Dawoud Bey, *Untitled #15 (Forest with Small Trees)*, 2017

History and Memory

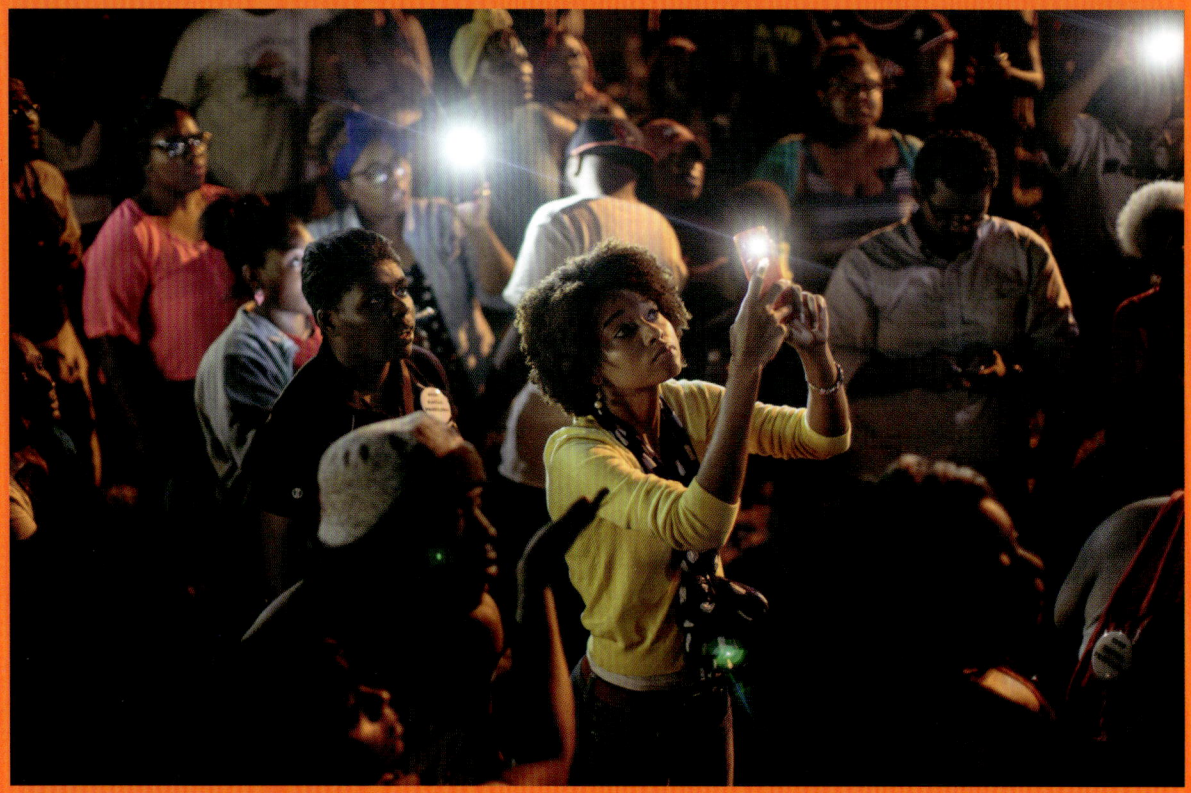

Whitney Curtis, Members of the community gather in Dellwood, Missouri, to protest the fatal police shooting of Michael Brown. The unarmed eighteen-year-old was killed on August 9, 2014.

Witnessing:
Images as Catalysts
for Change

# CHAPTER FOUR

# Meditation on President Obama's Portrait

Published July 25, 2014

Dawoud Bey's photograph of the man who would soon be president was taken on a Sunday afternoon in early 2007, at Barack and Michelle Obama's Hyde Park home in Chicago. The portrait is at once stately and informal. Mr. Obama's hands are folded gracefully in his lap. He wears an elegant suit and white shirt, but no tie. He stares intensely into the camera.

The Museum of Contemporary Photography had commissioned Mr. Bey the year before to take a portrait of a notable Chicagoan. He had known the Obamas for several years and saw them periodically at social gatherings. Impressed with Mr. Obama's keynote speech at the 2004 Democratic convention, Mr. Bey sensed a "growing air of expectancy" about him. "When I was asked who I wanted to photograph," Mr. Bey said, "it took me but a second to decide that I wanted to photograph him."

Mr. Bey posed Mr. Obama at the head of the dining room table, light reflecting off its polished surface, and photographed him from an angle. "I wanted an interesting animation of the body, and finally through camera positioning and having him turn himself slightly I figured it out," Mr. Bey said.

The photographer and his subject were comfortable with each other. Mr. Bey recalls that he asked Mr. Obama, who intended to be photographed in shirt sleeves, to put on a jacket. "I told him that I didn't want the portrait to be that informal, and he was fine with that," Mr. Bey said. The portrait, which was featured in the Whitney Biennial this spring, reminds us how much has changed in the intervening seven years. Looking back, we grasp the physical toll the weight of presidential responsibility has taken on Mr. Obama. His hair is considerably darker and his expression more serene than in photographs of him today.

"It's an unguarded intimate moment that Barack's becoming president made less possible," Mr. Bey said. "Certainly the ease with which the photograph was made, the lack of security, hanging out in the kitchen afterwards, all of that changed."

The photograph depicts its famously private and introspective subject only months before he was to step into the abyss of presidential politics. And it defines him free of the stereotypes and myths that have come to characterize his presidency.

Idolized by supporters and attacked by enemies, presidents to a great extent lose control of their public image. They inevitably become the one-dimensional clichés that underwrite popular conceptions of them: John F. Kennedy as the tragic hero of an unattainable Camelot, for example, or Richard Nixon as the faithless "Tricky Dick."

Mr. Obama's race has rendered him particularly vulnerable to this kind of mythmaking. Right-wing extremists see him as an exemplar of what is wrong with America. He has become a symbol of a dark and foreign otherness, a threat to white supremacy and racial purity. To some, he is a Muslim conspirator, bent on dismantling American mores and traditions. To others, he is an angry Black man covertly intent on avenging slavery and other historic injustices.

This mythmaking has not been limited to conservatives. A year after Mr. Bey photographed Mr. Obama, the candidate was rousing messianic fantasies on the left, stoked by the election's most memorable image: Shepard Fairey's "Hope" poster.

Distributed independently by the artist and later adopted by the Obama campaign, the poster was visually dynamic and politically effective. It radiated an aura of confidence and optimism. But Mr. Fairey's schematic rendering of Mr. Obama—branded by a single, amorphous word—reduced the candidate to a cartoonlike, racially ambiguous cipher.

Raking across Mr. Obama's face, in a picture devoid of the color brown, was a broad swath of off-white paint, a metaphoric blank screen onto which voters were invited to project their dreams and aspirations. The "Hope" poster visually transformed a man who unambiguously defined himself as Black into an icon of the unthreatening "post-racial" politician.

The poster foreshadowed the myriad ways the image of this president would be appropriated, for better or worse, for political effect. In hindsight, Mr. Bey's nuanced portrait—intimate and complex—provides a corrective to history. Rejecting political clichés and symbols, the artist reveals a dimension of Mr. Obama rarely evident in his politically charged public image: his humanity.

"The portrait conveys a degree of complexity, a sense of engagement, comfort, and a hint of weariness," Mr. Bey observes in retrospect. "It breathes with the sense of a real person being described. That's always what I hope to come away with: not merely the visualization of Barack Obama, but a momentary sense that a full and dimensional person is being described and looking back at you."

Chapter 4

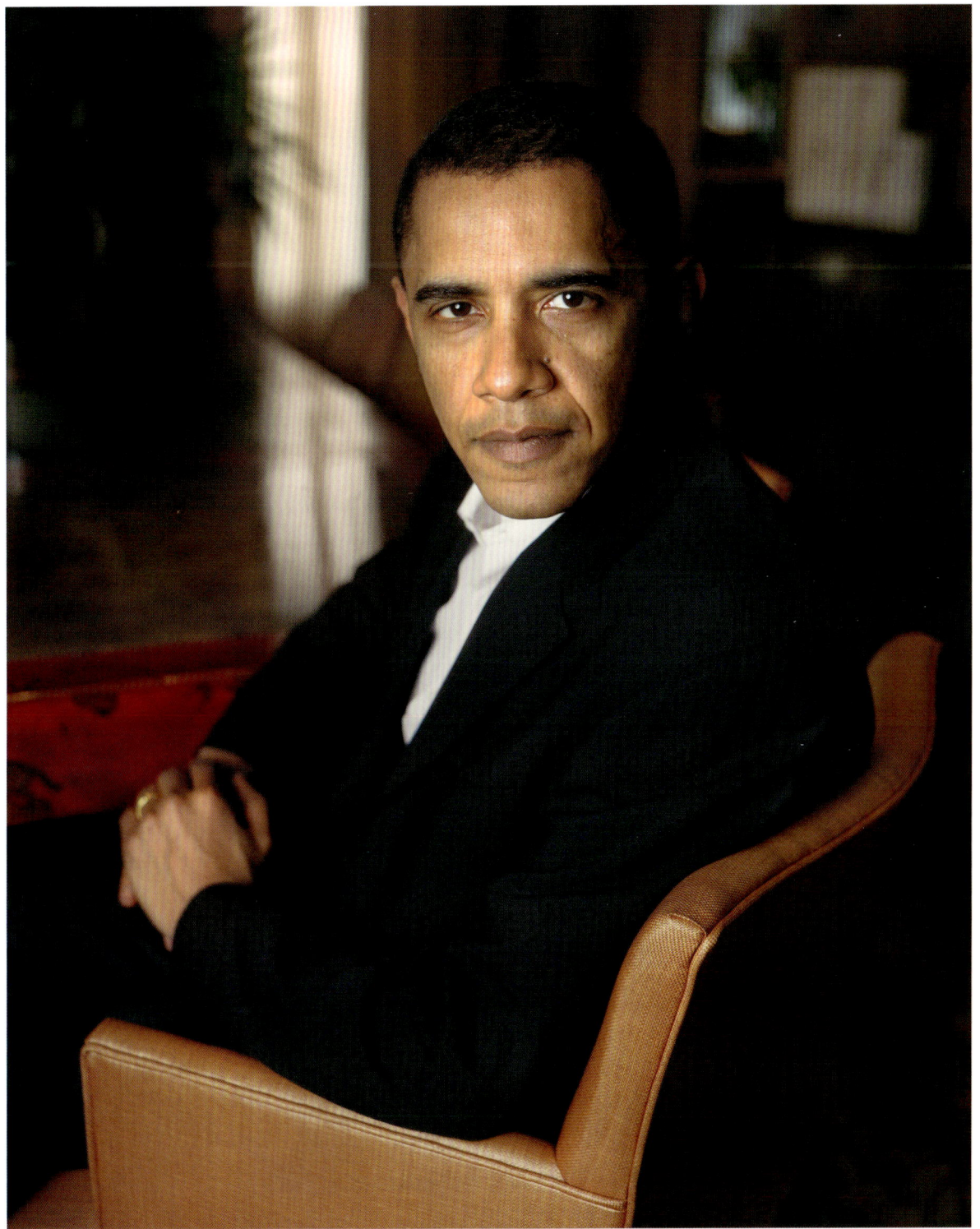

Dawoud Bey, *Barack Obama*, 2007

# A Meditation on Race, in Shades of White

Published September 17, 2015

The photograph of a round-faced white Southerner appears almost ordinary, except for a few unusual details: He wears a scruffy hairpiece, and his nails are painted. The man, publisher of the county newspaper, represented his community in the Georgia Legislature.

He was also a card-carrying member of the Ku Klux Klan.

The portrait reminds us that white supremacy comes in many forms. Taken in 1949 by the photographer Marion Palfi, the image appears in her consequential but relatively unknown photobook, *There Is No More Time: An American Tragedy*. Its unpublished manuscript resides in the Center for Creative Photography in Tucson, the largest repository of Ms. Palfi's material.

Ms. Palfi set out to document racism and segregation in Irwinton, Georgia, the small town where Caleb Hill Jr., in the first reported lynching of 1949, was murdered.

Later that year, Ms. Palfi spent two weeks in Irwinton documenting its residents, both Black and white.

Juxtaposing portraits, Ms. Palfi's written observations, and interview excerpts, *There Is No More Time* chronicles the many faces and viewpoints of white supremacy in Irwinton: the obedience to God and family; the religious and pseudoscientific justifications for believing that Black people were inherently inferior; the resentment of outside intervention in the South's racial affairs; and the determination to protect the legal authority of white people.

The book also demonstrates that white racial attitudes were neither uniform nor without ambivalence. Some qualified their prejudices by also voicing disdain for poor whites. Others unconsciously revealed the

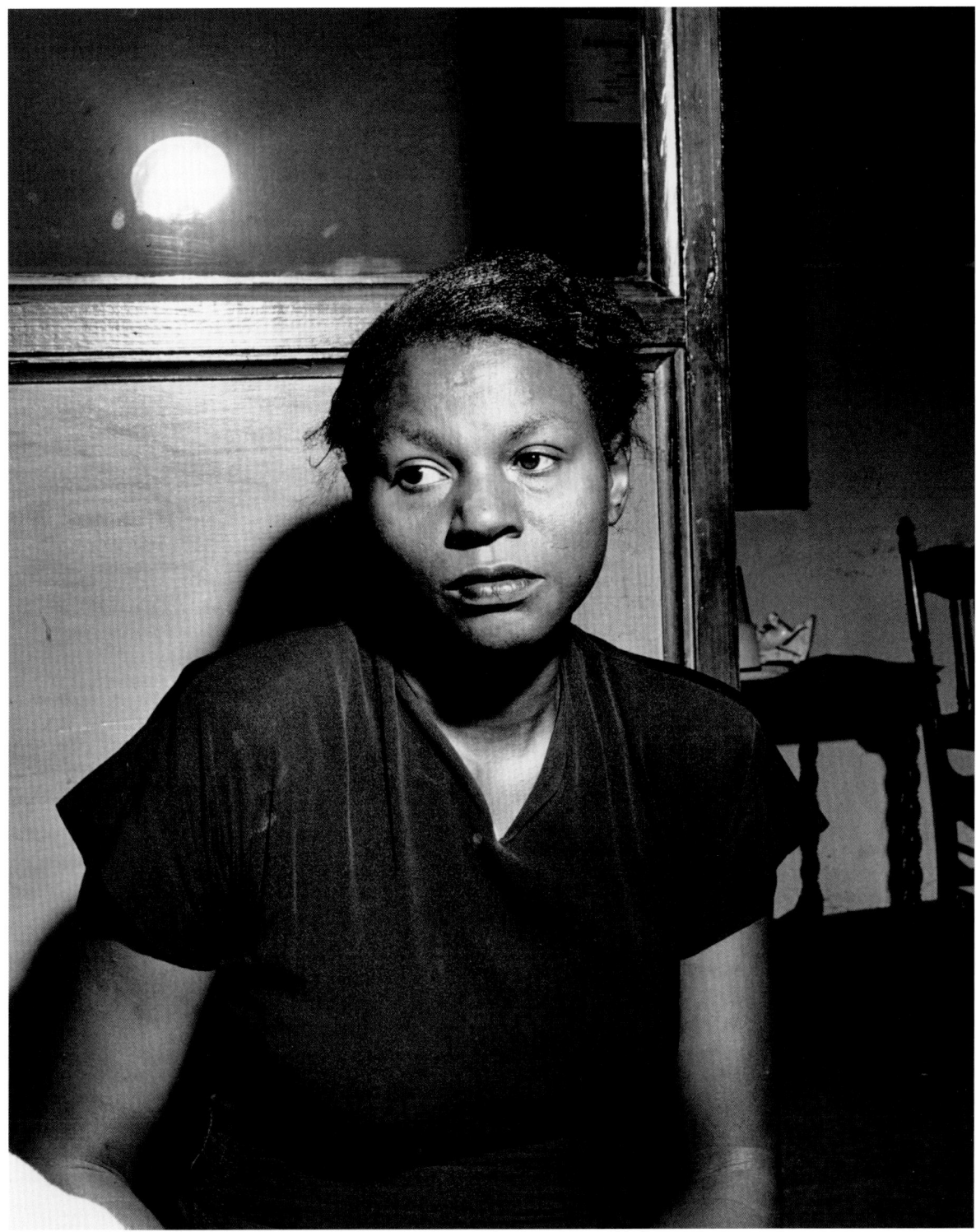

Marion Palfi, *Wife of a Lynch Victim, Irwinton, Georgia*, 1949

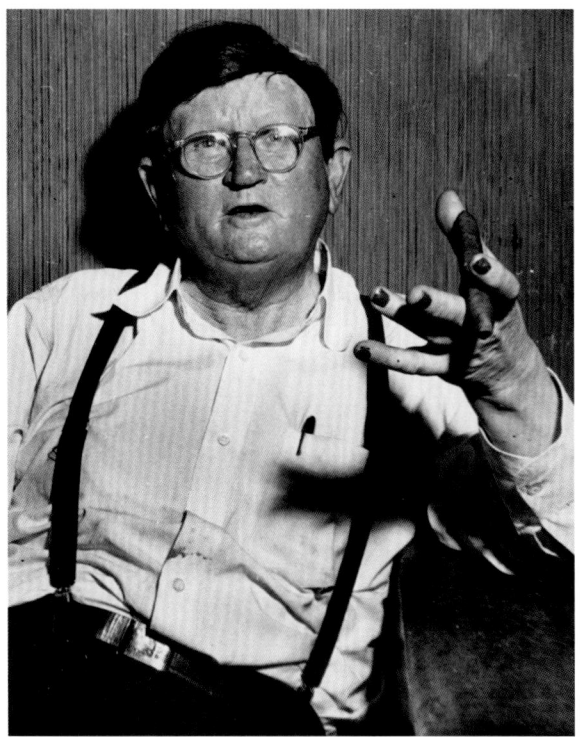

Marion Palfi, *Alexander S. Boone, Irwinton, Georgia*, 1949

insecurity and self-doubt that fueled their bitterness and, by extension, bigotry. Some discreetly criticized the biases of their neighbors, while others attacked them as traitors for doing so.

The town's African American residents appear in the book less frequently but to great dramatic effect. Their images make clear the tragic consequences of racial prejudice, their lives compromised and shattered in innumerable ways. This was no more evident than in the haunting portrait of Mr. Hill's widow or in the text of an anonymous letter from Black prisoners, unceasingly abused and dehumanized by their white jailers.

Born into an aristocratic family in Berlin in 1907, Ms. Palfi began her career as an actress and model. Distressed by Germany's increasingly reactionary politics, she turned to photography as a form of personal expression and activism. In 1935, she opened a

photo studio in Amsterdam. Five years later, having married an American serviceman, she immigrated to New York.

A member of the activist Photo League, Ms. Palfi believed that photographs, beyond merely representing problems, could influence social change. "A Palfi photograph brings us face to face with hidden realities that its surface only causes us to begin to explore," wrote the American poet Langston Hughes, a friend and admirer of her work. Ms. Palfi produced photo-essays on a range of pressing social issues, including child abuse and delinquency, the neglect of seniors, Native American displacement, prison inmate rights, and the ways poverty, segregation, and racism imperiled democracy. She died in 1978.

The backstory of *There Is No More Time* reveals much about Ms. Palfi's sophisticated and prescient understanding of American race relations. The manuscript met with considerable resistance from publishers. Contending that the subject matter "in these sticky times would not be very well received," one rejection letter subtly accused her of overstating the problem of segregation.

In order to make her book more appealing, the photographer offered to collaborate with a well-known author. Although her choice, Lillian Smith, ultimately declined, and Ms. Palfi wrote the text herself, the selection was telling. Five years earlier, Ms. Smith rose to prominence with the publication of her best-selling novel *Strange Fruit*, on the then controversial subject of interracial romance. But it was *Killers of the Dream*, her more recently published analysis of the origins and persistence of racism in the Jim Crow South, that undoubtedly caught Ms. Palfi's attention.

In contrast to other race books of the period, *Killers of the Dream* examined prejudice not just from the perspective of its

Chapter 4

victims, but also through the candid autobiographical observations of its Southern white author.

The most significant lesson of *Killers of the Dream*, one echoed in *There Is No More Time*, was that we must alter our expectations about who was responsible for talking about race. By focusing on the social and cultural mores of white Southerners—and by providing a platform for ordinary people to speak honestly about a difficult and controversial subject—both books exposed the attitudes, fears, and rationalizations that underwrote racial prejudice.

They challenged the myth that racism was exceptional, perpetrated only by monstrous or evil people. As Ms. Smith argued, few were spared the "grave illness" of prejudice. "The mother who taught me what I know of tenderness and love and compassion taught me also the bleak rituals of keeping Negroes in their 'place,'" she observed about the banality and ubiquity of racism.

Similarly and with uncompromising honesty, *There Is No More Time* revealed an enduring secret of American race relations: that ostensibly good people—men and women much like our neighbors, our family, and ourselves—could also harbor virulent prejudices. For Ms. Palfi, this revelation was necessary and urgent.

"There is no more time, we must act now—the whole world is looking on," she wrote in the book's foreword. Sixty-five years later, the problem remains dire and far from resolved as we cling to the belief that it is always, inevitably, the others who hate and discriminate.

# Bearing Witness to Jim Crow in Mississippi with Uncompromising Candor

Published February 19, 2019

Lillian Smith did something seventy years ago that was unusual for a white writer: She delved into the world of Southern gentility to reveal the bigotry, both casual and virulent, that lay beneath. In her controversial book, *Killers of the Dream*, she unflinchingly lays bare racist sensibilities, taboos, and behavior—of her neighbors, family, and herself.

She used her status as a privileged insider to expose and detail the paradoxes and complexity of racism. "The mother who taught me what I know of tenderness and love and compassion taught me also the bleak rituals of keeping Negroes in their 'place,'" Ms. Smith wrote.

Inspired by *Killers of the Dream*, Florence Mars, a white woman from Mississippi's landed gentry, did with her camera what Ms. Smith accomplished with her pen: She made visible, with uncompromising candor, the racial nuances, injustices, and contradictions

of the South. Her photographs are the subject of a new book by James T. Campbell and Elaine Owens, *Mississippi Witness: The Photographs of Florence Mars*, which includes more than one hundred images, most unpublished until now.

Ms. Mars began photographing in 1954 in and around her hometown, Philadelphia, in Neshoba County, Mississippi, partly in response to *Brown v. Board of Education*, the Supreme Court case that outlawed racial segregation in public schools. Many white residents responded with outrage and vindictiveness. Disturbed by their vitriol, and wanting to bear witness to changes taking place in her community, Ms. Mars bought a camera, built a darkroom in her home, and began taking pictures. For the next decade, she documented a fading but no less virulent racial order—from the humanity of Black residents beset by discrimination and

Chapter 4

poverty to the outward decorum of white life, racial rage, and panic seething just below the surface.

The pictures reflect the photographer's attempt to grasp "her own background, to come to terms with a world that she loved and loathed, a world awash in beauty and rife with violence and cruelty," Mr. Campbell observed. "Having lived so long on the border between insider and outsider," he wrote, "she saw herself as uniquely qualified to help fellow Philadelphians to understand and adapt to the changes they saw bearing down on them."

These photographs depict Mississippi when forces beyond its control were gradually dismantling its system of legalized segregation. They suggest both the inevitability of, but also the intense resistance to, this change: Some are hopeful, like that of Black and white children playing together in a sandbox. Others confirm racism's stubborn hold and its psychic and spiritual damage: farmers being entertained by a stylishly dressed man in blackface, or the somber all-white jury that, after only one hour of deliberation, acquitted the killers of Emmett Till, the Black teenager battered beyond recognition, his body tied to a cotton-gin fan and thrown into the Tallahatchie River. Many more images, in their ordinariness, underscore the pervasive, and sometimes casual, place of racism in Southern life, perpetrated by seemingly upstanding citizens.

Ms. Mars also represented the individuality and complexity of a Black community routinely stereotyped and demonized by white supremacists. Her images of African Americans are as precise and subtle as her portrayals of white people, from searching portraits of elders to scenes of well-dressed townspeople at work and leisure. These photographs also underscore the vital role Black Southerners had in the region's economy, culture, and daily life, in the face of segregation.

Despite threats and ostracism, Ms. Mars became increasingly vocal. In the summer of 1964, after three young civil rights workers were murdered near Philadelphia—a pivotal event in the civil rights movement—she cooperated with the FBI, publicly condemned the Ku Klux Klan, and denounced the fear and intimidation that wracked her community.

In retaliation, the Klan initiated a boycott that forced Ms. Mars to sell her cattle farm. She was pushed out of her leadership post at church. Vigilantes bombarded her home with bricks. And she was even arrested and jailed on trumped up drunken-driving charges. Ms. Mars recalled the murders and their aftermath in her 1977 memoir, *Witness in Philadelphia*.

When she died in 2006, her book was lauded by many. But few understood, or even acknowledged, her introspective photographs. Ultimately, they represented one of her greatest achievements, offering a candid insider's take on life in the waning years of the Jim Crow South that alters our perceptions about racism and segregation.

"Her passing elicited tributes and testimonials in newspapers all over the country, from the *Neshoba Democrat* to the *New York Times*, a chorus of praise for a courageous woman," wrote Mr. Campbell. "What the reports lacked was any consideration of what Mars would have called 'the background,' the confluence of place and time, character and circumstance, that allowed her to see what others could or would not. To understand that, look—really look—at her photographs."

Florence Mars, Performer in blackface entertaining farmers at the stockyard that Ms. Mars owned, Philadelphia, Mississippi, 1955

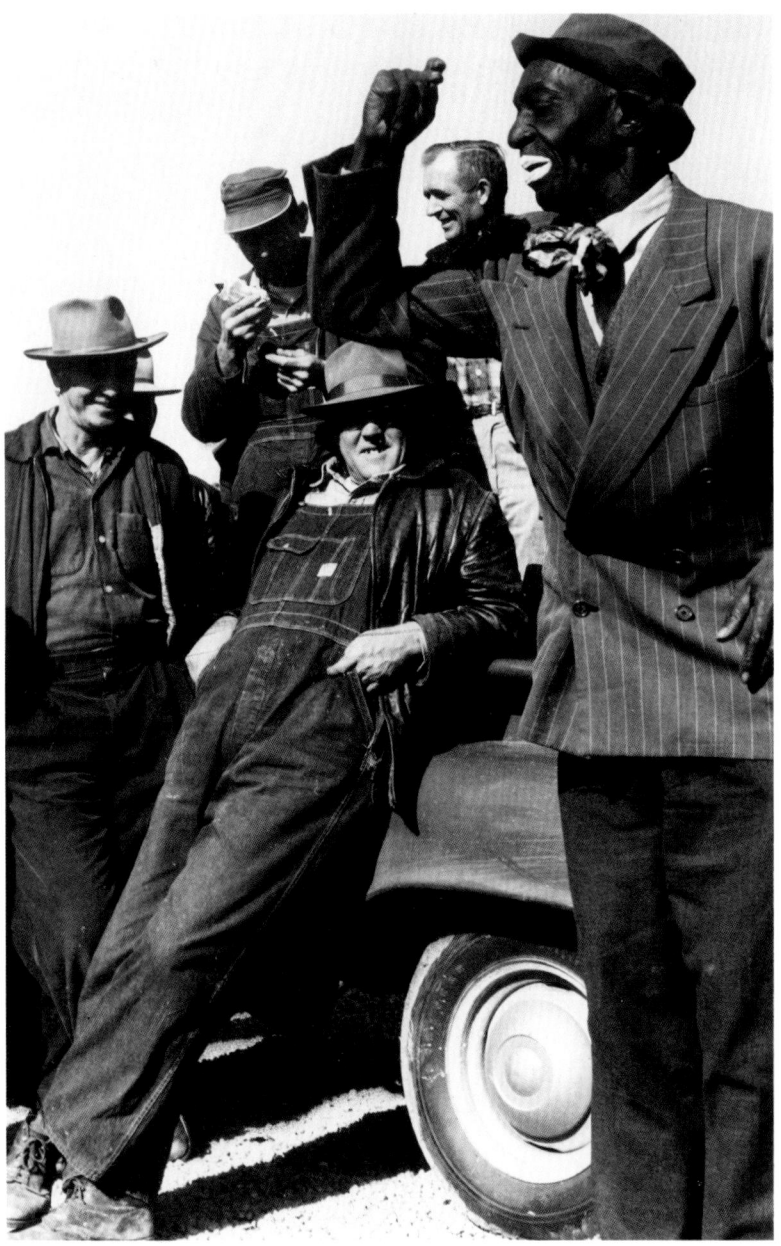

Chapter 4

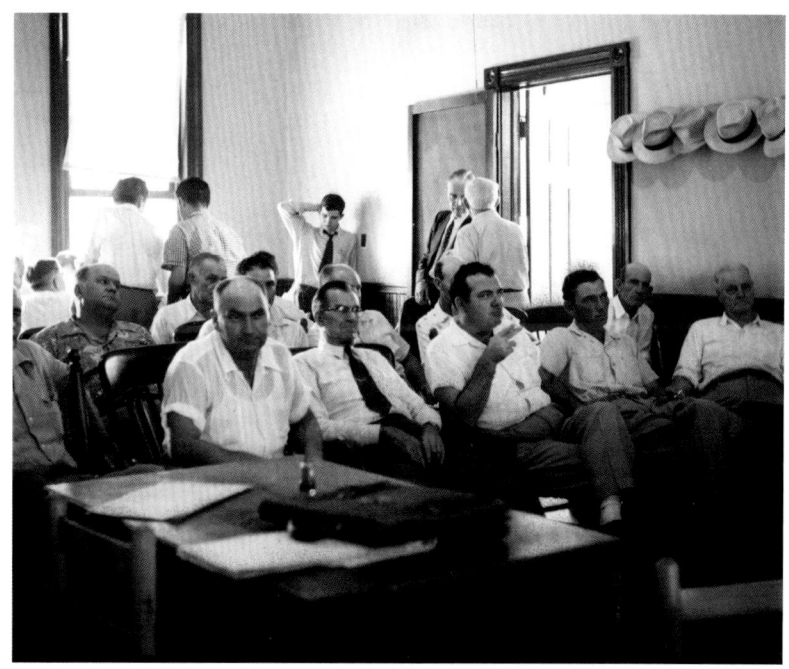

Florence Mars, Jurors during a recess of the Emmett Till murder trial at the Tallahatchie County Courthouse, Sumner, Mississippi, 1955

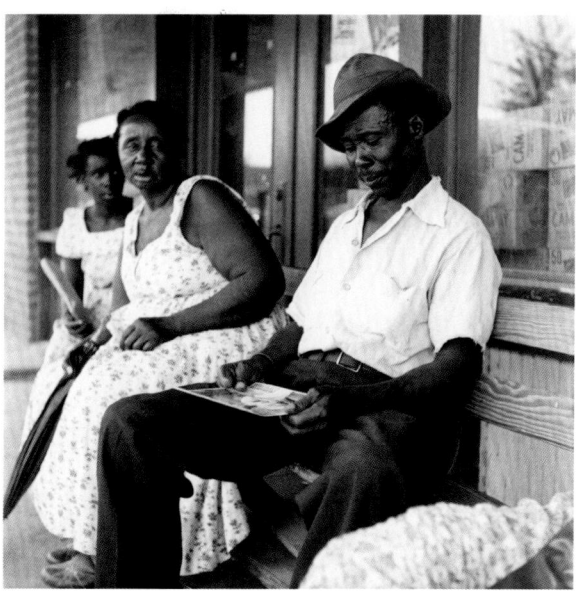

Florence Mars, John Mack Bell examining a photo of himself, Philadelphia, Mississippi, 1955

# Documenting Selma, from the Inside

Published March 2, 2015

A timely new show at the Steven Kasher Gallery in New York, *Selma March 1965*, reminds us that not all civil rights photographs were created equal. Commemorating the fiftieth anniversary this month of the historic Selma to Montgomery marches, the exhibition features the work of three documentarians of the protests: James Barker, Spider Martin, and Charles Moore.

While the photographs of Mr. Martin and Mr. Moore are well known, those of Mr. Barker are far less so. The most famous images of Mr. Martin and Mr. Moore—usually depicting civil rights leaders or dramatic milestones—are also more typical of the pictures we have come to associate with the movement.

On the other hand, Mr. Barker's images are more intimate, focusing on volunteers and their everyday activities. The gallery believes his photographs are the only ones known of the Selma demonstrations that were taken from the viewpoint of a participant observer rather than a journalist.

Working as a technical photographer at Washington State University, where he studied as an undergraduate, Mr. Barker was selected by an ad hoc committee at the university to travel to Selma, Alabama, to support marchers and document their activities. In March 1965, activists would make three attempts to complete a five-day, fifty-four-mile march to Montgomery, Alabama. The first was thwarted by state troopers, who mercilessly attacked protesters with clubs and tear gas as they attempted to cross the Edmund Pettus Bridge. The second was voluntarily suspended by demonstrators to avoid another "Bloody Sunday," as the first clash was called.

Mr. Barker's photographs depict the strategy sessions, meetings among activist groups, and the efforts to support and sustain hundreds of protesters.

"I was not trying to create a narrative of events, but rather to reveal the nature of the people, their emotions and developing relationships as they experienced the march," Mr. Barker said. "My intent was that their expressions and body language exhibit the context of the event."

His images reveal the resourcefulness, cooperation, and skill that allowed activists to pull off a historic event of this magnitude: organizers sitting around a table, engrossed in conversation; media-savvy demonstrators reading newspaper accounts of the march; a teenager stacking boxes in a chapel basement, the site of a makeshift kitchen, infirmary, and meeting hall; and a news conference with the Reverend Andrew Young, shown not from the perspective of its subject but from the behind-the-scenes scrum of cameramen.

Underscoring his insider status, Mr. Barker photographed the memos and directives that lined the walls of the office of the Student Nonviolent Coordinating Committee, a key organizer of the march. One note, attempting to locate the owner of an Oldsmobile, was particularly chilling. As Mr. Barker later discovered, the car belonged to Viola Liuzzo, the Michigan housewife and activist murdered by the Ku Klux Klan the night after the march concluded.

But mainstream publications rarely ran understated civil rights imagery. The relationship between the news media and political activists was symbiotic: Intentionally or otherwise, photojournalists provided dramatic images that demonstrated the gravity of the problem and appealed to a sense of fairness and justice, helping to sway public opinion. The activities of the movement offered those publications a continuing and

dramatic story told through enthralling images that helped sell magazines and newspapers. The more dramatic the photograph, the more desirable it was to editors and publishers.

Free of these constraints—and the need to sell pictures—Mr. Barker focused on the movement's backstory rather than its edgier public face. "When photographing an event, I only do so when I can wander about and shoot what interests me, and not be burdened with any thoughts about how the photos will be used or fitted to a page," observed Mr. Barker, who has lived in Alaska since the 1970s, where he documents Native communities.

Mr. Barker's insider access, and the trust it engendered, allowed him to represent his subjects as complex beings rather than as nameless icons of the struggle. Many of the most famous civil rights photographs depicted events impassively and from afar—lines of demonstrators marching across barren fields, a sea of humanity on the Washington Mall, jets of water knocking children to the ground in Birmingham. Mr. Barker's photographs portrayed something considerably more nuanced and allusive: the intensity, fear, weariness, tedium, and determination that registered on the faces and in the body language of Selma's brave foot soldiers.

When marchers finally reached the steps of the Capitol building in Montgomery on March 25, 1965, they had not just made history, they had also changed it. Photographs and television footage of "Bloody Sunday" would convince a skeptical nation of the justness of the civil rights struggle. These disquieting images were instrumental in the passage of the Voting Rights Acts later that year.

But as demonstrators changed the world, helped by photojournalists committed to providing the news media with what they believed were the most potent and effective images, Mr. Barker remained steadfast in his personal mission to document the prosaic, but no less important, actions and events that empowered a movement. In doing so, he believed he could most effectively gain the viewer's trust and empathy.

"In comparison with other images of the march, mine would be thought of as the adjectives and the adverbs of the story," Mr. Barker said. "I would like people to put the historical narrative in the background and identify with the people in the images. If I am successful, I'd hope the viewer feels a direct connection with the march participants."

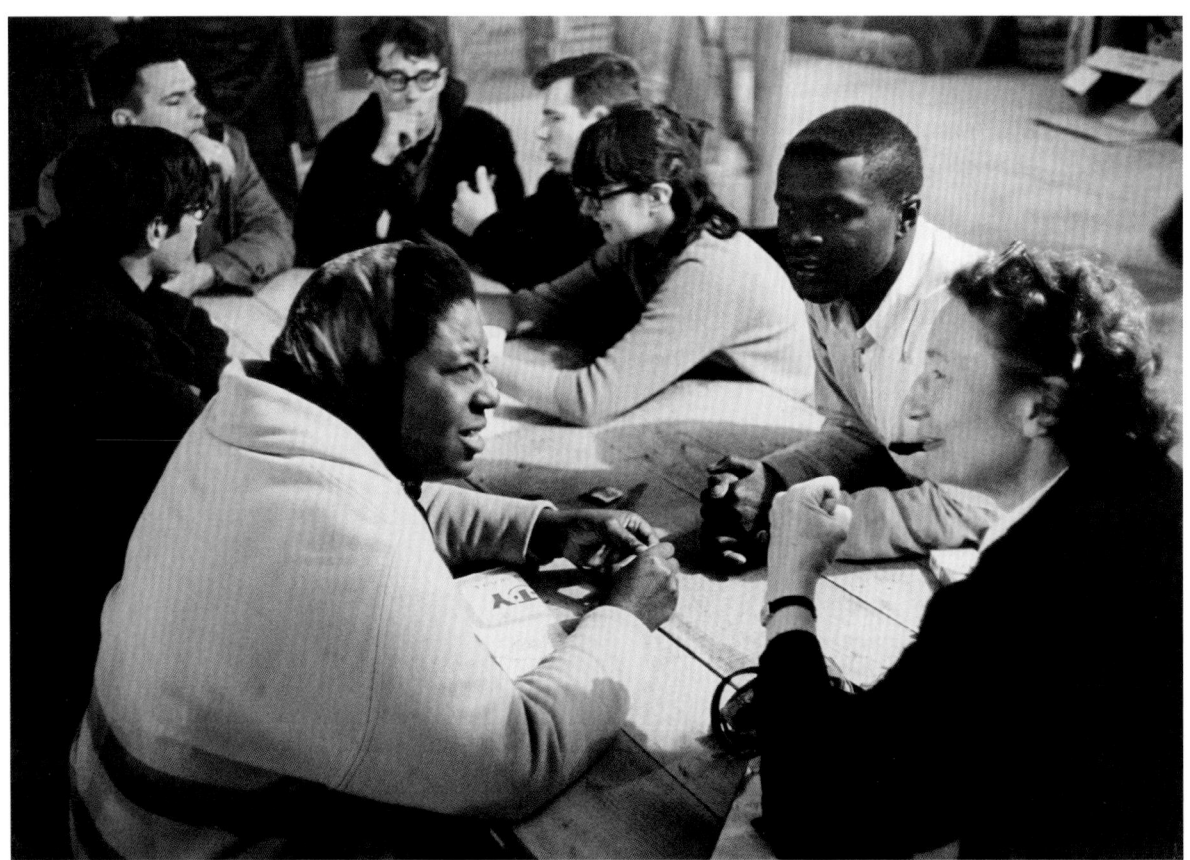

James Barker, March participants gathering in the basement of Brown Chapel, 1965

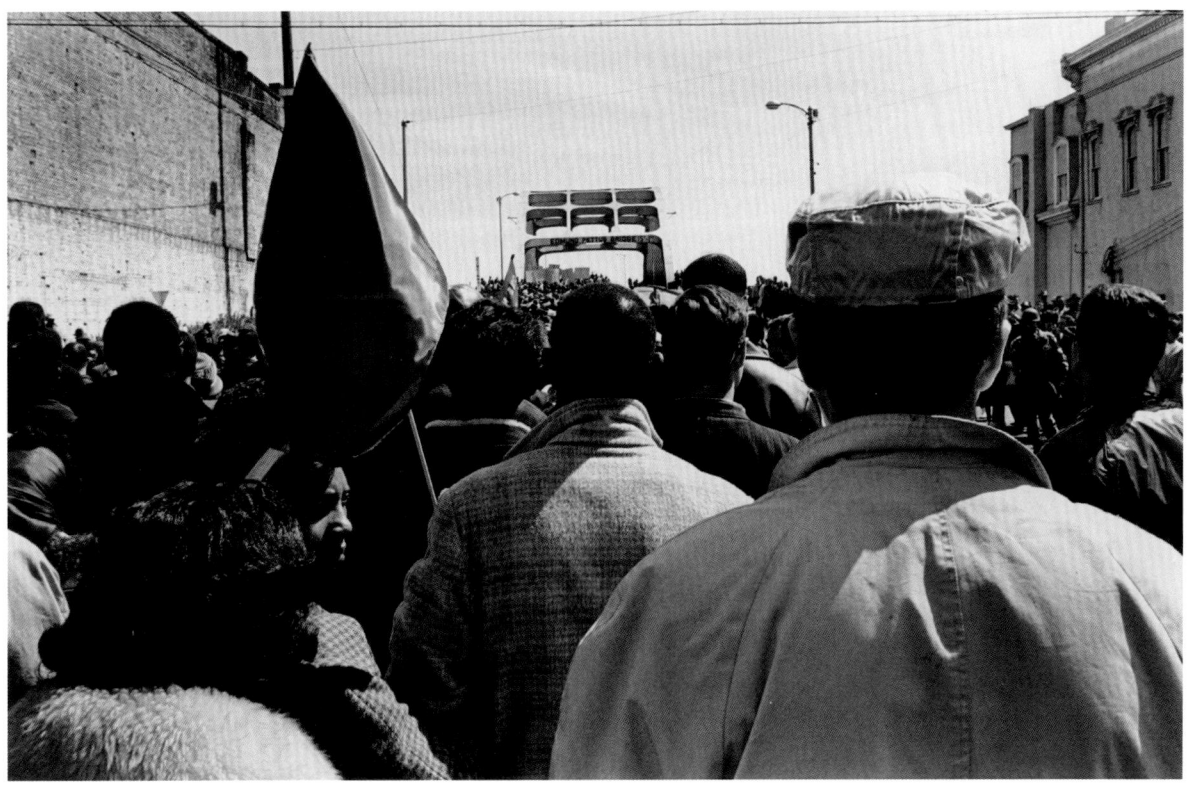

# Photos That Challenge Stereotypes about African American Youths

Published July 19, 2016

In *Double Exposure*, a series of small books published by the Smithsonian's soon-to-open National Museum of African American History and Culture, the complexities and nuances of African American life suffuse images made from the medium's birth right through today. *Picturing Children*, the fourth volume, features some fifty images from the museum's growing collection of more than 20,000 photographs.

These pictures resonate with the joy, contentment, resistance, determination, dissent, and the routines of everyday life: a photograph by Jason Miccolo Johnson of boys and girls singing in the choir of Shiloh Baptist Church in Washington; a pensive photograph by George Krause of a child sitting alone in a church pew; and James Karales's image of a young demonstrator, waving a flag at the Alabama march from Selma to Montgomery in 1965.

Through images and words by photographers and writers, Black and white, *Picturing Children* challenges the stereotype of the broken Black family and examines the family's crucial role "in shaping who we are." Images of the famous or the disenfranchised—Nina Leen's photograph of the pioneering baseball player Jackie Robinson with his wife and son, or James E. Larkin's Civil War–era picture of enslaved women and their children near Alexandria, Virginia—document situations that are simultaneously personal and universal, affirming the "importance of an engaged and committed family."

Among the book's five chapters, one examines how the African American community, from schools and churches to sports and fraternal organizations, supported "the development of children physically, intellectually, emotionally, and socially." The chapter on play expands the theme, featuring children having fun, an important aspect of early development that spurs mutual understanding and self-confidence.

Starting in the nineteenth century, Black-owned photo studios allowed African Americans to represent themselves as they wanted to be seen, and the book's section on portraiture reflects that revered status.

The studio was especially important for children, who endured withering attacks on their self-worth by stereotypical depictions. A study in the 1940s by an African American psychologist, Dr. Kenneth Clark, demonstrated the fragility of Black children's self-image when he showed Black grade schoolers photographs of Black and white dolls, identical in every way except for skin color. A majority of them chose the white doll as the one they would "like to play with,"

considering the white doll "nice" and the Black doll "bad." No wonder portraits, and the very act of being photographed, played an important role in bolstering the self-confidence of Black children in a culture awash with grotesque caricatures.

The book's final chapter looks at how African American children empowered themselves through political activism. Pictures include Gertrude Samuels's photograph of a meeting of teenage members of the Little Rock Nine, who tried to integrate Central High School in the Arkansas city in 1957 against ferocious opposition from white supremacists, and Devin Allen's contemporary image of a young girl holding a Black Lives Matter sign at a Baltimore rally in 2015.

Children have long played an important role in the struggle for civil rights. The

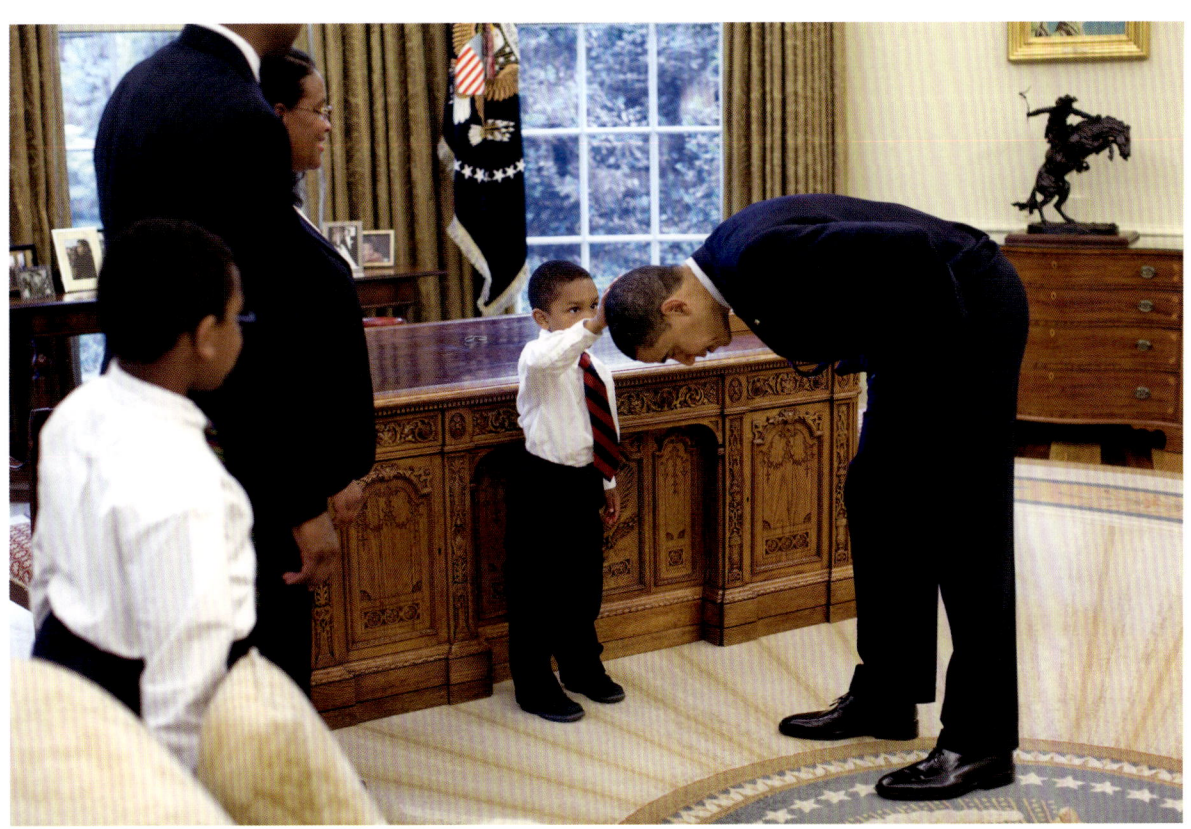

Pete Souza, President Obama allowing a child, Jacob Philadelphia, to touch his head, May 2013

1963 images from the Children's Crusade in Birmingham, Alabama, vividly demonstrated to a national audience the depravity and cruelty of the police and opponents of civil rights who attacked youths engaged in nonviolent protest. Stark photographs of them being attacked by dogs and knocked to the ground by water cannon shifted public opinion in their favor, persuading long-skeptical white Americans of the inherent indecency of segregation and its peril to democracy.

*Picturing Children* also makes clear that African American children have not been any less nurtured than those of other ethnic and racial groups. Indeed, the reality of racism and the potential for discrimination have made caring for and educating Black children even more vital.

"African American adults have long done their very best to protect their children from a society that does not always value them highly and to remind them that, no matter what the outside world says, they have dignity and sacred worth that no outside force can touch," wrote Marian Wright Edelman, the founder and president of the Children's Defense Fund, in one of the book's essays.

She also offers a reminder that despite significant gains and the election of our nation's first Black president, considerable work remains: "A toxic cocktail—poverty, resegregation, unequal schools, massive illiteracy and innumeracy, racial disparity in every child-serving system, violence, and a pipeline to prison that feeds a mass incarceration system—is sentencing millions of children of color to dead-end, powerless, and hopeless lives."

It is in this context that photography, as current events confirm, has become even more important for African American communities, both as a means of documenting these problems and as a catalyst for hope and change.

"We know that children are the only real Progress, the sole Hope, the sure victory over Evil," the seminal Black intellectual and activist W. E. B. Du Bois wrote in 1922. "Properly reared and trained and there is no Problem or Wrong that we cannot withstand."

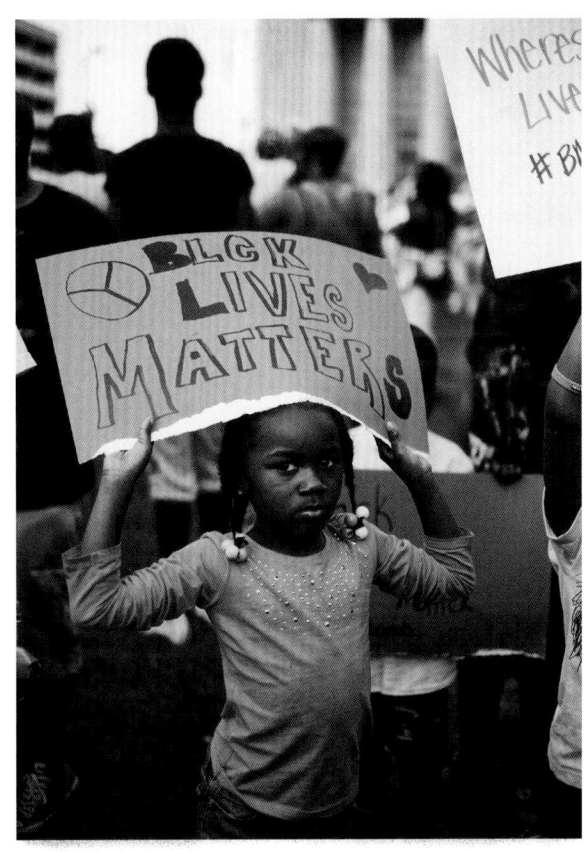

Devin Allen, A young girl at a Baltimore City Hall rally, May 3, 2015

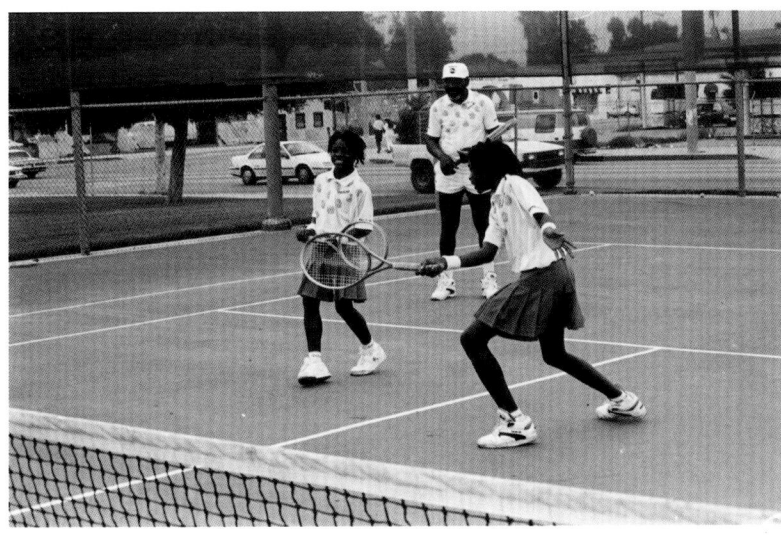

Roderick Lyons, Serena and Venus, 1991

Witnessing

# Intimate Photos of Community and Resilience in New York's Chinatown in the 1980s

Published January 2, 2019

In 1981, the photographer Bud Glick began documenting Chinatown in Lower Manhattan during a pivotal time in its history, when waves of immigrants from Hong Kong, Taiwan, and China were arriving, supporting different cultures and linguistic backgrounds but sharing the dream of a new life in a new world.

Back then, Chinatown was a decidedly different neighborhood than it is today. Over the ensuing decades, it would transform from a tightknit and largely self-supporting community—home to a robust garment industry and fading bachelor society shaped by earlier immigration policies—into a bustling neighborhood centered on young people and families.

Mr. Glick's Chinatown project began when he was commissioned by the Museum of Chinese in America—then known as the New York Chinatown History Project—to photograph local residents. Relocating from his native Wisconsin, he embarked on a three-year mission of representing the public and private lives of a community long misunderstood or stereotyped in the mainstream media and popular culture.

In retrospect, Mr. Glick did more than depict the street life, people, and domestic scenes of a New York neighborhood. He also sensitively documented a community at the cusp of dynamic change. His project is now the subject of an exhibition, *Interior Lives: Photographs of Chinese Americans in the 1980s*, organized by the Museum of Chinese in America in conjunction with the Museum of the City of New York exhibition *Interior Lives: Contemporary Photographs of Chinese New Yorker*s. Both shows are on view through March 24.

Intent on portraying Chinatown honestly and with complexity, Mr. Glick did so as an

Chapter 4

outsider respectful of a community he did not know from the inside. "I was a documentary photographer, with the responsibility of learning, understanding, making connections, gaining access, and documenting what I saw, felt, and understood—communicating what was occurring around me—telling the story as I understood it," Mr. Glick wrote in an email. "My role was to keep my eyes open, learn as much as I could, make connections, and follow wherever my connections took me."

Mr. Glick's photographs are at once vivid and intimate, a window into the everyday lives of their subjects: the male residents of so-called bachelor apartments, quietly reading newspapers or eating meals; a worker pressing clothes in one of the city's then ubiquitous hand laundries; a chaotic garment factory, piles of fabric strewn on tables; children playing, interacting with parents, or hanging out on the street; and a young man sporting a T-shirt from the punk rock band the Ramones, a harbinger of Chinatown's impending demographic and cultural shifts.

These photographs provided much-needed detail and context for a community all too often defined by stereotypes: the exotic tourist mecca replete with golden dragons and inexpensive restaurants; the booming business district, crowded with shopkeepers hawking ethnic foods, gaudy trinkets, and mysterious potions; or the lurid, opium-fueled world of *Chinatown Nights*, a 1929 gangster film directed by William A. Wellman about a white socialite caught up in San Francisco's Chinese underworld.

Beginning in the late-nineteenth century, a series of federal laws—built on stereotypes, anxieties about white racial purity, and the fear of lost jobs—greatly restricted Chinese immigration to the United States. The Chinese Exclusion Act of 1882, for example, was the first to bar a group on the basis of nationality or race. It placed draconian restrictions on prospective immigrants, including the exclusion of the wives and children of Chinese laborers already living in the country.

But the easing of immigration laws and quotas in the 1950s and 1960s precipitated an upsurge in Chinese settlement in the United States, dynamically altering Chinatown's demographics, physical character, and geography. Shops and small business were established, shuttered, and reborn. Old buildings were demolished and replaced. The neighborhood's boundaries expanded beyond its historical core streets. And Chinese communities arose and flourished in other parts of the city.

"All communities change," wrote Mr. Glick. "However, looking at it now, the incredibly rapid growth and change distinguishes Chinatown from many other communities. What felt big at the time now seems small. Chinatown has expanded tremendously. It seems qualitatively different now. Today's Chinatown is a dynamic community created by a new generation of immigrants."

*Interior Lives* represents these shifts not just through historical photographs, but also through audio and written excerpts from recently recorded interviews with some of their subjects. Mr. Glick perceives these interviews, which are featured in the exhibition and can be accessed through visitor's mobile phones, as a vital continuation of the project he began almost forty years ago.

"My goal now, in terms of this project, is to connect with and interview more people that I photographed in the 1980s and produce a book that places the photographs within the context of people's stories," wrote Mr. Glick. "The photos together with the stories that people tell will inform each

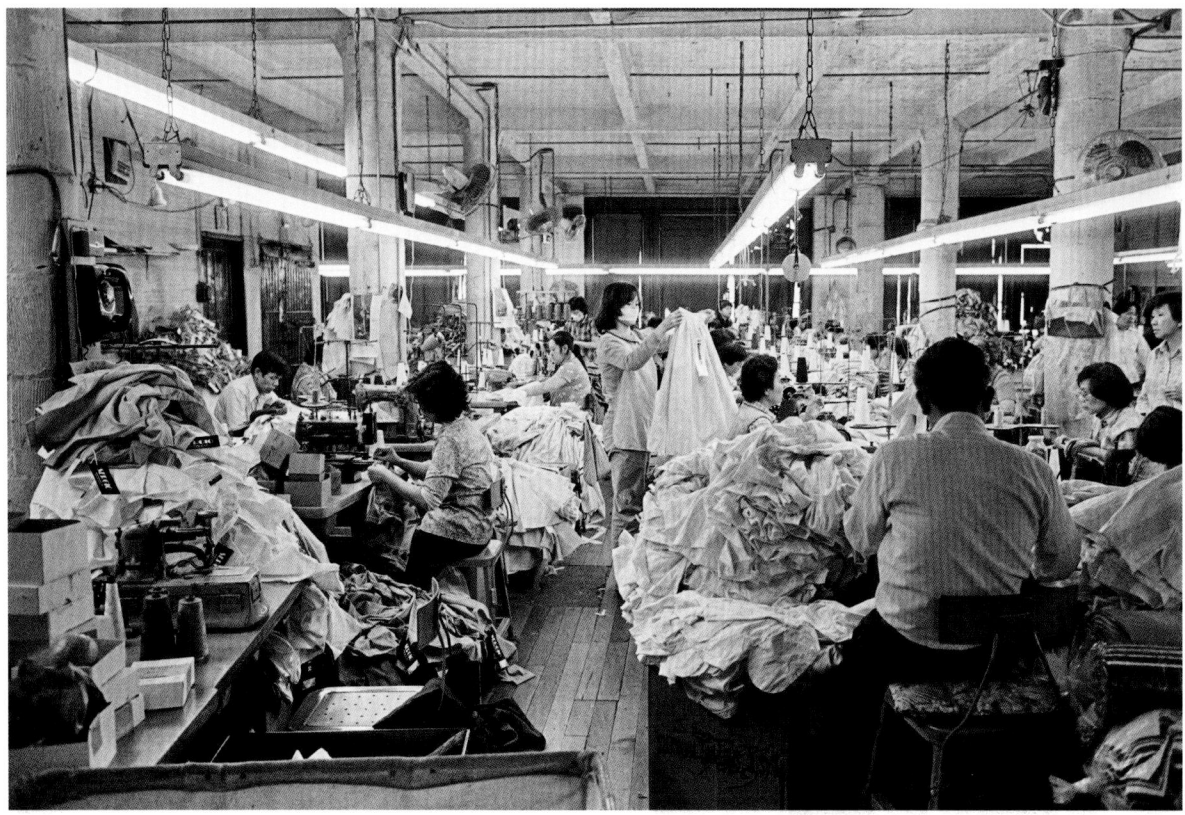

other and contribute to a deeper understanding of both the personal experience and the broader social history of New York's Chinatown."

Perceiving echoes of the Chinese Exclusion Act in our present-day politics, Mr. Glick believes the project is evermore urgent. In this regard, *Interior Lives* remains consequential and relevant during a time when immigrants are being demonized by the president and his supporters. Its testament to the strength and resourcefulness of an immigrant community belies the stereotypes, assumptions, and anxieties that fuel this regressive thinking.

"I hope that my Chinatown work can stand as a refutation of that bigotry," wrote Mr. Glick. "The photographs tell a quintessential American immigrant story of persistence to gain a foothold in a society that excludes them racially, socially, economically, and culturally. We know that the past is present. The same racist, anti-immigrant politics that led to Exclusion are alive and well in our current, toxic times. It was wrong then. It is wrong now."

Chapter 4

Bud Glick, *Columbus Park, New York City*, 1983

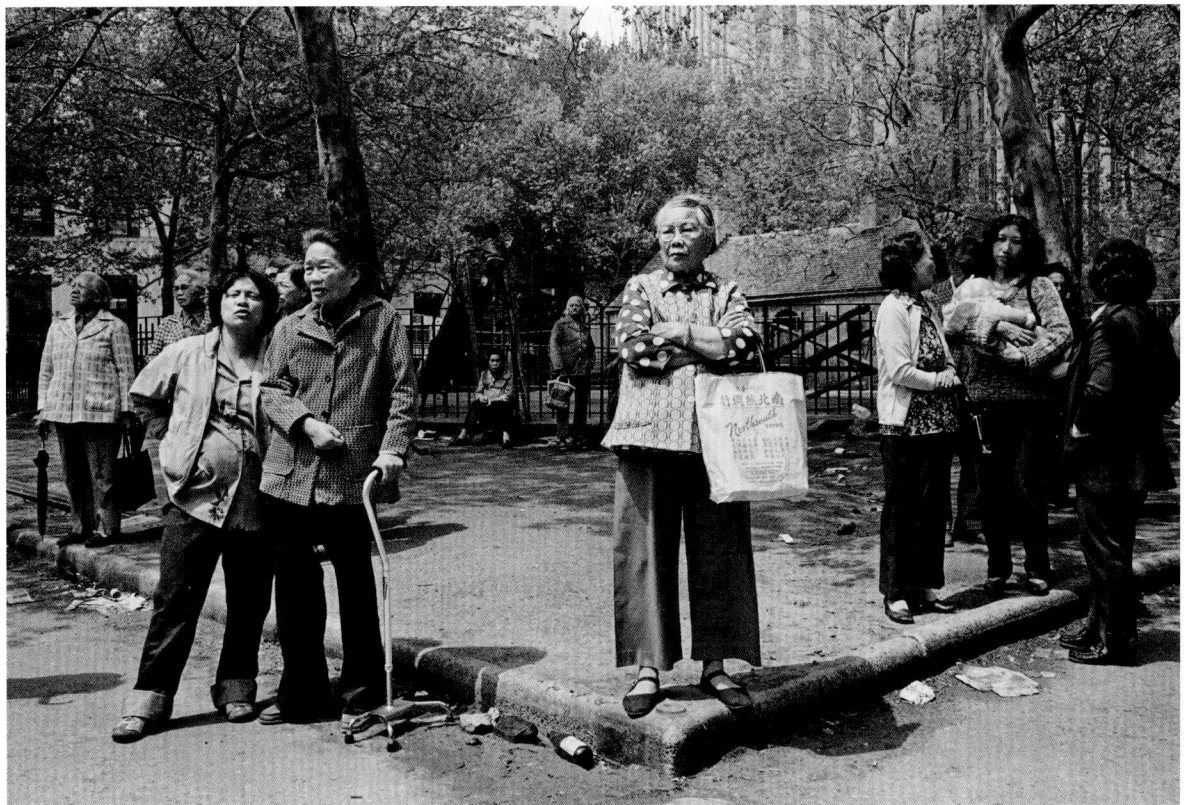

# In Ferguson, Photographs as Powerful Agents

Published August 20, 2014

Thousands of photographs continue to flood out of Ferguson, Missouri, some by photojournalists, but many more by local residents on social media. While these images document quickly unfolding events, they serve another purpose: providing the African American community with an important outlet for reporting on—and taking control of—the chaos around it.

Within hours after Michael Brown was killed by the police, photographs began surfacing, both in mainstream and social media, depicting residents, many of them teenagers, raising their hands in an ironic gesture of surrender, but also of passive resistance. These images—like those of people wearing hoodies in the aftermath of the Trayvon Martin killing—quickly went viral, inspiring other photographs of people across the country raising their hands in solidarity.

"Some of these photographs of young people with their hands up underscore visually their understanding of what it means to be economically marginalized, to be targeted because of the bodies they inhabit," said Barbara Krauthamer, coauthor, with Deborah Willis, of the groundbreaking study *Envisioning Emancipation: Black Americans and the End of Slavery*. "There is something politically and aesthetically profound about creating these photographs. The word *protest* diminishes the intellectual depth and political sophistication that these young people are exhibiting."

This would not be the first time African Americans have used the camera this way. Historically, photography was integral to the fight against racism and segregation. Leaders from Sojourner Truth to Malcolm X embraced the photograph's potential as evidence and its ability to combat stereotypes.

Chapter 4

But sometimes, as in Ferguson, the camera has served as a more spontaneous "weapon of choice," as the photographer Gordon Parks called it, wielded by the oppressed in moments of anger, fear, or frustration.

In the summer of 1955, Mamie Till Mobley embarked on a personal campaign to distribute to the press photographs of the mutilated corpse of her murdered son, Emmett Till. The fourteen-year-old Emmett had been abducted, beaten, and shot by white supremacists in Money, Mississippi, allegedly for whistling at a white female shopkeeper.

When Mrs. Mobley tried to make these images public—ultimately, only Black periodicals would publish them—she understood their ability to astound and disarm viewers. "I knew that I could talk for the rest of my life about what had happened to my baby, I could explain it in great detail," she later recalled, ". . . I could do all of that and people would still not get the full impact. They had to see what I had seen. The whole nation had to bear witness to this."

In the end, those stark and terrifying pictures inspired a political revolution, rousing thousands of young Black men and women to action, the brave soldiers of the "Emmett Till Generation," as the sociologist and activist Joyce Ladner has called them.

In recent years, social media has provided more immediate and alternative outlets for both political action and the distribution of images.

"We are living in an amazing time, when media is being taken into the hands of the people," observed the artist Hank Willis Thomas, whose work deals with issues of African American representation. "New

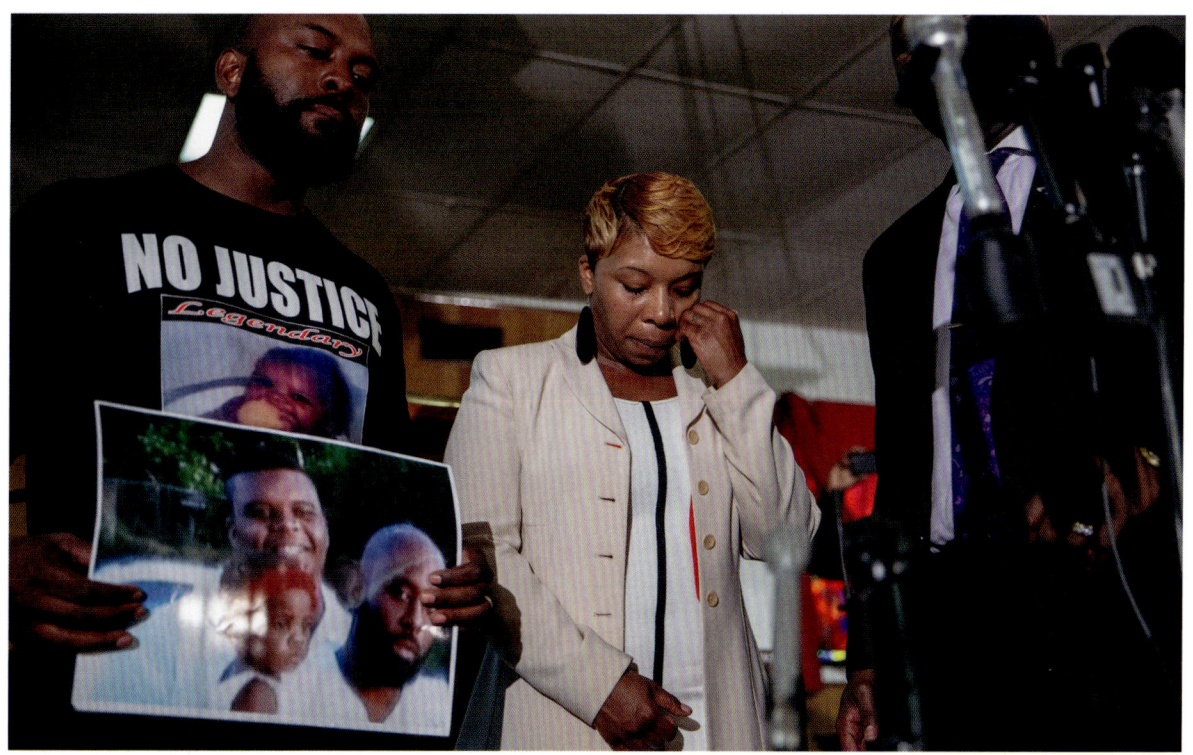

Whitney Curtis, Michael Brown Sr., left, and Lesley McSpadden listen as the lawyer Benjamin Crump spoke at a news conference about the shooting death of their son, Michael Brown, by a police officer, August 11, 2014

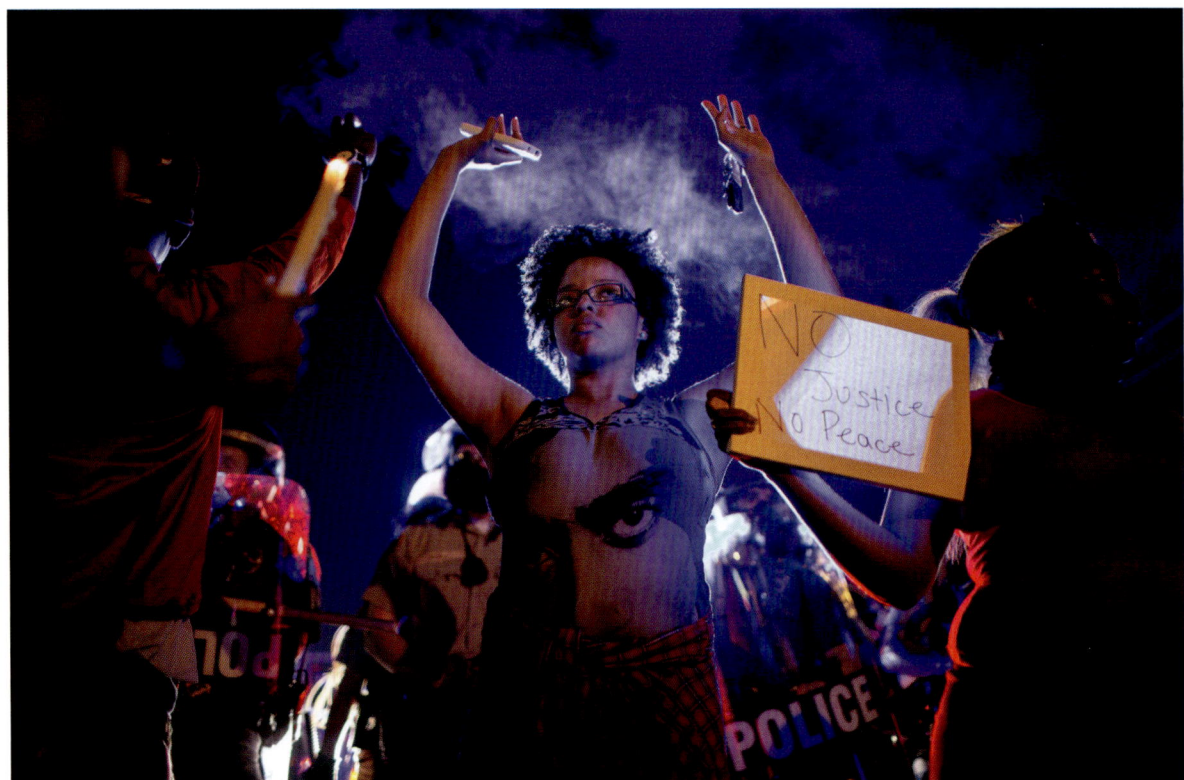

ways of using media are being applied on a daily basis. Through various means, and very much like artists, people are using found images and staging events or photographs. It's almost overwhelming to witness this rising awareness of the power of creative expression in people's hands."

But well before these advances, the camera has served as a vital force of communication and empowerment for African Americans. Ms. Krauthamer notes that the photographs emanating from Ferguson are "evocative of what Frederick Douglass wrote about in 1861, about the power of being able to represent yourself and to tell your own story through pictures. Douglass made the argument that when Black Americans represent themselves, then their fundamental humanity cannot be denied."

If the internet and social media, like the camera and television before them, have transformed the way we communicate, they have also made us more critical of the media images we cannot control. Millions of cameras in hand, we now have the potential to change the story of a major media event by providing pictures that question or counter it.

In our present media world, citizen photography not only reports on a story but can also become its subject. Some of the most extraordinary photographs created in the aftermath of Mr. Brown's shooting, for example, have centered on the role played by negative media portrayals of young Black men in perpetuating tragedies like Ferguson.

In the days following the shooting, thousands of Twitter users, under the

Chapter 4

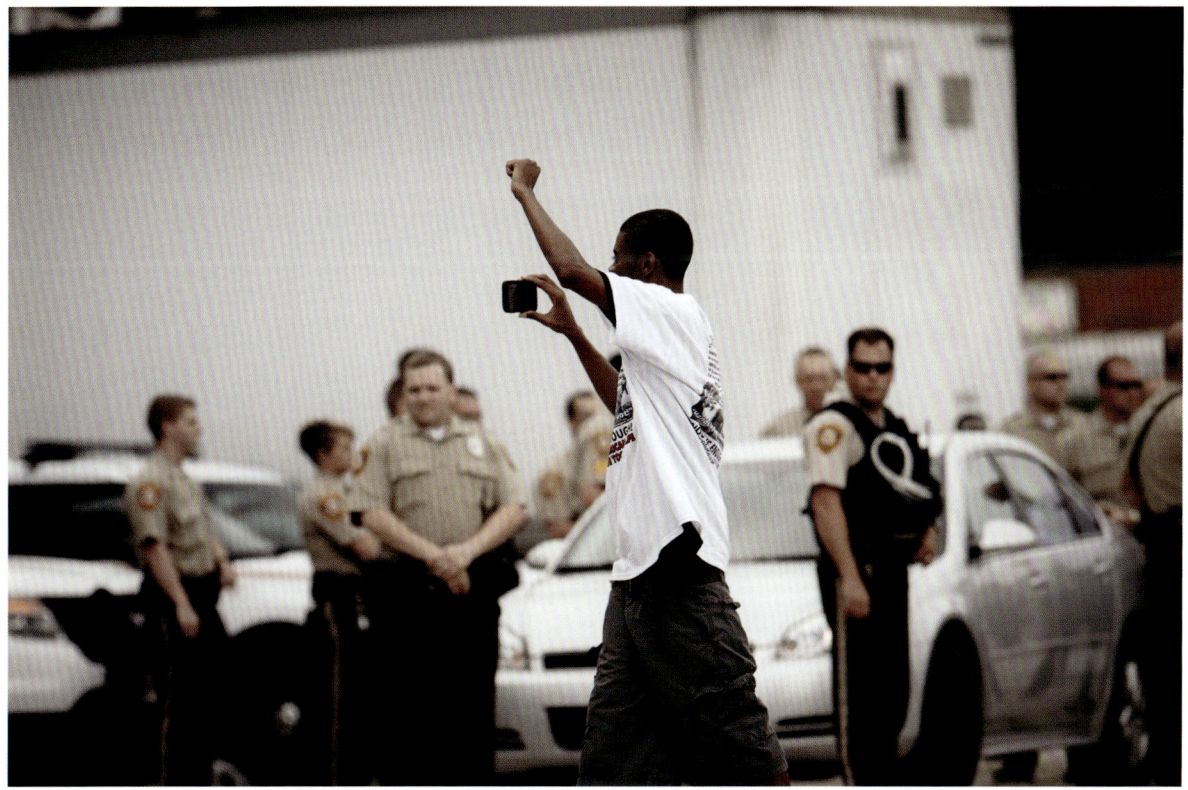

hashtag #IfTheyGunnedMeDown, posted contrasting photographs of themselves. One was in a positive context, like attending graduation, playing a musical instrument, or wearing a military uniform; the other, enacting a common stereotype, like loitering with other Black men or menacingly pointing at or staring into the camera. The campaign underscores—and contests—the habit of mainstream journalists to concentrate on images of the latter.

For more than a century and a half, the history of Black representation in the United States has resonated with the types of self-generated images now prevalent in social media. Whether in 1950s Mississippi or Ferguson today, the camera has served nobly as witness, provocateur, and agent of change.

Speaking about historic civil rights photographs at a symposium at the University of Maryland, Baltimore County, in 2012, Julian Bond attested to their importance in the lives of African Americans: "They summon the bravery of ordinary people to do extraordinary things. To risk life and limb. To secure democracy for themselves and their neighbors. They remind us of what we were and of what we hope we can be again."

"They are more powerful now," Mr. Bond wistfully concluded, words with profound implications for the story of Ferguson.

# Capturing the Struggle for Racial Equality, Past and Present

Published October 15, 2018

The dark sky casts an ominous haze over a demonstration in Ferguson, Missouri. Protesters congregate in front of a firehouse. In the foreground a man stands guard, his back to the camera, a metal baton in one hand, multiple handcuffs dangling from the other.

The tense image by Sheila Pree Bright evokes civil rights photographs of the past. But the clothes and hairstyles mark it as contemporary, taken at a 2015 demonstration against police brutality and the killing a year earlier of Michael Brown, a Black teenager.

The past often resonates in Ms. Bright's photographs, which are collected in a new book, *#1960Now: Photographs of Civil Rights Activists and Black Lives Matter Protests*. Committed to documenting recent activism through the lens of history, she reminds us that the struggle for racial equality and justice in the United States has been longstanding and ongoing. The book includes portraits of past and present activists, photographs of Black Lives Matter demonstrations and meetings, and texts by Ms. Bright, Alicia Garza, Deborah Willis, Kiche Griffin, Aaron Bryant, and Keith Miller.

Ms. Bright said the inspiration for *#1960Now* was the 2012 fatal shooting of Trayvon Martin by neighborhood watch volunteer George Zimmerman, an event that sparked the Black Lives Matter movement. "I was unwilling to sit on the sidelines," she wrote in an email. "I took a stand documenting the tensions, conflicts, and responses between communities and police departments, which have resulted from police shootings in Atlanta, Ferguson, Baltimore, and Baton Rouge, Louisiana. I've observed young social activists taking a stand against continued injustice that closely resembles what their parents and

Chapter 4

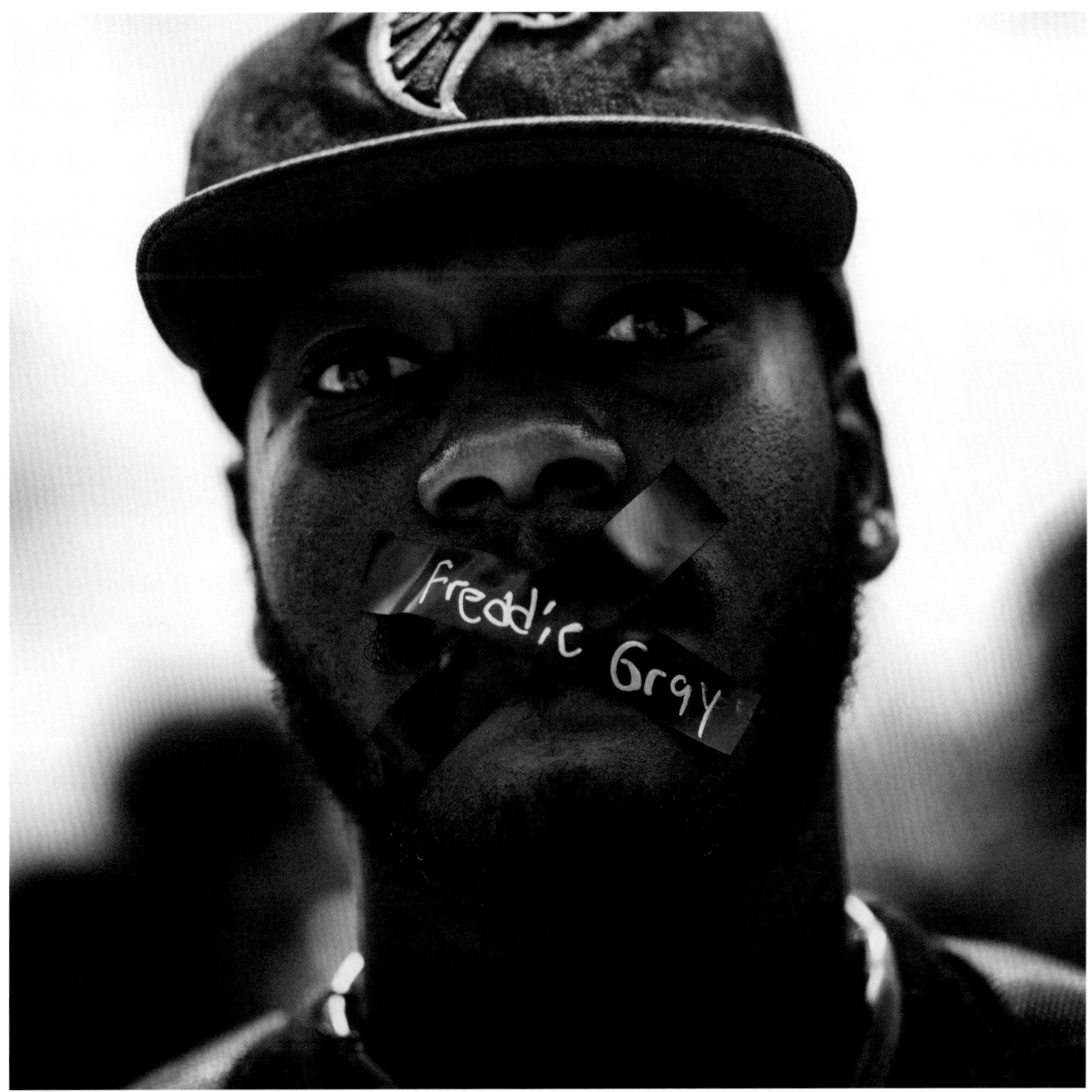

grandparents endured during the era of Jim Crow."

In her work, Ms. Bright focuses not only on movement leaders, but also on the thousands of grass-roots activists on the front lines of protest. She is likewise committed to representing people historically overlooked in mainstream depictions of Black political action, including mothers, women, and LGBT

activists. "Bright's work challenges what we see and how we see it," wrote Mr. Miller.

"Within the current context of momentous changes that surround us, her work refreshes our sense of the possible and expands our notions of what is beautiful."

Ms. Bright's photographs offer an intimate and humanistic view of Black protest: a demonstrator staring mournfully into the camera, a tear running down his cheek; a somber activist, his mouth covered by tape inscribed with the name of Freddie Gray, the twenty-five-year-old African American man killed while being transported by police in Baltimore; a marcher in rapt attention, his eyes closed, his hands clapping as if almost in prayer; and a moving juxtaposition of portraits—the artist Bree Newsome, who took down the Confederate flag at the South Carolina Capitol in 2015, and Roslyn Pope, a member of the 1960s Atlanta Student Movement.

The historical connections in *#1960Now* affirm that the fight for civil rights has taken many forms beyond the modern movement, the campaign from the early 1950s through the late 1960s to secure legal rights for Black

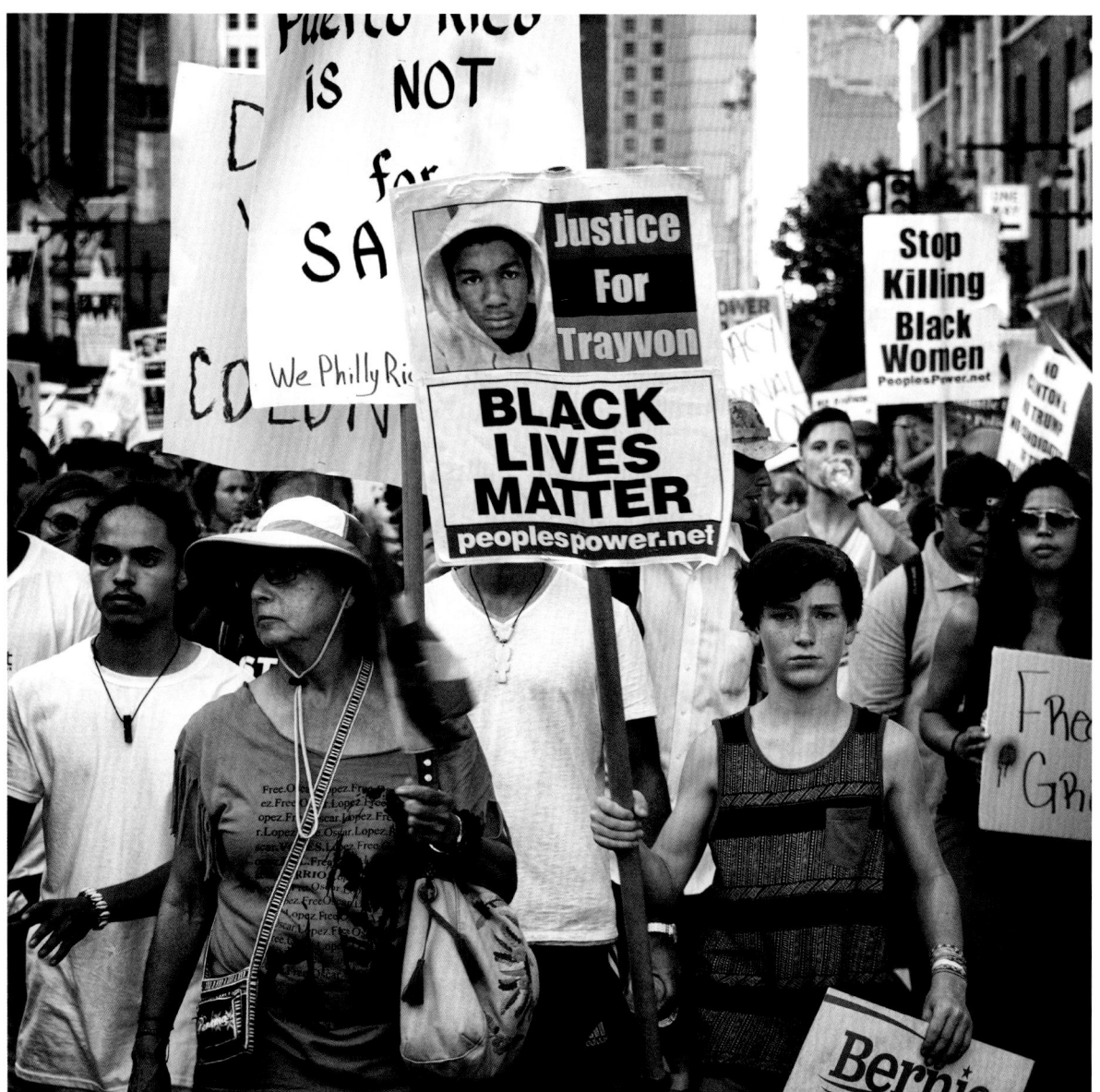

Sheila Pree Bright, *Shut Down the DNC*. Black Resistance March Against Police Terrorism & State Repression, 2016

Chapter 4

Americans. "The search for racial equality is like a perpetual revolution never ending," Ms. Bright wrote. "The struggles that continue now have taken on different shapes and forms throughout each generation."

The fight has progressed through such disparate movements and events as the abolitionism of the nineteenth century, the birth of the African American press in the early twentieth century, the Harlem Renaissance of the 1920s, the civil rights demonstrations of the 1950s, the Black Is Beautiful movement of the 1960s, and Black Lives Matter today. Despite different motivations and strategies, all belong to a shared legacy of African American resistance to prejudice, white supremacy, and oppression.

"The movements of now are faced with the same and worsening challenges that organizers and activists encountered in the 1960s—substandard conditions in Black communities, a lack of political power, and an amnesia that says that Black suffering is a product of our imagination rather than our lived experiences," wrote Ms. Garza, a cofounder of the Black Lives Matter Global Network.

Implicit in *#1960Now* is another common historical thread: the role of photography itself in recording historic events, motivating political action, and empowering African Americans. That several of Ms. Bright's portraits are of photographers—Robert Houston, who documented the 1968 Poor People's Campaign in Washington, DC, for example, or Devin Allen, whose dramatic image of the Baltimore uprising was published on the cover of *Time* in May 2015—speaks to the importance of the medium to the struggle.

By embracing the lush black-and-white aesthetic of legendary civil rights photographs, Ms. Bright underscores this historical continuity. While millions of cell-phone photos are generated each day—some forceful testaments to racial violence and injustice—few possess the grace and quiet lyricism of her images.

Ms. Bright hopes that her pictures will broaden our understanding of today's struggle for racial equality and justice, and the history that inspired it. She is heartened, too, by the conversations her photographs have generated about race, prejudice, police brutality, and social justice in the United States.

"I see my role as photographic artist as the messenger to bring about awareness," she wrote. "Photography has always brought awareness about racial injustices that exist in this country. However, there are questions that weigh heavily on my mind: Have we learned from the past? And who are we as a country?"

# A Photographer Who Made "Ghosts" Visible

Published January 11, 2017

It is the often oblique details in Ming Smith's photographs that provide their most profound meaning. Consider the eerie photograph of a person walking on a Harlem street, a blur moving across the image's surface. The street is urban and depressed; graffiti mars steel gates and a portentous crucifix-like shadow rakes across the cold pavement. But other details imbue the picture with additional levels of meaning and irony: a set of grinning faces on a doorway and the words *no money* that run across the top of the picture.

The image reminds us that the urban landscape is neither singular nor without contradiction. It affirms that sadness coexists with humor, that poverty is mitigated by culture and ideas, and that the absence of money cannot define a community.

This photograph appears in the first major retrospective of Ms. Smith's work, which opens on Friday at the Steven Kasher Gallery in New York. The exhibition, featuring more than seventy-five vintage black-and-white photographs from the 1970s to the present, offers a significant opportunity to appraise the work of a less-known but important and aesthetically adventurous artist.

After graduating from Howard University, Ms. Smith moved to New York, where she began working as a model. A friendship with the photographer Anthony Barboza affirmed her interest and talent in a medium that had captivated her since childhood. She was the first female member of the influential Harlem-based photography collective Kamoinge, and in 1975, she became the first African American female photographer whose work was acquired by the Museum of Modern Art. Her subjects have been diverse, from portraits of Black cultural figures to children in Europe and Africa and Harlem

Chapter 4

street scenes to abstract images of architecture and nature.

The mysterious, ethereal quality of Ms. Smith's photographs affirm her aesthetics and view of the medium. "Photography is definitely an art form," she recently observed. "You're using light, you're composing, even to the type of print paper you're using." Her work, personal and expressive, draws from a number of artistic sources, preeminently Surrealism. She has employed a range of Surrealist techniques: photographing her subjects from oblique angles, shooting out of focus or through such atmospheric effects as fog and shadow, playing on unusual juxtapositions, even altering or painting over prints.

Ms. Smith's evocative pictures summon up dreamlike states to tease out complex emotions and ideas deeply embedded in the places and consciousness of her subjects. We see this in *Lil' Brown Baby wif Spa'klin' Eyes, Harlem, NY*, the child's back to the camera, standing in a ramshackle crib left out on a graffiti-strewn street. We see this in the raking shadows and sense of isolation in the 1973 portrait *Old Man in Robe, New York, NY*. And we see this in the godlike countenance of James Baldwin, his face hovering in the clouds over Harlem, looking down on the fraught nation he left to live as an expatriate in a more stolid, but no less problematic postwar France.

Gordon Parks wrote of the transcendent quality of Ms. Smith's work, praising her ability to make visible the "ghosts" that remained imperceptible to most of us: "The camera, with its special attention to detail, enables one to hold on to a lifetime full of ghosts that might otherwise crumble to dust," he wrote. "What the memory often holds is not exactly what the camera records . . . Wondrous imagery keeps cropping up, stuffing themselves into [Ms. Smith's] sight. She grasps them and

gives eternal life to things that might well have been forgotten."

Ms. Smith's photographs, like the most profound Surrealist imagery, are not without social purpose or commentary. Her imagery of African American urban life, for example, typically documents the "alienation of individuals within the constructs of city living and at the same time celebrates the communal love and pride within those conditions," as the photo historian Deborah Willis wrote. They transform the cityscape into tense, motion-filled images that sometimes simultaneously reveal the disturbing, ironic, discordant, joyful, or affirming aspects of life.

Ms. Smith's subjects are often suspended between visibility and invisibility: faces turned away, or are blurred or shrouded in shadow, mist, or darkness, a potent metaphor of the struggle for African American visibility in a culture in which Black men and women were disparaged, erased, or ignored. Her pictures recall Ralph Ellison's epochal novel, *Invisible Man*, a title employed by Ms. Smith for one of her series. The novel recounts the enduring quest for equality and justice of a Black man whose skin color renders him invisible. Throughout the narrative, Mr. Ellison, like Ms. Smith, plays on alternate themes of darkness and illumination. In the instances when light shines, it breaks through ignorance or invisibility, serving as a metaphor for moral and intellectual enlightenment.

Ms. Smith's images are at once spontaneous, personal, and quivering with visual surprise. She positions her varied subjects—male or female, Black or white, anonymous or famous—as "intimates feeling their way through specific conditions and circumstances, and deliberately invokes this exchange in her images," wrote the art historian LeRonn P. Brooks. By deeply engaging the world around her, and ironically through the haze of blur, mist, or shadow, Ms. Smith makes visible not only what can be seen, but the complex psychological and social factors that lurk below.

In the end, Ms. Smith's work as a photographer aspires to and parallels James Baldwin's objective as a writer: "A writer is never listening to what is being said, he is never listening to what he is being told. He is listening to what is not being said, he is listening to what he is not being told, which means he is trying to discover the purpose of the communication."

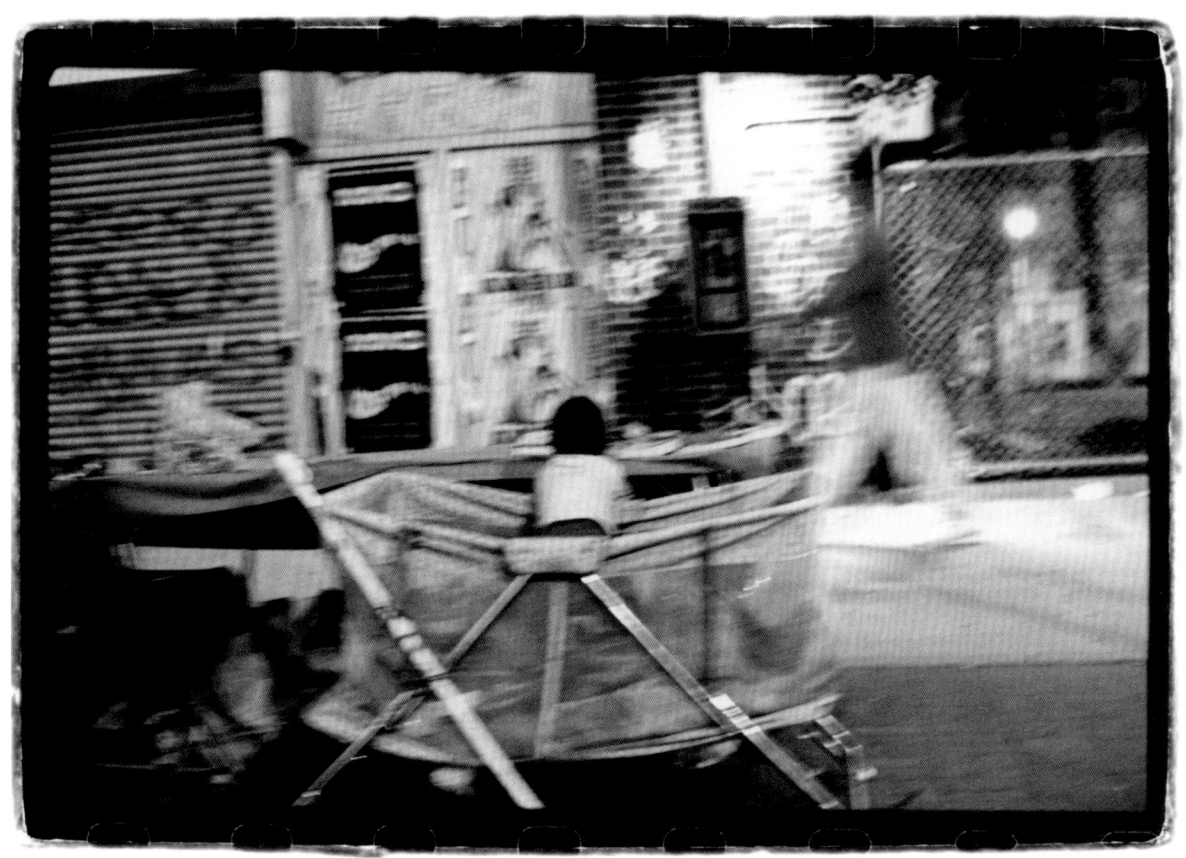

Ming Smith, *Lil' Brown Baby wif Spa'klin Eyes*; from the series *Invisible Man, Harlem, New York City*, ca. 1991

Chapter 4

Ming Smith, *Sun Ra space II*, New York, 1978

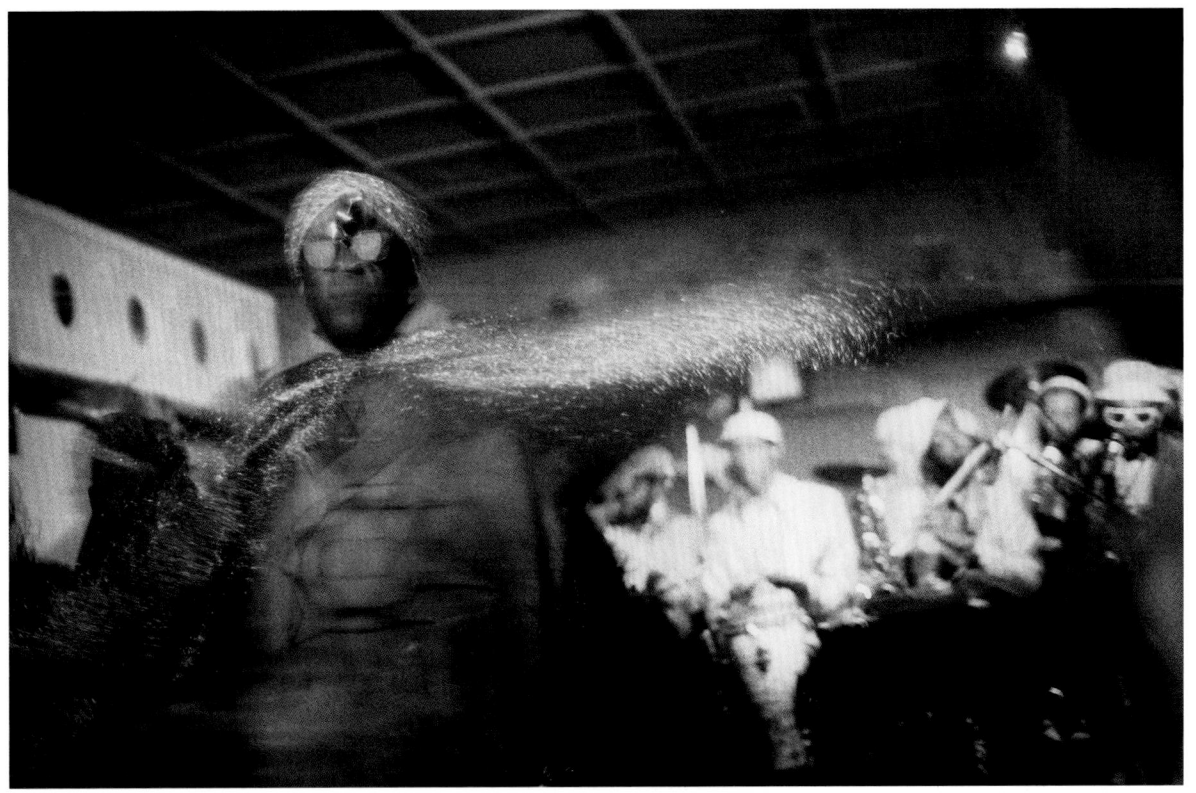

# The Holocaust's Paradox of Good and Evil, in Photographs

Published November 19, 2018

With the rise of white nationalism, racial violence, and domestic terrorism in the United States, photographers have increasingly had to document their brutal aftermath—from the mug shot of Dylann Roof, who killed nine Black parishioners as they prayed in a Charleston church in 2015, to the makeshift memorial in front of a Pittsburgh synagogue where eleven Jewish congregants were slaughtered last month by an avowed white supremacist and anti-Semite.

Photographers have also chronicled the resistance to racism and anti-Semitism, showing how Americans protest and resist bigotry in ways that can be quiet or outspoken, but always principled.

The juxtaposition of these distinct types of images shows the reality of hate, the possibility of defeating it, and photography's role in spurring change. The photographer Judy Glickman Lauder explores that contrast between the human capacity for virulent bigotry and the courage necessary to transcend it in *Beyond the Shadows: The Holocaust and the Danish Exception*. In her examination of this paradox, Ms. Glickman Lauder looks not to the present, but to an earlier and different era, when the Nazis exterminated millions in their demonic quest for religious and racial purity.

*Beyond the Shadows*, which includes text by Ms. Glickman Lauder, Michael Berenbaum, Judith S. Goldstein, and Elie Wiesel, alternates between two types of images. There are dark and evocative photographs, taken over the past thirty years, of Nazi concentration and extermination camps in Germany, Poland, and Czechoslovakia, as well as portraits and stories of Danish citizens who, under German occupation seventy-five years ago, bravely resisted the Third Reich by transporting to

Judy Glickman Lauder, A gas chamber at Auschwitz concentration camp, Poland, n.d.

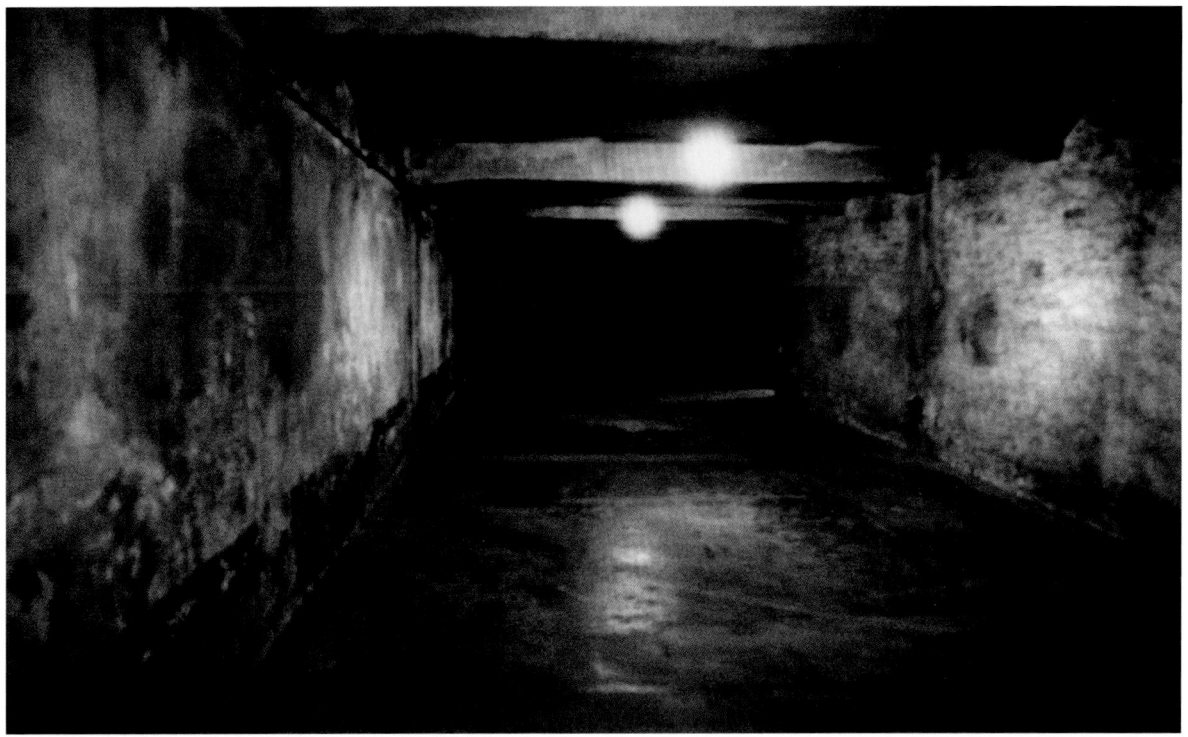

safety the country's Jews, some of whom are also profiled.

Ms. Glickman Lauder's haunting photographs of death camps—many rendered through the otherworldly glow of infrared film—make visible the mechanics of genocide: the Nazis's gas chambers, dissection tables, and crematories. Other images preserve the disturbing relics of those who died, from piles of shoes and luggage to a mound of human ash. These stark, atmospheric photographs are devoid of people, yet resonate with history and humanity. They are inhabited by ghosts—not only of innocent victims, but of the men and women who imprisoned, tortured, and murdered them.

"In the late 1980s, when I first visited Warsaw and Krakow, Auschwitz and Birkenau, I could almost hear the cries and feel the presence of what had occurred before me," Ms. Glickman Lauder wrote. "The

buildings, the rooms, the objects, the earth itself, the stones, the trees, the mass graves, and the ashes—all bore witness to the darkest period in our recent human history."

Ms. Glickman Lauder's photographs of Denmark's survivors tell another story, one of considerable daring and fortitude. The only country in World War II to defy Hitler's order to deport its Jews, Denmark shielded the vast majority of its Jewish population thanks to a network of Danish resisters who used small boats to spirit some 8,000 Jews to politically neutral Sweden.

Beyond the rescue, the Danish government, despite its accommodation with the Germans, took the unusual step of refusing to acknowledge its Jewish population as different, undermining a central tenet of Nazism: that Jews were racially inferior. "In Denmark, we were always regarded as normal citizens," Rabbi Bent Melchior recalled in a

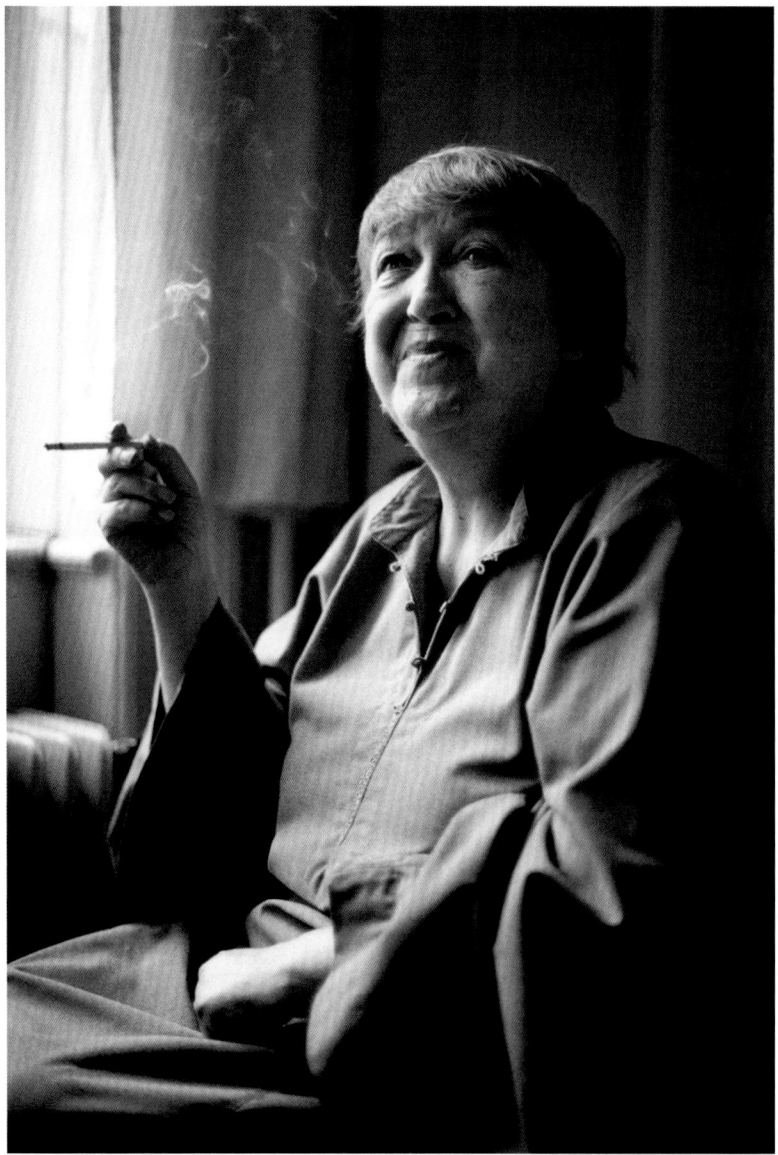

Judy Glickman Lauder, Karen Lykke Poulsen organized rescue operations and handled the transport of hundreds of Jews from the southern coast of Zealand, n.d.

2017 interview. "If a neighbor was being persecuted, you helped your neighbor."

Ultimately, the Danish resistance was a unique effort to stand up to Nazi degeneracy. "In the service of Christian and Democratic ideals—through a unique configuration of individual and institutional initiatives—Danes achieved collective morality in the pursuit of collective resistance, resilience, and rescue," Ms. Goldstein wrote.

Ms. Glickman Lauder's photographs and stories document how the Danes achieved this: Dr. Ebba Lund, while a student, defied the Gestapo by hiding escaped Jews; Svenn Erik Osterholm safeguarded religious texts from the main synagogue in Copenhagen; Bernt Hjejle, a well-connected lawyer, raised funds for the Jewish transport; and Karen Lykke Poulsen, active in the communist underground, oversaw the passage of hundreds of Jews from the southern coast of Zealand.

The photographs and stories in *Beyond the Shadows* are not just a reminder of how racism and anti-Semitism can foment violence and murder, but a warning for our uneasy present, when white nationalism and neo-Nazism are on the upswing. These stories are also a primer on how to stand up to prejudice, transcend tribalism, and embrace our shared humanity.

"Hatred, injustice, and genocide did not end with World War II, and evil is present with us today in too many parts of the world," Ms. Glickman Lauder wrote. "'The other' continues to be vilified. We must challenge ourselves to step out of the comfortable role of bystander, and to stand in the way of all forms of hate. We need the moral courage to act against all injustice."

In a sad twist, the book is also a reminder that history is not always destiny. As Ms.

Goldstein observed, the righteousness of the Danish rescue, once seen as a model of minority protection, no longer endures: "Today Denmark has closed its borders to refugees to preserve its welfare state and cohesive tribal identity," she wrote. "European countries are in crisis over diversity and national cohesion and security. The stability of Europe, torn over diversity, is once again at stake."

# The Faces of Bigotry: When the Hoods Come Off

Published August 21, 2017

The photographs from Charlottesville, Virginia, last weekend tell multiple stories. They document a rally, Unite the Right, where a protest over the removal of a Confederate monument served as a smokescreen for spewing racist and anti-Semitic hate. They show the counterprotesters who gathered to uphold the values of democracy and justice. They depict the murder and injury of some of these courageous individuals.

Some of the most fascinating and telling photographs focus on groups of enraged men carrying tiki torches and shouting racist and anti-Semitic slogans as they marched through the streets of Charlottesville. Perhaps the most significant implication of these images is the extent to which neo-Nazism and white supremacy have entered a new era—a movement mainstreamed by its followers and enabled by a sitting president.

These photographs and startling video footage portrayed neo-Nazis and white supremacists not as abstract figures lurking in shadows or concealed by hoods but as proud men and women openly displaying their bigotry. Their visibility also made them identifiable, so much so that a Twitter account, Yes, You're Racist, circulated photos of them in an effort to publicly expose and shame them.

The photographic documentation of hate has typically stressed the consequences of bigotry, violence, and genocide to demonstrate its gravity: the shattered, glass-strewn German streets, Jewish businesses, and synagogues that were photographed as the sun rose on the devastation of Kristallnacht in November 1938; stark pictures of young people clinging to a building as Bull Connor's troops targeted them with forceful water jets during the Children's Crusade

Chapter 4

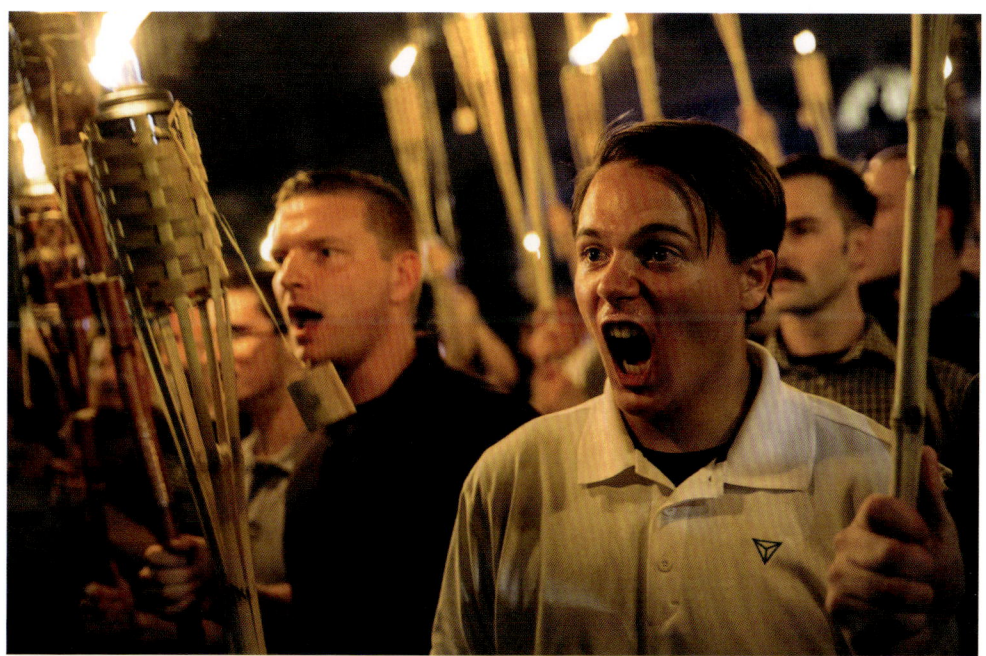

Samuel Corum, After marching through the University of Virginia campus with torches Peter Cvjetanovic (right) along with Neo Nazis, Alt-Right, and White Supremacists encircle and chant at counter protestors at the base of a statue of Thomas Jefferson, Charlottesville, Virginia, August 11, 2017

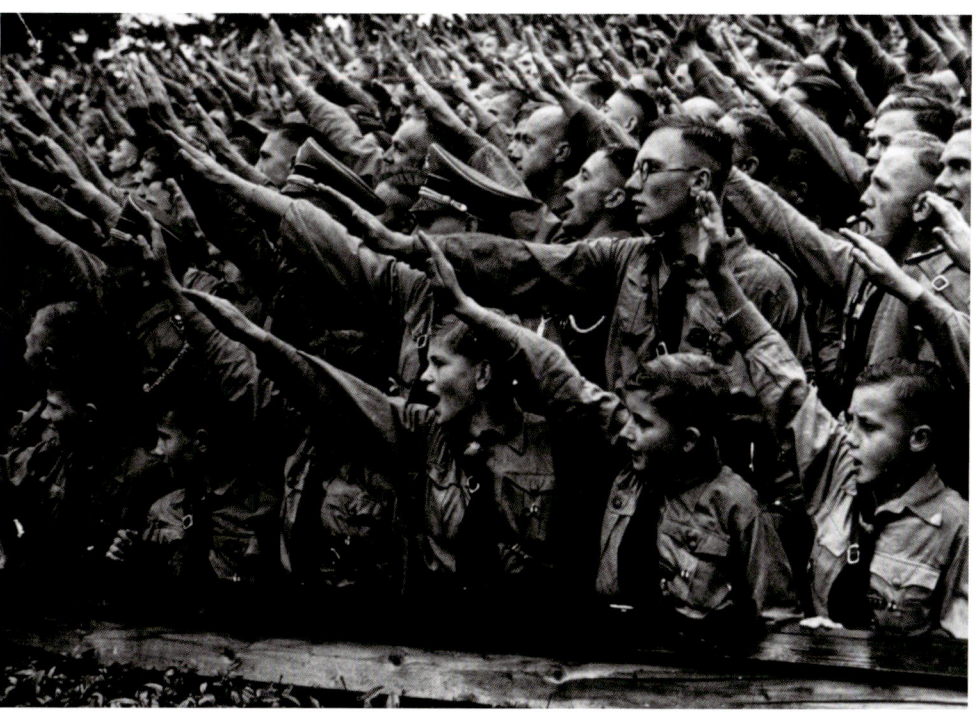

Photographer unknown, Hitler Youth. Some of the 48,000 boys and 5,000 girls who attended the Nazi Party Congress rally cheering and saluting Adolf Hitler's speech, Nuremberg, Germany, n.d.

in Birmingham, Alabama, in 1963; a dying Philando Castile, his bloodied and lifeless body live-streamed last summer by his girlfriend after he was shot by the police during a traffic stop near St. Paul, Minnesota.

But some of the most consequential photographs of racial discord, like the images out of Charlottesville, focus not on the victim but on the perpetrator. They reveal what pictures of oppression, violence, and destruction generally do not: the ordinary people who typically perpetuate white supremacy. These people are sons and daughters, siblings, spouses, and parents who today have traded Klan hoods for polo shirts and khakis. Many are college educated and employed in white collar jobs. They look like people we know—friends, coworkers, neighbors, and family. And they have one thing in common: an allegiance to a scurrilous ideology bent on intimidating, disempowering, and even annihilating African Americans, Jews, and others they view as foreign or racially impure.

A former FBI agent, Michael German, who went undercover with neo-Nazi and white supremacist groups, observed on CNN that the most perilous threat comes from activists who blend into mainstream society. "It wasn't necessarily the skinhead with the tattoos and the club who was dangerous," Mr. German said, "but somebody who wore a suit and went to work in an office and was college educated and much more capable as a threat than some drunk skinhead."

The mainstreaming of hate is not new. Cameras have revealed the ordinariness of racist and anti-Semitic agitators: the fresh-faced zealots of the Hitler Youth; the family-minded Nazi sympathizers of the German American Bund; the well-dressed lynch mobs, posing before Black and Mexican bodies dangling from trees; or the unrequited rage of a white teenager, her face contorted in fury, as she screams at an African American student integrating a high school in Little Rock, Arkansas.

But now President Trump's seeming inability to forcefully condemn as terrorism the actions of domestic hate groups enables them in ways that are unprecedented. To ignore, dismiss, or manipulate the implications of these photographs is to further the injustices they represent. As Donald J. Trump draws moral equivalence between the forces of racist and anti-Semitic hate and the men and women who stood up to them, he reveals a distorted sense of right and wrong.

We cannot ignore the logic of President Trump's words, which would equate the rebellious inmates of the Warsaw Ghetto with the Nazi collaborators who imprisoned and murdered them or condemn the brave young people of the Children's Crusade as they rose up against the noxious belief system of Jim Crow segregation. Can we credibly argue that these courageous people were morally equivalent to their oppressors?

The photographs of white supremacist rage and resentment in Charlottesville do more than affirm that unrepentant bigots live next door to us, date our sons and daughters, and work in our institutions. They also remind us that blindly supporting a president committed to stoking the flames of white supremacy and bigotry is itself an act of complicity.

A vast majority of Americans are good people who are clearly repulsed by what they have witnessed in the photographs of Charlottesville. But the very ordinariness of the people these images bluntly represent underscores that bigotry is not solely perpetrated at the extremes and as something exceptional. It is everywhere, having infiltrated every corner of society and culture, in places and institutions on the right, left, and in the middle.

Will Counts, Students of Central High School, including Hazel Bryan, shout insults at Elizabeth Eckford as she calmly walks toward a line of National Guardsmen. The Guardsmen blocked the main entrance and would not let her enter, Little Rock, Arkansas, September 4, 1957

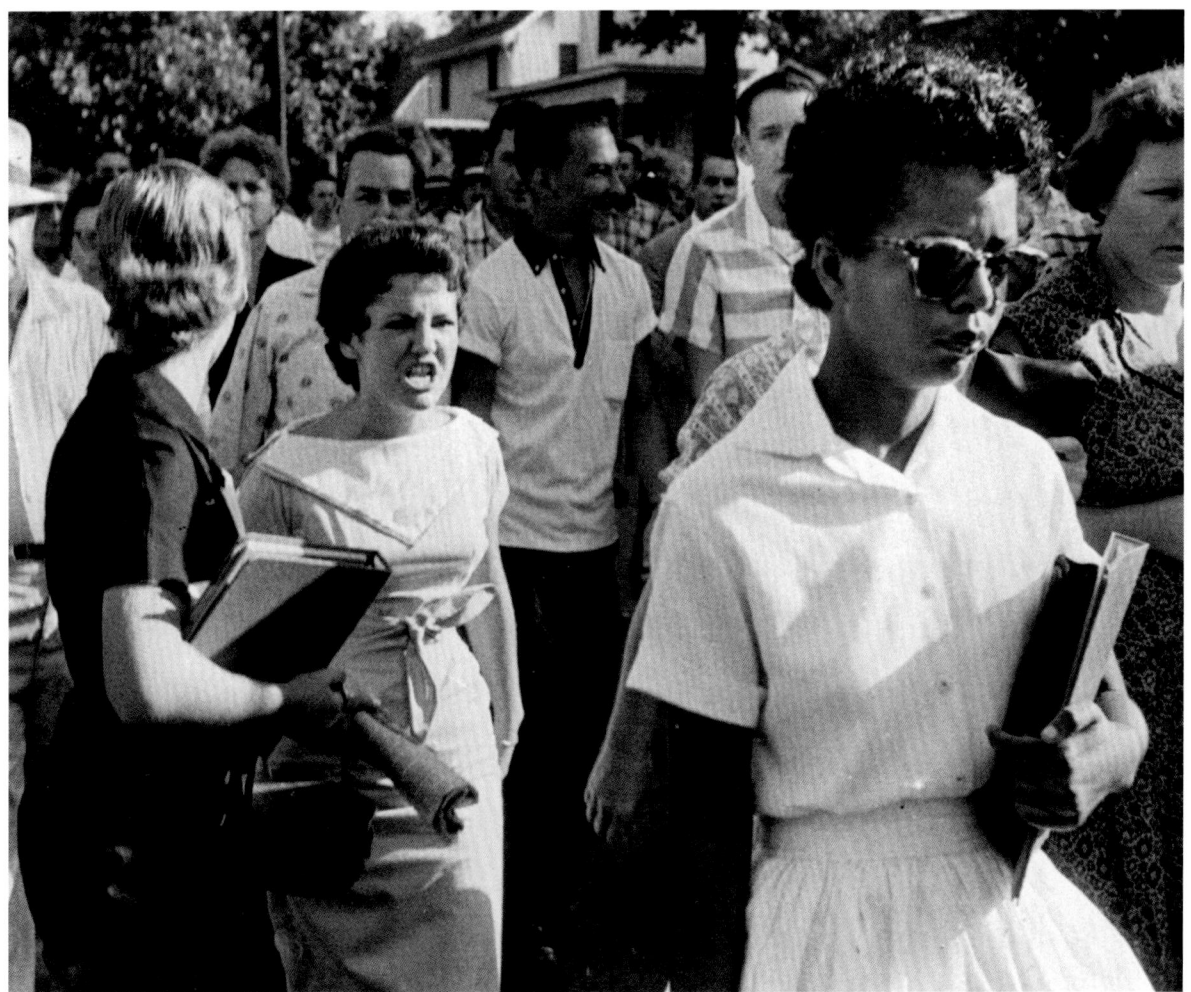

# Civil Rights, One Person and One Photo at a Time

Published April 22, 2013

The hands of the father and his young daughter wave emphatically: The two are not in agreement. The man, looking down, speaks. The child listens, but continues to take a cookie from the plate on the dinner table.

The scene is not unusual: A father is telling his daughter that she will not be going to an amusement park. But he is doing so not because it is a school day, or because he is punishing her. He fears for her safety.

The father is Martin Luther King Jr., the child is his seven-year-old daughter Yolanda, and the two are engaged in a conversation that no parent wants to have. He is explaining to the girl for the first time the hazards of segregation and the reasons she cannot visit Fun Town, a popular but restricted theme park in Atlanta.

This photograph, which first appeared in a 1963 photo-essay in *Look* magazine, is emotionally intimate and psychologically insightful, like many of the images in *Controversy and Hope: The Civil Rights Photographs of James Karales.* The book, by Julian Cox, provides a singular opportunity to reevaluate the innovative work of Mr. Karales, who died in 2002, at age seventy-one.

As Dr. King's aide and confidante Andrew Young notes in the book's foreword, Mr. Karales's photographs were distinguished by their ability to reveal the "complexity of emotions intertwined with the hopes and hardships of the struggle." Their personal, contemplative approach was not always in step with a mainstream press enthralled by the high drama of historic speeches, conflagrations, and demonstrations. This approach may also have been the reason Dr. King, who was fiercely protective of his family, granted the photographer unprecedented access to them.

Chapter 4

Mr. Karales typically favored the individual over the collective, and his photographs are more like artful portraits than the straightforward documentation of momentous events. In his reporting on the Selma to Montgomery march for voting rights in the spring of 1965, for example, he frequently photographed participants—the famous and the unknown—up close, carefully rendering their individuality and state of mind.

His images of the march resonate with nuances of emotion and psychology: a tight, brooding shot of a young demonstrator in profile; the bitter, scowling face of a segregationist being arrested; a Black child nestled contently on the shoulders of a bearded white man; the indelibly memorable photograph of an African American teenager staring wearily into the camera, the word *vote* emblazoned on his whitewashed forehead.

This intimate viewpoint aligned Mr. Karales more with the strategies of the Black press than those of the mainstream media. Just as the mainstream media dispensed profiles about white people—relegating people of color to stereotypical, sensationalistic, or communal reporting—publications owned and operated by African Americans covered the private lives of ordinary and famous people alike.

These profiles, accompanied by photographs or drawings, were the mainstay of one of the earliest Black pictorial magazines, the *Crisis*, edited by the civil rights leader W. E. B. Du Bois. In the civil rights era, the profiles continued to have a central role in the periodicals of the Johnson Publishing Company—*Ebony*, *Jet*, and *Tan*, the first Black women's magazine—subtly challenging the status quo by emphasizing, rather than concealing,

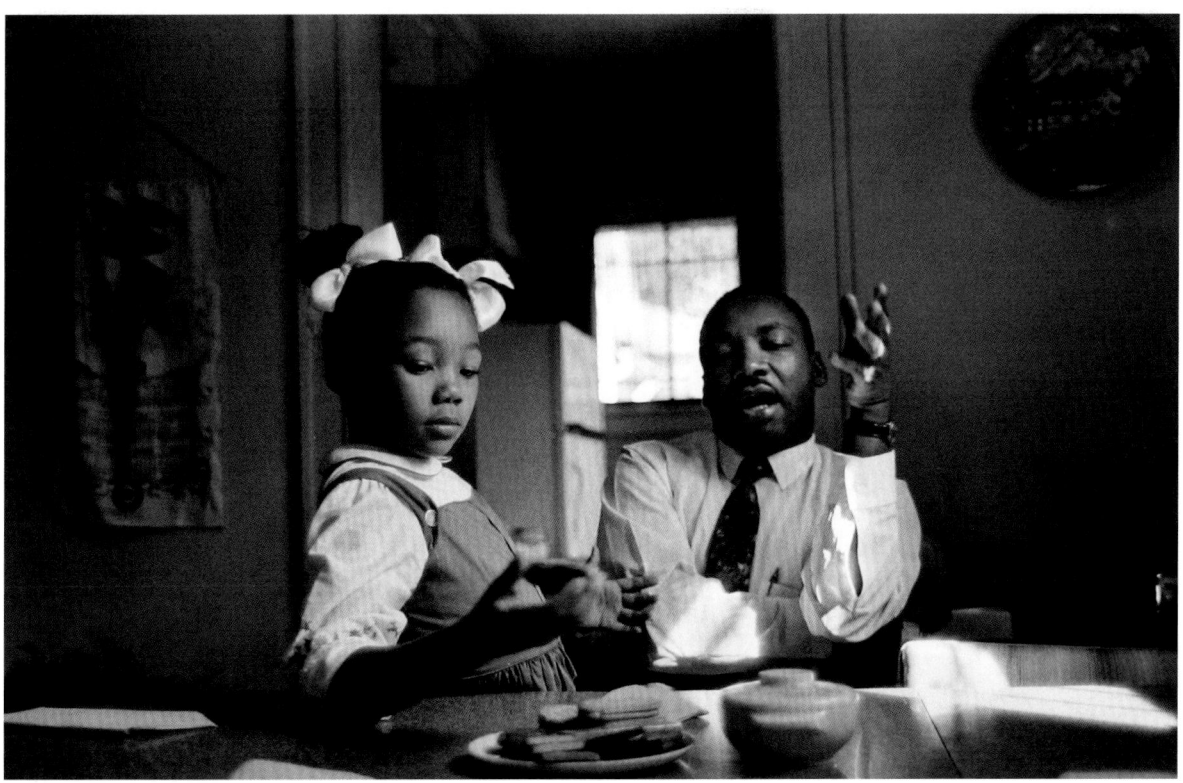

James Karales, *Martin Luther King Jr.*, 1962

African American humanity, individuality, and psychological nuance.

If Mr. Karales's method was akin to that of the Black press, it was driven not by sympathy—the motivation Mr. Cox ascribes to it—but by empathy. Born into an immigrant Greek family in Canton, Ohio, in 1930, Mr. Karales struggled to learn English. He experienced firsthand the hardships of a community routinely viewed as exotic, inferior, and not quite American. After working blue-collar manufacturing jobs, he enrolled in Ohio University and studied photography.

Mr. Karales was determined to use his camera in the service of social justice. From his first photo-essay—a tender, keenly observed profile of Canton's working-class, Greek American community—he strove to reveal the complexity of his subjects by stressing the individual details lost amid collective stereotypes and biases.

Over a half-century career, including a staff position at *Look* that gave him a national platform, Mr. Karales continually fixed his lens on the marginal, the besieged, and the politically fraught: coal miners in the racially integrated but economically depressed town of Rendville, Ohio; racial discrimination in organized religion; the quagmire of the Vietnam War; and segregation in New York City. (Those last photographs went unpublished, perhaps because they upended the era's myth of Northern racial tolerance.)

Nowhere is Mr. Karales's defiance of racial clichés more apparent than in his 1960 *Look* profile of Richard Adams, a pioneering speech therapist and social worker. The photo-essay inverted racial typecasting: Adams was Black, his students were mostly white, and they coexisted not in a Northern city but in rural Iowa. These images of adoring youngsters and their dedicated teacher spoke to the possibility of racial harmony. But they also called into question an abiding myth of integration: that African Americans had the most to gain from it.

Mr. Karales's focus on the individual succeeded—paradoxically, as Mr. Cox notes—because it added to his work "some sense of a common, shared humanity." By affirming our fundamental similarities, his images implored Americans, in an age of turmoil and transition, to reexamine their own humanity. Rather than presenting predictable scenes of racial disunity, they challenged a nation to face the individuals it had reduced to collective symbols of fear, condescension, and hate. There, in the midst of crowds and chaos, he found one person, one image.

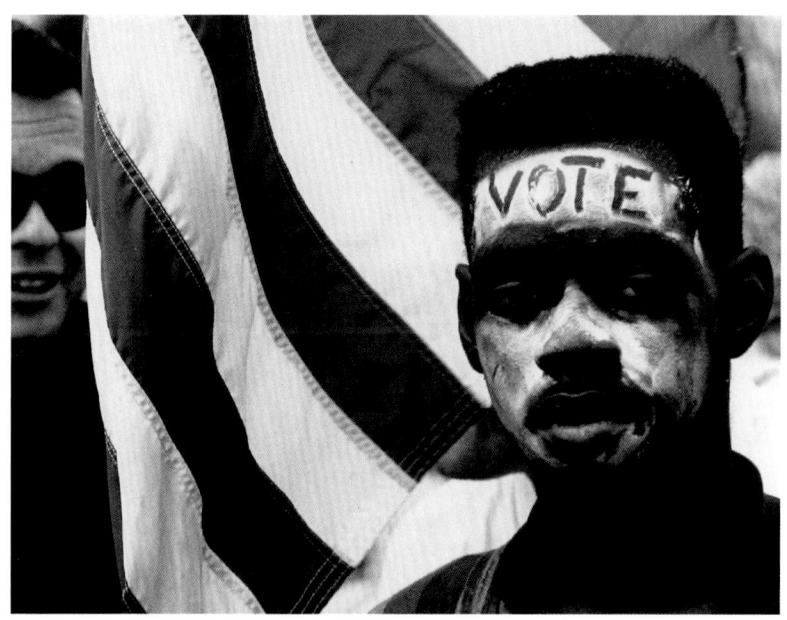

James Karales, *Vote, Selma*, 1965

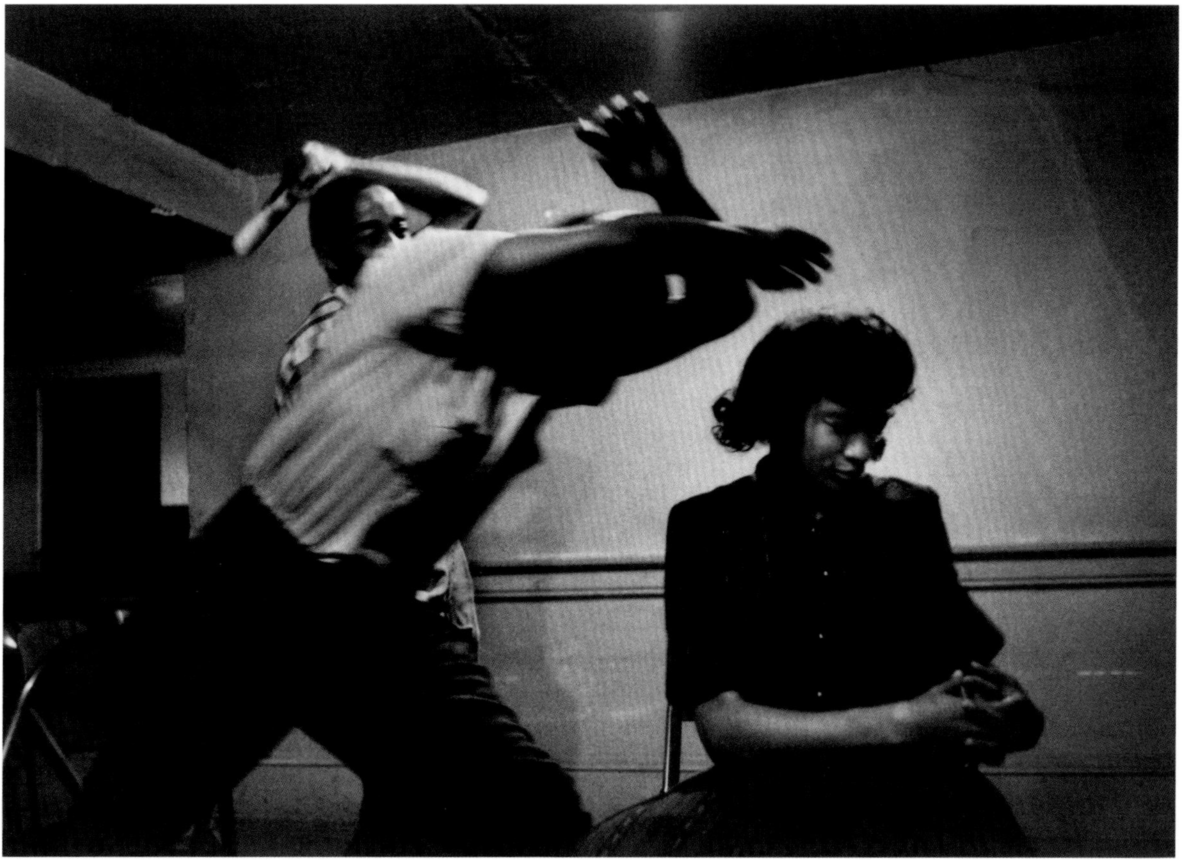

James Karales, *Passive Resistance Training, SNCC*, 1960

Witnessing

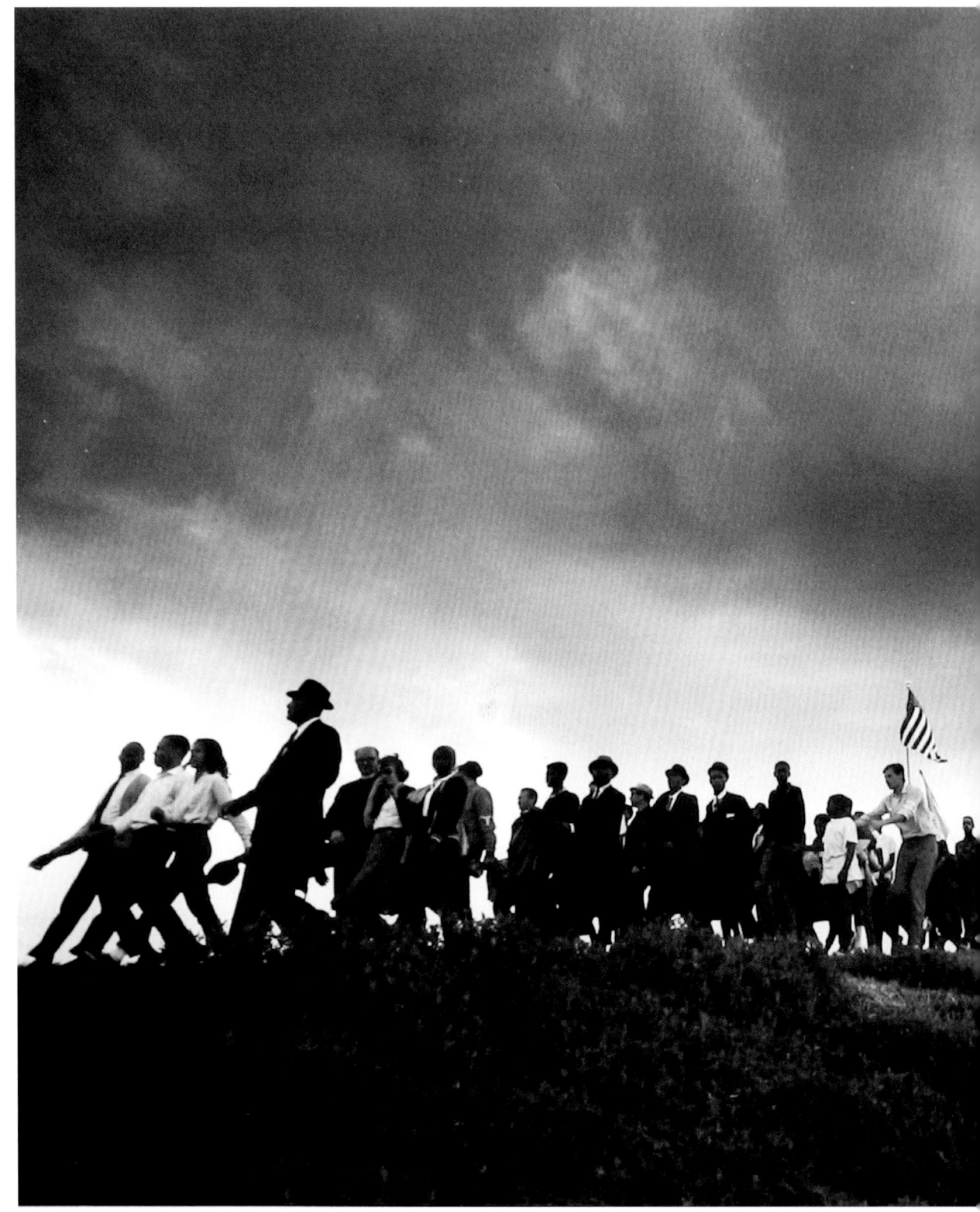

James Karales, *Selma to Montgomery March, Alabama*, 1965

Chapter 4

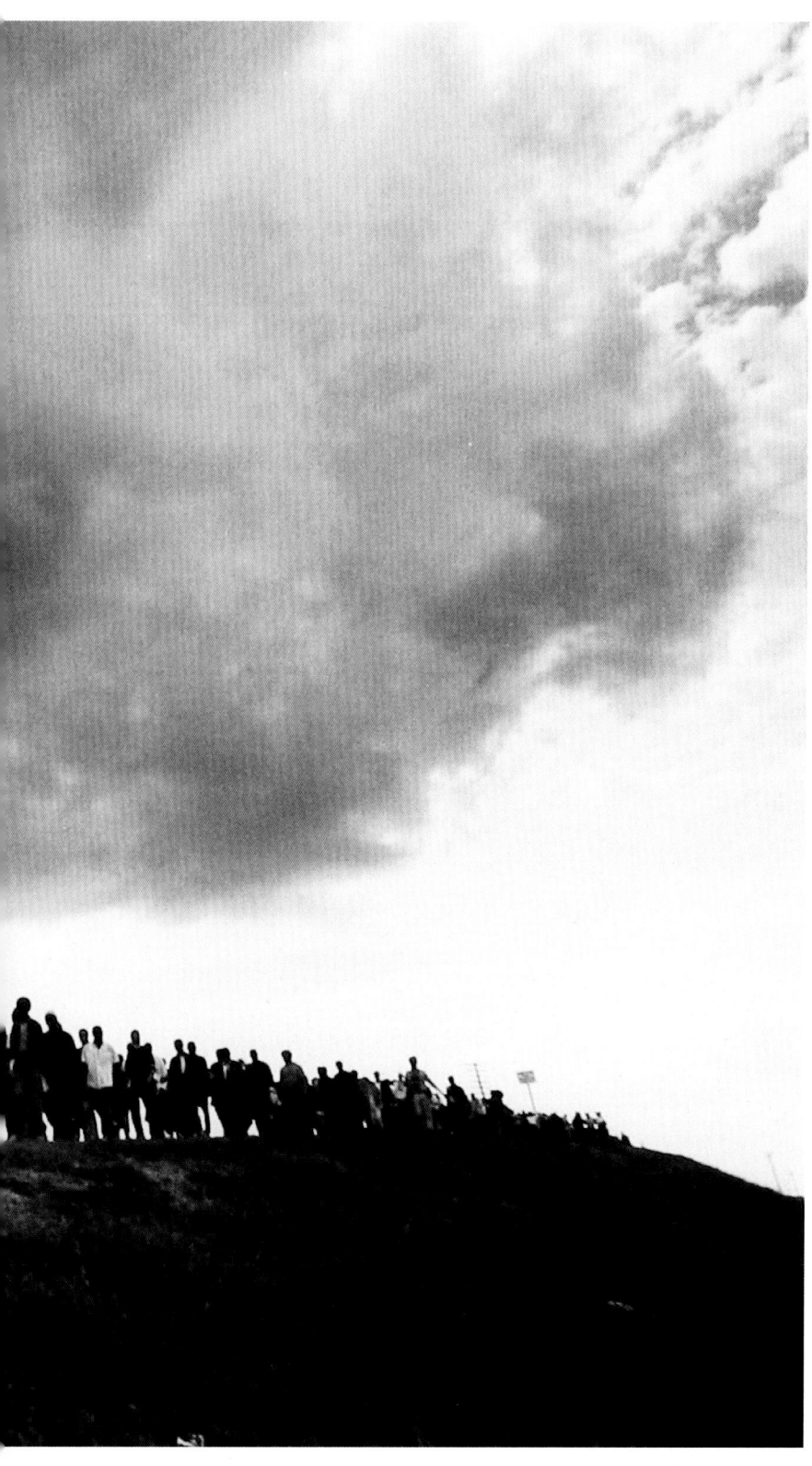

Witnessing

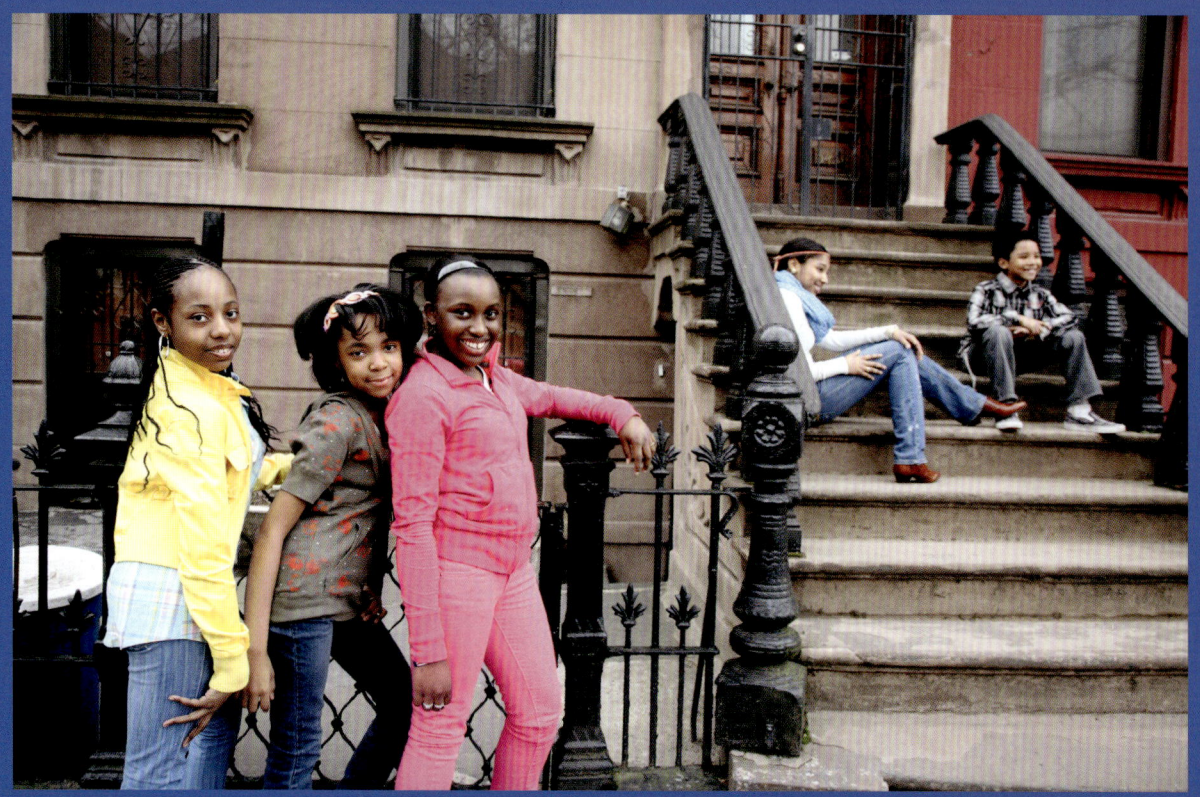

Jamel Shabazz, *The Youth, Clinton Hill, Brooklyn*, 2007

Community:
Visualizing
the Connections
between Us

# CHAPTER FIVE

# Jamel Shabazz's Forty Years of Sights and Styles in New York

Published May 2, 2017

When Jamel Shabazz began photographing New York in 1980, the city was recovering from one of its most tumultuous periods. By the late-1970s, New York was facing a faltering economy, a serious drug problem, and the physical deterioration of many neighborhoods. New York was ripe for sociological analysis and hand-wringing.

But where others saw danger and decay, Mr. Shabazz saw an opportunity: to represent the complexity of an imperiled generation of Black and Latino young people who were creating an empowering and influential urban culture.

It is not surprising, then, that Mr. Shabazz has called his new book—which chronicles life in New York over the past four decades—*Sights in the City: New York Street Photographs*, taking the title from a song by one of his favorite hip-hop artists, the rapper Keith Elam, known as Guru, who died in 2010.

Focusing on communities of color, including a generation of younger African American men who grew up in the city as he did, Mr. Shabazz has produced an epochal work that explores the power of style, fashion, music, and culture to uplift and enrich urban life.

Mr. Shabazz's interest in photography began as a child in the 1960s, growing up in the Red Hook section of Brooklyn. His father had been a Navy photographer in the 1950s. At home, he was surrounded by images, including his father's photos and picture magazines like *Life* and *National Geographic*. He borrowed his mother's camera when he was fifteen and photographed his friends in junior high school. His commitment to photography intensified when he entered the army.

After serving three years in Germany, Mr. Shabazz, who went on to a career as a correction officer, came back to a city transformed.

Chapter 5

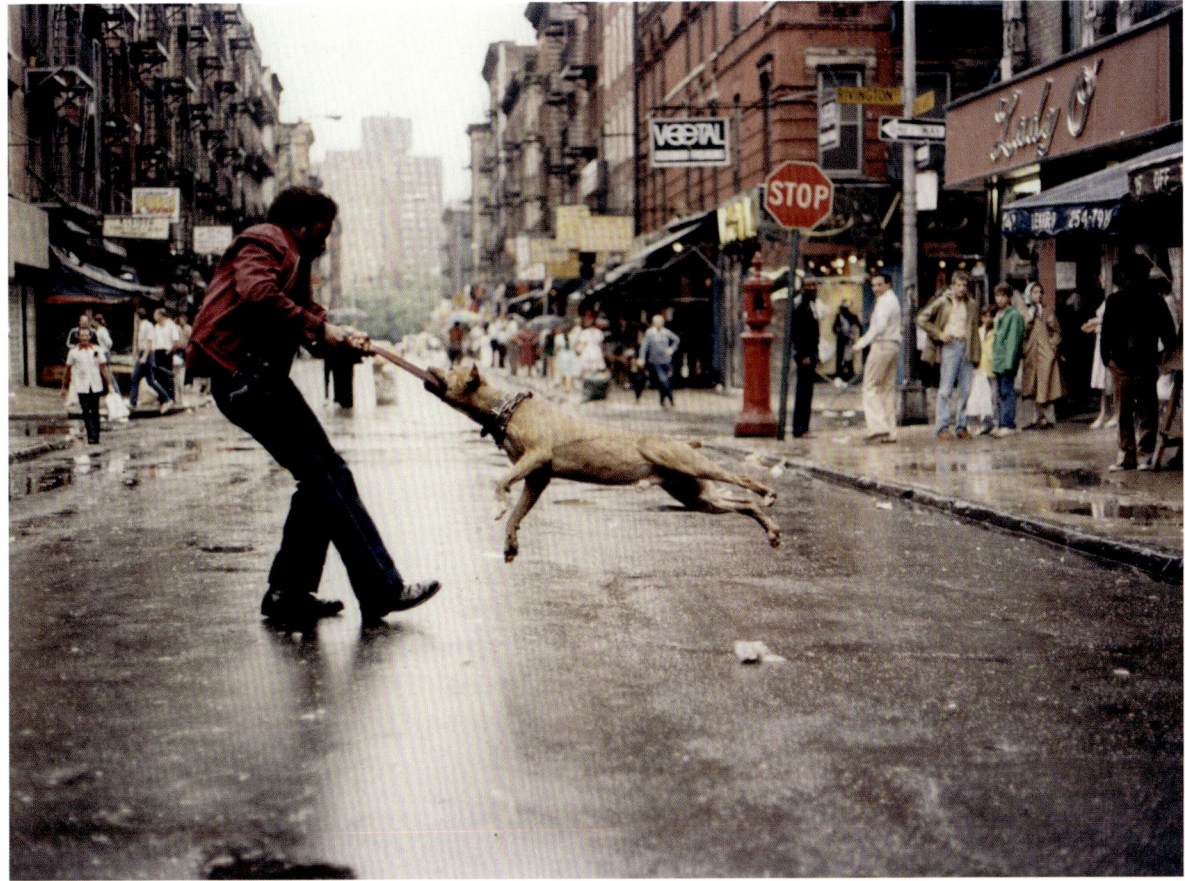

"I returned home to the United States with a new camera and with a new vision to try to capture a part of my life that was gone," Mr. Shabazz recalled. "During the time period in which I was away, so much had changed in my community, so I came back thirsting to catch up with people and, in a sense, to establish a vision diary—photograph people and engage in conversation about what had been going on." The resulting pictures from this period challenged prevailing stereotypes by concentrating on the personal style of his subjects, some of it influenced by an emerging hip-hop culture.

"Clothing in most cases is the central item that reflects one's cultural identity," he said. "I speak mainly about the Black and Brown communities here in this city, because I have photographed them more than any other demographic. The Flatbush section of Brooklyn, for example, is a diverse community that is home to people from various Caribbean islands. Each has their own style and culture that can often be identified by certain items that they wear such as beads or trinkets representing the colors of their island's flags."

Mr. Shabazz's imagery is wide-ranging. Photographs of young people, radiating with hip-hop style, are juxtaposed with images that address social problems: the scantily clad backside of a prostitute leaning into a car; a homeless man sleeping in the doorway of a shuttered Holiday Inn in Chinatown; and a suspect apprehended by the police in an attempted robbery.

But Mr. Shabazz uses his camera predominantly to challenge stereotypes and negative perceptions about urban life—and especially about New York's Black and Brown residents—by focusing on the vitality, diversity, and dignity of his subjects. He shows young Black men performing on a Midtown street; hijab-clad mannequins in a shop; a Hasidic Jew, a Black man, and an Asian American teenager standing alongside one another in Union Square; people talking in front of the elaborately decorated facade of the Ethiopian Orthodox Coptic Church in Harlem; soldiers taking instruction from their commander; and a teenager posing in front of a wall covered in effervescent red graffiti.

Mr. Shabazz considers himself a social documentarian, aware that city life and culture are inevitably infused with political and social meaning. "As a child coming of age during the turbulent 1960s, I became a witness early on to political and social issues in America," he said. "Later, it was the work of documentary photographer Leonard Freed that first exposed me to what a social documentarian was on a more personal level. In his award-winning book and personal diary *Black in White America*, it became clear to me how a photographer could use his or her abilities to capture images that address an array of social and political issues. Freed was skilled in that area, and provided me with a template for what I would do later on."

A photograph Mr. Shabazz took last year suggests how drastically New York's neighborhoods have changed since he began photographing them almost forty years ago. Aptly titled *Representing*, the photo shows a Harlem apartment building, its fire

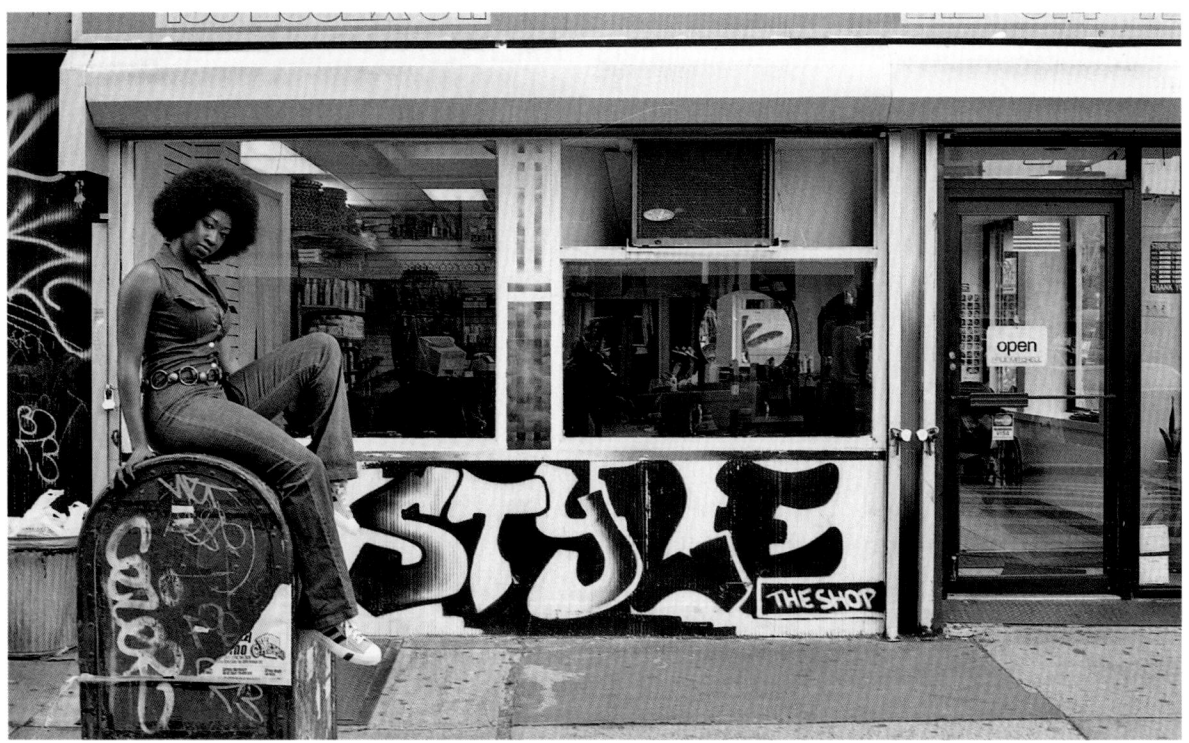

Jamel Shabazz, *Style, Lower East Side, Manhattan*, 2002

Chapter 5

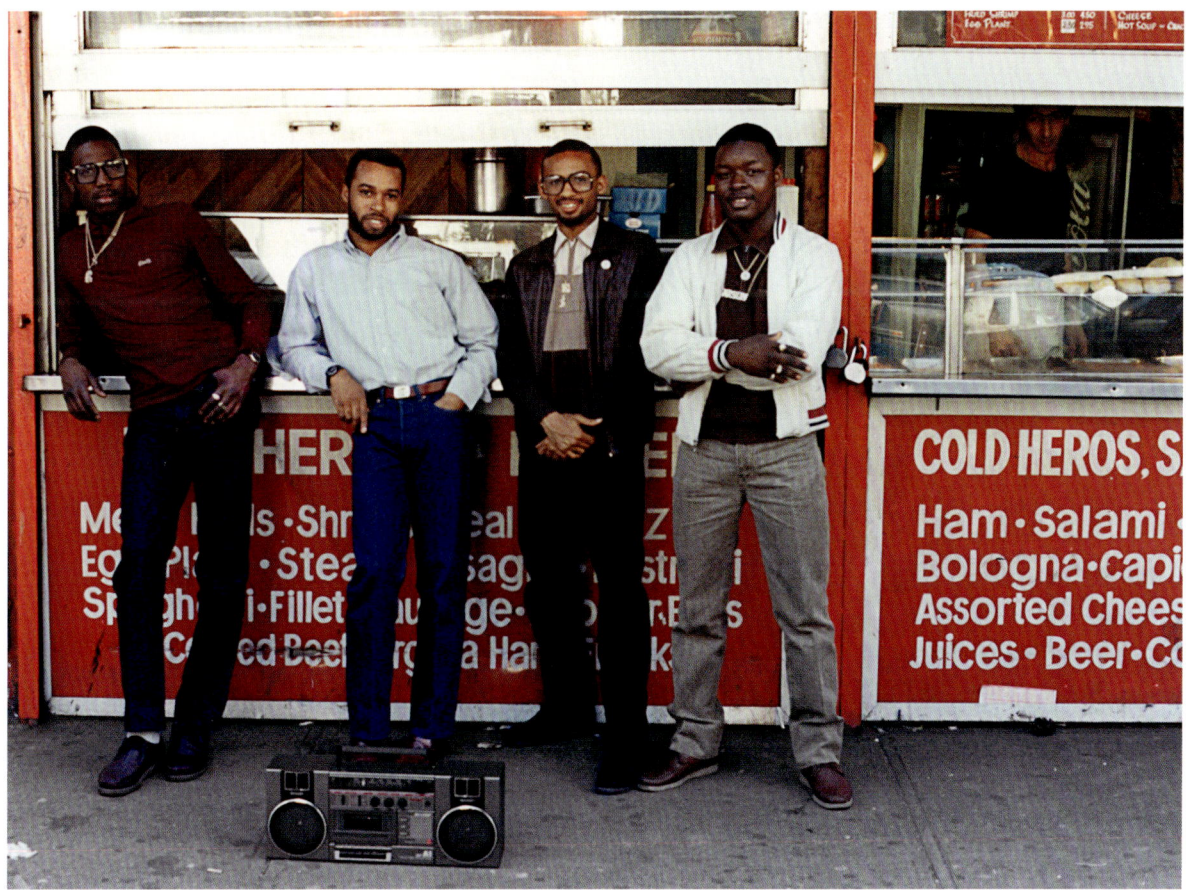

escapes adorned with large flags, including those of the United States, the Dominican Republic, and Panama. As he did in his early years, Mr. Shabazz again captures the social and cultural implications of a city in flux, this time observing New Yorkers as they navigate their future in neighborhoods that are becoming increasingly gentrified and diverse.

"When I was coming up, communities were pretty much separated across racial lines," he said. "In documenting Harlem for nearly three decades, for example, many of the people from that community that I once crossed paths with on a regular basis are no longer there. Many have been priced out by the high cost of rents and have since moved on to more affordable areas. So in looking at some of my more recent work from that particular neighborhood, you will find a lot more diversity than you would have seen in the 1980s."

# Complicating the Picture of Urban Life

Published February 23, 2015

The 1980 image of Paul Newman, taken in the South Bronx during the filming of *Fort Apache, the Bronx*, could be a production still or a publicity photo. But the photograph was taken on location for more consequential reasons: Its photographer, Joe Conzo Jr., the teenage son of activists, was there to document a film that many in the community believed would hurt and embarrass it.

Perhaps Mr. Newman sensed that. The famously liberal actor—an outsider slumming on Mr. Conzo's turf—glared at the camera while a production assistant tried futilely to wave off the photographer.

This image appears in a provocative new exhibition at the Bronx Museum of Art, *Three Photographers from the Bronx: Jules Aarons, Morton Broffman, and Joe Conzo*, which opens February 26. The disparate subjects of its three Bronx-born, socially conscious photographers—the civil rights movement, life outside Manhattan, and community advocacy—would at first seem to have little in common.

According to the exhibition's curator, Antonio Sergio Bessa, what ties their work together is a shared interest in "photography as a form of activism that informs our awareness of community." But these photographs do more than make us aware of the role and power of community. They also illuminate the transitions, displacements, and complexity of urban life, as well as the conventions or biases that color our understanding of it.

Mr. Broffman's images may at first appear irrelevant to city life. Taken during the height of the civil rights movement, they document some of its most historic events, including the Selma, Alabama, to Montgomery, Alabama, march in 1965; the last Sunday sermon of the Reverend Dr. Martin Luther King Jr.; and the Poor People's Campaign in Washington.

Chapter 5

Mr. Broffman engaged the movement during a time when most white people regarded it with anxiety, indifference, or outright hostility. Like many activist photographers, he embraced a strain of progressive urban politics that argued for the interrelated interests and destinies of Americans North and South, Black and white.

"While his perspective is undeniably that of a documentarian looking into the epic struggle of African Americans for social justice," Mr. Bessa wrote about Mr. Broffman, "his images exude the sense of kinship and camaraderie that was a hallmark of the civil rights movement." This kinship drove activists of all races to temporarily leave the relative safety and comfort of Northern cities to work in the noxious environment of the Jim Crow South.

The images of Mr. Aarons, who was both an astrophysicist and a photographer, suggest another kind of displacement. Taken between the 1940s and 1970s, the photographs relocated street photography from the hustle and bustle of the central city to quieter outer precincts, including Rockaway Beach, the Bronx, and the ethnic enclaves of Boston's West and North Ends. Rather than showing romanticized meditations on life in the big metropolis, Mr. Aarons depicted prosaic but consequential moments, in ways befitting a scientist in his precise, though humanistic, appraisal of urban life.

Significantly, Mr. Aarons's photographs of the Bronx testify to the migration of upwardly mobile Jewish families from the tenements of the Lower East Side and East Harlem to the desirable Art Deco buildings along the Grand Concourse. In so doing, they remind us of the shifting fortunes and transformations of neighborhoods as well as the ways they enter into our collective imagination, as wells of possibilities or as symbols of urban decay.

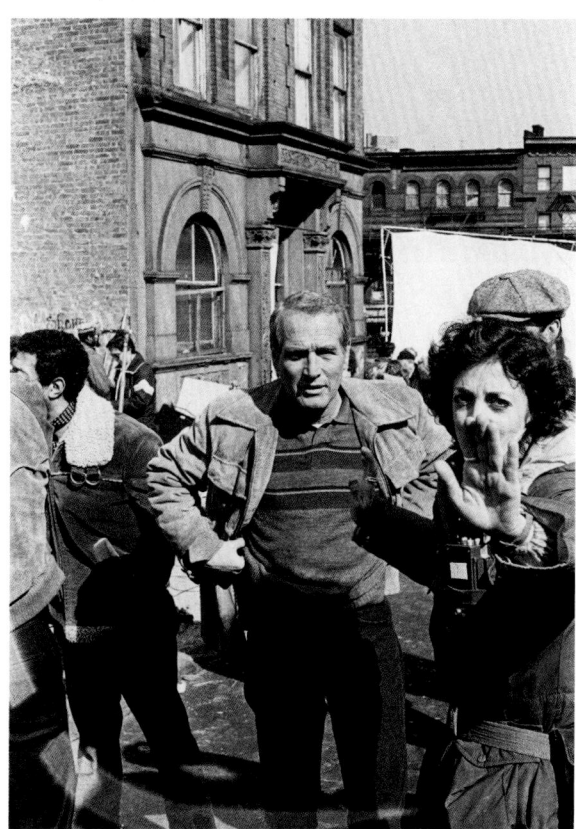

Joe Conzo, *Paul Newman on the Set of "Fort Apache, the Bronx,"* 1980

Over the past forty years, our collective view of the Bronx has all too often embraced the media-driven myth of its inexorable decline. For many, the blight, addiction, and poverty that plagued parts of the South Bronx in the 1970s have come to symbolize the whole borough. But as Mr. Conzo's photographs suggest, the reality of the Bronx has been far more complicated. They demonstrate the power of courage, cultural expression, and political advocacy to sustain even the most endangered neighborhoods.

Mr. Conzo, who is best known for his pioneering documentation of hip-hop's early years, is represented in the exhibition by his photographs of the Committee Against Fort Apache, a grass-roots coalition that challenged the distortions and ethnic stereotypes of the 1981 movie. In it, Mr. Newman starred as a conflicted police officer assigned to South Bronx's 41st Precinct—Fort Apache—depicted in the film as teeming with murderers, prostitutes, and drug addicts.

The committee was spearheaded by the activist Richie Pérez and Mr. Conzo's grandmother, Dr. Evelina López Antonetty, a legendarily outspoken advocate for Puerto Rican families. The young photographer, still in high school, tagged along to demonstrations as well as shooting locations, becoming the principal chronicler of committee activities.

Mr. Conzo's prodigious images testify to a focused and media-savvy movement, from committee representatives meeting with studio executives to a news conference by the activist and writer Gerson Borrero at Lincoln Hospital. By concentrating on sophisticated political activism—in the service of ethnic and community pride—Mr. Conzo's photographs tell a different story about the Bronx, one as meticulous as Mr. Aarons's and as socially conscious as Mr. Broffman's. In so doing, they brighten our collective imagination of a place often left for dead by the media.

"Community is predicated on a narrative, and consequently susceptible to control," Mr. Bessa wrote in the catalog. "Indeed, as one starts to ponder the shape and boundaries of community, the delicate balance between inclusion and exclusion, between belonging and otherness, becomes apparent and complicate the picture."

In the end, three talented Bronx-born photographers managed to complicate the picture, creating a more textured and less static view of urban life—the ever-changing metropolis rich with activism, self-possession, and hope.

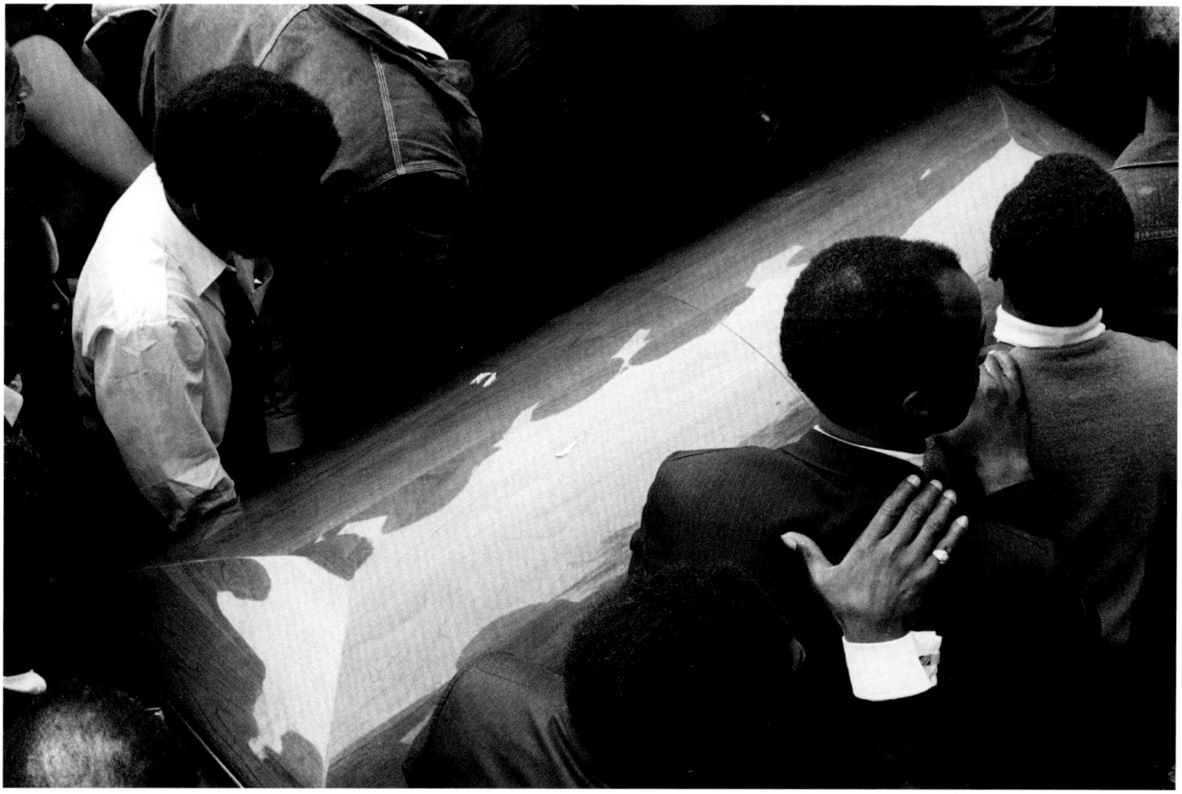

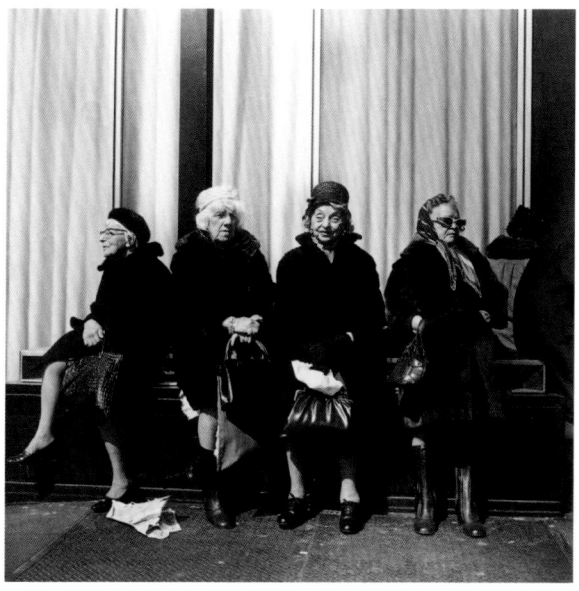

Morton Broffman, *Martin Luther King Jr.* The casket of Dr. Martin Luther King Jr. being carried by pallbearers in Atlanta, Georgia, April 5, 1968

Jules Aarons, *Other Women in the Bronx, 170th Street*, ca. late 1960s

# Born by a River, Watching the Change

Published February 21, 2014

The interplay of images in LaToya Ruby Frazier's *Landscape of the Body (Epilepsy Test)* is haunting: a portrait of the artist's mother in a disheveled hospital bed hooked up to monitors, juxtaposed with a shot of the Braddock, Pennsylvania, hospital's demolition taken shortly after her stay, its tangled wiring exposed.

This work is being exhibited at the Seattle Art Museum in *LaToya Ruby Frazier: Born by a River*, a powerful show about the lives of the artist's imperiled hometown. Ms. Frazier, thirty-two, currently a fellow at the American Academy in Berlin, is the latest recipient of the museum's Gwendolyn Knight and Jacob Lawrence Prize, a biannual award to an early-career Black artist that culminates in a solo exhibition.

Braddock, in the Pittsburgh suburbs along the banks of the Monongahela River, was once a flourishing steel town, home to Andrew Carnegie's first steel mill and the first Carnegie Library. As of the 2010 census, it had not quite 2,200 residents, a ninety percent decline from its 1920s heyday.

As *Born by a River* documents, the quality of life in the largely African American town has deteriorated over the years, a victim of lost jobs, toxic waste, political neglect, redlining, and white flight. Braddock's lone hospital—the scene of Ms. Frazier's mother's portrait, the town's largest employer and main provider of medical care—closed in 2010 when its owner relocated it to a more affluent suburb.

*Born by a River*, organized by Sandra Jackson-Dumont, a curator at the Seattle Art Museum, functions on three visual levels. Large color aerial photographs taken from a helicopter represent Braddock from a distance. Smaller black-and-white images record its broken land and buildings. And portraits,

Chapter 5

also in black and white, document the private lives of Ms. Frazier and her family, who have lived in Braddock for three generations.

The colorful and rhythmic patterns of buildings, lots, and roads spied from above at first suggest a flourishing town. Closer inspection reveals signs of deteriorating infrastructure and aggressive redevelopment: the modest home of a longtime resident and activist, Isaac Bunn, assessed by the town as worthless, vacant land, is seen in bird's-eye view as the last holdout on a street overtaken by the industrial storage of large white bags of shredded rubber tires.

Ms. Frazier's stark black-and-white photographs zero in on the details of a community engulfed by privation, illness, and ruin: barely habitable homes surrounded by decaying buildings and abandoned construction sites; a forlorn recliner, the walls above it marked by the ghosts of long-gone artifacts and mirrors, the floor below littered with detritus; the unsmiling faces of people coping with chronic pollution-borne diseases, including Ms. Frazier herself, who has lupus.

The project's title was inspired by Sam Cooke's "A Change Is Gonna Come," an epochal civil rights–era song in which the protagonist, "born by the river" in a time of rampant segregation and racism, imagines a better and more just world. Glimmers of optimism and self-possession shine through the gloom of Ms. Frazier's pictures—from the splendor of her deceased grandmother's doll collection to the determination on her young cousin's face—rescuing her subjects from the visual stereotypes of Black poverty.

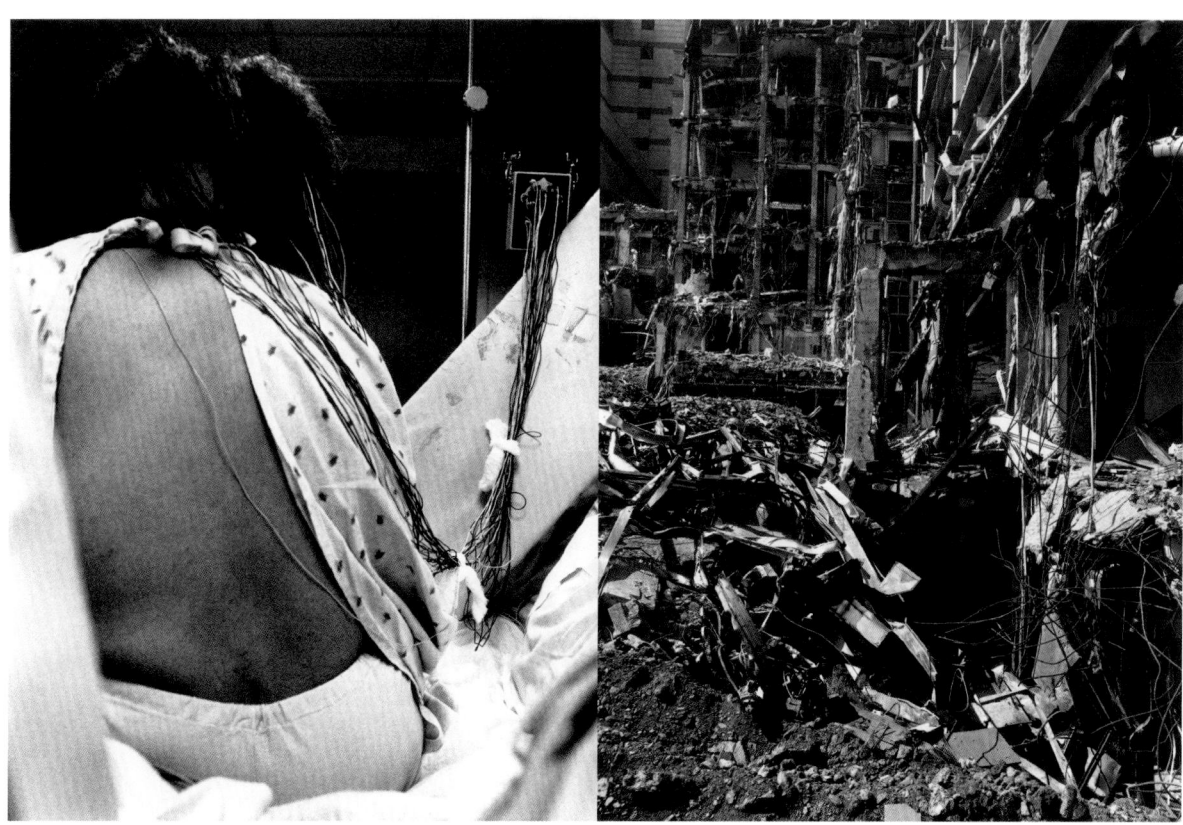

LaToya Ruby Frazier, *Landscape of the Body (Epilepsy Test)*, 2011

As part of an initiative to revitalize Braddock's faltering economy, its ambitious, Harvard-educated mayor, John Fetterman, has supported the development of green industries and partnerships with nonprofit organizations. But it is the transformation of Braddock into a thriving cultural hub that has been the cornerstone of his administration. Widely reported in the news media, his efforts have attracted artists with the promise of affordable housing and studio space.

Offers to shoot major films there soon followed, including *Out of the Furnace*, a 2013 thriller starring Christian Bale as a steelworker avenging the murder of his Iraq War–veteran brother, and *The Road*, based on Cormac McCarthy's Pulitzer Prize–winning novel about a father and son on a post-apocalyptic journey. Back in 2010, Braddock was chosen by Levi Strauss & Company as the setting of its "Go Forth: Ready to Work" advertising campaign. The stylized print and television ads highlighted the plight of the Rust Belt, featuring local residents and a slogan that was as dubious as it was patronizing: "Everybody's work is equally important."

As the unrelenting adversity documented in *Born by a River* affirms, however, gentrification and the cultural activity of outsiders rarely alleviate the underlying problems of poverty and racism. In a video produced by the PBS series *Art21* and included in the Seattle exhibition, Ms. Frazier is filmed in performance in Manhattan in front of a Levi's pop-up store in a former SoHo art gallery, which displayed images from "Go Forth." In it, she rends the Levi's jeans she wears by repeatedly scraping her legs against the sidewalk.

On one level, the performance counters Levi's romanticized view of work and of Braddock as an icon of blue-collar fortitude and solidarity. On another, it speaks to the insidiousness of gentrification, which can tear a community apart by driving up rents and property values and displacing its poorest residents.

For Ms. Frazier, a gifted artist who has been photographing her hometown since she was sixteen, it is self-determination that provides the most just and durable path to renewal.

"What I feel an urgency to do at this moment is to return back home," she says in the *Art21* video. "Not as the artist, LaToya Ruby Frazier, but as the citizen of Braddock, Pennsylvania, LaToya Ruby Frazier . . . [and] do something about what they've done to my community."

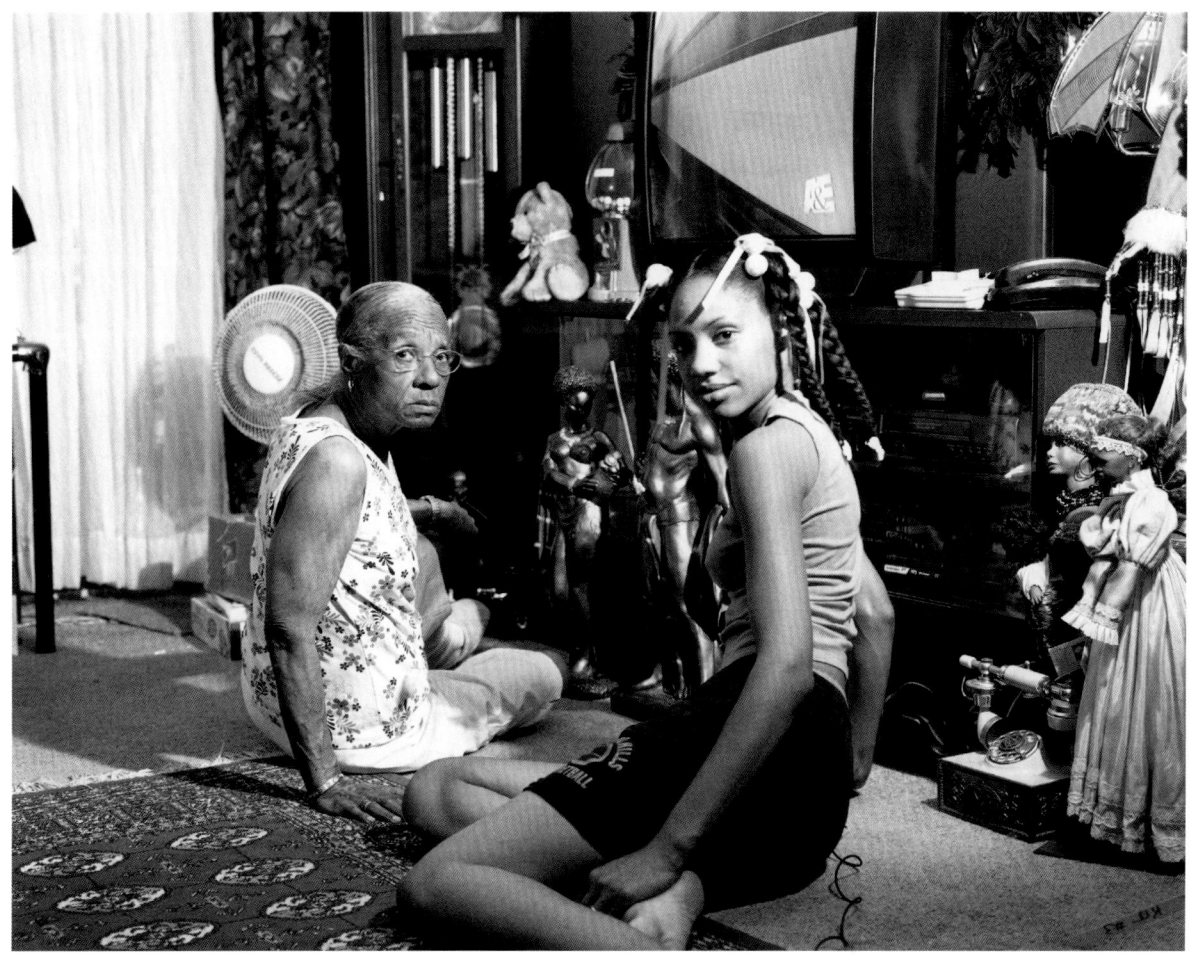

LaToya Ruby Frazier, *Grandma Ruby and Me*, 2005

# Past and Present Collide in Pittsburgh

Published June 2, 2015

Sometimes it takes a connection to the past to better understand the present. For essayists exploring African American life in Pittsburgh, a trove of 80,000 photos taken by Charles "Teenie" Harris allowed them to immerse themselves in everyday life from the 1930s through the 1970s.

Mr. Harris took those pictures during his nearly forty-year tenure as a staff photographer for the weekly *Pittsburgh Courier*, one of the nation's leading Black newspapers, and they are now archived at the Carnegie Museum of Art. As a complement to an earlier exhibition, *Teenie Harris Photographs: Civil Rights Perspectives*, the museum asked writers—including poets, playwrights, and historians—to respond to "the social, cultural, and political content" of Mr. Harris's photos.

Edited by Matthew Newton, associate editor at the museum, the series continues with the exhibition *Teenie Harris Photographs: Cars*. The project represents an imaginative effort by a preeminent American art institution to rethink its historical holdings and make them relevant.

Motivated by the increasing demand for visual reporting, the *Courier* appointed Mr. Harris its first staff photographer in 1941. Enterprising, well-dressed, and charming, he was an eminent presence in Pittsburgh's Black community, producing one of the most comprehensive visual records of mid-twentieth-century African American urban life. Whether photographing everyday events, political demonstrators, or the rich and famous—Mr. Harris was invariably present whenever Black entertainers, sports figures, and business and political leaders appeared in Pittsburgh—he had a knack for capturing the humanity and grace of his subjects.

Known as "One Shot Teenie," Mr. Harris, who died in 1998, also had a talent for

Chapter 5

taking the perfect picture in a single shot. Flashbulbs, both expensive and difficult to handle—once discharged, they smoldered—were one reason for his efficiency. (The paper did not cover the cost of equipment or supplies.) Another was his camera. As news organizations in the late 1940s began switching to 35 mm cameras, allowing for quick multiple shots, Mr. Harris remained loyal to his relatively slow and cumbersome Speed Graphic.

Mr. Harris's work centered on the Hill District, encompassing a group of largely run-down neighborhoods, segregated by restrictive housing covenants, which historically served as the center of African American life in Pittsburgh. To augment his modest income at the paper, Mr. Harris opened a photo studio, which did brisk business.

"Set against this everyday backdrop, vividly captured by Harris's lens, were the special moments—marriages, graduations, baptisms—that mark the cycles of change in life," wrote the historian Laurence Glasco. In the online essay series, Mr. Harris's photographs served as a historical frame of reference against which a racially fraught present was rethought and reevaluated. "I wonder what images Teenie might have captured had he traveled to Ferguson during the protests," pondered the literary artist Tameka Cage Conley, for example, about the unrest last year in Missouri.

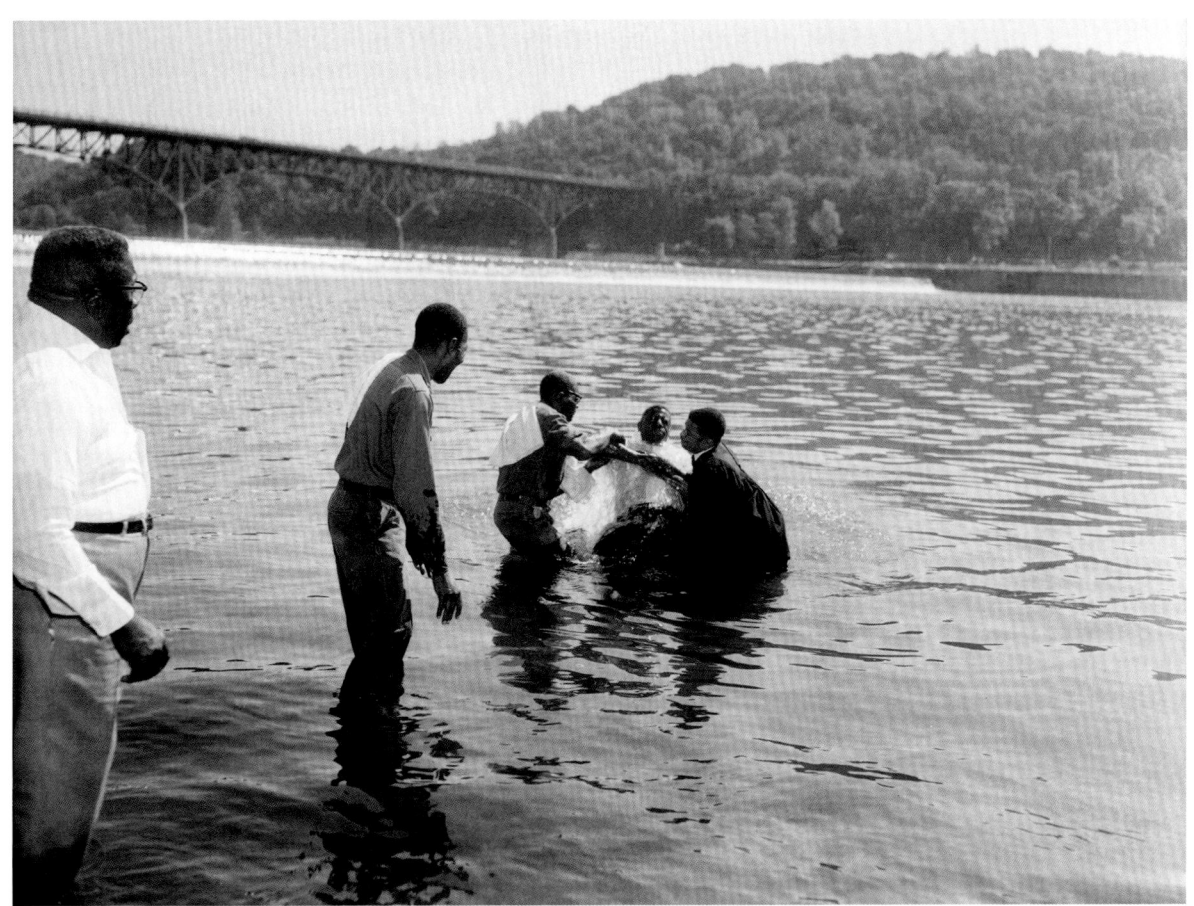

Charles "Teenie" Harris, *River Baptism*. Calvary Baptist Church Deacon Clinton Robinson, Deacon Henry Robinson, and Rev. James M. Allen, baptizing man in Allegheny River, Pittsburgh, Pennsylvania, October 1969

The poet and creative writing professor Yona Harvey described a workshop in which third graders were asked to select a photograph by Mr. Harris and compose a poem about it. She recounted the students' focused engagement with images that stoked their imagination and motivated them to make poignant connections across time. "The past is echoed within the present," Ms. Harvey wrote. "The present echoes the past."

The writer and oral historian Yvonne McBride repeatedly turned to Mr. Harris's photographs for inspiration while working on a novel set in the Hill District during the golden age of jazz. For Ms. McBride, these images offered a retrospective view of Pittsburgh, one that suggested a troubling irony about present-day efforts at urban renewal.

The city's African American residents have long struggled with inadequate housing and crumbling infrastructure. In his panoramic view of Black life, Mr. Harris documented a complex reality that acknowledged both the destructive effects of racism and poverty and the possibility of resistance, achievement, and self-possession.

In recent years, redevelopment has improved the quality of life in the Hill and other Pittsburgh neighborhoods. But progress often has been at the expense of African Americans, forced out of their gentrifying neighborhoods by escalating property values, redlining, and other practices that promote the influx of young white urban professionals.

"I am both fascinated and disturbed by how the problems of the past come back to haunt us through the lens of his camera," Ms. McBride observed about Mr. Harris's photographs. "Who could have imagined that fifty years later we would still need to argue the case for employment opportunities, business opportunities, and affordable housing for both new and lifelong residents—especially when that development takes place within our own communities?"

This terrible paradox, highlighted by the essay series's potent collision of historic images and present-day words, impelled another contributor to question how much African American lives matter, even in the liberal urban enclaves that sustained the electoral victories of the nation's first Black president.

"I imagine that the thousands of people photographed by Teenie Harris in the 1940s and 1950s—schoolteachers and bandleaders; coal miners and Pittsburgh Crawfords; nurses and nannies; politicians and Charlie Parker—would have predicted a better Pittsburgh in 2015," wrote Damon Young, cofounder and editor in chief of *Very Smart Brothas* magazine. "And they would have been right. The city is better. Much better." The signs of improvement are many, he observed, from a growing population and cleaner air and water to the nimble transition from steel town to technology and culture hub.

"It's one of the best cities in the country," Mr. Young concluded. "And it's even better if you're not Black."

Charles "Teenie" Harris, American singer and actor Eartha Kitt (1927–2008) steps through a poster as she is introduced to a crowd at Vine and Colwell Streets in the Hill District neighborhood. Among those also pictured is police officer Harvey Adams (fore right). She was there to help launch a self-help program sponsored by the Citizens Committee on Hill District Renewal, Pittsburgh, Pennsylvania, May 1966

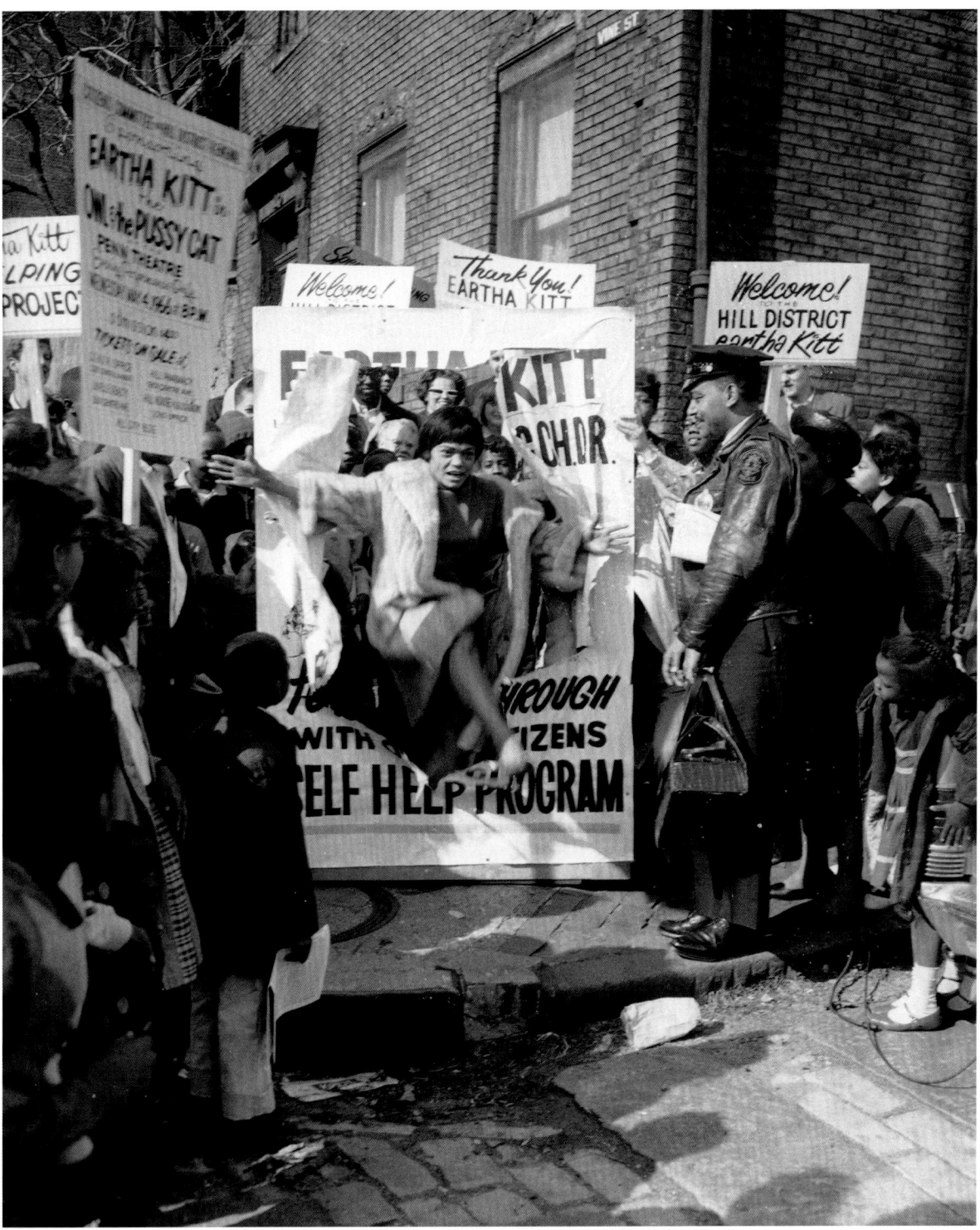

# A Photographer's Search for the Magic in Everyday Life

Published January 9, 2018

As a young man growing up in Harlem, Shawn Walker was shaped not just by what he saw at museums, but also what he heard in clubs. "I grew up as a jazz kid," Mr. Walker, seventy-seven, said. "I heard all the avant-garde players, major influences like John Coltrane and Lee Morgan . . . Jazz takes something ordinary and changes it. Jazz was the background music to my life."

These influences led him to see photography as more than just visual reporting. As a founding member of the Kamoinge Workshop, the influential Black photo collective, he was inspired by his colleagues, especially Roy DeCarava. "Roy opened my eyes to photography as art," recalled Mr. Walker. "I've always considered myself an artist. It's not just talking about a social condition. I'm trying to approach it artistically."

With a career spanning half a century, Mr. Walker is just now having his first retrospective in a show opening this week at New York's Steven Kasher Gallery. The images reflect his belief that "photography has always been magic" for him, ever since his teenage years in Harlem, with his uncle, a photographer, being an early influence. He pursued his passion at Benjamin Franklin High School in East Harlem, which had a photography program and darkroom.

Mr. Walker's photographs are aesthetically rich, even as he documents the lives of regular people engaged in everyday activities and rituals. His images reveal the paradoxes and nuances in his subjects' lives: a woman in a stylish hat asleep on the steps of a Harlem tenement; the words *Black Power* scrawled across a rundown Romanesque-style facade; children in Halloween masks standing in darkened and ominous doorways; a Batman logo, hovering apparition-like on a paint-splattered wall; the ramshackle door of a church marked

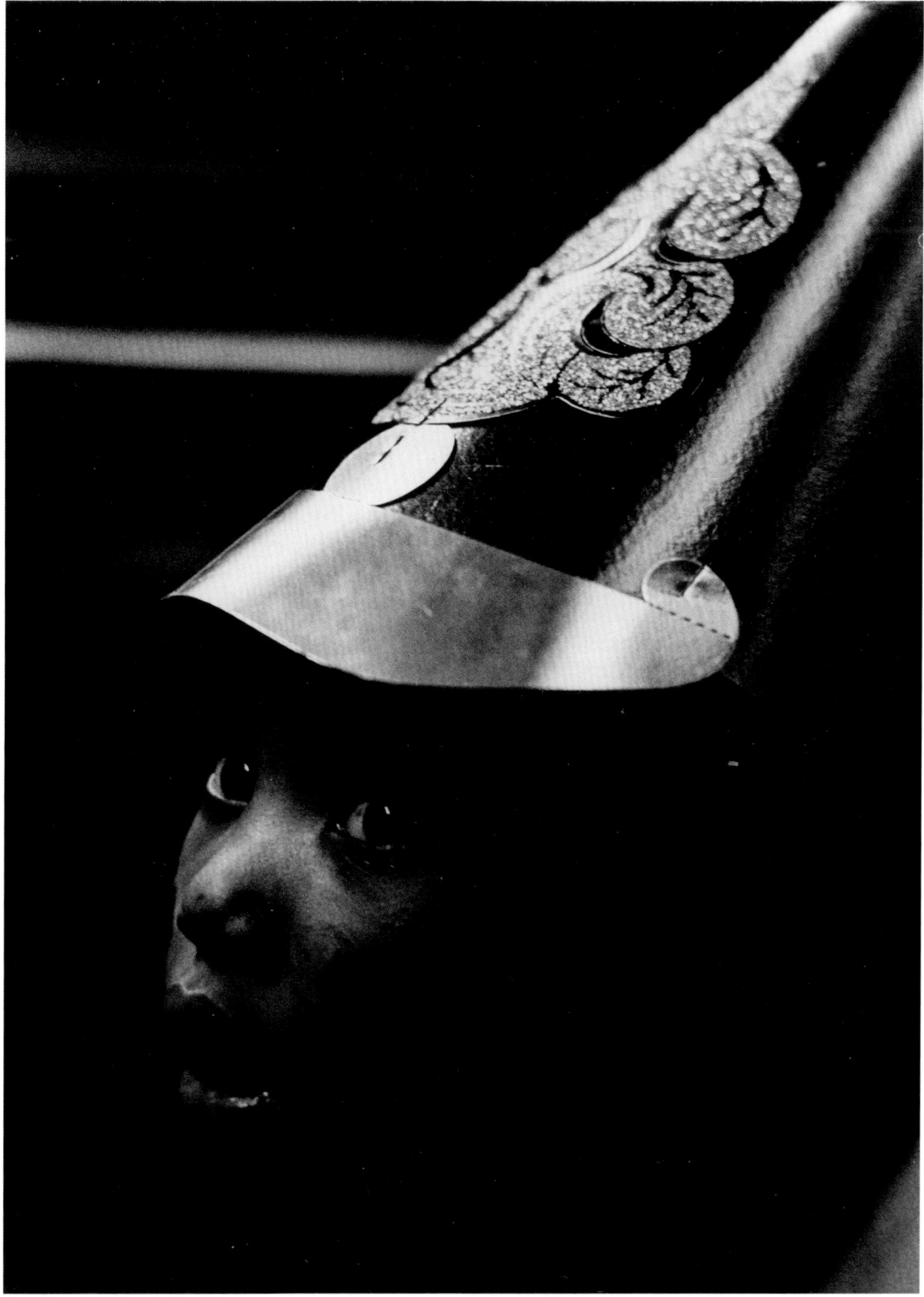

with a cross; and regal women in evening gowns seated on parade floats.

Mr. Walker's layered and complex images are influenced by a range of artists and photographers who, in addition to Mr. DeCarava, include Charles White, Romare Bearden, Jacob Lawrence, Henri Cartier-Bresson, and Minor White. Above all, he sees himself as a latter-day Surrealist, pushing the formal and conceptual boundaries of photography. "I've always been taken by Surrealism," Mr. Walker said, fascinated by its penchant for teasing out the extraordinary in commonplace things and situations.

Mr. Walker refers to his photographs as "found images," echoing the Surrealist concept of the found object—a random artifact that inspires deeper aesthetic or cultural meaning. "I always wanted to make the distinction that I'm not creating images," he said. "These are images that I find, that catch my eye, that I see something I'm interested in."

Mr. Walker's interest in Surrealism includes its popular manifestation in film noir, especially the raking shadows and histrionic lighting of the stylish Hollywood crime dramas of the 1940s and 1950s. His photographs resonate with these flourishes, transforming the cityscape into multifaceted and haunting pictures: a mysterious pointing hand, silhouetted against a light-dappled street; the face of a child in a metallic party hat, illuminated by an intense streak of light; the roof and turrets of a Harlem building encircled by dramatic sky; or dismembered mannequins in a Harlem store window, their lower torsos discreetly draped in rags.

Ultimately, there is also a political dimension to these photographs—exemplified by the image of the photographer's ghostlike reflection in a shattered window, a play on the tension between Black obscurity and presence in *Invisible Man*, Ralph Ellison's epochal novel. "I always want to be recognized as a Black photographer," Mr. Walker said. "I am an African American first and a photographer second. I derive my creativity from an African aesthetic." His photographs reflect this sentiment, examining everyday Black life and exploring its culture with a depth rarely seen in mainstream art. It was extremely important, he said, to "have people see themselves photographed by their own kind."

In these images, Mr. Walker liberates his subjects from stereotypes and invisibility, no more so than in his continuing *Parade* series. For thirty years, he has photographed ethnic parades, focusing on their cultural and ceremonial details, from clothing and costumes to marching bands and elaborate floats. In their inclusiveness and range, these photographs track the similarities and differences of public celebrations of identity across racial lines.

For Mr. Walker, who was a picture editor of the *Black Photographer's Annual* from 1973 until 1980, photography can tell us much about the world in which we live and the ideals to which we aspire. "I look for truth within the image, for the multi-layers of existence, for the ironies that are our everyday lives," he wrote in an artist's statement. "I try to reflect on the positive aspects of my community and to see the relationship between various communities of color. My work reflects a Black aesthetic, but tries to speak to everyone."

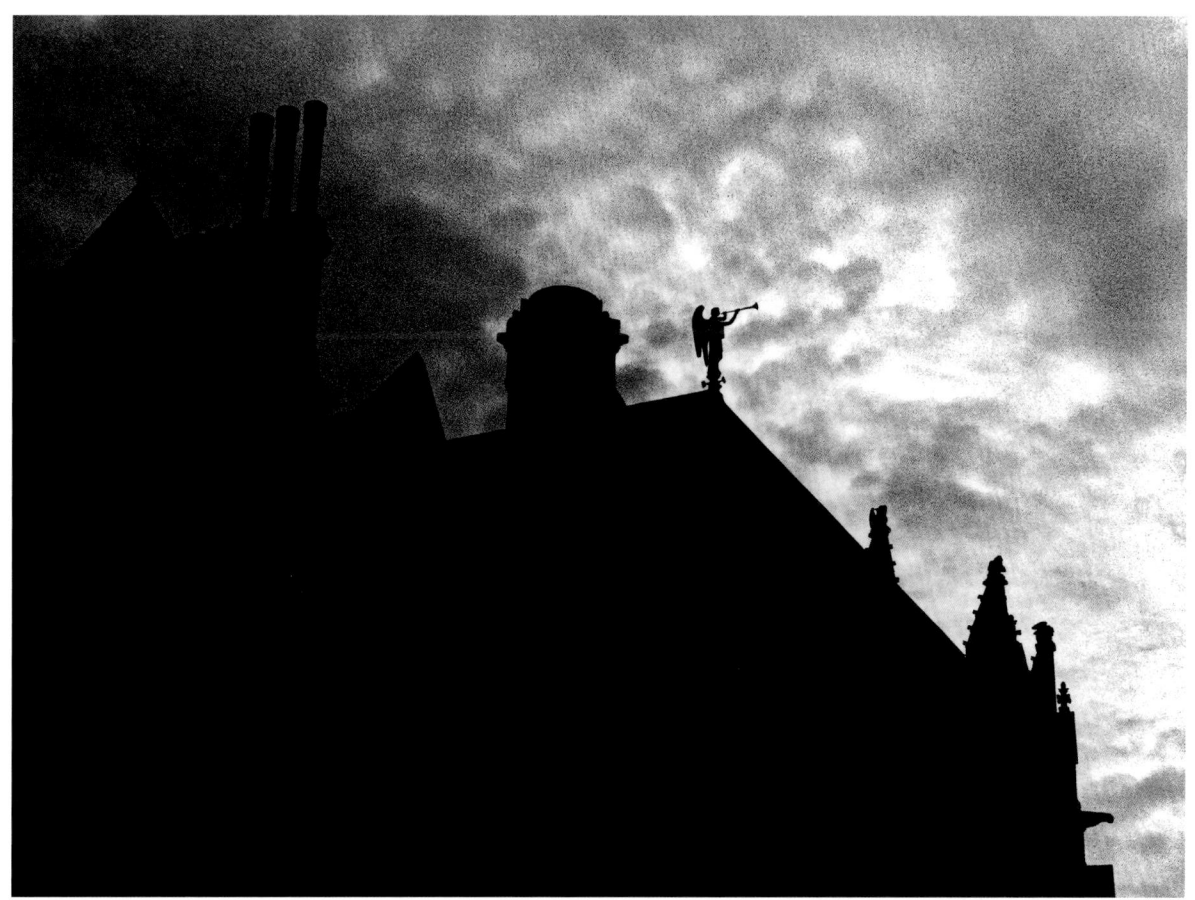

Shawn Walker, *Cloud Series, Riverside Church, Harlem, New York*, 1992

# Artists of Color as Avatars of Originality

Published April 2, 2019

A glamorous woman, dressed in jeans, a shirt and a vest, looks into the camera. Her full-on Afro and styling are retro, a homage, perhaps, to 1970s Blaxploitation stars like Pam Grier and Tamara Dobson. But one telling detail, the high-school yearbook she is holding, reminds us that the image is more than a fashion photograph. The school's location, Braddock, Pennsylvania, is the struggling hometown of the subject, LaToya Ruby Frazier.

Elia Alba photographed Ms. Frazier, an artist, on an ornate staircase at the Braddock Carnegie Library. Ms. Alba thinks the image alludes not to movie stars but to a political figure: Kathleen Cleaver of the Black Panther Party. In this context, the portrait honors Ms. Frazier as the "patron saint of Braddock," as Ms. Alba calls her—an activist photographer who uses art for social change. In *The Notion of Family*, her 2014 book, for example, Ms. Frazier photographed her own family to document the decline of a once-flourishing steel town and the lives of its residents, largely African American, beset by poverty, gentrification, and discrimination.

The photograph is in her new book, *The Supper Club*, edited by Sara Reisman with George Bolster and Anjuli Nanda Diamond, which documents Ms. Alba's project, reimagining artists of color as A-list celebrities.

Ms. Alba is influenced by art history, Afrofuturist aesthetics, and contemporary media, and her fantasy portraits echo spreads in *Vogue*, *Harper's Bazaar*, and other glamour magazines. "Fashion photography is fascinating to me due to its construction of image; the likeness is real time but it's completely hyperreal with many elements of fantasy," she said in a recent interview. But Ms. Alba also acknowledged that mainstream publications have historically ignored or marginalized people of color and still do.

Chapter 5

Riffing on *Vanity Fair*'s "Hollywood Issue," Ms. Alba assigns artists literary names that describe their philosophy, sensibility, or reputation—"The Alchemist," for example, or "The Oracle"—and photographs them in environments reflective of their art. She designs costumes and either constructs sets or photographs her subjects on location, and she adopts the visual devices of posing and styling common to the publications that inspired her. But her interests transcend fashion.

"These portraits go beyond merely a record of the subject," she wrote in an artist's statement, and convey "a deeper meaning or vision of the sitter, through their art." Arnaldo Morales ("The Machinist"), for example, is posed against the machines and gadgets that inspire his futuristic sculptures. Maren

Hassinger ("The Spiritualist") appears as a dancing Orisha in the forest, echoing her themes of spirituality and nature. And a series of portraits represents artists who challenge conventional notions of masculinity, including Angel Otero ("The Romantic"), whose paintings recast the male body as sensual and vulnerable, and Kalup Linzy ("The Star"), sultry in drag as Marlene Dietrich.

Ms. Alba's project also relates to the history of artists who use other artists as their subjects. At the height of the New York School in the 1950s and 1960s, for example, the photographer Hans Namuth made many such portraits. Much like Ms. Alba, his pictures were stylish and glamorous, displaying a sensibility rooted in his training with Alexey Brodovitch, the renowned art director of *Harper's Bazaar*. Typically depicting his subjects in their studios, Mr. Namuth described his photographic process as akin to "the feeling of being in a theater, of watching and directing." But his portraits, unlike those of *The Supper Club*, were neither theatrical nor art directed.

While *The Supper Club* both perpetuates and challenges this legacy, it rejects one sensibility inherent to these projects: their view of the art world as largely white. It highlights the accomplishments of contemporary artists of color through work that also reflects the consequential issues engaged by their art. It does so not only through portraits but also through a series of dinners that Ms. Alba hosted—the "supper clubs" of the project's title—in which artists discussed the social, cultural, and aesthetic issues reflected in their work and worldview.

Challenging the cliché of the artist as hermetic and socially insular, these dialogues explored the motivations and intentions of the participants as well as the impact of real-life events and issues on their lives and art.

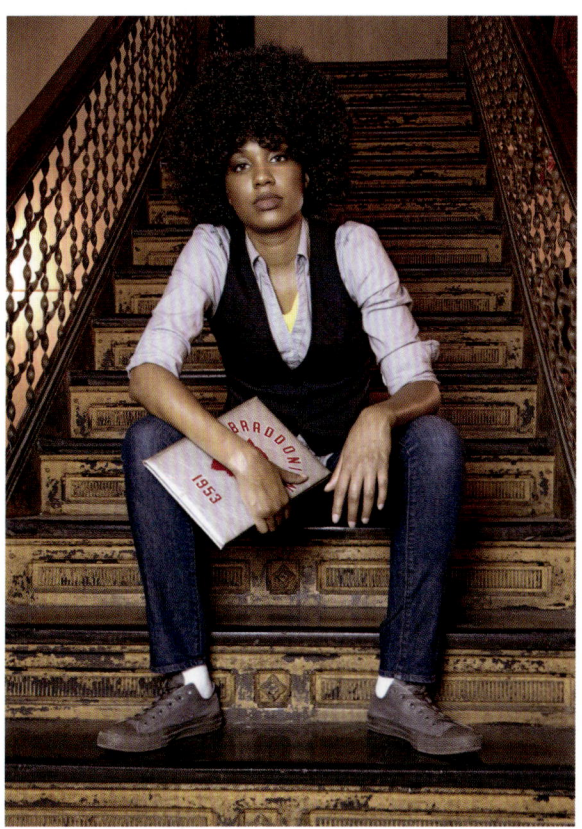

Elia Alba, *The Braddonian (LaToya Ruby Frazier)*. Photographed at the Carnegie Library, Braddock, Pennsylvania, 2012

In the end, Ms. Alba's project—which recasts the artist's portrait as a complex reflection of artists and their work—underscores the interplay among persona, politics, and aesthetics in much contemporary art.

If the typical celebrity portrait aggrandizes its subject, the photographs in *The Supper Club* give artists of color a place of honor in a mainstream art world that continues to ignore, underestimate, or play down their accomplishments. They honor these artists on multiple levels: as icons of originality and brilliance, as interpreters of a changing culture and society, and as role models for people long erased from the history of art. In the end, these vibrant portraits represent their subjects not simply as culturally expressive, but also as embodying the potential of a refreshed and relevant cultural world unencumbered by racism.

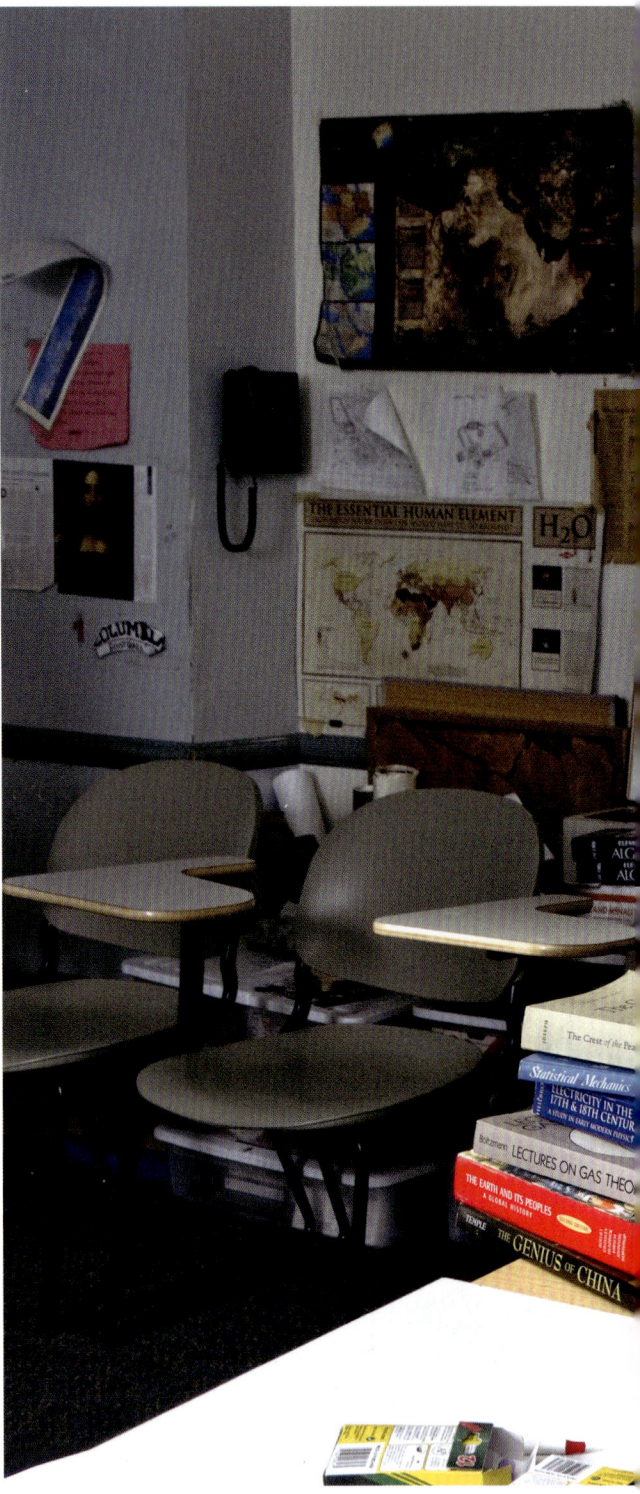

Chapter 5

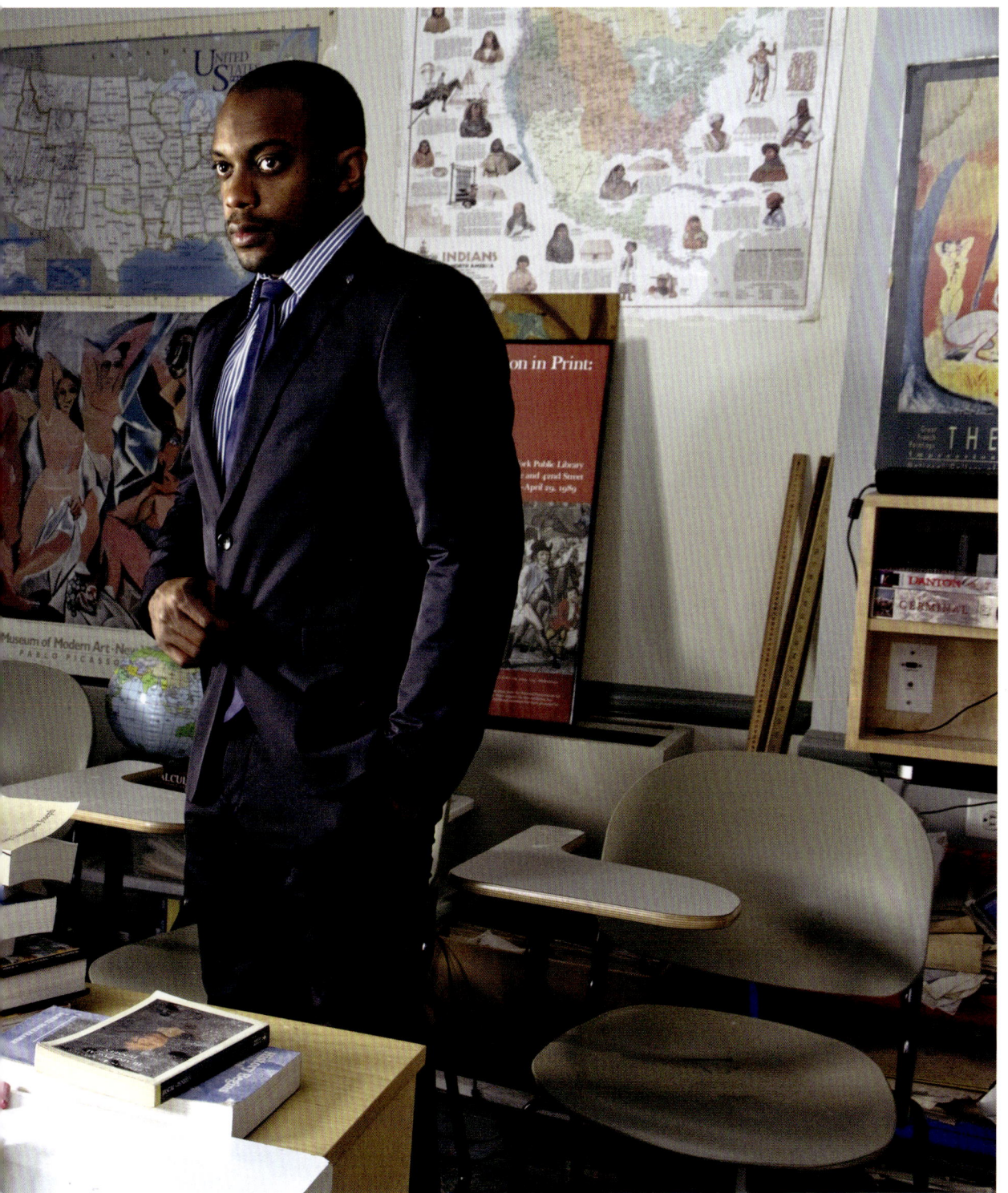

Elia Alba, *The Professor (Hank Willis Thomas)*. Photographed at Saint Ann's School, Brooklyn Heights, New York, 2014

Community

# American Culture, Riding a Mushroom Cloud

Published December 24, 2014

The photographer Shomei Tomatsu was drawn to ninja and samurai movies as a child in post–World War II Japan, even though teachers forbade students from seeing them. They called them "disreputable." He found them irresistible.

Even when he had no money, he found the huge, showy billboards that dotted the theater district a suitable substitute. They "were exaggerated to grab people's attention, and the colors were always gaudy and vivid," he said. "To a boy who loved the movies, it was a blindingly surreal world."

Years later, Mr. Tomatsu was drawn to another, equally striking world: the "garish, heavily made-up" entertainment districts that catered to American soldiers just outside of United States military bases in Japan. "Whenever I'd go into one of these base towns, I'd feel slightly dizzy," Mr. Tomatsu wrote in a 1972 essay. The vertigo, he later realized, was caused by his inability to reconcile the nostalgic passion he felt for forbidden places.

This tension between desire and revulsion pervades *Chewing Gum and Chocolate*, a powerful survey, edited by Leo Rubinfien and John Junkerman, of Mr. Tomatsu's iconic photographs of the American presence in postwar Japan. One of that nation's foremost photographers, Mr. Tomatsu, who died in 2012 at the age of eighty-two, was also its preeminent chronicler of the seismic cultural impact of the Allied occupation.

From the late 1950s through the 1970s, Mr. Tomatsu embarked on a "pilgrimage," as he called it, across Japan, photographing United States military bases. For him, the interplay between the two countries was as much cultural as martial: "Culture, riding a mushroom cloud, came in from across the sea. People called it 'occupation,'" he wrote in 1959.

Chapter 5

Shomei Tomatsu, *Koza, Okinawa*, 1978

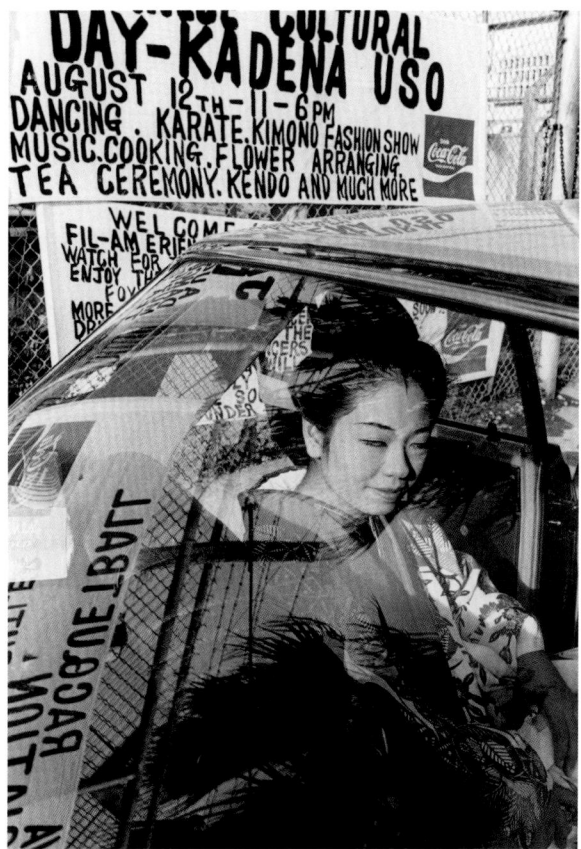

Despite Mr. Tomatsu's misgivings about this cultural encroachment, he remained fascinated by its influence. The chocolate and chewing gun that American soldiers in jeeps showered upon eager Japanese children may have been empty calories. But as Mr. Rubinfien wrote in his intelligent and sensitive essay for the book, "the ideas, styles, and manners that they disseminated were not, and these invigorated two generations or more of younger Japanese."

Mr. Tomatsu personally "cherished those delights—romantic love, jazz, surrealism, the freedom to make up one's own mind, or to not make it up—which, if they had not entirely been anathema to the spartan mind of the militarist period, could only be tasted freely after its demise."

Nevertheless, as Mr. Rubinfien wrote, if Mr. Tomatsu appreciated Americans as liberators from totalitarianism and Japanese cultural dogmatism, he felt "an intense wish to be rid of them" and their aggressive usurpation of land and resources. Even as a child, with the Allied war machine closing in on Japan in 1944 and 1945, he imagined Americans to "have noses hooked like beaks, and to wear hats that had sharp points, like rotten teeth."

Arriving in Okinawa in 1969, its sprawling military bases a key staging point for United States operations against North Vietnam, Mr. Tomatsu felt tremendous antipathy about American domination. During that period, violent protests erupted over these military sites as well as the renewal of the Japan–United States defense treaty. In solidarity, Mr. Tomatsu emblazoned a slogan of the liberation movement across the cover of his first book on the island: "The bases are not [situated] within Okinawa, Okinawa exists within the bases."

Given Mr. Tomatsu's tangled and contradictory point of view, it is not surprising that his first love was film. It is almost as if photographs were too static to depict this incongruity. The images in *Chewing Gum and Chocolate* are distinctly cinematic—formally complex, full of movement and grit, and, given the photographer's emotional reaction, dizzying. The surfaces of some appear fluid; others are blurred, nearly to the point of abstraction.

Mr. Tomatsu's images resonate with the visual energy of colliding cultures, tastes, and histories: an American soldier revealing a tattoo as gaudy as the graffiti on the wall behind him; a strip mall at dusk, outside a military base; walls plastered with grotesque posters of naked, huge-breasted women; mixed-race children; a seemingly endless Okinawan field of rubble; an American woman in a Western-style wedding dress being tended to by a Japanese woman; a Japanese boy in a white suit, like a buttoned-up, world-weary Tony Manero in *Saturday Night Fever*.

If Mr. Tomatsu documented the ambiguous relationship of the Japanese to an invading culture, he was also aware of the contradictions and hypocrisy of the occupiers. In a multipart series published in 1960 in the magazine *Asahi Camera*, he focused on the segregated Black units of three United States military bases in Japan. In so doing, he questioned the power relations and paradoxes of cultural occupation, both within Japan and the United States.

*Chewing Gum and Chocolate* contains similarly ironic pictures of African American soldiers flashing the Black Power salute at the height of the Vietnam War. "The fists the Black soldiers raised to the Okinawan sky," Mr. Tomatsu speculated, "might have been an expression of antiwar sentiment by people who are extremely unfree and know the stupidity of fighting a war 'for the sake of freedom.'"

In the end, Mr. Tomatsu's ambivalence never diminished: "I always say that my Occupation series is on the border between love and hate. I can neither reject nor affirm the occupation. Of course, I reject it, but there are many elements that I have to affirm. Immediately after the defeat, some people called the occupying forces an army of liberation. Those words imply an affirmation, and I experienced that very feeling."

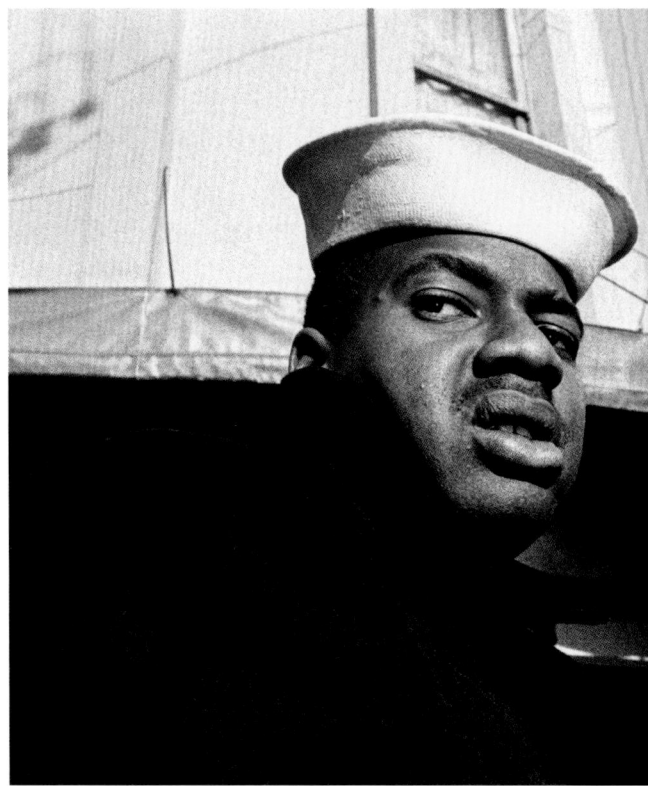

Shomei Tomatsu, *Yokosuka*, 1966

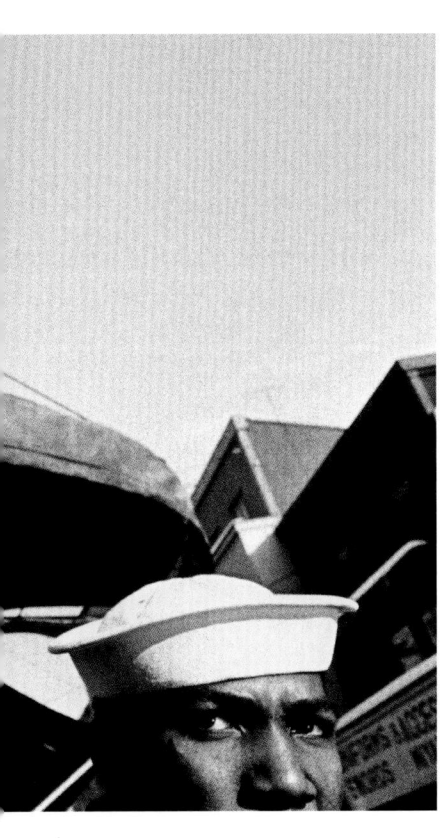

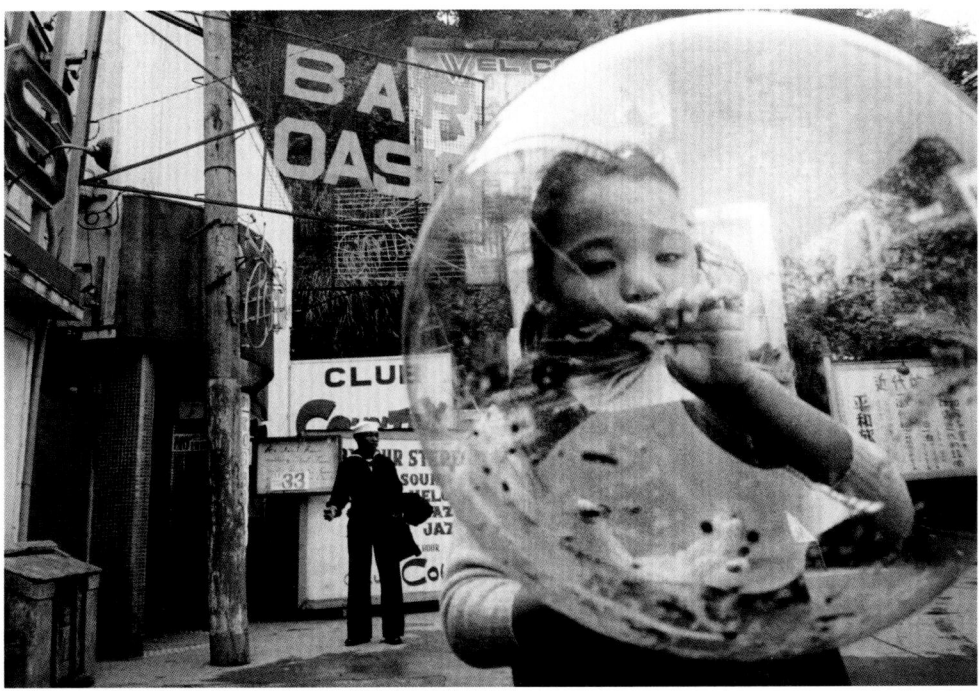

Shomei Tomatsu, *Yokosuka*, 1959

# A Russian American Photographing Native Alaska

Published July 17, 2013

The black-and-white photograph taken in Killisnoo, Alaska, at the turn of the twentieth century depicts a group of fishermen reeling in a gigantic halibut. The image is light-hearted and almost comical: workers smile as the imposing creature writhes perilously close to them.

What makes the photograph unusual is not its subject matter but its subjects. The fishermen, working in apparent harmony, represent a cross section of the population of Killisnoo, an island off southeastern Alaska that was an important outpost for American businesses and tourism. Several of the men are white; at least two are Native American, members of the Tlingit community; and one is Asian. Taken when racial integration was the exception and not the rule in the United States, the image—by Vincent Soboleff, a Russian American amateur photographer— is noteworthy.

As the Dartmouth anthropologist Sergei A. Kan argues in his new book, *A Russian American Photographer in Tlingit Country: Vincent Soboleff in Alaska*, Mr. Soboleff's images of the United States territory, especially its Native population, are also significantly different from others of the period.

Mr. Soboleff, who was born in Killisnoo in 1882, the son of the town's well-regarded Russian Orthodox priest, set out to document his community almost as soon as he commandeered his family's small Kodak camera as a teenager. His project ended in the late 1910s, when the need to help support his family after the death of his father drove him to seek more gainful employment, first as a postal worker and later as the owner of a popular general store and movie theater. While Mr. Soboleff later made some of his photographs into hand-tinted postcards and permitted a handful of local business to use

Chapter 5

Vincent I. Soboleff, Kichnáalx, left, and Kharlampii Sokoloff wore ceremonial shirts belonging to Kichnáalx and depicting his clan's crest, the diving raven, Angoon, Alaska, ca. 1900

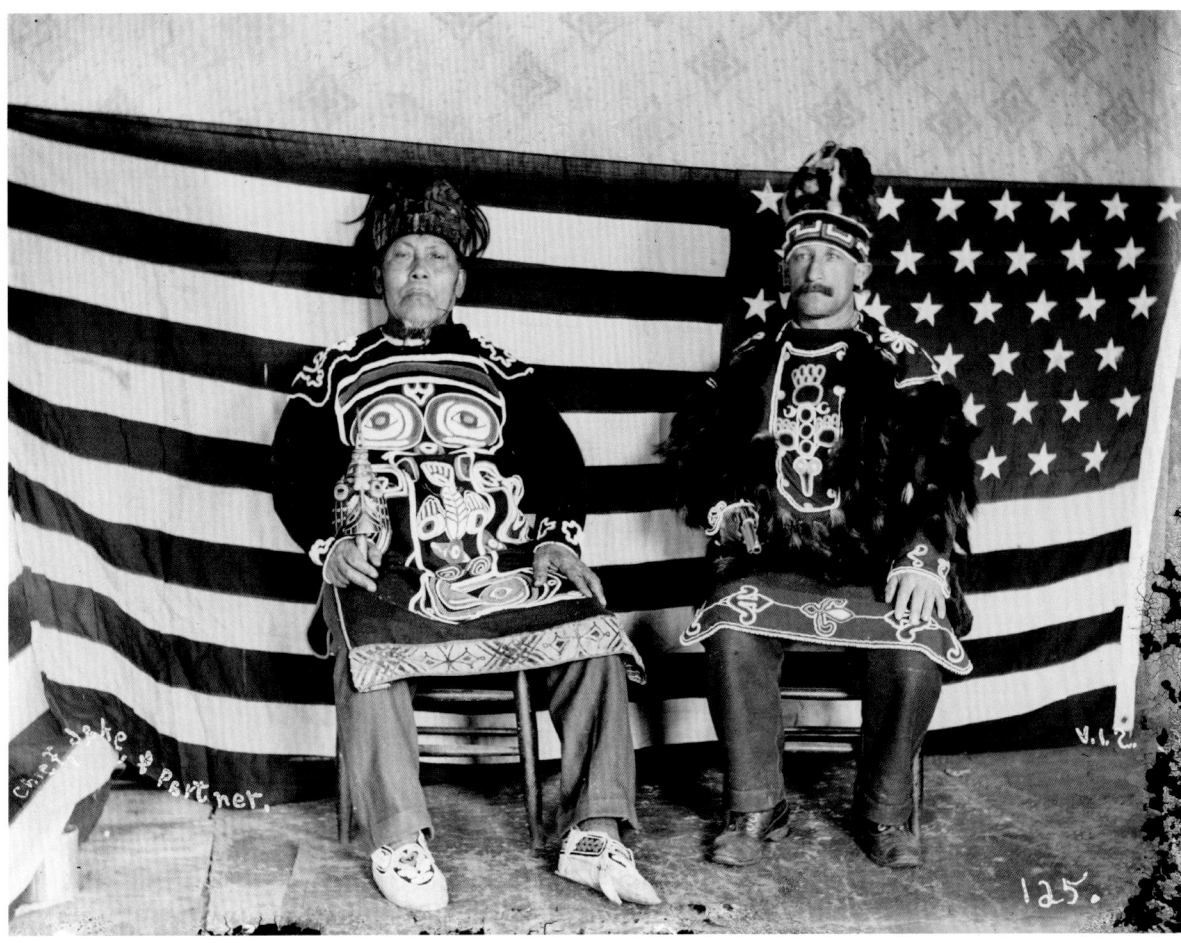

his images as logos, he remained disengaged from the medium until his death, in 1950.

Mr. Soboleff approached his subjects familiarly, with youthful enthusiasm. Nevertheless, he was reasonably knowledgeable about Native social organization, ceremonial life and history, a facility aided by his close relationship with the Tlingit community and his ability to speak its language fluently.

His pictures are competent but not artful or studied, unlike the work of more commercial photographers of Alaska's Native population, like William Case and Horace Draper. This informality was part of his unconventional point of view. He rarely staged

photographs or posed his subjects, favoring natural settings and straightforward depictions of everyday life and customs.

As nineteenth-century Native Americans were forced to adapt to a world dynamically altered by war, racial brutality, disease, and displacement, photographic depictions of them habitually trafficked in stereotypes built on an implicit comparison between the new, "civilized" Indian and the tradition-bound "savage." Mr. Soboleff's pictures were more respectful of, and ultimately more informative about, his subjects, despite the fact that the Russian Orthodox Church, which began working in Alaska in the

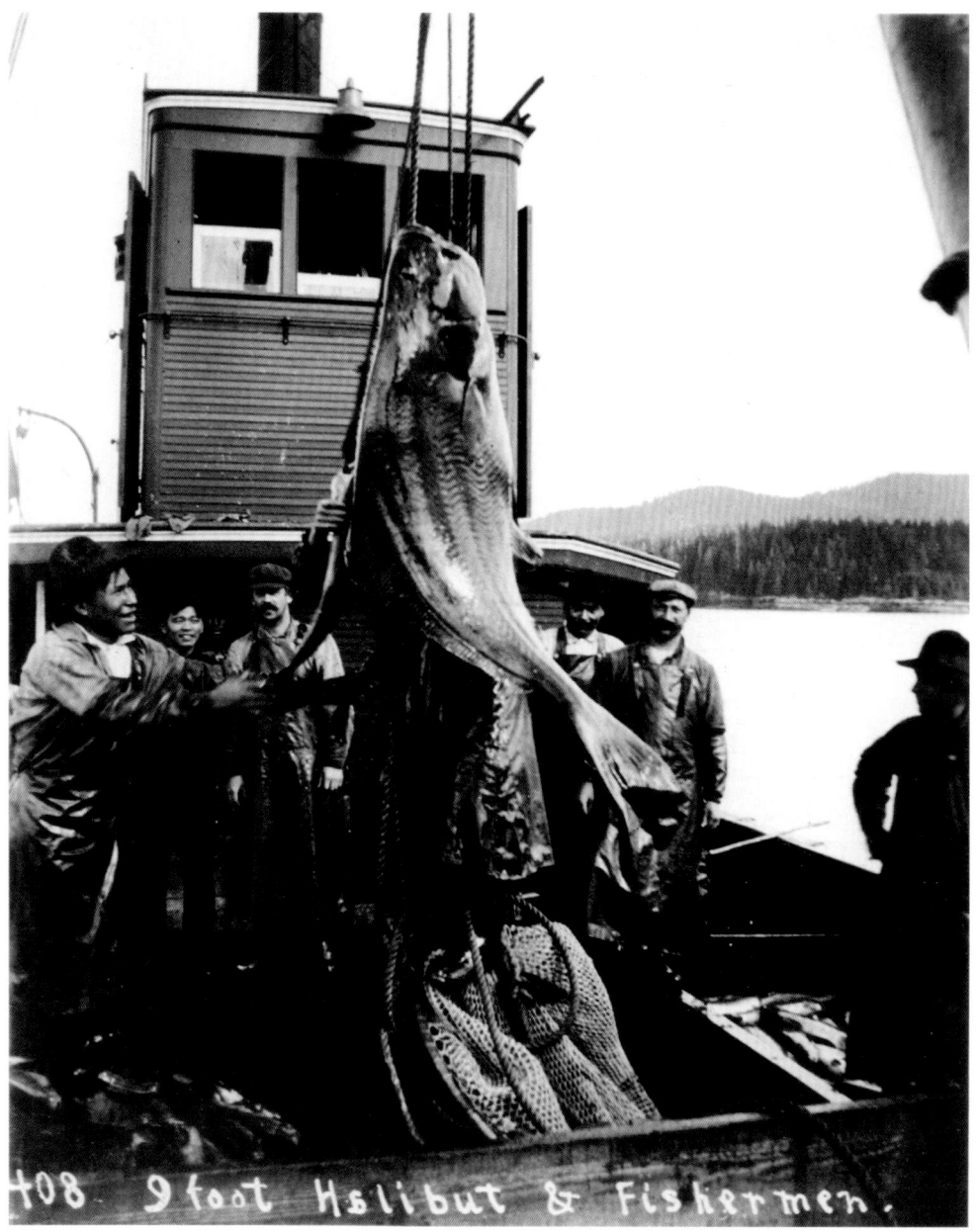

408  9 foot Halibut & Fishermen.

Vincent I. Soboleff, A nine-foot halibut caught by the crew of the Killisnoo company vessel SS Dolphin, ca. late 1890s–1910s

mid-eighteenth century, was actively proselytizing in the Tlingit community.

The contents of Mr. Soboleff's archive, some 780 plate negatives donated to the Alaska State Library by his sister in 1968, suggest that he was interested in capturing a wide-ranging view of life in Alaska. His photographs depict local buildings and landscapes, maritime culture, and the Tlingit, Russian American, European American, and Asian American residents of Killisnoo and a nearby town, Angoon. Mr. Kan's rigorous study focuses on the pictures of people, particularly scenes of work, celebration, and play, as well as of the interface between Native and non-Native populations.

This interaction was not as sanguine as it first appears in the photos. On the surface, Killisnoo seems like a racial paradise. Tlingit and Russian American men labor together in factories, and the Russian Americans—then referred to as Creoles and seen as not quite white by the nation at large—seem to be more empathetic to the plight of their Native coworkers. A leader of the Russian Orthodox Church poses with a Tlingit aristocrat in traditional Native ceremonial vestments. White and Native villagers participate in a Fourth of July celebration.

But closer inspection of that last image reveals disharmony. Although the white men are active participants, their Native counterparts are relegated to the sidelines as passive spectators. While workers of all races did labor together, Mr. Kan says, their leisure time was often spent apart: a number of photographs depict whites hunting, fishing, boating, hiking, and playing in a small orchestra, largely without their Tlingit coworkers. Even in employment, integration went only so far. Jobs requiring specialized technical knowledge were restricted to whites.

Mr. Soboleff's intimate portraits, especially of Tlingit aristocrats, are his most visually compelling images. The aesthetics of these photographs reside less in their formal or stylistic mastery and more in the artfulness of their subjects and environment. Such images afforded a culturally marginalized people an uncommon opportunity to represent themselves as they wanted to be seen, surrounded by stunning artifacts, especially the ceremonial objects and garments bearing the crests of individual clans.

Instead of transforming his subjects into exotic and anonymous icons, the nineteenth-century standard for images of American Indians, Mr. Soboleff treated them as individuals, identifying many by name in his captions. His subjects were also solicitous: "Local clan leaders, like most Tlingit people in general, were quite fond of being photographed," Mr. Kan writes, valuing the images as "permanent proof of their high rank and status" or of the richness of their lives.

"Try putting yourself inside these photos," writes Edwin Schupman, a citizen of the Muscogee Nation of Oklahoma and an educator at the National Museum of the American Indian, and "you might begin to understand the world from their points of view." Mr. Schupman speaks to the importance of empathy in interpreting photos of Native peoples. For Mr. Soboleff, an honorary citizen of Tlingit country, an intimate understanding of his subjects was an important prerequisite for photographing them as well.

# Documenting the Dynamic Black Community of 1940s Seattle

Published March 27, 2018

The radiant photograph shows Duke Ellington at the piano, his hands dancing across the keyboard. Behind him, a drummer lifts his arms joyously in the air. It is the type of club photo we have seen many times, often taken in famous venues like the Savoy Ballroom, Café Society, or the Cotton Club.

Except this one was taken in Seattle, a city known more for grunge than great jazz.

The image appears in *Seattle on the Spot: The Photographs of Al Smith*, an exhibition at the Museum of History and Industry in Seattle, a city that played only a modest role in American jazz history. Mr. Smith's photos tell a compelling story, not just about the city's jazz scene but also about the complexity of life in an African American community cloistered within a largely white, and for many decades, de facto segregated city. Organized by Howard Giske, the museum's curator of photography and a friend of

Mr. Smith's, the exhibition is accompanied by a catalog with essays by Mr. Giske and the historians Jacqueline E. A. Lawson and Quin'Nita Cobbins; the jazz critic Paul de Barros; and the photographer's son, Al Smith Jr., known as Butch.

Photographing clubs in the 1940s, Mr. Smith documented a heroic period for Seattle jazz, a scene that jump-started the careers of luminaries like Quincy Jones, Ray Charles, and Ernestine Anderson. Unlike other nightclubs, where patrons of color were barred except on designated nights, the integrated establishments of Jackson Street, in the city's predominantly Black Central District, embraced African American performers and customers.

Mr. Smith, who died in 2008 at the age of ninety-two, was born to Jamaican immigrant parents and grew up in the Central District in a close-knit West Indian community. "When

Chapter 5

my father . . . was given a Kodak camera as a preteen, he fell in love with photography," noted the younger Mr. Smith. "From then on, he always had a camera. It was like a universal key that opened doors and gave him license to go anywhere."

After traveling the Pacific as a steward on steamships, Mr. Smith returned to Seattle in the 1940s, raising a family in the District. Documenting Seattle's after-hours jazz scene, the enterprising and self-taught photographer started On the Spot, a business that sold photographs to club patrons. Through Mr. Smith's lens, we witness an impressive range of jazz musicians performing, including Louis Armstrong, Dizzy Gillespie, and Lionel Hampton.

After the jazz nightclub scene largely shut down in the mid-1950s, Mr. Smith, who remained a letter carrier by day, became the go-to photographer for events, celebrations, and gatherings in the African American community. These intimate images also chronicled the broader cultural and demographic shifts of the Central District.

While segregation was not legally sanctioned in Seattle, the Central District emerged in the shadow of discrimination.

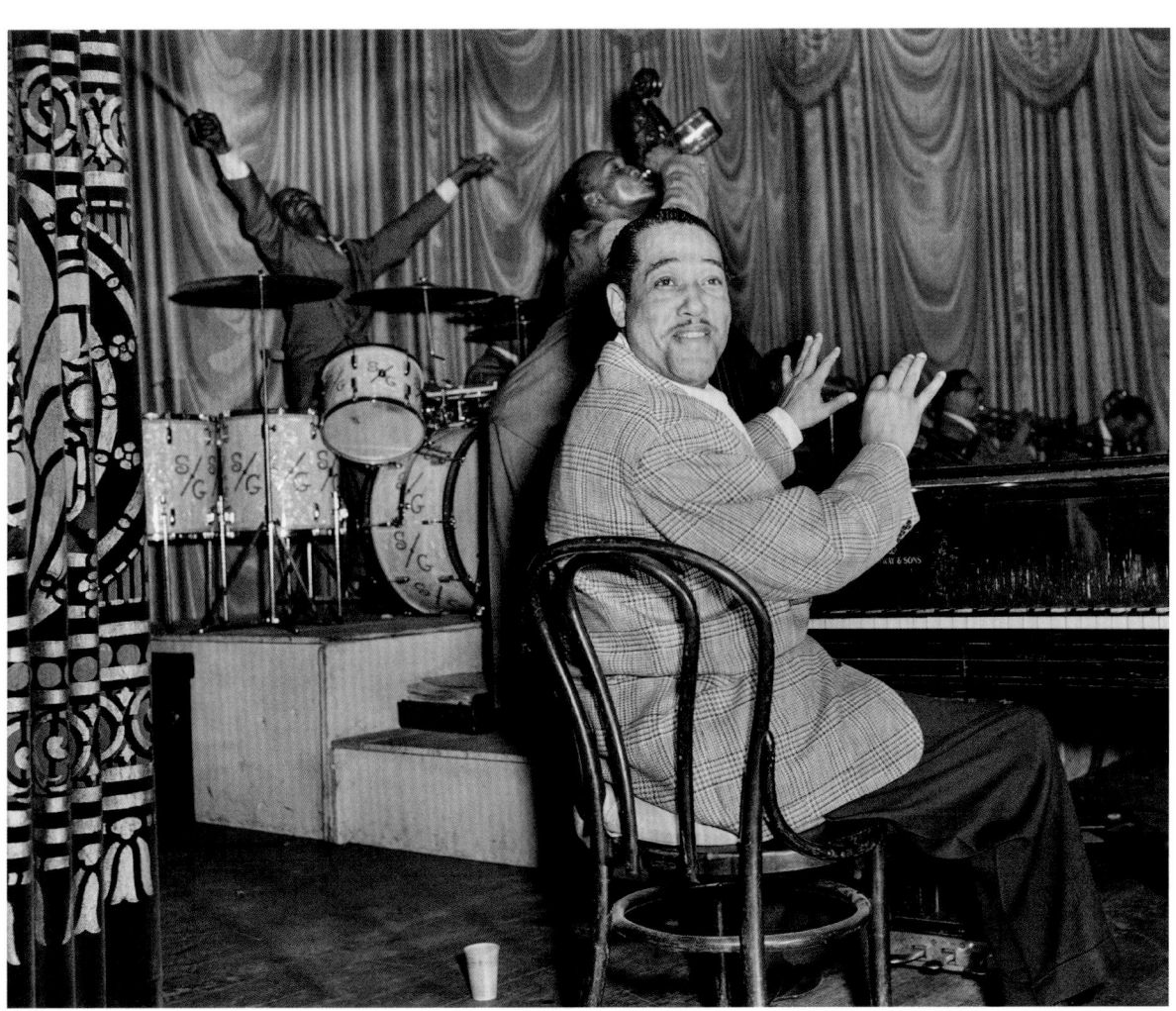

Al Smith, *Duke Ellington at the Civic Auditorium*, ca. 1948

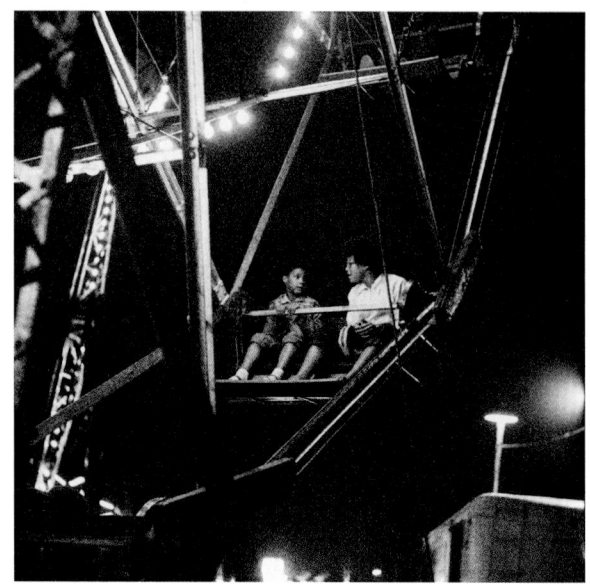

Al Smith, *Cheryl Smith and Frances Lane Riding a Ferris Wheel*, ca. 1953

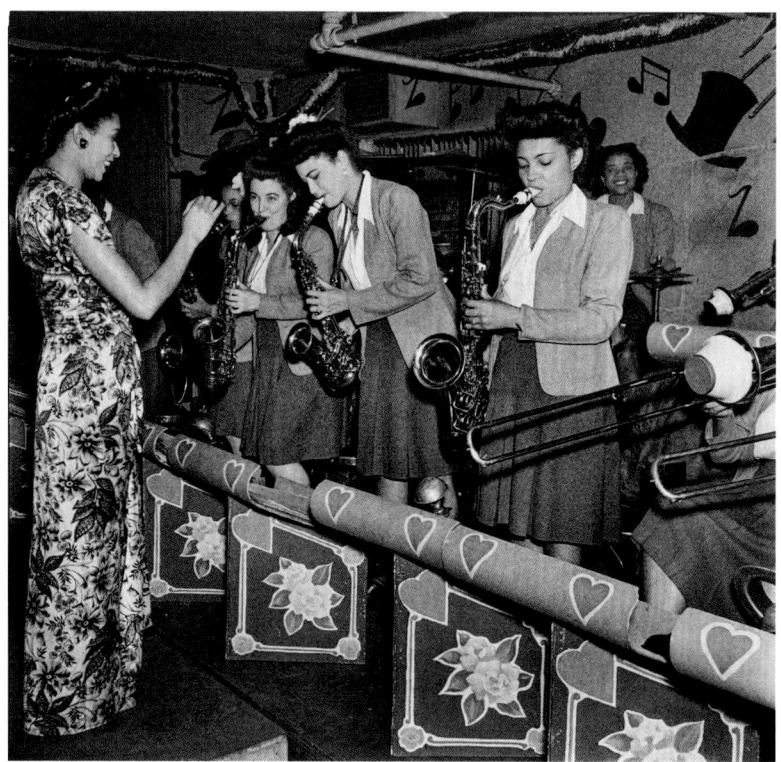

Al Smith, *International Sweethearts of Rhythm*, 1944

As Black Americans migrated to the Pacific Northwest during World War II—with Seattle's Black population more than tripling to over 15,000 from 4,000—banks, real estate agencies, and neighborhood associations engaged in redlining and other discriminatory practices. "The isolation of African Americans in the Central District," wrote Ms. Cobbins, resulted in a "geographically concentrated Black community within Seattle, where African Americans fashioned their own cultural, social, political, and economic spaces with meager resources."

Mr. Smith's photographs bear witness to this social and cultural transformation: the beauty parlors and barber shops that were vital to the district's business sector; the local chapter of Alpha Phi Alpha, the nation's first intercollegiate African American fraternity; the "International Fighting Irish" youth football team, sponsored by the Japanese American Veterans Association and open to children of all ethnicities; Mardi Gras, a weeklong summer festival evocative of its New Orleans counterpart; and the singer and pianist Hazel Scott, who refused to perform in segregated venues, playing the Civic Auditorium in 1947.

The photo of Ms. Scott is a reminder that Seattle's African American jazz scene was not immune to racism. While the Jackson Street clubs drew renowned musicians, the mainstream press did not cover them, focusing instead on the classical music venues favored by white people. As prejudice banished a rich and flourishing music scene from the cultural mainstream, Mr. Smith faithfully documented it for posterity.

His photographs tell us as much about the present as they do about the past. The once bustling and self-sufficient neighborhood he documented for more than half a century has changed dramatically.

Gentrification, the decline of affordable housing, the influx of young, mostly white tech workers, and the continued legacy of racism and segregation have transformed a predominantly Black neighborhood into a mostly white one: In 1970, the Black population of the Central District was seventy-three percent. By 2014, it had dwindled to less than twenty percent.

"To be Black in Seattle requires an ability to hold your own in mostly white spaces," Tyrone Beason wrote in the *Seattle Times* in 2016. "You have to get used to representing not just your own idiosyncrasies as a person but an entire race. It can be draining work, and it can detract from the obvious benefits of living in a region with good-paying jobs, a mix of lifestyles and otherwise easygoing people."

In this context, Mr. Smith's documentation of Seattle's African American community testifies to the possibilities of the past as well as the diminished opportunities of the present. "It surprises me why there weren't more people taking these pictures back then," he once remarked. In light of the vanishing of a dynamic community, it is fortunate that at least one talented and devoted photographer saw fit to embrace this responsibility.

# What the Camera Sees, and Doesn't See

Published June 27, 2014

The photograph from January 2013 is ethereal: a close-up of goldfish swimming in an aquarium. The water that sustains them is ominously cloudy. Yet, they survive.

This image appears in *Seen, Unseen*, a compelling photo series of ninety images about an extended Southern Black family. It stands as a metaphor of the perseverance not just of its subjects, but also of its creator, Kim Weston.

Less than a year earlier, while undergoing brain surgery, Ms. Weston had stopped breathing. Doctors labored to resuscitate her. Although she was unconscious and in peril, she has primal memories of that event being serene and peaceful.

It was also life altering.

"Coming so close to dying made me realize that life is short, and that I had a choice," Ms. Weston said. "I wasn't doing what I loved, and I was determined to go after my dream."

Ms. Weston, forty-five, had spent years as a freelance photographer and graphic designer, working mostly in the music industry. But her dream was to return to being an artist. "Art can have a voice, it can have personal meaning," she said.

To aid her recovery, her wife bought her a new camera: "Go back to doing what you love. Photography makes you smile. It makes you happy," Ms. Weston recalled her saying.

Six months after her surgery, Ms. Weston enrolled in the International Center of Photography–Bard program in advanced photographic studies. She found the program challenging, more so than her undergraduate training at Cooper Union. A mother of two young children, she was now considerably older than her classmates. But the program helped her to find herself as an artist.

*Seen, Unseen*, Ms. Weston's contribution to her class's thesis group show, focuses

Chapter 5

on her mother's family in Cheraw, South Carolina. The artist, who is part African American, Native American, and Irish, initially found the process of photographing her relatives daunting. "I was afraid of violating their privacy. I didn't want to be seen as exploiting them."

Though she completed the series in relative secrecy—she told no one at school about it—she ultimately embraced it as a celebration of "the people who made me who I am."

At first glance, Ms. Weston's images appear candid, like mundane family snapshots. A closer look reveals their complexity. The power of *Seen, Unseen*, as its title suggests, resides in its ability to make visible not just what the camera sees but also the intangible things it usually cannot see, or the things society doesn't want it to see.

Propriety, for example, typically forbids photographing the dead. Yet one of the most gripping images in the series is of the artist's grandmother lying in repose. "It is not unusual in African American culture to photograph the dead, as James Van Der Zee had done in *The Harlem Book of the Dead*, to create a lasting memory of a person through a final image," Ms. Weston said.

*Seen, Unseen*, while grounded in the present, conjures the stories of a lost and sometimes disquieting past: A withered and blackened cornfield is all that remains of a once robust family farm driven out of business by corporate farming; a pile of burning trash, "a metaphor of life and death and everything in between," as Ms. Weston puts it; and the gutted house built by her great-grandfather, its wooden elements the "last remnants of what he physically touched."

For Ms. Weston, these images expose the fault lines of American society: the messy divisions of race, class, and geography that many would rather not see. The story of

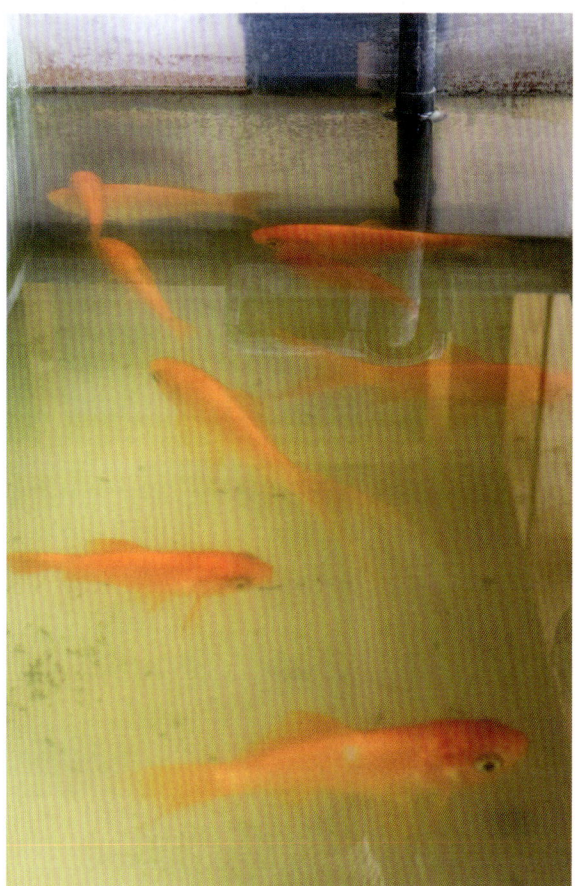

Kim Weston, *Seen, Unseen*, 2013

her family is a microcosm of Black life in the South, a history beset by discrimination and privation and uplifted by extraordinary acts of determination and fortitude.

Ms. Weston's brush with mortality has left her fascinated by indeterminate states, not just between past and present, but also between life and death and the worldly and the spiritual. While photographing her late grandmother's bedroom, for example, her camera continually recorded a vibrant haze of light invisible to the naked eye. A recent addendum to *Seen, Unseen* consists of diaphanous images that evoke transcendent states, like trails of light left in the wake of dancers performing in Native American ceremonies.

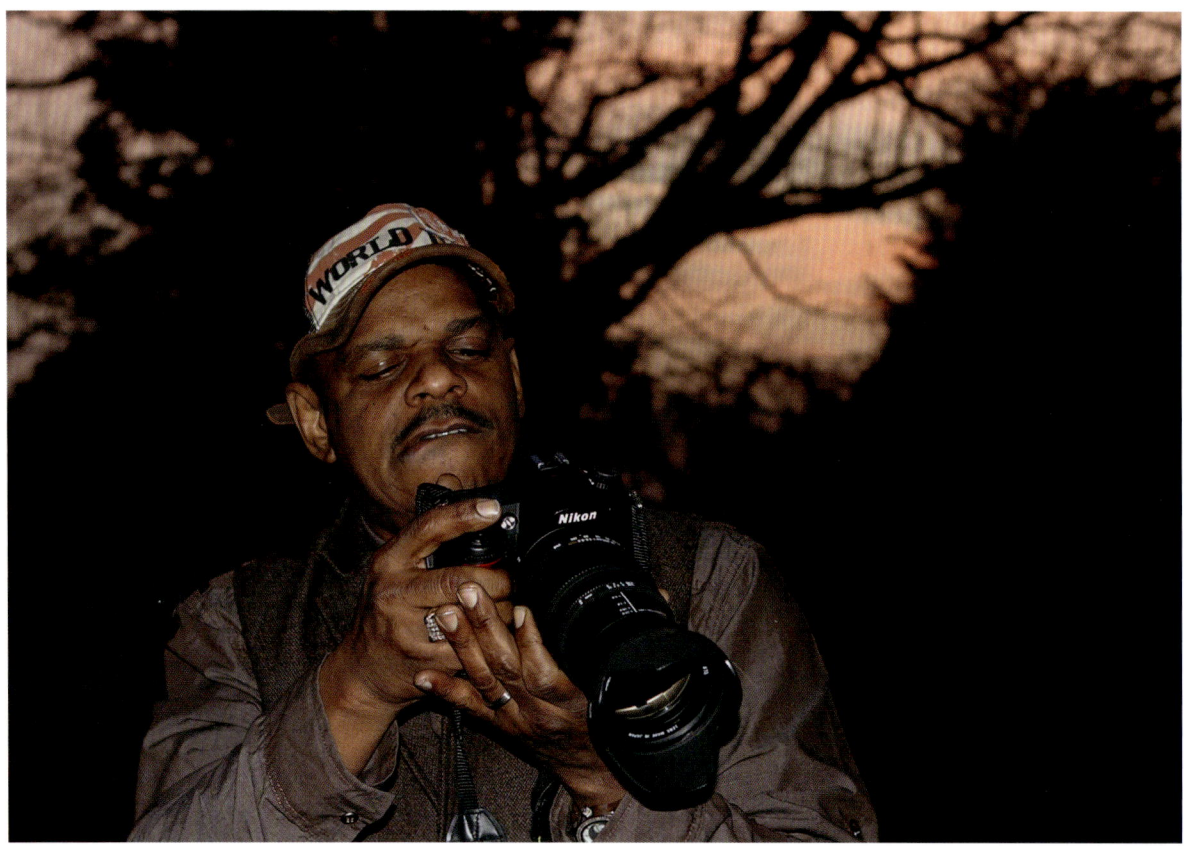

At ICP-Bard's Midtown Manhattan campus this April, Ms. Weston installed her family pictures salon-style, against a backdrop of embossed white wallpaper. Understood in this context, *Seen, Unseen* commemorates the historical, almost sacred status of photography in the lives of people of color.

In many African American homes in the Jim Crow era, for example, photographs were juxtaposed in arrangements on walls or on mantels as "altars," much like Ms. Weston's installation. Studio portraits memorializing the dead were displayed alongside snapshots celebrating the history, activities, triumphs, and celebrations of family and community. These shrines were vital to the development of a "sense of self and identity as a family," as the cultural critic bell hooks wrote,

documentation meant to affirm and enhance oral history, like maps guiding a people "through diverse journeys."

In *Seen, Unseen*, Ms. Weston honors the ways photography has supported her subjects through their diverse journeys: a weathered, old snapshot of unknown ancestors, an image that the artist characterizes as "grounding the series"; a cousin, an amateur photographer, peering through the viewfinder of his camera; and an aunt proudly displaying framed pictures of her parents.

In the end, there is no family member more enriched by the camera than Ms. Weston. "Photography has opened so many doors for me. I often wonder where my life would have gone if I had not had the privilege to experience its power. I know it saved me."

Chapter 5

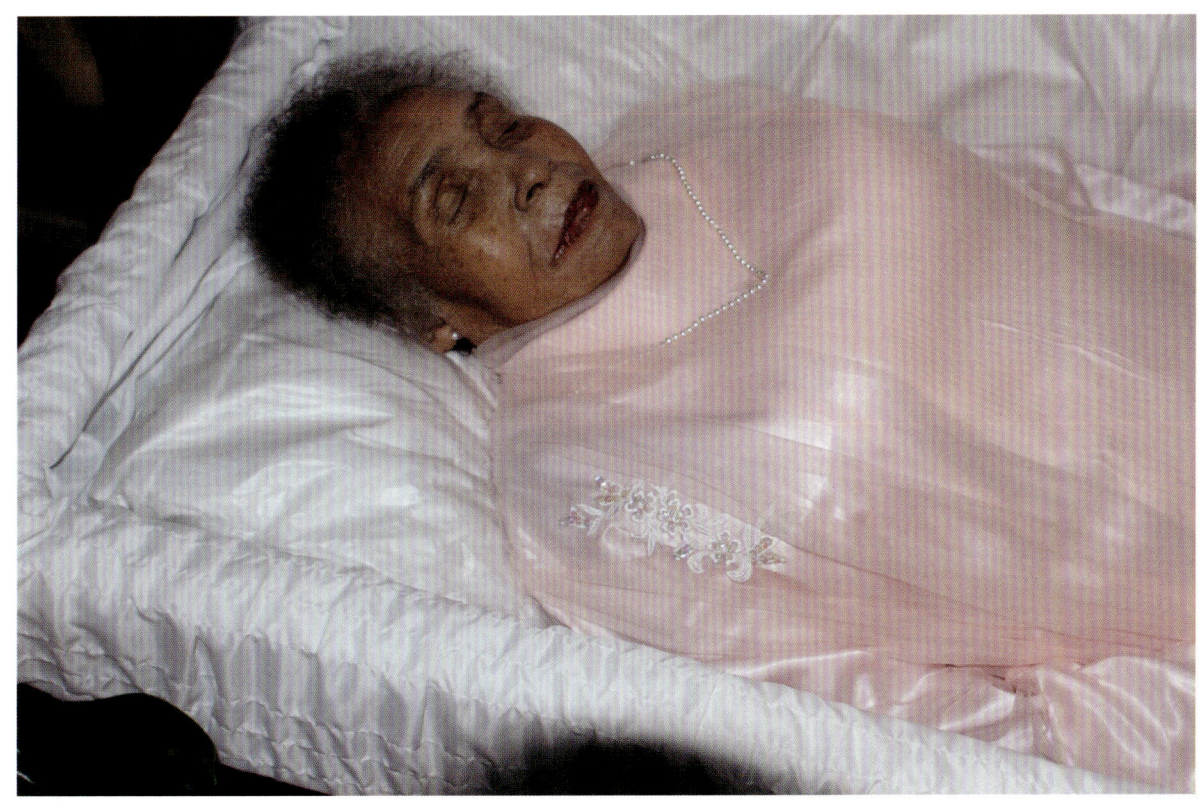

Kim Weston, *Seen, Unseen*, 2013

# LaToya Ruby Frazier's Notion of Family

Published October 14, 2014

LaToya Ruby Frazier was perusing a recently published photobook about her hometown, Braddock, Pennsylvania, when she realized something was missing: any trace of the African American residents who had contributed much to the town and who were now its majority population.

Once a bustling steel town in the Pittsburgh suburbs along the banks of the Monongahela River, Braddock has declined over the past half-century, a result of mill closings, chronic unemployment, toxic waste, redlining, and white flight. Recent efforts at gentrification have further marginalized the town's African American residents. And Braddock's lone hospital and largest employer closed in 2010, its owner, the University of Pittsburgh Medical Center, relocating to a more affluent suburb.

"This continued omission, erasure, invisibility, and silence surrounding African American sacrifices to Braddock and the American grand narrative," Ms. Frazier said, motivated her to explore the town's history, and present-day reality, through the visual narrative of her family. Five years later, she has produced an epochal book—*The Notion of Family*—about the largely forgotten Rust Belt town.

Ms. Frazier, who teaches at the School of the Art Institute of Chicago, was inspired by Gordon Parks's idea of using the camera as a "weapon" of choice against racism, intolerance, and poverty. She does not pretend to speak for African Americans or even Braddock's Black community in this project. Instead, she typically photographs herself and her mother and grandmother, three generations of women whose "lives parallel the rise and fall of the steel mill industry," and who endured despite "thirty years of disinvestment and abandonment by local, state, and federal governments."

Chapter 5

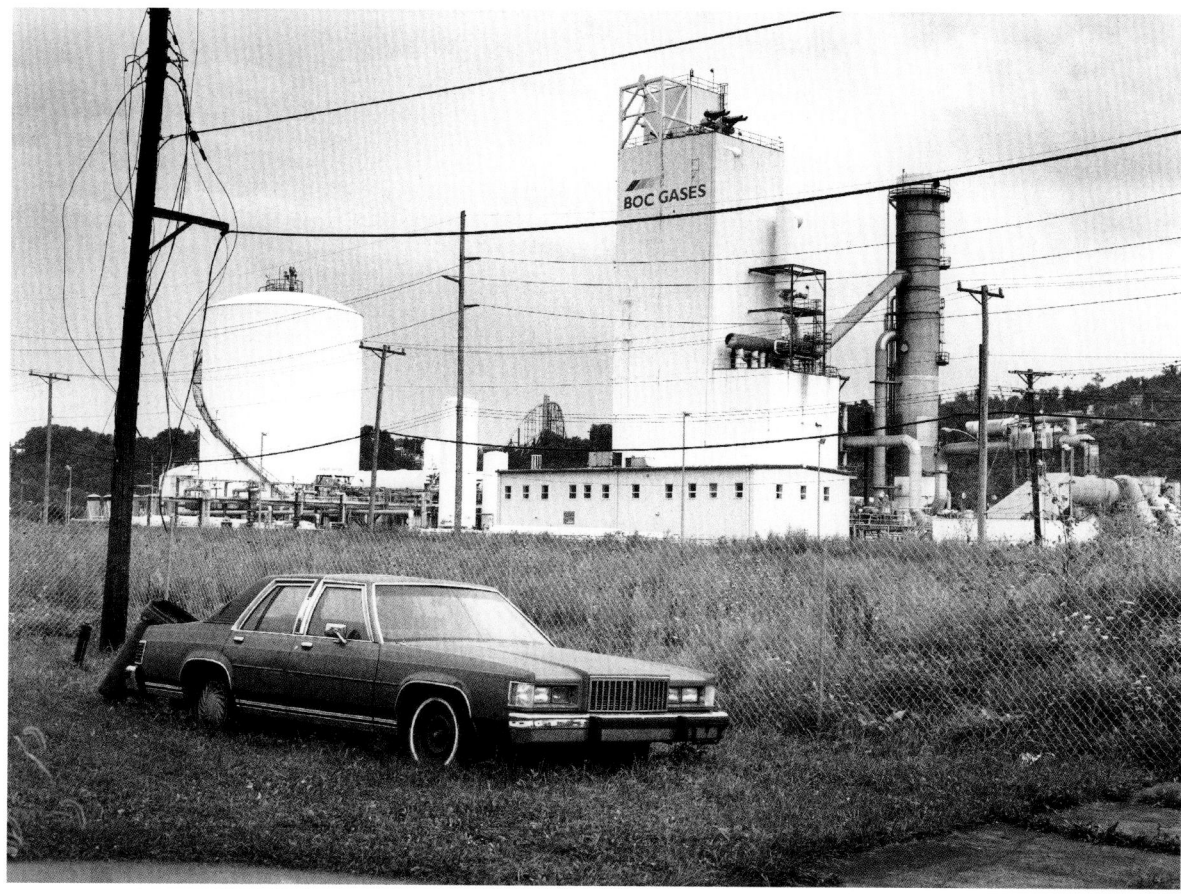

By representing the substandard living conditions, hardships, and withering effects of the pollution-borne illness that have beset the three women—as well as their struggles to survive—Ms. Frazier makes visible the human cost of political indifference and neglect.

"We need longer sustained stories that reflect and tell us where the prejudices and blind spots are and continue to be in this culture and society," Ms. Frazier said. "This is a race and class issue that is affecting everyone. It is not a Black problem, it is an American problem, it is a global problem. Braddock is everywhere."

Her book conveys the magnitude of the problem through desolate and haunting images: Ms. Frazier in her grandmother's or step-great-grandfather's pajamas, lingering like an apparition in the rooms of the latter's dilapidated and abandoned home; Braddock's dramatic skyline, shrouded by a haze of noxious pollutants; boarded-up facades of grocery stores and other local businesses; bleak portraits of Grandma Ruby, a towering presence in Ms. Frazier's life, dying from pancreatic cancer.

Ms. Frazier reimagines the tradition of social documentary photography by approaching a community not as a curious or concerned outsider but as a vulnerable insider. But like other trailblazing works about poverty in America—James Agee and Walker Evans's *Let Us Now Praise Famous Men*, for example, or Mr. Parks's *Moments without Proper Names—The Notion of Family* is both a cautionary tale and a force for educating the public and motivating reform.

As *The Notion of Family* affirms, it is principally family, both immediate and extended, that holds the key to survival in Braddock, nurturing each other as the world around them crumbles. Ms. Frazier collaborates with her mother, for example, in the book's most poignant and affirmative images. In these emotionally intense portraits, the women pose together or photograph each other, employing the camera as a potent vehicle of self-expression and self-possession.

The title of Ms. Frazier's book recalls *The Family of Man*, an exhibition organized by the photographer Edward Steichen at the Museum of Modern Art in 1955. The show documented life in sixty-eight countries through more than five hundred images taken by an international team of photographers.

*The Family of Man* played down cultural and national differences in favor of Cold War platitudes about the "essential oneness of mankind throughout the world." But it also echoed a sentiment shaped by the New Deal, and espoused by nearly every president from Franklin D. Roosevelt to Jimmy Carter: that the survival of humanity was dependent on how well we respected and took care of each other.

*The Notion of Family* testifies to the ominous consequences of rejecting this idea. The ascendance of neoconservatism in the 1980s ushered in an era of brazen self-interest, one that defined the notion of family as more a matter of blood than social responsibility. Braddock's decline was exacerbated during Reagan-era policies favoring trickle-down economics, union-busting, and diminution of social welfare programs, which foreshadowed the ever-widening gap between rich and poor Americans.

Ms. Frazier's wistful words and images, despite their focus on close relatives, speak to the value and necessity of altruistic notions of family, exemplified by the community of activists who fought to save Braddock Hospital and who continue to advocate for a better quality of life for the town's residents.

In the end, Ms. Frazier, who suffers from lupus and who lives part time in Pittsburgh to care for her mother, refuses to succumb to pessimism. The struggle for her is continuing and embodied by her work. But it is also sustained by a hopefulness informed by her endurance.

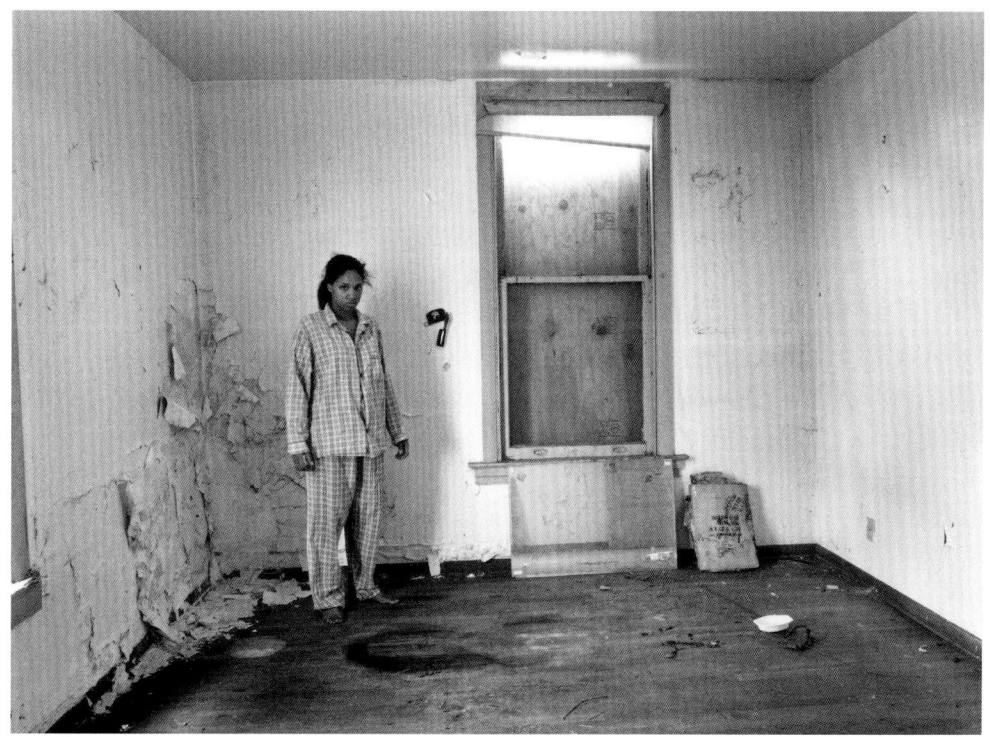

LaToya Ruby Frazier, *Self Portrait in Gramps' Bedroom (227 Holland Avenue)*, 2009

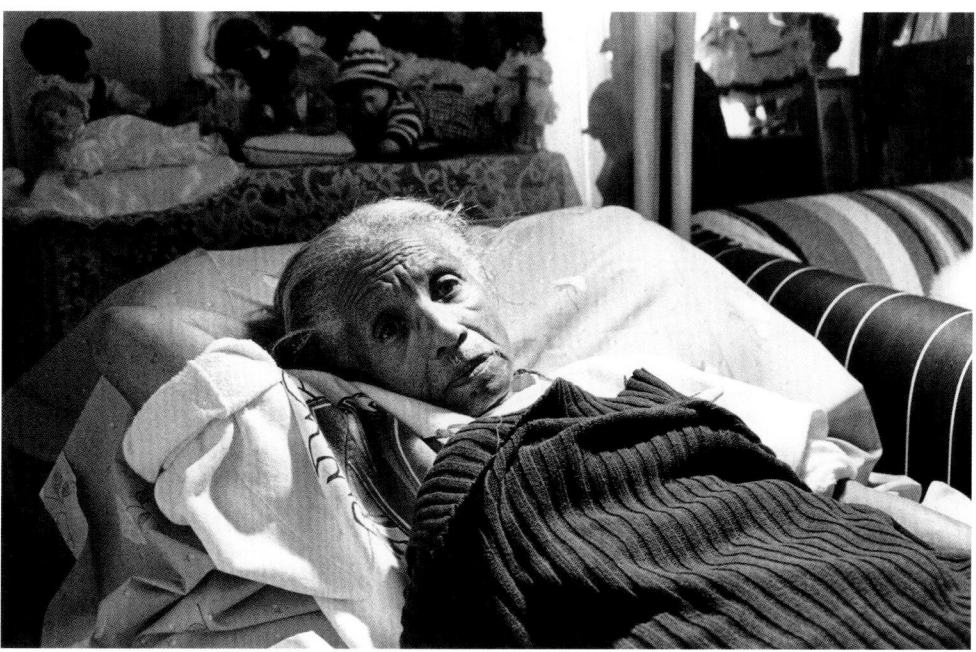

LaToya Ruby Frazier, *Grandma Ruby on Her Recliner*, 2002

# Kamoinge's Half-Century of African American Photography

Published January 7, 2016

In the early 1960s, when African American photographers were keenly aware of their isolation in a field dominated by white men, two collectives held a joint meeting. The result of that encounter was a decision to merge and form a more robust group they called Kamoinge, which in Kenya's Kikuyu language means a group of people acting together.

"We saw ourselves as a group who were trying to nurture each other," Louis Draper, a founding member of the Kamoinge Workshop who died in 2002, once wrote. "We had no outlets. The magazines wouldn't support our work. So we wanted to encourage each other. . . . to give each other feedback. We tried to be a force, especially for younger people."

To commemorate its fiftieth anniversary, the workshop has published *Timeless: Photographs by Kamoinge*, a survey of its evolving and wide-ranging work and an important contribution to the history of photography.

"We speak of our lives as only we can," Mr. Draper wrote about the personal and individualistic perspective of Kamoinge's African American photographers, and the book affirms that with a multifaceted, richly textured, and global view of the Black experience. Today, even as media depictions of people of color continue to rely on negative stereotypes and clichés, these pictures resonate with complexity.

Founding members of the workshop included Mr. Draper, Albert Fennar, Ray Francis, Herman Howard, Earl James, James Mannas, Calvin Mercer, Herbert Randall, Larry Stewart, Shawn Walker, and Calvin Wilson. Roy DeCarava, who helped shape the group and give it direction, was voted its first director.

As the group expanded and its roster changed—Mr. DeCarava left the workshop in 1965, and its first female photographer,

C. Daniel Dawson, *Amiri Baraka*, 1970

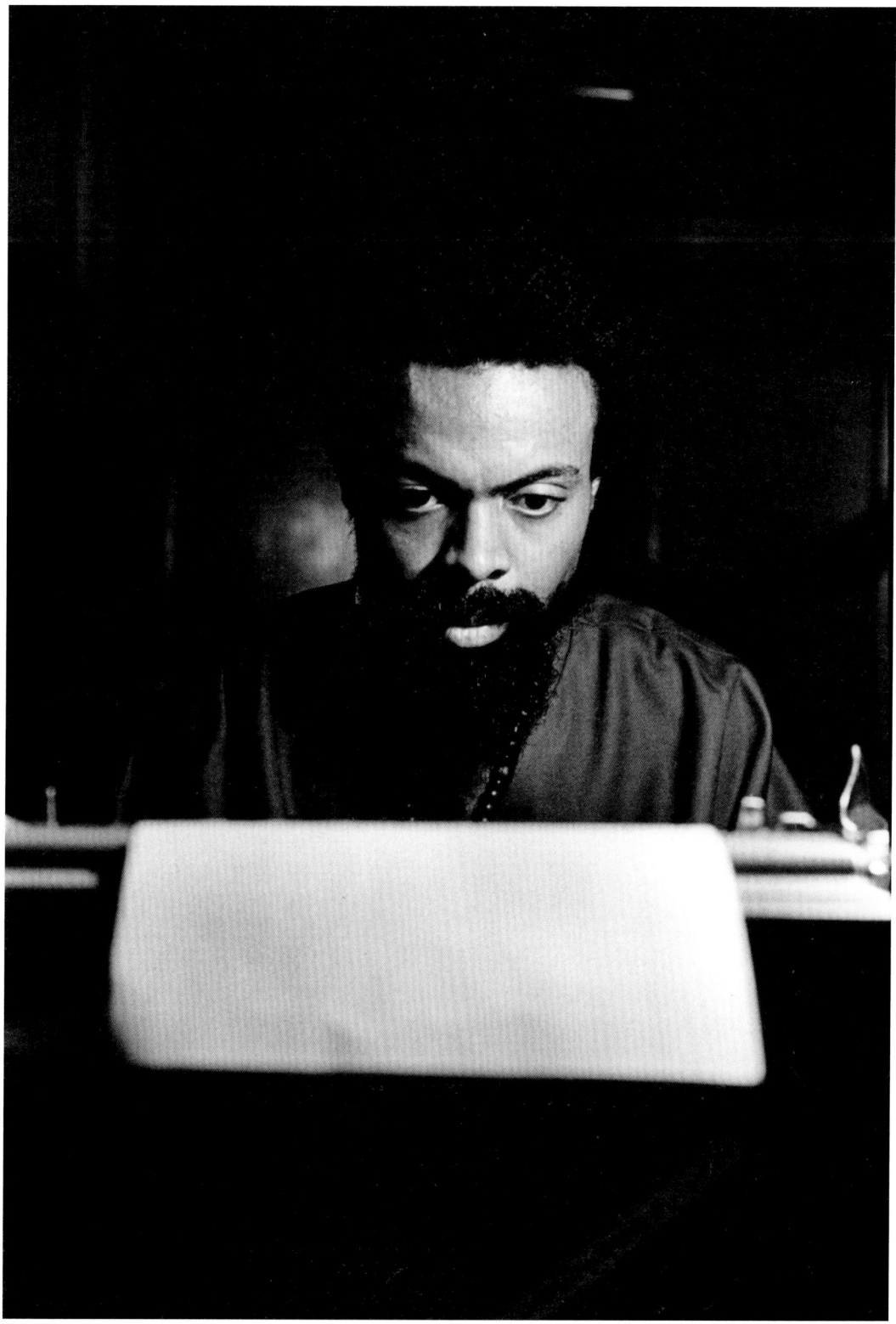

Ming Smith, joined in 1972—it supported a range of projects. These included exhibitions, initially at the gallery and meeting space the workshop rented in a Harlem brownstone and later at the Countee Cullen Library, the Studio Museum in Harlem, the International Center of Photography, and other sites. The workshop also hosted lectures and group critiques and published portfolios, which it distributed to museums.

The book includes a brooding and elegant portrait of the writer and activist Amiri Baraka; a silhouette of bass players in a Lower East Side club; an austere bird's-eye view of a city park in winter; a photo of a child in Bedford-Stuyvesant learning how to tie a necktie; a haunting image of a sheet hanging on a clothesline, evoking Ku Klux Klan hoods; an arid Malian landscape, camels resting in the distance; a jarring photograph of a mother holding a toddler in Louisiana, an electronic monitoring device strapped to her leg; a dapper gentleman in a white fedora, his clothes an essay in bold contrasting patterns; and a study of children playing in a Rwandan refugee camp.

"The photographs are a rich contrast to the 'headline' images that have circulated worldwide about Black communities known only as the roughest and toughest neighbor-hoods to live in," the photographer and photo historian Deborah Willis wrote in the book. "We have seen countless images of Black life across the diaspora and I consider these photographs to be a mosaic of the Black experience; they expand our consciousness and challenge what we think we know about Black life."

Embracing abstraction, Conceptualism, Surrealism, portraiture, social documentary, performance documentation, and landscape, cityscape, and street photography, this work challenges the myth of a unified African American aesthetic. Nevertheless, its interpretation has sometimes been limited by this idea: A Kamoinge portfolio published in the July 1966 issue of *Camera*, a leading Swiss photo magazine, was titled "Harlem" by an editor, despite its range of locations, content, and viewpoints.

Despite this misconception, Kamoinge photographers have approached their subjects from differing emotional, political, and cultural perspectives. As the art historian Erina Duganne observed in an article on the diversity of the group's imagery, "rather than speak for African Americans as a group or act as a corrective lens, the Kamoinge members used their photographs to explore how the particularities of their individual circumstances—including their collective experience of racial difference—informed and complicated their art."

If Kamoinge members worked together and learned from one another in order to change how global Black life was represented, their photographs were also influenced by, and produced in dialogue with, eminent artists of all races. It is in this context that their work helps us to better understand not only the people and communities they engaged, but also aesthetic, cultural, and social issues germane to the broader history of modern art and photography, a history from which these artists have been largely excluded.

The workshop has evolved over the last half-century: Some participants have died, including Mr. Draper and Mr. Francis. New members were welcomed. Solo and group exhibitions were mounted and articles written about the group. Members opened studios, became college teachers, and took on magazine and advertising assignments. But even as the Kamoinge Workshop grew in stature, its members remained focused on their profoundly individualistic creative mission.

"Kamoinge photographers have never followed the latest trends, but nonetheless we have been influenced by what is around us," wrote Anthony Barboza, the current workshop president. "As artists, we are moved by all that happens every day; artists are sponges that absorb the feelings of the self and the world and reflect back what we see. Within each photograph is what the artist has lived, and you see the individual's truth that has been breathed into the art form."

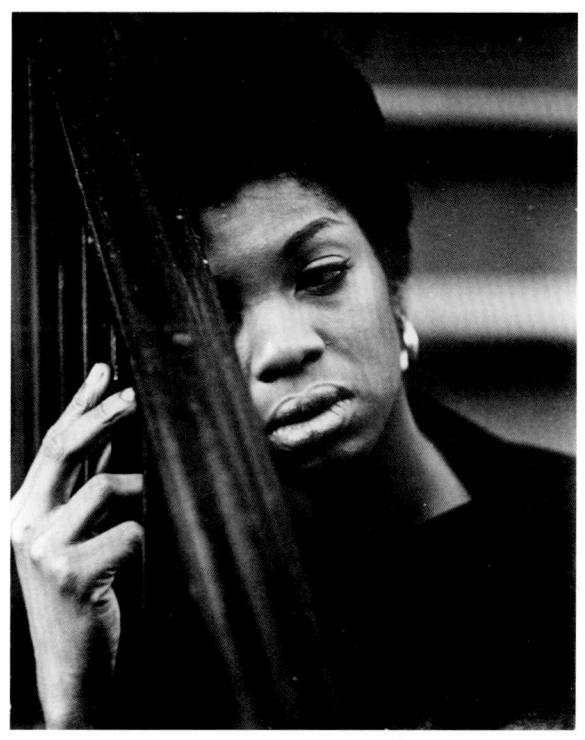

Calvin Wilson, *New York*, 1960s

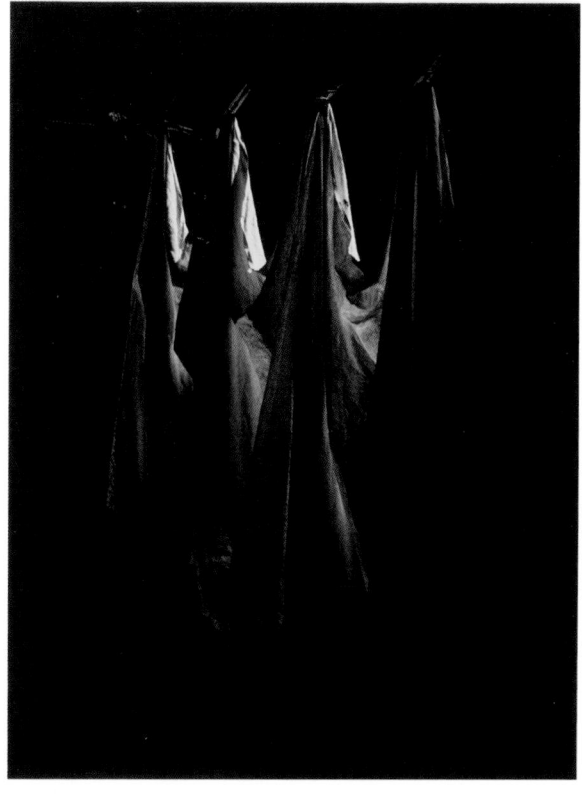

Louis Draper, *Congressional Gathering*, 1959

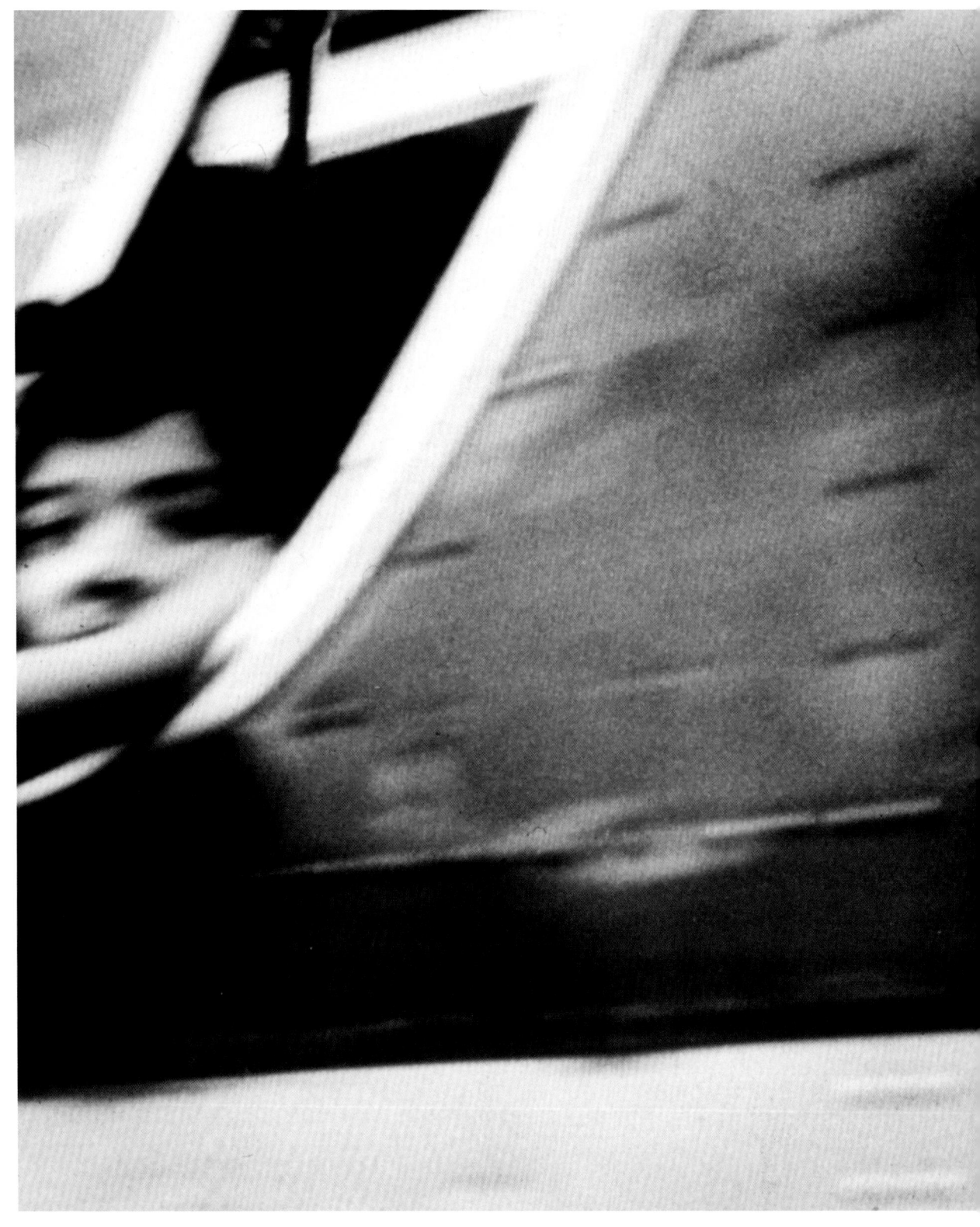

Anthony Barboza, *Bus Boy, New York*, 1973

Chapter 5

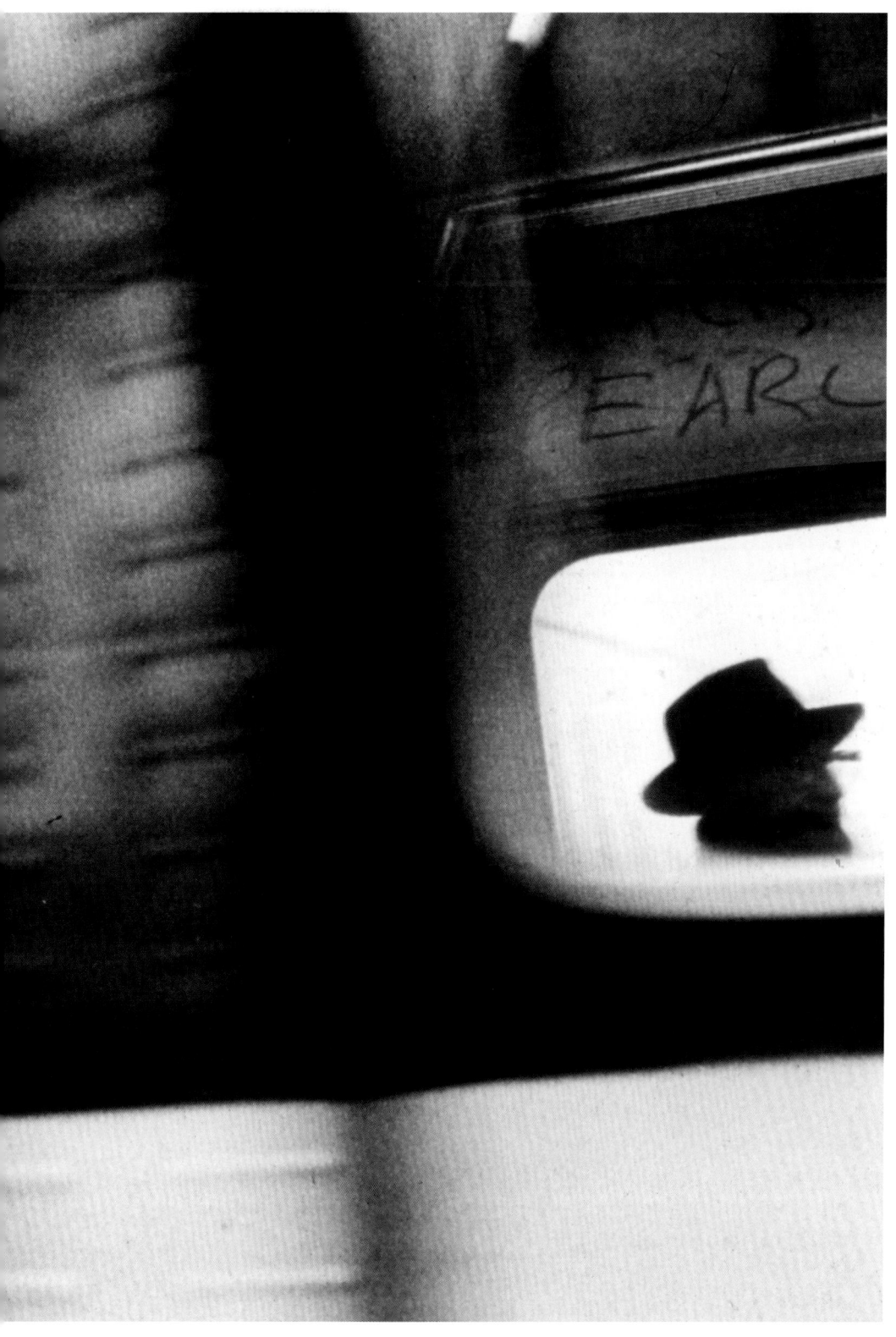

# Afterword:
# Reflections on
# Maurice Berger
# and His Work

Nona Faustine, Peter W. Kunhardt, Jr., and Dawoud Bey

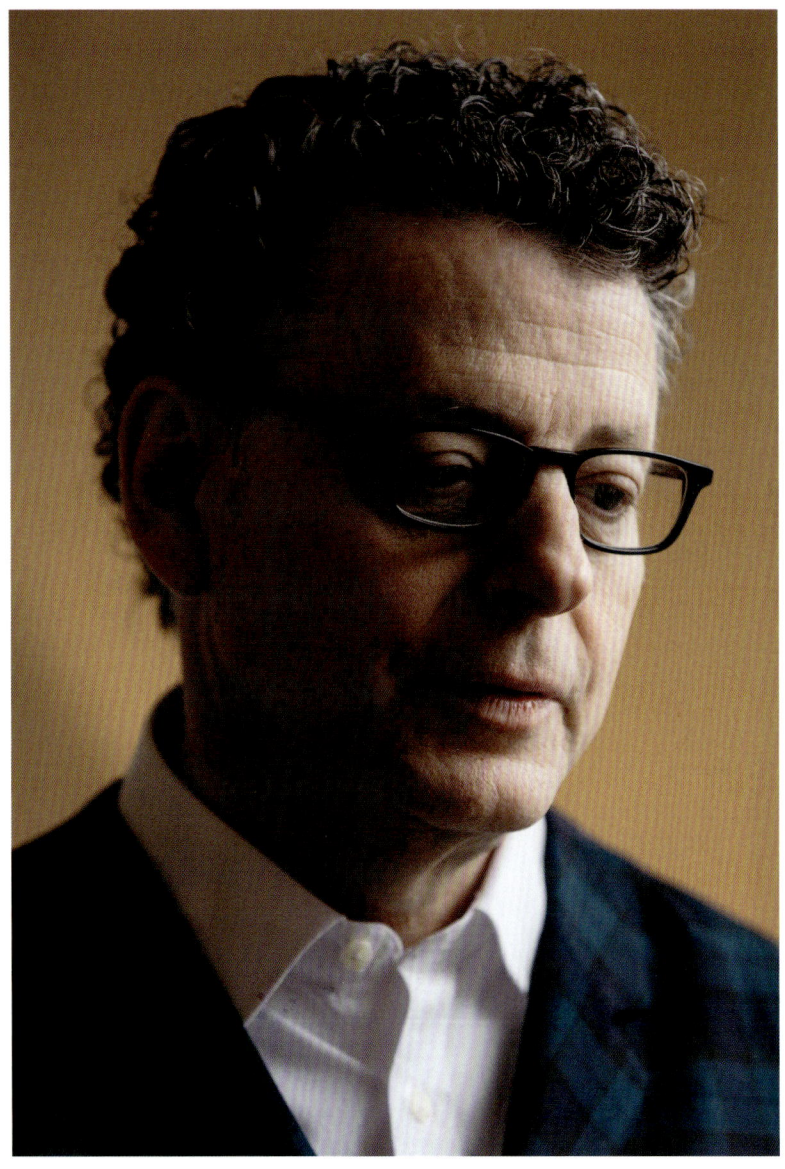

Seher Sikander, Portrait of Maurice Berger, 2019

# Nona Faustine

I was a first-year graduate student in 2012 when, after an evening event where students presented their work, Maurice came over to say how much he liked and admired what I was doing. I still remember the personality and energy he had as we talked about what I felt I needed to do in my work. He urged me not to be deterred or swayed by those around me. Maurice, knowing about race and how things go in grad school, sensed I was drowning in the program. And I was: overwhelmed, singled out, and bullied. That night, I felt like Maurice became, instantly, my fan-club president.

I'd almost tuned him out, thinking, "Who is this guy?" Then something in me said, "No, calm down for a second. Listen to him." From that moment on, he was a mentor to me. We would talk over social media. We would inbox each other. During my second year in grad school, Maurice was the person who gave me the name for the photographic series that eventually grew out of my thesis project. I had originally called it *Reconstruction*, but he said, "No, that sounds too academic. Let it be *White Shoes*." And I thought that was perfect. After I graduated and was making my first museum sale, to the Studio Museum in Harlem, Maurice was the first person I turned to for advice.

In his pieces for the Lens blog, Maurice often featured work in recent exhibitions or books. He couldn't write about *White Shoes* because the *Times* didn't publish nudity at that time. (They published a piece, years later, after Maurice died, when the series was shown at the Brooklyn Museum.) So, when some works from my earlier *Mitochondria* series—a visual diary of family pictures I made as a single mother living within a household of three generations of Black women—were on exhibit, he wrote about those.

Thinking about my own work in a progression of images made by African American picture-makers, like Gordon Parks, Roy DeCarava, and Marilyn Nance, was not something I was doing then. All of those photographers who came before me, they're incredible. I never thought I might be in that canon. You do your best work. You pay your dues. Everybody has their stories, you know. But really, someone else still needs to come along and help you. What Maurice did was like saying, "I know what you're doing *and* why you're doing it." Maurice was one of the people who came along and helped me.

I read Maurice's column because I knew him and how phenomenal his writing about photography was, and because his *Times* column gave visibility to work that wouldn't necessarily get that kind of audience or be contextualized so well. To be written about by him, there, to have my work seen in a broader history of art and politics, elevated me as an emerging artist.

# Peter W. Kunhardt, Jr.

Born generations apart, Gordon Parks and Maurice Berger both keenly understood how art can be used as a tool to enact social change. Although Gordon and Maurice never met, their work engaged in a dialogue on racism that confronted systemic injustices and advocated for progress. When Parks passed away in 2006, he left behind an archive of his groundbreaking work in photography, film, music, and writing that became the heart of the Gordon Parks Foundation. In a career that spanned over fifty years, he made visible Black life in America with a visual language that was poignant, humanistic, unexpected, and at times revolutionary. Maurice's research and writing on that archive introduced a perspective on Parks's versatility and approach that was likewise extraordinary, and his illuminating scholarship left an indelible mark on our understanding of the lasting impact of Parks's work.

In 2013, Maurice did a story for the *New York Times* Lens blog on Joanne Wilson, the woman pictured standing with her niece in front of a movie theater in downtown Mobile, Alabama, in Parks's 1956 photograph for *Life*. Maurice's interview with Mrs. Wilson and his writing on the larger series of color transparencies—once thought to be lost, but recently recovered—helped to establish and contextualize the significance of that body of work. By highlighting the humanity of Parks's approach and his focus on details—from the choice of using Kodachrome film to the strap of Mrs. Wilson's slip—Maurice's writing revealed the photographs as some of the most important images of the civil rights era. He forever transformed our perception of Parks's legacy and the ways in which we carry it forward at the Gordon Parks Foundation.

Parks famously described his camera as his "choice of weapons against what I hated most about the universe: racism, intolerance, poverty." In 2019, Maurice participated in an interview included in the 2021 documentary *A Choice of Weapons: Inspired by Gordon Parks*. There, he shed further light on the significance of that phrase and the impact Parks's photographs had on those that viewed them: "Gordon used the term 'weapon of choice' as a way of describing the power of the camera to do what almost no other object, vehicle, form of expression could do, which was to produce a picture of the world that

would be so moving and so persuasive, that it could move people to change their views, to push back against the racism that they saw around them, to give themselves a sense of pride in the face of that racism."

# Dawoud Bey

For all of its supposed liberalism, the art world has been a hotbed of racism, with an unspoken yet active policy of benign neglect for Black, non-white, and non-male artists who have, for decades, sought to gain access and show their work in its institutional spaces. Through sheer persistence and principled erudition, Maurice Berger called out this reality in the most public of ways. For example, when he published his essay "Are Art Museums Racist?" in the September 1990 issue of *Art in America*, it set off an explosion from inside the art world, which was then only inching toward tokenism, at best. Maurice called them out . . . forcefully. It got a lot of people's attention, including mine.

My exchanges with Maurice were somewhat clandestine affairs, tinged with a kind of irony and humorous anger. He would share news of yet another encounter with someone who had only now become a vocal cheerleader for the substantive changes that he had been advocating for, for years. They were the very same people who excoriated him in the past for pushing too hard and too fast for changes to systemic practices that a long struggle and resistance had finally made untenable and, yes, unfashionable. We have Maurice to thank for constantly prodding the forces that love to drag their feet and prolong the insidious joys of privilege and exclusivity. Belatedly, art institutions have increasing started to look like the broader social communities in whose midst they sit. Maurice was the annoying pebble inside the polished shoes of the privileged that we all so needed.

Maurice's interest in my own work was effusive and consistent. It was his brilliant critical mind I always sought in the midst of a project or upon its completion, knowing he would fully appreciate both the impetus that drove the work and the studied rigor that informed it. Maurice would also ask questions that helped buoy me when I had moments of lingering doubt before the work was publicly presented. When I had the opportunity to publish a forty-year survey of my work in 2017, I immediately knew that I wanted Maurice to write the essay for the chapter on *The Birmingham Project*, which I had completed in 2012. He would more than do justice to the work through his ability to excavate the history that the work addressed, both socially and through the visual history of the civil rights movement in the South. He understood the ways in which that moment of racial repression and resistance had been photographically represented. The essay he penned, "A Remembrance of Lives Lost," was not only a full display of Maurice's regard for the project, but also of his astute and heartfelt grasp of the histories that preceded this work. He also wrote about *The Birmingham Project* in his *Race Stories* column for the *New York Times* Lens blog, knowing that platform could provide the wider exposure the project deserved.

I miss Maurice. He was a singular presence, someone free from pretense whose friendship and support came with no expectation of quid pro quo, only a mutual desire to continue to remake the world into the more equitable place that we both passionately agreed it needed to be. How wonderful it was to have been in partnership with him on this path.

# Contributor Bios

**MAURICE BERGER** (1956–2020), a cultural historian, curator, and writer, spent much of his career studying and teaching racial literacy through innovative visual-literacy projects. In influential essays, books, and provocative museum exhibitions, Berger presented compelling photographic images to engage and challenge readers and viewers into reconsidering both cultural and personal assumptions and prejudices. Berger's unique perspective first came to public attention in 1990, when his now-landmark essay "Are Art Museums Racist?" was published in *Art in America*. Over the years, he wrote for a diverse range of specialized and general-interest periodicals, including *Artforum*, *Aperture*, the *Village Voice*, *Brooklyn Rail*, *PEN America*, *Wired*, *National Geographic*, the *Los Angeles Times*, and the *New York Times*. Berger's books include *White Lies: Race and the Myths of Whiteness* (2000), a finalist for the Horace Mann Bond Book Award of the W. E. B. Du Bois Research Institution, Harvard University, and *For All the World to See: Visual Culture and the Struggle for Civil Rights* (2010). He received honors and grants from the National Endowment for the Humanities, National Endowment for the Arts, Association of Art Museum Curators, International Association of Art Critics, and an Emmy Award nomination. For the *New York Times* "Race Stories" column, Berger was awarded a 2014 Creative Capital/Andy Warhol Foundation Arts Writers Grant, as well as the International Center of Photography's Infinity Award for Critical Writing and Research in 2018.

**DAWOUD BEY** has for decades made groundbreaking and evocative work about the histories of Black communities. His numerous honors include a MacArthur Fellowship, Guggenheim Fellowship, and National Endowment for the Arts Fellowships. A major career retrospective of his work, *An American Project*, was coorganized by the Whitney Museum of American Art, New York, and the San Francisco Museum of Modern Art (2020–22). Bey is professor of art and a former distinguished college artist at Columbia College Chicago. He also serves on the Board of Trustees at Aperture. His books include *Class Pictures* (2007), *Seeing Deeply* (2018), *Dawoud Bey on Photographing People and Communities* (2019), and *Elegy* (2023).

**NONA FAUSTINE** is a photographer and visual artist. Her work evokes a critical understanding of history, identity, and representation by revealing underrepresented narratives throughout history and today. She is a graduate of the School of Visual Arts, New York, and the International Center of Photography at Bard College's MFA program. Faustine is the recipient of the Rome Prize, a NYSCA/NYFA Artist Fellowship, the Colene Brown Art Prize, and the Anonymous Was A Woman grant. Her photographs are in numerous collections, including the Museum of Modern Art, New York; Los Angeles County Museum of Art; Studio Museum in Harlem; San Francisco Museum of Modern Art; and Museum of Fine Arts, Boston. Her work has been exhibited at the National Portrait Gallery, National Gallery of Art, both in Washington, DC, and the Carnegie Museum of Art, Pittsburgh, among others. In 2024, the Brooklyn Museum exhibited Faustine's first solo museum show, *White Shoes*.

**HENRY LOUIS GATES, JR.** is the Alphonse Fletcher University Professor and director of the Hutchins Center for African and African American Research at Harvard University. An Emmy Award–winning filmmaker, literary scholar, journalist, and cultural critic, Gates has published numerous books, including, most recently, *Stony the Road: Reconstruction, White Supremacy, and the Rise of Jim Crow* (2019) and *The Black Church: This Is Our Story, This Is Our Song* (2021). He has produced and hosted over twenty documentary films, including *The Black Church* (PBS),

*Black Art: In the Absence of Light* (HBO), as well as *Finding Your Roots*, his groundbreaking genealogy series for PBS. Gates was a member of the first class awarded "genius grants" by the MacArthur Foundation in 1981, and in 1998 he became the first African American scholar to be awarded the National Humanities Medal. He earned a BA from Yale University and an MA and PhD from Clare College at the University of Cambridge. A former chair of the Pulitzer Prize board, he is a member of the American Academy of Arts and Letters and serves on many boards, including those of the New York Public Library, NAACP Legal Defense Fund, Aspen Institute, Whitney Museum of American Art, Library of America, and Studio Museum in Harlem.

**MARVIN HEIFERMAN** creates onsite, online, and publication projects about photography and visual culture for institutions, including the Smithsonian Institution, Washington, DC; Museum of Modern Art, International Center of Photography, Whitney Museum of American Art, and New Museum, all in New York; and Carnegie Museum of Art, Pittsburgh. Heiferman has written for numerous publications, monographs, magazines, and blogs, including the *New York Times*, CNN, *Artforum*, *Design Observer*, *Art in America*, and *Aperture*. He has authored or edited over two dozen books on visual culture, including *Photography Changes Everything* (2012) and *Seeing Science* (2019).

**PETER W. KUNHARDT, JR.** is executive director of the Gordon Parks Foundation and series editor for Steidl/Gordon Parks Foundation publications. Under his leadership, the foundation has established such major educational initiatives as a scholarship and fellowship program for students and artists. He has edited and contributed to more than twenty-two publications, most recently *Devin Allen: Baltimore* (2024); *American Gothic: Gordon Parks and Ella Watson* (2024); *Gordon Parks: Born Black* (expanded edition, 2024); *Jamel Shabazz: Albums* (2023); *Ralph Ellison: Photographer* (2023); *Gordon Parks: Stokely Carmichael and Black Power* (2022); *Gordon Parks: Segregation Story* (expanded edition, 2022); *LaToya Ruby Frazier: Flint Is Family In Three Acts* (2022); and *Gordon Parks: The Atmosphere of Crime, 1957* (2022). Kunhardt also coedited the multivolume *Gordon Parks: Collected Works* (2012).

**SARAH LEWIS** is the John L. Loeb Associate Professor of the Humanities and associate professor of African and African American studies at Harvard University and the founder of Vision & Justice. Her books and edited volumes include *The Rise* (2014), *The Unseen Truth: When Race Changed Sight in America* (2024), *Carrie Mae Weems* (2021), and the "Vision & Justice" issue of *Aperture* magazine (2016), which received the Infinity Award for Critical Writing and Research from the International Center of Photography. She is also the recipient of the Andrew Carnegie Fellow and the Freedom Scholar Award, presented by the Association for the Study of African American Life and History, for her body of work and its "direct positive impact on the life of African Americans." She has held curatorial positions as the Museum of Modern Art, New York, and the Tate Modern, London. Lewis's writing has received fellowship and grant support from the Ford Foundation; Hutchins Center for African and African American Research at Harvard University; Gilder Lehrman Center for the Study of Slavery, Resistance, and Abolition; Beinecke Rare Book & Manuscript Library; Whiting Foundation; Lambent Foundation; and the Dorothy and Lewis B. Cullman Center for Scholars and Writers at the New York Public Library. She received a BA from Harvard University, an MPhil from Oxford University, an MA from Courtauld Institute of Art, and a PhD from Yale University.

LEIGH RAIFORD is professor of African American studies at the University of California, Berkeley, where she teaches and researches about race, gender, justice, and visuality. At Berkeley, Raiford is also codirector and coprincipal investigator with Tianna S. Paschel of the Black Studies Collaboratory, a three-year initiative to amplify the world-building work of Black studies funded by the Andrew W. Mellon Foundation. Raiford is the author of *Imprisoned in a Luminous Glare: Photography and the African American Freedom Struggle* (2011), a finalist for the Berkshire Conference of Women Historians Best Book Prize; coauthor of *Collaboration: A Potential History of Photography* (2023), conceived with Ariella Aïsha Azoulay, Wendy Ewald, Susan Meiselas, and Laura Wexler; coeditor with Heike Raphael-Hernandez of *Migrating the Black Body: The African Diaspora and Visual Culture* (2017); and coeditor with Renee Romano of *The Civil Rights Movement in American Memory* (2006).

DEBORAH WILLIS is a curator, photographer, and leading scholar of photography and Black studies. She is university professor and chair of the Department of Photography and Imaging at the Tisch School of the Arts at New York University, where she is also the director of the NYU Institute for African American Affairs and the Center for Black Visual Culture. Her research examines photography's multifaceted histories, the photographic history of slavery and emancipation, and contemporary women photographers. She is a MacArthur and Guggenheim Fellow. Willis received the NAACP Image Award in 2014 for her coauthored book *Envisioning Emancipation: Black Americans and the End of Slavery* (with Barbara Krauthamer), and in 2015 for the documentary *Through a Lens Darkly*, inspired by her book *Reflections in Black: A History of Black Photographers 1840 to the Present* (2000). Willis has also served as a consultant to numerous museums, archives, and educational centers. In 2024, President Biden announced Willis as a nominee to be a member of the National Council on the Humanities.

# Acknowledgments

*Race Stories* represents and celebrates the lives and work of many: image-makers, those they've photographed, and those who look at the pictures after they're made. The essays survey the powerful roles images have had and continue to play in shaping the ways race is represented and understood. *Race Stories*, too, pays homage to the brilliance and legacy of Maurice Berger, whose influential essays, books, online projects, and museum exhibitions challenge readers and viewers to recognize and explore how profoundly the picturing of race impacts much of what we feel, think, and do.

Many people helped to produce this volume. Thanks to Sarah Lewis, Leigh Raiford, and Deborah Willis—the editors of the important and ongoing Vision & Justice Book Series that *Race Stories* inaugurates—for their unwavering encouragement, support, and respect for Maurice's work.

The essays in *Race Stories* owe their existence to James Estrin and David Gonzalez at the *New York Times*, who conceived of and edited the newspaper's online Lens blog and gave Maurice a venue and unprecedented opportunity to explore intersections of race and photography and to engage readers in images and ideas on a scale he'd only dreamt of. I'm also thankful to those in licensing and book development at the *New York Times* who guided the project through a long process to copublish *Race Stories* as a book with Aperture: Gregory Miller, Erik Borenstein, Caitlin Roper, Trish Daly, Caroline Que, and Erika Sommer.

At Aperture, my sincere and special thanks to Denise Wolff and also to Jessica Lynne and Iesha E. Coppin-Forde for their editorial expertise and passionate dedication to this project. Thank you to Susan Ciccotti, Zack Hatfield, Claire Voon, and Freddy Martinez for their careful text editing; and to Minjee Cho and Andrea Chlad for their supervision of the book's production. I'm thankful to Sarah Meister and Michael Famighetti at Aperture as well, whose belief in and support for this volume were essential. I'm grateful for the work of Jon Key, whose graphic design for *Race Stories* captures the rigor and freshness of style that characterized Maurice's thinking and work.

We are honored that Henry Louis Gates, Jr., whom Maurice counted as a friend and colleague, has written the foreword to this volume. It's wonderful to hear from Dawoud Bey and Nona Faustine, artists Maurice championed, and Peter W. Kunhardt, Jr., whose stewardship of the Gordon Parks Foundation Maurice greatly admired. The essays in this book were written while Maurice was the senior curator of the Center for Art, Design, and Visual Culture and a research professor at the University of Maryland, Baltimore County, where directors Symmes Gardner and Rebecca Uchill advocated for his ambitious projects and goals. Thanks to Carin Kuoni (chief curator and director of the Vera List Center for Art and Politics at the New School) and to Charles Traub (chair of the School of Visual Arts' MFA program in photography, video, and related media) and for programming they sponsored to honor Maurice's work and legacy and, more recently, to Joanne Leonhardt Cassullo, who's been instrumental in establishing the Maurice Berger Memorial Archive and Library at the Center for Studying Structures of Race at Roanoke College in Virginia, where Dr. Jesse Bucher is director.

Finally, this book could not have happened without the love and support of friends and family, including: Ron Heiferman and Judy Miller, Dan Feigelson and Suzy Stein, Therese Lichtenstein, Steve Miller, Saul Ostrow, Katherine Dieckmann and Brian Wallis, Dana Hoey and Oliver Wasow, Mason Klein and Elizabeth Sacre, Barbara Buhler Lynes, Laura Blanco, Steve Kasher, Chelsea Adewunmi, Courtney Baker, and Kinshasha Holman Conwill.

Marvin Heiferman

# Image Credits

Front cover: © and courtesy The Gordon Parks Foundation; Frontispiece: © Estate of Jack Manning, image courtesy, Collection of the Smithsonian National Museum of African American History and Culture; page 4: © Nona Faustine, courtesy the artist; page 9: © Charles "Teenie" Harris, courtesy Carnegie Museum of Art/Getty Images; page 11: © and courtesy The Gordon Parks Foundation; page 12: © The Art Institute of Chicago; page 13: © and courtesy The June Leaf and Robert Frank Foundation, from *The Americans*; page 15 (top): Courtesy Collection of the Smithsonian National Museum of African American History and Culture, Frances Albrier Collection; page 15 (bottom): © and courtesy Museum of History and Industry, Seattle, Al Smith Collection, 2014.49.010-019-0039; page 16: © Twenty Eight Ink, New York, NY, courtesy the artist; page 17: © Matt Herron, 1963, courtesy Take Stock/TopFoto; pages 18–25: © and courtesy The Gordon Parks Foundation; page 27: © Fred R. Conrad/*The New York Times*; pages 29–30: © Stephen Shames, 2024, courtesy the artist/Polaris Images; pages 33–37: © Bruce W. Talamon, 2018, All Rights Reserved; pages 39–40: © and courtesy Collection of Greg French; page 43: © Bob Adelman, courtesy the artist; page 44: Courtesy Library of Congress, Prints & Photographs Division; page 45: © John Vachon, photographer, *LOOK* Magazine Photograph Collection, Library of Congress, Prints & Photographs Division, LC-L9-56-6595-U2, no. 36; page 47: © Gillian Laub, courtesy the artist; page 48: Courtesy Pete Mauney; page 49: © Wendy Ewald, courtesy the artist; pages 51–53: © Adger Cowans, courtesy the artist; pages 55–57: © Carrie Mae Weems, courtesy the artist and Gladstone Gallery, New York, Fraenkel Gallery, San Francisco, and Galerie Barbara Thumm, Berlin; pages 59–61: © and courtesy The Gordon Parks Foundation; pages 63–65: © Leonard Freed/Magnum Photos; page 67: © and courtesy The June Leaf and Robert Frank Foundation, from *The Americans*, reproduction image © National Gallery of Art; page 69: © and courtesy The June Leaf and Robert Frank Foundation, from *The Americans*; page 70: © Harry Ransom Center, the University of Texas at Austin, image courtesy the Collection of the Smithsonian National Museum of African American History and Culture; pages 74–75: © and courtesy The J. Paul Getty Museum, Los Angeles, Gift of the Flora Family, reproduction image © Bettmann Archive/Getty Images; pages 77–79: © Zanele Muholi, courtesy the artist and Yancey Richardson Gallery, New York; page 81: © Peter Hall/Hulton Archive/Getty Images; page 82: © William Lovelace/Express/Getty Images; pages 86–89: © John G. Zimmerman, courtesy John G. Zimmerman Archive; page 91: © Reuters Pictures; page 93: © Richard Ellis, courtesy the artist; page 95: Courtesy UCLA Chicano Studies Research Center; page 97: © Patricia Borjon-Lopez, courtesy UCLA Chicano Studies Research Center; pages 99–101: © Nona Faustine, courtesy the artist; pages 103–4: Courtesy the artist and Dr. Yaba Blay; pages 107–9: © Zun Lee, courtesy the artist; page 111: © Rose Callahan, courtesy the artist; page 112: © Kia Chenelle, courtesy the artist; pages 115–17: © Deborah Willis, courtesy the artist; pages 119–20: © Raphael Albert, courtesy the artist and Autograph, London; pages 123–24: Courtesy Trent Kelley; pages 127–29: © and courtesy The Gordon Parks Foundation; page 131: © Don Cravens/The LIFE Images Collection/Getty Images; pages 132–33: © Flip Schulke/Corbis/Getty Images; page 134: © Leonard Freed/Magnum Photos; pages 137–39: © Dawoud Bey, courtesy Stephen Daiter Gallery; pages 141–43: Courtesy U.S. National Archives; pages 145–47: © Nandita Raman, courtesy sepiaEYE; pages 149–50: © Barbara Karant, courtesy the artist; page 153: © Library of Congress, Prints & Photographs Division; page 154: © Chicago-Sun/Associated Press; page 155: © Associated Press; page 157: Courtesy Collection of the Massachusetts Historical Society; page 161: Courtesy West Virginia and Regional History Center WVU Libraries; page 162: Courtesy Collection of the Massachusetts Historical Society; page 166: Courtesy Collection of the Smithsonian National Museum of African American History and Culture; page 167 (top and bottom): Courtesy Library of Congress, Prints & Photographs Division; pages 169–70: Jon Lewis Photographs, Beinecke Rare Book & Manuscript Library, © Yale University; pages 174–75: © Jill Freedman, courtesy the artist; pages 177–79: © Matt Herron, 1976, courtesy Take Stock/TopFoto; page 181: Courtesy Collection of the Smithsonian National Museum of African American History and Culture, Gift of James E. Brown; page 183: Courtesy Collection of the Smithsonian National Museum of African American History and Culture, Gift of the Scurlock family, Robert Scurlock; pages 185–86: © Ken Gonzales-Day, courtesy the artist and Luis De Jesus Los Angeles; page 190 (top): Courtesy the Archives and Records Service Division, Mississippi Department of Archives and History; page 190 (bottom): Courtesy Eric Etheridge, from *Breach of Peace: Portraits of the 1961 Mississippi Freedom Riders* (Vanderbilt University Press, 2018); page 191 (top): Courtesy the Archives and Records Service Division, Mississippi Department of Archives and History; page 191 (bottom): Courtesy Eric Etheridge, from *Breach of Peace: Portraits of the 1961 Mississippi Freedom Riders* (Vanderbilt University Press, 2018); pages 193–94: © Lee Friedlander, courtesy Fraenkel Gallery, San Francisco, and Luhring Augustine, New York, image courtesy Eakins Press Foundation; pages 197–99: © Dawoud Bey, courtesy Stephen Daiter Gallery; page 200: © Whitney Curtis, courtesy the artist; page 205: © Dawoud Bey, courtesy Stephen Daiter Gallery; pages 207–8: © Center for Creative Photography, Arizona Board of Regents; pages 212–13: Courtesy the Archives and Records Services Division, Mississippi Department of Archives and History; pages 216–17: © James H. Barker, courtesy Steven Kasher Gallery; page 219: © Pete Souza/The White House; page 221 (top): © Devin Allen, courtesy the artist; page 221 (bottom): © Roderick Lyons, courtesy Collection of the Smithsonian National Museum of African American History and Culture, Gift of Roderick Lyons; pages 224–25: © Bud Glick, courtesy the artist; pages 227–29: © Whitney Curtis, courtesy the artist; pages 231–32: © Sheila Pree Bright, courtesy the artist; pages 236–37: © Ming Smith, courtesy the artist; pages 239–40: © Judy Glickman Lauder, courtesy the artist; page 243 (top): © Samuel Corum/Anadolu Agency/Getty Images; page 243 (bottom): © Hulton Archive/Stringer/Getty Images; page 245: © Will Counts/*Arkansas Democrat-Gazette*, image courtesy Associated Press; pages 247–51: © Estate of James Karales, courtesy Howard Greenberg Gallery, New York; pages 252–57: © Jamel Shabazz, courtesy the artist; page 259: © Joe Conzo, courtesy the artist; page 261 (top): © Morton Broffman/Getty Images; page 261 (bottom): Courtesy the Estate of Jules Aarons/Gallery Kayafas, Boston; pages 263–65: © LaToya Ruby Frazier, courtesy the artist and Gladstone Gallery; pages 267–69: © Charles "Teenie" Harris, courtesy Carnegie Museum of Art/Getty Images; pages 271–73: © Shawn W. Walker, courtesy the artist; pages 275–77: © Elia Alba, courtesy the artist; pages 279–81: © Shomei Tomatsu, courtesy Taka Ishii Gallery; pages 283–84: © and courtesy Alaska State Library, Vincent Soboleff Photo Collection, PCA0001-7 and PCA0001-312b; page 287: © and courtesy Museum of History and Industry, Seattle, Al Smith Collection, 2014.49.002-013-0040; page 288 (top): © and courtesy Museum of History and Industry, Seattle, Al Smith Collection, 2014.49.002-028-0103; page 288 (bottom): © and courtesy Museum of History and Industry, Seattle, Al Smith Collection, 2014.49.006-012-0036; pages 291–93: © Kim Weston, courtesy the artist; pages 295–97: © LaToya Ruby Frazier, courtesy the artist and Gladstone Gallery; page 299: © C. Daniel Dawson, courtesy the artist; page 301 (top): © Calvin Wilson, courtesy the artist; page 301 (bottom): © Louis H. Draper Preservation Trust, courtesy Bruce Silverstein Gallery, image courtesy The J. Paul Getty Museum, Los Angeles; pages 302–3: © Anthony Barboza, courtesy the artist; page 304: © Seher Sikander, courtesy the artist

**RACE STORIES: ESSAYS ON THE POWER OF IMAGES
BY MAURICE BERGER**

A Vision & Justice book edited by Marvin Heiferman

Series Editors' Note by Sarah Lewis, Leigh Raiford,
and Deborah Willis
Foreword by Henry Louis Gates, Jr.
Afterword by Dawoud Bey, Nona Faustine, and
Peter W. Kunhardt, Jr.

Cover: Gordon Parks, *Department Store*, Mobile,
Alabama, 1956

Editor: Denise Wolff
Associate Editor: Jessica Lynne
Editorial Assistant: Iesha E. Coppin-Forde
Designer: Morcos Key (Jon Key, Chuck Gonzales)
Production Director: Minjee Cho
Production Manager: Andrea Chlad
Copy Chief: Susan Ciccotti
Copy Editor: Zack Hatfield
Proofreaders: Freddy Martinez, Claire Voon
Work Scholars: Isabella Convertino

Additional staff of the Aperture book program includes:
Sarah Meister, Executive Director; Michael Famighetti, Editor in
Chief; Sang Patten, Managing Editor, Books; Caroline Foulke,
Editorial Assistant; Karina Eckmeier, Designer and Project
Manager; Thomas Bollier, Production Consultant; Kellie
McLaughlin, Director of Sales and Outreach; Richard Gregg,
Director of Book Sales and Operations

Special thanks:
*Race Stories* was made possible, in part, with generous support
from the Ford Foundation through its grant to the President
and Fellows of Harvard College's "Vision & Justice: The Art of
Citizenship" initiative.

Aperture also wishes to thank Agnes Gund for her contributions
to making this project possible.

Additional thanks to Dawoud Bey for his support.

This volume is part of the Vision & Justice Book Series. Created
and coedited by Drs. Sarah Lewis, Leigh Raiford, and Deborah
Willis, the series reexamines and redresses historical narratives
of photography, race, and justice.

# Vision & Justice

The *Race Stories* essays by Maurice Berger were originally
published in the *New York Times* Lens blog. Publication dates are
noted with each essay. With few exceptions, the essays in this
book retain the *New York Times* styling.

First edition, 2024
Printed in China
10 9 8 7 6 5 4 3 2 1

Library of Congress Cataloging-in-Publication Data available
upon request.

ISBN 978-1-59711-562-9

Copublished by Aperture and *The New York Times*

**The New York Times**

To order Aperture books, or inquire about gift or group
orders, contact:
orders@aperture.org

For information about Aperture trade distribution worldwide, visit:
aperture.org/distribution

**aperture**
548 West 28th Street, 4th Floor
New York, NY 10001
aperture.org

Aperture is a nonprofit publisher dedicated to creating insight,
community, and understanding through photography.